DONALD *of China*

"DONALD OF CHINA"

William Henry Donald photographed
shortly before his death

DONALD

of China

EARL ALBERT SELLE

HARPER & BROTHERS PUBLISHERS
NEW YORK AND LONDON

For Two Courageous Women
BETTE AND RUTH

2-8

DONALD *of China*

Copyright, 1948, by Earl Albert Selle
Printed in the United States of America

FIRST EDITION

A-X

Contents

Memo to the Reader

You've heard about William Henry Donald, the "Donald of China," fabulous, an almost legendary character, who for four decades sought by example, by a strangely mild bluntness to knit together the loose and sprawling land of China and to give it dignity. But you have not heard much, and much of what you've heard is hearsay, for few of the facts have been written about this publicity-shy world figure who served the Manchus in days of monarchy as brilliantly as he did Dr. Sun Yat-sen and Generalissimo and Madame Chiang Kai-shek.

Before you now is set the story of Donald as Donald himself told it to me. I offer it to you simply as a piece of journalism, as a reporter presenting a story—one of the truly big stories of the century. There is little in this book that is not developed from the voluminous notes he gave me. I have rounded off corners, filled in gaps with history where it was needed and with observations of his friends where they, too, were needed. No doubt there will be those who know the story of Donald somewhat differently than it is written here. I will not quarrel with them. This is the story of Donald as Donald himself told it. Further, other characters in this book may emerge contrary to the accustomed treatment of them. But you must remember that Donald knew them as no one else did.

In January, 1946, I found him in a naval hospital in Honolulu, dying. He was as aware of the ominousness of the doctor's prognosis as I was: Perhaps a month to live, perhaps a few days. Who could say? The octopuses of cancer had grabbed at his lungs. Time which had moved with the leisureness of China herself across his span of seventy-one years was racing to a close. Yet he had an infectious smile for all. He was facing death with customary good humor.

For nearly two decades publishers had sought to tempt this mystery man of the Orient with lavish offers for his memoirs. But he had no wish to tell on his friends—the little men and the big men of China.

The only foreigner since Marco Polo to live and to break bread with China's rulers, as a member of the inner circle, he had their confidence and their trust. He would not write a book.

Now, in the eleventh hour, he agreed that he must not take history with him to the grave, although I think that he might have liked it better if he had. And so in the quiet, numbing atmosphere of chloroform and tiptoeing nurses, this maker of exciting history, this man whose mark upon China and perhaps the world even now cannot be assessed, began to talk for the first and the last times on the heretofore sealed chapters in his life. Outside his hospital window the earth was alive with the freshness of the early Hawaiian spring. He looked with calm wonderment at a bedside calendar and said:

"You know, if I had ever written a book about China, I would have begun it this way: 'This is a book about a people who are thoroughly human.' I think the second sentence would have been: 'It does not purport to be a treatise on the likes, the customs, the habits or the morals of the Chinese people.'" He watched a white dove flutter down from a poinciana tree to his window sill. Then he said, "The third sentence would be: 'It is written with sympathy and understanding.'"

Thus our brief encounter began, he short of breath, aware that death might come at any moment.

I have tried to keep faith with Donald. Yet I have had to face the painful truth of these thoroughly human people who do thoroughly human things in such abundance. Even Donald, China's kindest friend, never refrained from being her severest critic.

He was as reticent about the details of his own personal life as he was about the lives of others. He said that he was married to an Australian girl in Hong Kong in 1905. Their daughter was born a few years later. Around 1912, his wife had said to him, "Don, you are married more to China than to me." With the daughter, she had left him forever.

This book does not pretend that its story is set forth as a solution to China's ills and her problems. I am sure that Donald would have advised leaving that to the experts who have been trying to do so for so long.

For myself, I am deeply and forever indebted to Miss Ruth Nagle for her kindness, her intelligent understanding and for her devotion to this manuscript. Without her, and the assistance of my wife, this book might never have been written. I am also indebted to Commodore M. D. Willcutts, Lt. Col. Wilson Gaddis, Mr. Raymond S. Coll, Con-sul-General King Chow Mui, Mr. H. B. Elliston, Mr. and Mrs. N. Peter Rathvon, Mr. Harold Hochschild, Miss Alix Ungern, Mr. and Mrs. Henry B. Congdon, and Mrs. Frederick W. Thomas.

EARL ALBERT SELLE

PROVIDENCE, R. I.
JANUARY 3, 1948

The Japanese "gestapo" swept into the internment camp.

Their demand: Produce W. H. Donald.

Reason: Japan wanted him.

Japan, of course, wanted him, wanted this man who suddenly and mysteriously had become lost to the world, this man she had christened The Evil Spirit of China. In Tokyo, the dossier on him was thick. Without him, Japan might have sabotaged China's 1911 revolution. Without him, Japan might have swallowed China in 1915. Without him, China might never have entered World War I, nor would she have been ready to hold off Japan in World War II. Without him, there might have been no Manchurian Incident in 1931, nor would China have found what little unity she eventually did.

The "evil spirit" had done a thorough job.

The "gestapo" chief was tough. He barked at the commandant: "Make no mistakes! We want this man. There is a price on his head!"

chapter

1

TO THE EAST FROM DOWN UNDER

*He who rides in the chair is a man; he who
carries the chair is also a man.*

✲

HONG KONG rose coolly pontifical on the right. On the left, a small
arm of the China mainland—Britain's Kowloon—drooped down a
half mile from the island.

At the rail of the steamer stood a stocky, brown-haired young man
with sharp blue eyes set in a strong, ruddy face marked by a willful
chin and a large nose. He was William Henry Donald, newspaperman,
late of Melbourne, Australia.

As he gazed at the shore Donald was thinking: No matter where I
look, there is England.

The man on his left said, "It's a fine bit of rock now. We put our
flag here sixty years ago after a tiff they called an opium war. We had
another go at the Chinamen a dozen or so years later and the beggars
gave us that strip over yonder called Kowloon. When we set up at
Hong Kong, it was barren and treeless." He pointed to the slopes thick
with green trees.

"There were only boulders and matted grass there," he went on. "It
had been a pirates' den. That's the only bloody history the island had
until we came along."

The man on Donald's right cleared his throat and spat.

From the ship's bow they could see the roads that cut and wound
through the red-dirt hills. On Kowloon and Hong Kong's skirts were
hems of busy wharves, and from them a motley traffic of steam launches,
sampans and barges swarmed like birds among a forest of ships
at anchor.

1

"Hong Kong," the man on the left was saying, "is a monument of British enterprise. It's the realization of the British ideal of colonial government. It is an asylum for the oppressed. It is Britain!"

Donald said, "Oh? And where is China?"

The man on the left gestured in the direction of Kowloon.

"Is that China?" Donald asked and added drily, "Do they boil you in oil over there?"

"Boil you in oil? They don't boil you in oil in China—they skin you alive."

"Well, where do I find out about that?"

The man swept his arm airily in a great circle. "Oh," he said, "anywhere in there."

The man on the right knocked the ashes from his pipe with vigor.

Before them now rose "the Peak," its head poking into a mist eighteen hundred feet above the sea. From the city of Victoria at the base, echelon upon echelon of homes and buildings beautifully terraced advanced in a cone of shimmering splendor.

"There's tradition and prestige there," said the man on the left. "The higher you climb on the Peak the finer the homes, the finer the people, the higher their social position. There are, of course, no Chinamen living on it."

"Oh," said Donald, "and who lives at the top?"

The man on the right spoke for the first time. "I think God does," he said, and walked away.

The ship·put in at Kowloon, and Donald crossed to Hong Kong by ferry. He stepped ashore on Ice House Street wharf into a strange and bewildering world. A stench billowed over him. It came from the sweat of straining, garrulous wharf coolies, from the urine-soaked piling, the soured foods and stale peanut oil odors in sampans, the masses of humanity corrugated in squat, slatternly dwellings and narrow furrows of streets.

The incongruity of Donald's dress, dark clothes and black bowler hat, was swallowed up in the confusion of Hong Kong's streets. He stopped for a moment and filled his mind with a quickly tumbling avalanche of new and fascinating pictures. Then he walked on, avoiding little clusters of sedan chair carriers and ricksha pullers and moved uncertainly through streets where a tide of humans flowed.

Faces crossed and crisscrossed. Determined and haughty ones. Ugly and scarred, ivory and oval and beardless. Tired and expressionless faces. Donald stopped once more under an arched granite building. The sun blazed down on the listless rivers of humanity. Korean and Japanese faces, Portuguese, Parsi, Hindu and Malayan faces swam through seas of weary Chinese faces. Here and there the uniforms of British army or marine trooper, Indian cavalryman or a Scotsman in kilts. Other Europeans, immaculate in white, seemed adept at not touching anyone or anything.

At a street intersection Donald asked a white-clad Sikh policeman, "Which way is Wyndham Street?" The tall, bearded man touched his colored turban in elaborate respect, pointed and said, "The flower street is that way, sahib."

Donald found the foot of Wyndham Street which wound tortuously up the Peak riotous with crowds upon crowds of bright flowers. Here was the flower market. He began the climb and stopped when he saw a weather-beaten sign which read, THE CHINA MAIL. It hung on a sagging building built on a decline. A balcony overlooked the street, and the paint on its railing was curled and peeling. Donald walked up the stairs and entered the editorial room.

A short, squat man jumped down from a high chair and said, "The editor? That's me. Name's George Hurd Reid. Presume you're Mr. Donald. Happy you have come. Your desk is over there." He pointed to a desk on which old papers were stacked, yellowed and dusty.

Donald walked over, then turned and looked at the bluff, cryptic little man.

"How did you happen to send for me?" he asked.

Reid already had climbed back onto his high chair. He spoke over his shoulder, looking at the street more than at Donald. " 'Member Petrie Watson?" he called. "When he was here, I said: Somewhere in the world find me a man. Find me a printer, a journalist, a teetotaler—above all, a teetotaler. I said I wanted them all in one package. Four weeks later he telegraphed that he had found my man. Here you are, Mr. Donald."

Donald was surprised and greatly amused. Petrie Watson. He remembered him very well—an odd-looking, travel-stained Englishman who, the previous Christmas day, had walked into the office of the Sydney *Daily Telegraph*, where Donald was subeditor, asking for a loan. He was, he had said, a reporter on the Kobe *Chronicle* in Japan, and was returning to England by way of Hong Kong, Australia and South Africa. Donald had taken him out for a bite, had been surprised when Petrie Watson asked for tea, but not so impressed, apparently, as Watson had been to hear that Donald also would have tea—that, in fact, the twenty-seven-year-old Donald had never had a drop of liquor in his life and doubted whether he ever would. Donald remembered that Petrie Watson had looked at him intently, as if he were scribbling a memorandum somewhere on the shirt cuffs of his mind.

As they drank their tea, Donald had plied him with questions about Japan, and for an hour Petrie had talked of the turbulence of Japanese politics, of what he termed their so-called culture, and the limitlessness of their one-track minds. He spoke convincingly, with the authoritativeness of one who had lived long in the country—not maliciously, Donald thought, but as one whose patience had been rubbed thin. He pointed out that, in his view, they were an insidious, hypocritical people.

"Never trust them," he had warned. "Doubt everything they say. Watch them always."

Donald felt a distaste growing for the Japanese. He never lost that feeling.

Donald had asked, "Well, what about the Chinese?"

"Ah," Watson had replied, "the gospel truth is that they're a bit of a mess, too. They are people who spend so much time acquiring wisdom they never find time to apply it. They are sprawled all over like a spilled bowl of soup and they never mop themselves up. The heavy flesh of inertia weighs them down. They are like a mother who eats its young. They wallow in extremes of wealth and filth, and over all is the curdle of vanity. They are worm eaten. They are like a tired and broken old house with its rump over the mud. They are to topple by themselves or someone is to topple them."

Petrie had hesitated. "There's power there," he went on finally.

"Like that under a sleeping old volcano. Indefinable, intriguing, exasperating in its apathy."

After a last swallow of cold tea he had added, "They need someone to put starch in them. They need someone to take hold of them like a Dutch uncle and tell them which is up wind and which is down."

They had gone back to the *Daily Telegraph* and at Donald's invitation, Petrie had written an article which Donald captioned, "The Hegemony of the Pacific."* It outlined the ambitions of the Japanese and their advance toward militaristic power. When he finished, the cashier had gone for the day. Donald had seventeen shillings. He gave them to Petrie Watson. The Englishman left, and Donald never saw him again.

About two weeks later, Donald received an offer of a job as political writer on the Melbourne *Argus*, at a higher salary. At that time, he had been a reporter on the *Daily Telegraph* for about two years, and had become subeditor only shortly before Petrie Watson arrived. At the customary rate of promotion, he could look forward to becoming editor possibly in twenty years. So he accepted the *Argus*' offer with alacrity, but he had been at his new post only two weeks when he received a telegram from Hong Kong. It offered him the subeditorship and eventual editorship of Hong Kong's big afternoon paper, the *China Mail*. The telegram added laconically:

APPLY AT CHINA NAVIGATION COMPANY MELBOURNE FOR TICKET AND EXPENSE MONEY.

Donald carried the telegram with him most of the day before he went to the steamship office. There he said to a clerk: "I think I've been the victim of a hoax."

He was assured that he had not, and was asked when he might be leaving. Donald replied that he'd let him know later and walked off, the clerk thought, as a man in a bit of a stew. A block from his office he halted, hesitated a moment, then marched down Collins Street into the *Argus* and finally to the editor's desk.

* It is interesting that Watson's article, published in the Sydney *Daily Telegraph* thirty-nine years before Japan began her abortive march to conquest in the Pacific, detailed with a high degree of accuracy the hopes of Tokyo.

"I'm going to China," he said and waited.

The editor looked up. Even though their association had been short, he had had a chance to appraise Donald. One thing stood out: He was a man who talked sense with a remarkable plainness of expression, sometimes with brutal frankness. The editor saw that Donald was eyeing him in the quiet way that invited no challenge. He said:

"Isn't it a bit sudden, Mr. Donald? Really, you just got started, and I should hate to lose you. I'm sure that the *Argus* is your place. Anyway, what do you know about China?"

Donald smiled. The question was irrelevant. What did he know about China? Nothing except what Petrie Watson had told him. Must man always know the answer before he seeks? Problems, algebraic or otherwise, are not worked in reverse. One starts with X and goes on from there.

He said, "China could be my place. I will go and find out for myself."

That night the Sydney *Daily Telegraph's* correspondent in Melbourne, a stanch friend of Donald's, walked him up and down Collins Street for nearly an hour, arguing against going to China.

"Look," he pleaded, "you have your foot on the rung of the ladder here. The old *Argus* is the mecca of journalists in Australia. This is what you've worked for. You've got a good chance. Distance has a way of making parched grass look green, old man. Anyway, in China they boil you in oil."

"Ah," said Donald, "that's why I want to go there."

He sailed from Melbourne in May, 1903, and, as Reid had just pertinently remarked, here he was.

Reid turned back to the copy he was editing. "Never have trouble with a sober man," he said. "Drink myself, though. Edition time is in an hour. Here are late telegrams from London. Please read and caption them, Mr. Donald." He was back at work before Donald could take the sheaf of papers.

As the Australian turned to his desk, the top telegram slid to the floor. He was about to retrieve it when Reid said quickly, "Mr. Donald! You need not pick it up!" He clapped his hands. "Boy!" he shouted, "pick up that blasted paper!"

The "boy" had gray hair about his ears and in his queue. He handed the telegram to Donald. He said politely, "Here, master."

Donald walked thoughtfully back to his desk.

The *China Mail*'s proprietor, George Murray Bain, had just entered and had witnessed the scene. He went over to Donald and said, "You're new here, but you'll get the hang of custom soon enough. The first rule for living in the tropics is: Don't exert yourself. Never walk if you can ride. You may find this hard to believe, Mr. Donald, but I've hardly taken a step outside my office or home in ten years. I find the sedan chair bumpy but adequate."

Donald had been a printer before he became a journalist, had first learned to set type on the Lithgow *Mercury*, a paper in which his father, a prominent Australian building contractor had been chief shareholder. His father, descendant of a Scottish engineer, and a stern but kindly disciplinarian, had insisted that his son learn a trade "because no boy of mine will be brought up so that he cannot use his hands." To a man with such a heritage, to a man from vigorous Australia, the world into which Donald had now stepped was only short of incredible. It was a world of the privileged, a circumspect yet casual world on one hand; on the other, a world where no problem was too small to cause a British, American or French gunboat to come boiling hell-for-leather up a Chinese river or to heave to menacingly off a Chinese coastal city. It was a world of expedient diplomacy where gun turrets pointed in the right direction could write treaties in a hurry and set down quicker than the pen the desired commercial advantages. In business and territorial aggrandizement, the nineteenth century had been productive for the Powers.

The first of modern Asia's fires had been ignited by opium. The Dutch and Portuguese had secured early toeholds in the drug traffic, the Americans joining in later. Eventually, however, Britain had dominated the market by reason of big production in India. Thereafter, two wars to foist the drug on China, one ending in 1842, the other in 1856, resulted in Britain's acquisition of Hong Kong and Kowloon, and the payment by China of heavy and humiliating war indemnities. Out of the 1842 defeat also came treaties extending extra-territorial privileges in China to nationals of the United States, Britain and other European powers—privileges which placed these nationals above all Chinese jurisdiction. In the years that followed, China, economically weak, politically diffident, submitted to gunboat diplomacy.

There was also a less violent method employed for extracting favors, concessions and special advantages from these ancient and tired people. Japan used it profitably. Corrupt Manchu princes, the rulers of China, were willing to provide whatever the bargainer sought—if the bribe was attractive enough.

Yet even before the opium wars, the British had been the dominant foreign factor in China. The wars had enhanced their position commercially and from a point of political prestige. While China's defeats had given all Powers a stranglehold on Chinese customs, the British managed to emerge stronger than ever. Treaties provided that they were to head the customs, in addition to appointing commissioners and subordinates, as long as their trade exceeded the trade of other treaty states. Their dominance, aided and abetted by superior manufactured goods and a strong foreign policy, increased in the years that followed. By the beginning of the twentieth century, Britain's role in China had received such world-wide attention that the average man found that when he thought of China, he immediately thought of Britain.

This was the state of affairs in a land where even history was either confused or undecided. Where the Chinese had come from was a matter of conjecture. It was possible to vaguely trace China's beginning back to the third millennium before Christ when Asian tribes first began to wander, to coagulate finally somewhere in Central China.

Donald had come to a land whose exterior was as crumbling as its history, a land which had risen and fallen many times. But its past history, periodically tempestuous, was to pale before the history which China would soon make.

When the fierce June heat settled down on the tight colony of Hong Kong,[1] Donald understood what Bain had meant by his caution to take life in easy, unhurried strides. The air hung so heavy and still that he felt he could part it with his hands. Doors and windows of buildings and homes were flung wide open, and Europeans lived by day and night on their large verandas, punkahs swung wearily from the

[1] The 1903 population: 307,050 Chinese; 18,581 non-Chinese.

ceilings of offices and banks, while in the anthills of the Chinese sections men, women and children hardly stirred. Like the long cloth shop banners that hung listlessly over the slits of the streets, they lay half nude in doorways and on balconies.

Donald made an effort to fit into the rigid and conservative British community. Bain put him up at the exclusive Hong Kong Club whose palatial building sat in the city's heart. With its library, spacious grounds for tennis and cricket, it lacked nothing to satisfy a colonial gentleman. Donald spent an occasional evening there, listening more than taking part in conversations.

The talk varied little from one night to another. It concerned mainly the price of rubber, news from home, new shows in London, whether wheat or corn was the better buy on the Chicago market. China was rarely mentioned. Colonial officials and taipans, as the heads of the big foreign firms were known, whether English or French, German or American, were insensitive to the politics of the nation on whose doorstep they lived. China's history, her doings, were ignored. The trend of the country's economy stirred only little pockets of personal interest. Donald's paper and Hong Kong's two other dailies, the *South China Morning Post* and the Hong Kong *Telegraph*, mirrored a serenely stagnant community. What was happening in the House of Commons or House of Lords and cricket scores from home were adequate for the Hong Kong appetite. There were few local matters of sensation except for an occasional kidnaping. The efficient British police system kept the city prim and well behaved. Unlike the more scandalous Shanghai and Peking to the north, Hong Kong had few barroom roisterings, street brawls or bayonetings.

Donald found that he was not fitting well into Hong Kong life. He became conscious of the distinction, subtle as it was, that the colony made between one born in England and one who had emerged from the raw hinterlands of Australia. He even became conscious of his accent. Gradually, by his own decision, he began to restrict his social life. His job, with matters peculiar to Hong Kong, and an avid reading of Chinese history kept him busy. Unlike some of his acquaintances, there were no spare hours for what was up the hill, on Lyndhurst Terrace, just beyond the *China Mail*.

On the terrace lived about forty of Hong Kong's most beautiful girls

—red-heads, blondes and brunettes. They were prostitutes, all of them Americans. Sometimes he would be on the balcony of his office when they would come down the hill in the afternoon, clad in silks and riding in sedan chairs. They used to call out to him. One night he did stroll down Lyndhurst Terrace. He could see the girls through the lighted windows. He did not go in.

His eagerness to learn about China mounted daily, but Hong Kong offered only the most limited opportunity. As an experiment, he kept track of the three papers for three days running. There appeared no story or even an advertisement that concerned China. His impatience grew.

"What about China?" he would ask. "What about the Chinese?" He had not left Melbourne to go to a slice of Trafalgar Square, a bit of Piccadilly or Kensington Gardens. He thought: This is not my notion of China.

His deep interest in politics, the thrill of being a spectator to men and government at work pulled strongly. His father, a bare-knuckle sort of politician who rose from being mayor of Lithgow to membership in the New South Wales Parliament, had planted the seed. He had drawn his son into political discussions when he was young and from them Donald had learned much. At Sydney, covering the always ebullient sessions of Parliament at a time when Australian states federated, his political awareness had been heightened.

China's politics, at first glance, appeared strange and complicated, with government as devious as a tangled skein of yarn. It was top heavy with bureaus and bureaucratic mandarins who had no special ability for progressive administration but a singular talent for growing rich quickly at the expense of their districts. Against this, there was a deepening rumble and secret plotting by some Chinese. There was talk that they had panaceas for the ills of Peking, from where the Manchu conquerors had ruled China for two and a half centuries, despotically and with growing ineptness. Donald heard the murmurs, and he heard of a Dr. Sun Yat-sen whom the colonials referred to as a "revolutionary donkey."

The land that Petrie Watson had said sprawled all over like a spilled bowl of soup was a fascinating challenge.

He had been in Hong Kong only a few months when he accepted the challenge. He determined to pry open old doors that had been closed to foreigners—the barbarians—by an indifferent Manchu government. The nearest "old doors" were at Canton, the seat of Viceroy Chang Chen-chun, a Chinese whose authority for the Manchus extended over the big southern provinces of Kwangtung and Kwangsi. Canton itself was the biggest city in South China and second only to Peking in political importance. Late one afternoon Donald stopped by the desk of George Reid. He said, "I'm going to Canton tonight. I'm going to set my two feet on China." Reid went on with his work. "'Bout time someone did," he said.

The gray of dawn washed Canton in a soupy light as Donald's steamer ended its overnight trip up the Pearl River from Hong Kong. The air hung fetid and heavy from the morning's harvest of stools. When Donald walked down the Bund, he could hear the clankings of bowls and cans from a thousand and one alleyways where night-soil was being dumped into pushcarts.

A solitary foreigner, immaculately attired, was walking aloof to a disorderly parade of oxcarts, wheelbarrows and ragged Chinese, who scuffed around him as if still half asleep. He stopped when he saw Donald. It was Paul King, a Britisher, commissioner of customs at Canton. Donald had met him a number of times at the Hong Kong Club.

King asked what Donald was doing in Canton, in a voice that indicated a conviction that newspapermen were not expected to emerge from behind paste pot and scissors.

"I've come down to see the viceroy," Donald replied. His bluntness, as usual, was accompanied by a twinkle.

"Have you an appointment?"

"Appointment?" Donald asked slowly. "Where do you get an appointment?"

"Oh," King replied matter-of-factly, "from Mr. Everard Fraser, the British consul, of course. If you don't, you can't see the viceroy for two or three days."

Donald stared at the commissioner. "The British consul?" he asked.

"I've got to go to the British consul to see a high Chinese official? What's the matter with this damn country?" He added that it was his intention to see the viceroy that day and return to Hong Kong that night.

King bristled. "Well," he said, "you can't do it." With the knob of his cane he tapped a Chinese on the shoulder, motioned him from his path and strode on.

Donald boarded a sedan chair and was carried to the viceroy's yamen. It was half past eight when he alighted at the sprawling government house, interlaced with courtyards. A cordon of servants barred the way at the gate, impassively regal in their round white hats and red plumes. Donald sought to pass them, but they sputtered sentences that seemed to have no end and finally pointed abruptly to a tier of steps. He sat down, his back against one of the big pillars. He had no way of knowing then that Chinese officials never appeared at their offices until one or two o'clock in the afternoon.

An hour passed.

Donald made up his mind to wait, all day if need be. He thought: If patience is what is needed in this country, then I'll have it! I'll find me more patience than the most patient of Chinese. If necessary, I'll learn to outsit a mud idol.

The sun was hot now. It beat down on him. It accented the stench of filth until he fought hard not to gag. Coolies milled about, aimlessly. They expectorated. They jabbered and guffawed. They cleared their throats with noisy relish. If Donald had not decided to be patient, they would have driven him away. On a near-by street, men in gowns, women in trousers, both with pigtails, passed in phlegmatic, seemingly aimless streams.

At the main gate were two large earthenware urns. They were patronized constantly by men who lifted their gowns without embarrassment and urinated expertly and with elaborate unconcern. Through the welter of other odors, the smell of the urinals was sharp and acid. On the back of his steamer timetable Donald made the notation: "When China removes urns, she will have found progress."[2] Then, in

[2] Twenty years later they were removed, but not by man's hand. Fire destroyed the yamen and with it the same big urinals.

a characteristic change of mood, he scribbled a humorous limerick on the art of passing water skillfully. A prolific writer of such verse, he wrote it at odd times whenever a subject caught his fancy, and at home he had a box filled with limericks, printable and otherwise.

He sat there, a bit drowsy in the heat, thinking. Was this incongruity China? Were these stinkpots the companion-pieces of fine art and literature, of tapestries and exquisitely woven silks? What anachronism was this? What had some prankish god done to the clock that he should sit in a dung pile and loathe it while men around him wallowed in it, not caring that time had placed them in two worlds?

He recalled the drab picture as Petrie Watson had seen it. He wondered if a nation, like a man, could wear out and lie down by the roadside, unmindful, indifferent to the wheeling buzzards. Did the arteries and genitals dry up, did the heart pound to a stop, did the skin parch and wrinkle just because a nation had five thousand years of history?

The hours dragged. The stench was still about him. He knew that where he sat was no exception; that everywhere he might go, there would be the same ugliness, the same squalor.

He fretted uncomfortably on the hard stone steps. It occurred that they were as unyielding as China to the pressure of modernization, as unfeeling to man's discomfort as the Peak was to the lesser beings at its feet.

True, mistakes of Hong Kong, typical of those made by most foreigners in China, were plain. But error and bad judgment were not peculiar to the foreigner. The Boxer Rebellion of a few years before, in which foreign and Chinese Christians were massacred by fanatical Chinese, was a bitter dose for both sides.

While Donald sweltered awaiting a tardy government, he decided upon a line of conduct, which he never had to change: He would not be revolted by odiousness. He would look upon it as a nurse might look upon an ugly wound. He would have patience. He would concede to the Chinese the right to think as they liked. The country was theirs. He was only a guest.

It was past noon now. The heat was intense. Coolies no longer straggled about him. They lay, asleep, sprawled in the shade, empty rice bowls beside them. Soon, however, the courtyard's human medley began to stir as if a spoon had been taken to it. At the gate, the guards opened their eyes and stood up. Others moved into this doorway, out of that, carrying teapots and pails of hot, unclean-looking towels. It was nearly two o'clock when a keen-eyed young Chinese pushed his way through the mob. He stopped when he saw Donald.

"Hello," he said in perfect English, "what do you want?"

Donald jumped to his feet. To the young man who it later turned out was the tutor of the viceroy's son, he replied that he had come to make an arrangement with the viceroy whereby he could obtain Chinese views on international questions. He added that it had been his observation that the Chinese version had been ignored.

The tutor smiled gently. "Did Mr. Fraser give you an appointment? Have you seen the British consul?"

Five hours in the hot sun did not contribute to an appreciation of what seemed national apathy. "You are a Chinese," Donald blazed, "and you tell me to go through the British consul before I can see your viceroy? What's wrong with this blasted country?"

The tutor shrugged. He said that was the rule.

"Well!" Donald snapped. "I'll have to see about that!"

In short order and singly came a second, a third and a fourth official. Each hesitated before Donald, listened to his story, shook his head, and walked on into the yamen after advising a visit to the British consul. Finally he heard a voice say in a clipped British accent, "Well, my hearty, what can I do for you?"

Startled, Donald looked around to see a mandarin-coated, white-bearded old gentleman peering at him from behind white shaggy eyebrows. Donald thought: Good lord, what's this?

Good-naturedly he explained that he had come to see the viceroy without benefit of British blessing and he did not intend to get it. The man laughed. He was Admiral Wei Han, a graduate of Britain's Royal Naval College. He said, "It's irregular, old fellow, but we'll see what we can do about it."

He disappeared into the yamen and shortly a servant came out and motioned Donald in.

The Australian sat on one side of a long table. Across from him in mandarin dress were the five men with whom he had talked in the courtyard. At the far end was the tutor, Wen Shih-tsen. Next was a Yale graduate, Captain Woo Kwan-kien, in command of Canton's naval squadron, and, in order, a Mr. Yen, head of the salt administration in South China; Wen Tseng-yao, a thickset man in his early thirties, and Admiral Wei Han who sat next to Viceroy Chang Chen-chun and directly across from Donald. In the years to come, Donald's history and China's were to be interlaced with the lives of Tutor Wen, the scholarly Wen Tseng-yao, and others such as the viceroy who sat at the head of the table, fingering his great strings of beads. In his luxurious official robes, big red mandarin buttons, his mandarin hat and peacock feathers, he combined dignity and pomp. He had a big head with big ears, but Donald observed that the droop of his white mustache gave him a wise and kindly appearance.

A cork popped, a boy came in with champagne and set out glasses. Donald said quietly, "I have never drunk champagne in my life. I don't want to drink it now."

The tutor said, "You must. You must drink to the viceroy." They all nodded in agreement.

Donald, however, said determinedly, "I'm very sorry, but we'll have to find some way out."

Captain Woo said, "You pretend."

The viceroy looked perplexedly from one to another. He understood no English.

Donald said to the tutor, "I don't want to pretend. Will you please translate to the viceroy what I have to tell him?"

The tutor nodded, and Donald turned to the viceroy. "I have never drunk champagne or any other liquor in my life. I don't want to start now. But these gentlemen opposite suggest that I pretend. If I pretend, I am endeavoring to fool you. That is one thing I do not want to do. I hope to come here often. Now, let us make an understanding that we will never fool each other. No matter who else we fool, we will pledge ourselves to tell each other the truth."

The old viceroy let out a roar. He turned to the five men. "The man speaks wisdom," he explained. "He tells you: When men are really friends, then even water is sweet." He inclined his head as if in a bow to the Australian. "I like you, Mr. Donald," he said.

He leaned back and chuckled quietly. He tugged at his mustache. "I like it," he said slowly, "I like it! No matter who else we fool, we will not fool each other." He was enjoying the thought immensely. To Donald, he said, "Proceed, proceed!" and slapped the table.

From that hour, Donald never turned back in China. He had won the first round.

The viceroy listened attentively as he outlined his program, stressing the lack of connection between high Chinese officialdom and newspapermen.

"I want to know what is happening in China," Donald explained. "I want to educate foreign readers. I want them to understand the Chinese viewpoint."

These were strange words to the viceroy's ears. He had heard no foreigner speak them before, and to him it had been a matter of no concern whether the foreign devils cared what China thought. But the young man before him spoke earnestly and persuasively. Chang kept nodding his big head, his peacock feathers dancing crazily.

When Donald concluded, he promised that the yamen would be open to him at any time. The offer was unprecedented. Donald had rapped, and a door had opened in the old shuttered Celestial Empire.

That night he returned to Hong Kong. He had, as he had told George Reid he would, planted his two feet solidly on China. He had had a glimpse of "mysterious" Cathay, but it was not mysterious—only curious to the degree of one's choosing. His unorthodox visit had clearly shown his purposefulness, his determination. He had overcome the obstacles with a stubbornness deep set in his character. What he had accomplished, he had not stumbled into by chance. He had charted the course carefully and thoughtfully. Now he felt exhilarated, as Marco Polo must have when he began his long trek over the Burma Road into the vastness of China.

A few days later, he received a letter from Viceroy Chang Chen-chun. It stated that Mr. W. H. Donald had been appointed his adviser on all matters that pertained to government in South China. Donald realized that the honor was one of magnitude. The opportunity was two headed: the chance to serve and the chance to sit at the very core of news, to write about, to portray China from the inside, not from without.

He wrote in answer to the viceroy's letter: "I accept with gratitude. As for your question about what compensation I require for my services, the answer is that I require none. I want no reward. If I may be of service at any time, that alone will be enough."

It was autumn, 1903. Russia and Japan had begun to growl at each other over Manchuria. Donald was aware of the explosiveness of the situation in the North, but his interest of the moment was the development of his Chinese news sources. The pages of the *China Mail* were reflecting his efforts and for the first time Hong Kong residents saw in print what Chinese men of merit had to say. In addition to his own stories, missionaries, responding to Donald's requests, were contributing accounts of life and happenings in remote provinces.

Donald made frequent trips to Canton to offer advice on foreign relations. It was given without pretense of expertness, without a plea for its acceptance. The Chinese found it sound. They had a man upon whom they could depend. In turn, they telephoned him important information. He had a "leak," he had stories not available to other newspapermen.

Step by step, Donald learned more about China and the Chinese. Petrie had spoken of power asleep. He thought he sensed it, somewhere under the dust and mold, somewhere behind the naïveté. What was needed to rip the musty shrouds from a withering pomp? Was it a two-fisted Messiah, or a kindly saint? He remembered Petrie's words: "They need a Dutch uncle to tell them which way is up wind and which way is down."

Donald again and again found patience a good companion when the Chinese mind balked at finality, when it shied away from cold barren fact. A question was not walked into head on; the approach was oblique —and the Chinese understood. To bang the table, to speak in a loud voice was to affront them. Dignity ended with loss of temper or betrayal of emotion. Chinese said, "Beat your drum inside the house and your neighbors will not hear it."

Within a short period he understood China better than many who had lived in it a decade or so because he wanted to understand it. He was adjusting himself quickly to an association with the Chinese. It was easy, for he was a man of many facets. Purposeful, trustworthy, daring, blunt, at times gusty and stormy, at other times sympathetic, kindly and mellow, convivial or whimsical—he assumed whatever attitude the situation called for. He could pare the meat from a profound subject neatly and sharply and, a moment later, punctuate it with light and humorous remarks. He was full of vitality and laughter. He was a curious combination of rebel and diplomat, of sage and jester.

As months passed, the Chinese began to look upon him with awe and with warmth. Yet, as he delved deeper into things Chinese, it was inevitable that he should revolt against a condition he found prevalent among classes high and low: pretense and hypocrisy. In the language of the East, it was known as "face" behind which hid inefficiencies and medieval habits. He slashed at it continuously, felling friend if need be. Because of this, most of those who knew him or knew of him thought him strange.

One day at tiffin at Thomas' Grill Room, on Queen's Road, an acquaintance at the Hong Kong Club paused at Donald's table.

"You puzzle me," he said. "I can't figure you out. It seems you're going overboard on this Chinese business."

"Oh?"

"Quite. These people are immature. They're like children, you know. One can't go around treating what they have to say seriously."

Donald smiled and went on with his eating. He didn't give a damn whether or not people liked what he did.

The incident was typical. Even Reid one day, as he finished editing one of Donald's articles on China, had turned and asked, half over his shoulder, "Going to grow a pigtail, Mr. Donald?"

2

THE CZAR'S LOST FLEET

He who sits in a well can see but little.

✤

SMOKE, more than a wisp, was seeping again from the ancient Tinderbox—the plains of North Asia. The story was old; the participants new. From this uterus of world-shakers, men, girded for titanic plunder, had sprung forth century after century, and history had jerked back their descendants, marionette-like, again and again. The wild sweeps from the north had begun several centuries before Christ. Powerful Tartar tribes—the Turks, the Cathayans, the Kins and the Mongols, this khan and that khan—had stormed with bow and arrow the great caterpillar of a wall that crawled along fifteen hundred miles of China's border. Like the sand dunes that pyramid and level in a desert wind, the dynasties of China rose and subsided.

North Asia, land of roving nomads not peaceful farmers, bred a fierceness that had even cut deep into Europe in the thirteenth century and sent the people of Russia, Poland and Hungary onto their knees in churches. The Manchus had been the last to sally forth. They had come to Peking in 1644 by invitation of the Chinese to help rout an oppressor of the Ming emperor. It was a most opportune situation. The Manchus stayed to rule. Another dynasty had fallen. After that the blood of the warriors ran thin.

Russia's advance toward the Pacific—a stretching out for ice-free ports to compensate for lack of European outlets—had begun in 1579. Before the end of the nineteenth century, the czar had command of the Pacific from Bering Strait in the North southward to Korea's borders. But Japan sensed that Russia was not content. There were still the juicy plums of Manchuria, Korea, and Mongolia which, if acquired by Russia, would give her access to the Yellow Sea and to the lucrative China trade.

Japan had begun her major machinations on the Asiatic mainland in 1894 when, in a defeat of China, she secured through the Treaty of Shimonoseki the island of Formosa, the Pescadores, the prize naval base of Port Arthur and the Liaotung Peninsula on which it was located. But Russia, who had always coveted Port Arthur, enlisted France and Germany to help scuttle the treaty. Under such pressure, Japan had no alternative but to return to China all except Formosa. Smarting, she never forgot who master-minded the job.

The diplomatic surgeons then went to work elsewhere in Asia. In 1898, Germany scalpeled from weakened China a ninety-nine-year lease of Shantung's Kiaochow Peninsula, turning it into a base for German power. France sliced off Kwangchowan, a valuable port near French Indo-China; Britain, the important North China harbor of Weihaiwei. Nicholas II repudiated a previous pledge to respect China's territory and grabbed Port Arthur, bribed a Chinese statesman to legalize a twenty-five-year lease which was extended to ninety-nine years following the 1900 Boxer Rebellion. The United States took note of the scramble for Chinese ports and enunciated what it called the Open Door policy—equal commercial opportunity for all.

In the next few years, smoke from the Tinderbox thickened. Russia met evasively Japan's repeated demands for a clarification of her Manchurian policy. She proposed instead a neutral zone in Korea where for centuries Slav and Oriental ambitions had been in collision. Irritated by obvious smoke screens, Japan landed troops in Korea late in 1903, to protect, she said, her trade.

It was now January, 1904. The friction of the last several years between Russia and Japan had rung the alarm in world capitals. No new khan stood ready to burst out of the North's stony lands, but trouble was afoot.

Throughout the winter Donald had followed the drama in the North with growing excitement. Late in January, a Reuters telegram from Shanghai was set on his desk. It stated that the Japanese fleet under Admiral Togo reportedly had put to sea in the direction of Port Arthur.

He lit a cigar, read it slowly, and marked it for the typesetter. For awhile he sat. Then he walked over to Reid.

"I'm going to Japan," he said. "I'm going to cover a war."

Reid was sharpening a scrubby pencil. He blew noisily at the powdered lead. "War?" he echoed. "Haven't heard of any war. Heard someone rattling some windowpanes in Tokyo and St. Petersburg. That's all. Nasty climate up north. Better take some heavy underwear." The pencil was too short. He threw it away. "Boy!" he shouted, "bring me a blasted pencil." When the boy scampered over, he said to him more than to Donald, "Editorship this rum sheet coming up for you next year. Going home to live as God meant me to. Man can miss too many ships, Don."

Donald smiled. He said, "I'll go to Tokyo. We shall see what we shall see. I'll be back, have no fear."

Donald sailed January 31. Before he left Hong Kong he had wired his old paper, the Sydney *Daily Telegraph*, in addition to the Melbourne *Age*, Adelaide *Advertiser* and Brisbane *Courier*, stressed the imminency of war and had received an appointment from each to act as correspondent. He was to supply the *China Mail*, too.

When his ship put in at Shanghai several days later, the *North China Daily News* carried a story captioned in big type to the effect that the Japanese minister, Kurino, had left St. Petersburg abruptly. Soon after, on February 5, Donald arrived in Kobe, where Petrie Watson had worked.

The next day war broke out between Russia and Japan.

When Donald reached Tokyo, he checked in at the Imperial Hotel. Japanese army press officers informed him that as soon as other newspapermen arrived a correspondents' corps would be organized and he would be at the front in the thick of it. As yet, no front had opened. The first big blow came on February 9, when the Japanese admiral, Uriu, attacked at Chemulpho, on Korea's west coast. At the same time, Admiral Togo swept his torpedo boats in at Port Arthur and damaged three Russian warships.

By ones and twos and in groups, correspondents from all over the world drifted into Tokyo. Richard Harding Davis, of *Collier's Weekly*, arrived and his close friend, John Fox, Jr., Jack London, representing

Hearst, and many others who either already were, or were soon to be, world famous. There was Grant Wallace, of the San Francisco *Bulletin*, the world's first war artist and Lionel Pratt of Reuters. Within a month or two, more than ninety newsmen were lodged in the Japanese capital. Donald enjoyed them all, in particular the company of a rugged British free-lance journalist, Smiler Hales, whose tempestuousness saved many a dull day. They were all anxious for sound and fury. But the expected front in Manchuria did not open. To repeated questioning, Captain Tanaka, the army press officer, would grin broadly: "Maybe tomorrow you go. Maybe tomorrow."

As the boredom of inactivity settled down over them, the newsmen began dubbing themselves "Cherry Blossom Correspondents."

Togo attacked again at Port Arthur, crippling the Russian fleet. Japan then began to throw division after division into Korea. By May the land war was on with the Russians falling back. Weeks grew into months and no correspondent had witnessed battle. Official versions were being released, but correspondents in Tokyo knew no more, and often less, than the newspaper reader at home. They became more and more disgruntled. Togo promised a sea attack and a landing at Port Arthur which correspondents would be permitted to witness, but it did not materialize.

The barrooms by day, the Yoshiwara[1] and private gambling parties by night became routine for the correspondents. Such diversions as the Japanese theater and Suma wrestling soon lost their appeal. Frustrated, a stagnation set in, and tempers were shortened by alcoholic immersions. Incidents often resulted which barely escaped serious consequences. Donald could always be found somewhere in the center of them, a sober sort of Puck, prodding his friends on or holding them in check—whatever he thought the situation called for.

He never forgot the time when he was called upon to act as second in a duel between two bored and frustrated correspondents—a duel which, thanks to the intervention of a timely and sobering earthquake, never came off. On another occasion, through sheer force of personality, he managed to restrain an irate and thwarted British correspondent

[1] Government-licensed prostitution districts.

seriously bent on shooting his ambassador who he vowed was holding up his exit pass for the front. The correspondent was Smiler Hales.

As the half-drunken Hales reeled toward the British Embassy, Donald seized him by the arm and bluntly warned him to come to his senses.

"If I do, if I go back, you've got to have a drink with me, you damn teetotaler," he demanded.

Donald agreed, and in the bar at the Imperial, Smiler challenged, "Name it!"

Donald ordered, "Barmaid's Blush, please."

"What in the hell is that?" exclaimed Smiler.

"Oh," Donald answered, "it's a glass of soda with a teaspoonful of port wine."

Smiler burst out laughing. "You bastard!" he bellowed.

The next day Smiler received his exit pass and a few days later he was aboard a steamer for Manchuria.

The intensity of the war in Manchuria mounted as Japanese pressure increased. The Russian general, Kuropatkin, wanted to retreat as far north as Harbin, but St. Petersburg wanted the deciding battles fought on the seacoast, a tactic which Kuropatkin saw as fatal. With the Harbin retreat forbidden, he dug in and awaited the Japanese.

Numbering only a few men, the first column of the "Cherry Blossom Correspondents" finally sailed for Manchuria and the war. A second column followed in July, landing well in the rear of Japanese lines and staying there as the tempo was stepped up for the forthcoming battle. Donald and a large section of the news corps were still in Japan, however.

The battle blazed up at Liaoyang on August 23, and from then until September 2 the fighting was fierce. The Japanese with great losses succeeded eventually in breaking the Russian lines. Meantime, the siege continued at Port Arthur where the Russian fleet had twice sought to escape.

By late October, the Japanese army was pressing hard on the port. At this moment, Russia's Baltic fleet, under Admiral Rojestvenski was dispatched to the Far East. The hope was to make a junction with the beleaguered Port Arthur units. But in November, the Japanese destroyed these units and then began the assault which ended in Port Arthur's surrender on January 1, 1905. Mukden then fell on March 10, after the most tremendous battle in history to that time had taken place. Nearly one hundred and fifty thousand men were slain.

Finis now was nearly written to the land war, but the sea still held a storm. Rojestvenski's Baltic fleet's whereabouts were unknown. Almost five months had passed since it pushed off from Libau, on the Latvian coast.

But Donald, as had many others, had left Japan for home long before Mukden fell. A telegram had come from George Reid at Hong Kong:

HUSTLE ALONG STOP I'M BLIGHTY BOUND.

Donald departed with no regrets.

At Hong Kong he eased into the editorship vacated by Reid. Their ships had passed in the harbor. Reid was heading for England to live "as God meant me to"—among neat flower and vegetable gardens; dogs and grouse hunts; pubs; tea, the *Times* and muffins at breakfast; brisk walks through fogs that creep in from the moors.

Not long after Donald returned to Hong Kong, the London *Daily Telegraph* appointed him as its correspondent, and a few days later came cryptic instructions:

RUSSIAN FLEET REPORTED LOST SINCE LEAVING RED SEA STOP MAY BE SOMEWHERE YOUR AREA STOP GO FIND IT.

Donald dropped the telegram on the desk of George Murray Bain. The *China Mail*'s proprietor saw the unmistakable glint in his young editor's eyes. He said, despairingly, "Heavens, no, Mr. Donald, not again!"

"I've a hunch I'll find it. I'll have a go at it."

Bain looked bleakly at him. "Send in the new subeditor, then," he said. "I'll have him carry on."

Donald's gift of instinctively going about a job in the most straightforward way, without always knowing quite why he did it that way, carried him now with little hesitation aboard a French steamer for Saigon, in French Indo-China. The day before they arrived, Donald was standing at the rail. Camranh Bay was in the distance. Columns of smoke were billowing up against the sky.

Donald said to the captain, "What's that?"

The captain shot him a swift, sharp glance. "Oh, that's from big industries," he said and walked on. Donald looked long and hard at the smoke. Had the captain told the truth?

When Donald stepped from the ship, one of the first signs he saw read: THE HONG KONG SHIP CHANDLERY. It was weather beaten and hung on a faded and bent building. He went in, the "hunch" still tugging at him. The air was pungent with tobacco smoke, tar and hemp. From behind a counter, a Chinese, aged like his building, gazed at him in the calm penetrating manner which a Chinese reserves for a white man—a sort of dispassionate, detached scrutiny, as if wondering what particular sort of lunacy this particular lunatic was up to now!

Donald smiled. He said, "I want to know where the Russian fleet is."

The old man scuffed around from behind the counter, went to the door and looked out. He came back and looked searchingly at Donald. He said nothing.

From where they stood, the old man's sign was visible. It caught Donald's eye again. He said, "I'm from Hong Kong. I want to know where the Russian fleet is."

The Chinese filled his long thimble-bowl pipe and lit it from a charcoal burner. Then he spoke, and Donald was never able to explain fully what prompted a reply.

"Camranh Bay," he said.

Excitement almost like pain ran through Donald. "Well," he asked, "how do I get there?"

A buff-colored ship had eased up river and into her berth. The Chinese, his back to Donald, watched the fore line crumple on the wharf and a small battalion of coolies hustle it to a wooden bitt. "You go Hotel de Ville restaurant," he was saying slowly. "There you find captain of steamer called S.S. *Mance*. He go tomorrow."

At the hotel restaurant, Donald stepped into a hum of voices. It was tea and cocktail hour and at the tables men and women of a dozen nationalities sat in conversation. At the till, a fat French lady shrugged off Donald's inadequate French. He was about to turn elsewhere when he was tapped on the shoulder. A voice said, "I heard my boat mentioned."

At a table in a far corner they talked quietly, for the French had made the Russian fleet's whereabouts a top secret. By paying the captain handsomely, Donald secured passage aboard his grimy, stubnosed coaster, and in late afternoon they got under way.

They arrived that night off Nhatrang still some distance from where the fleet lay. "We part company here, my friend," the captain said and rowed Donald ashore. There was no sign of habitation. There was only the dark jungle that crept close to the beach.

The captain shook his hand. "You can't cut through that jungle tonight," he said. "If I were you I'd sit on the beach."

He looked amused and went on: "In the jungle, there are tigers. In the sea, there are sharks. If a tiger comes, run into the sea. If a shark comes, close your eyes."

He climbed back into his rowboat, and for awhile the only sound Donald could hear was the splash of oars. Then he heard the rustle of vines. A twig snapped. Somewhere behind him animals were on the move. He lay down, and after awhile he fell asleep.

At daylight, he found a tunnel through the jungles, reached a road and walked until he came to buildings and a sign that read: NHATRANG PASTEUR INSTITUTE. There, from the head of the institute, Dr. Vassal, he received additional information concerning the Russian fleet and also an invitation to make the institute his headquarters.

That night he made a quick trip to Camranh Bay and then wrote the dispatch which fluttered diplomatic dovecots in many parts of the world. He had found the Russian fleet! The French were hiding it!

France, sympathetic to Russia, was permitting the use of her facilities at Camranh for repair and coaling in excess of the twenty-four hours international law allowed ships of a belligerent nation to remain in a neutral port. Donald's stories, which told of Admiral Rojestvenski's tortuous six months' voyage from the Baltic to the hide-out at Camranh, were hastened to Saigon, from there to Hong Kong and the world. The London *Daily Telegraph* had a scoop of magnitude.

Rojestvenski had arrived April 14, Donald on May 1. At anchor in Camranh, he saw the imposing spectacle. Close in stood Rojestvenski's flagship, *Kniaz Suvaroff*, and among other battleships were *Oleg*, *Aurora*, and *Orel*. In the rear were rows of cruisers, torpedo boats, colliers, transports and a hospital ship. On their flank lay the French cruiser *Descartes*, as if to guard them. At this time the fleet already had overstayed by more than two weeks the lawful period, but Donald heard that Rojestvenski had no intention of moving. He would wait until Admiral Nebogatoff's Third Fleet, which was trailing him, caught up. The plan was to sail together in a direct line for Vladivostok.

Donald's revelation stirred up a tempest. The French officially denied the presence of the Russians, but from Paris came orders to the French naval command at Camranh to request their immediate withdrawal. It was May 5. At Nhatrang, Donald watched the beginning of an international farce. Under command of spare, sharp, gray Rear Admiral Jonquières, the cruiser *Descartes*, which Donald had seen at near-by Camranh, dropped its hook at Nhatrang. Through his information sources, Donald followed every step of the comedy. Jonquières sent his dispatch boat back to Camranh, and a lieutenant, with a twinkle, informed Rojestvenski that he would have to take his men-of-war to sea, that the harbor would be inspected the following day—but not thereafter.

When Jonquières swept his cruiser around Camranh Bay as planned he found only Russian colliers, no warships. To this effect, the French government was informed. Twenty-four hours later, Donald stood at Camranh and watched Rojestvenski's fleet slip back into harbor. The neutrality of France again was being compromised.

Donald hurried to Saigon and filed with the French telegraph office a dispatch to London, detailing the Russo-French burlesque. Two days later, the telegraph office sent word for him to drop in. A clerk said, "Monsieur, your money and your telegram," and handed him both.

Donald went to his hotel, put the message into code, and filed it again. In two days, he received another call. "Monsieur," said the same clerk, "your money and your telegram."

"Are you refusing this because I have exposed your confounded comedy?" Donald blazed.

The clerk shrugged. "*Je ne comprends pas,*" he said.

Donald dropped in at the British Consulate for a chat. The next day, both the *China Mail* and the London *Daily Telegraph* printed his dispatch.

The tempest, which had died down momentarily, blew again. For the second time, the French government denied Donald's story. It issued a yellow book which stated flatly that the czar's navy was not at Camranh. At this point, however, Admiral Jonquières appeared off the flagship *Kniaz Suvaroff* and went aboard. He was greeted by Commander Vladimir Semenoff[2] who escorted him to Rojestvenski.

"Messieurs," Jonquières said, "this is adieu. I can help no longer. You must go."

Rojestvenski and Semenoff looked through a porthole to where their patrols stood alert for the Japanese. They said nothing.

Jonquières went on, "It is inevitable that you go to fight. The Japanese attack on you is the first step to total expulsion of all Europeans from Asia. In any case, it is a step toward replacing the domination of the white races by a Pan-Asiatic league under the banner of the Rising Sun."

Rojestvenski poured champagne and passed two glasses. Semenoff toyed with his. He said to Jonquières, "You have been more fortunate than we."

"Oui. I was sure the first blow would be aimed at us in Indo-China. That would have been disastrous. We are weak here, you know."

He stood up, and Rojestvenski and Semenoff walked him to the ship's ladder. They exchanged salutes.

Jonquières said, "Tomorrow you go. *Il n'y a plus rien à faire!*" He shrugged and descended.

The Russian fleet wheeled out of Camranh Bay the next day and headed north. Rojestvenski was now less fearful of meeting the Japanese force, for at last he had word of Nebogatoff's Third Fleet. It was to join with him at any hour. He halted at Van Fong Bay, despite Jonquières' request to clear French waters, and waited. Nebogatoff arrived, and with a powerful armada now of fifty-two ships, the Russians started on the long haul toward Vladivostok. It was May 14.

[2] Author *Rasplata*, an account of Rojestvenski's voyage to the Far East in which he describes the farewell scene with Jonquières aboard the *Kniaz Suvaroff.*

The route they were to take was through Tsushima Straits—a decision after several nights of councils which had ended in drunken brawls.

From Van Fong, Donald watched the Russian Grand Fleet disappear to the north. He was convinced that they would make no creditable show against the tried and capable Admiral Togo. His early admiration for Rojestvenski's picturesque fleet had given way to skepticism for its chances of victory. It was honeycombed with vessels too ancient to stand against Japan's modern navy. Donald penciled a note: "These ships will be disgraced in their first engagement" and hurried away to write his dispatch. It was a story to capture the imagination of the world, full of suspense with promise of frightful consequences, as audacious as the dispatch in which he exposed the whereabouts of the "lost" fleet. It told the Japanese that their foe was charging northward to inevitable battle.

Three days later, his dispatch was printed in Hong Kong, flashed on to London, thence to Tokyo and in other directions. Everywhere the news was read avidly. The picture was awe inspiring. In the far Pacific, the great hulk of Russian naval might was hurling itself over a 2500-mile path from French Indo-China to Vladivostok. Somewhere along the way, the cunning Togo lurked. The world held its breath.

Donald returned to Hong Kong on the morning of May 27—the day of the great Battle of Tsushima. It was the battle for which Japan had readied herself, warned by Donald's story.

In Japanese waters, Togo waited and watched, anticipating that Rojestvenski would act just as he did. Scouts posted to the south discovered the Russians on the evening of May 26. At his secret naval base off the islands of Tsushima, Togo got the word at 5:30 A.M., May 27, that the Russians were approaching. In a heavy mist he got under way, halted and waited for Rojestvenski's eleven battleships, ten cruisers and other fighting craft. The flagship *Kniaz Suvaroff* was sighted first —at 1:45 P.M. Up went Japan's fighting flags amid cheers. Togo signaled, "The fate of the empire hangs solely on this battle, and all must use their best endeavors." Answers came from four other battleships, twenty-four cruisers and fifty-eight additional fighting ships.

The mist lifted, disclosing to the Russians the terrible trap into which they had run. At a range of seven thousand yards, Togo was cutting across their path, pitting them with fierce cannonading. The light funnels of their scenic ships clearly defined them as targets. Rojestvenski's men fought back confusedly, doggedly, but their firing was inaccurate; that of the Japanese excellent. Russian gun turrets were split and demolished. Shells tore into engine rooms and swept away bridges. Crippled ships exploded, turned over and sank. In forty-five minutes, Togo rendered the Russians ineffective as a fighting force. The next two days were spent in cleaning up scattered remnants. Few battles of World War II came close to equaling the destruction wrought. While Russia had lost most of its fleet, Japan, however, with its usual conservatism in such matters, stated officially that it had lost only three torpedo boats.

By late afternoon, the first dispatches out of Japan and Shanghai began to flow into Donald's office at the *China Mail*. They were fragmentary, but with his firsthand knowledge of the Russian fleet, he began to write a dramatic account of the great struggle in Japan's waters. His stories were detailed, charged with action. They sounded as if he had ridden into Tsushima on the bridge of Rojestvenski's ship. So exciting were the accounts that the editors on the *Telegraph*, in London, and on Australian papers could not help but believe that Donald somehow had been an eyewitness. The Melboure *Age* handled it this way:

THE BATTLE
OF TSUSHIMA

EYEWITNESS' STORY

New Light on the Conflict

But Donald, the "eyewitness," had sat in Hong Kong, twelve hundred miles to the south.

As it had in past warriors of North Asia, the blood of the fighting man ran thin in the Russian and the Japanese. They were tired and they wanted peace. Japan, though now in command of the sea and in possession of Korea and a large part of Manchuria, was at the bottom of the barrel of her resources of men and money. She could not hope to invade the vast territory of her enemy. Russia's resources still were enormous, and militarily it appeared she stood to gain by continuing the war. But the morale on Russia's home front was beginning to wobble due to the many reverses in the Far East. If the czar's government hoped to remain in power, termination of the war was imperative.

The United States now intervened. The deepening interest it had demonstrated since the war's beginning was manifested after the Tsushima battle. President Roosevelt took steps to halt the conflict. For this, he drew criticism from anti-Japanese groups that he was interfering; that he was preventing a Russian defeat of Japan. But Donald saw little evidence to support this, considering Russia's domestic situation.

Roosevelt arranged the peace conference at Portsmouth, N. H., and after negotiations which at times seemed likely to end disastrously, a treaty was signed September 5, 1905. Russia agreed to surrender to Japan the much-tossed-about lease of the Liaotung Peninsula, including Port Arthur, and to cede the southern half of the island of Sakhalin. Korea was to be a sphere of Japanese influence, and both parties were to evacuate Manchuria.

By now, Donald was solidly back in the editor's chair at the *China Mail*. This time with no interruptions, Bain hoped. For Donald, the experience had been rich. He had established himself as a foreign correspondent of high merit whose services in the days ahead were to be in demand. He had reported his story from Indo-China with the strict regard for fact of the neutral observer. That it had helped Japan was in no way to disturb him as years later he stood by China fighting Japan's sinisterness. It might have weighed heavily on the consciences of others, but Donald was only amused.

3

HONG KONG DAYS

The door of virtues is hard to open.

☫

THE passage of time failed to reconcile the man from a congenial, democratic Australia to the rigidity of Hong Kong's caste system. For the most part, however, he was not concerned with it for the editorship of the *China Mail*, in addition to his chores as correspondent for his string of Australian papers, kept him busy. His only relaxation was yachting. He was, in his own words, a "humdinger of a sailor" and a friend once wrote of him, "He's as buoyant as the sea he loves but always with an undercurrent of seriousness."

If the caste system affected him at all, it was in the attitude of officialdom, a large and aloof body which placed itself in an upper stratum and relegated all others to various subservient levels. Yet on one occasion he ran afoul of it in an encounter that was to have a long-range effect on his life. At the exclusive Royal Hong Kong Yacht Club of which he was a member, it was an unwritten law, observed religiously by those who did not wish to offend, that, with no exception, way had to be made for the yacht of one of the colony's governing body. If not, the foolhardy would stand in jeopardy socially and otherwise.

One Sunday Donald nosed his yacht, the *Sprite*, toward Hong Kong Harbor from the sea. He was winding up a day of sailing—a relief from the swelter on the island that now stood out like a giant baked dish. In the sun's brilliance, the city, Victoria, was a blinding glare.

Donald was on a starboard tack, with the right of way, as a yacht bore down harbor toward him. He could see the man at the tiller waving his arm, motioning him from his path. He recognized him as an official in the Public Works Department. Donald held his course. The yachts drew near. The man jumped to his feet and yelled, "Get out of my way, you damn fool!" Donald held his tiller firm, eyed him coldly. He knew his maritime law, and he was a strict observer of it.

Just in time, the man put over his tiller. Donald shot past him. Looking back, he saw him shake his fist angrily.

When he refused to give way to the official, Donald was aware he could expect retaliation. He was right. The man, thereafter, sought to hinder him in his newspaper work whenever possible and finally was responsible for Donald's resignation as editor of the *Mail*.

George Hurd Reid had passed on an old saying that one had to get a ticket for heaven to see any of the haughty bureaucrats, and Donald found this figuratively true, although it was not long before no doors were barred to him. He would state his business in his pleasant but abrupt manner and leave. However, he never mixed with them socially. He left them, as he put it, stiff necked behind their sacred lace curtains.

He worked until late at night, sometimes until one or two in the morning. On Sundays, the sound of his typewriter was superimposed on bell tones from churches. They did not disturb him, a churchless man, a religious devotee of ethics and principles, a religious avoider of pretense and hypocrisy. He saw others come down from the Peak, bearded, bowler hatted, white frocked, parasoled, Bibles in hand. He thought in good humor: There go the one-hour-a-week Christians.

In a dingy little office on Wyndham Street, Hong Kong, smug in tradition, was building an iconoclast. Donald's mind and tongue were sharp. So was his pen. To libel laws, he paid little or no attention, and when he felt he was right, he wrote what he thought.

Late one afternoon at about tea time, Hong Kong's quiet reserve was more than rumpled by the leader in the *China Mail*, just off the press. Donald was lashing out at the ponderous bureaucracy of the colonial government. It was a fight to extend electoral rights to the people, to permit election of representatives on the colony's governing body. He twitted the government for living in the lethargy of past governments, for the laxity of officialdom, for the nepotic-like way honors befell them.

A point in example was made. A few years before, bubonic plague had been rampant in the colony. Committees were formed to stamp it out, one being headed by an official who was paid for his time, the other by a Hong Kong barrister who gave up his practice and received no pay. At the end of the plague, the official was honored with a C.M.G.[1] and considerable fanfare. The barrister, who had worked hard and unselfishly, was given a silver inkwell.

The morning after the article appeared, an indignant letter lay on Donald's desk. It was signed by Sir Henry May, the colonial secretary. It read:

I take the strongest possible objection to your reference to the C.M.G. bestowed upon me by Her Majesty, Queen Victoria. It was not given to me for suppressing bubonic plague, but for correcting labor disputes.

Donald made a quick answer:

Since you seem to be unaware of the reason for your C.M.G., I refer you to the Laws and Courts of Hong Kong. There is a page which records a citation noting that your reward was given for suppressing bubonic plague.

For a long time Donald puzzled over the exchange of letters. Was it possible that Sir Henry, living in his clouds at the Peak, had never bothered to learn why he had received his C.M.G.?

Hong Kong's wealth and the supposed naïveté of those who possessed it attracted a variety of men who lived by their wits, scoundrels and crackpots, adventurers and get-rich-quick promoters. Their misfortune was to meet up with Donald—a man who, aided by his uncanny hunches, was quick to penetrate fraud.

In 1906, he tried to prevent before it happened, the fraud of the Junk Bay Flour Mill. The mill, a promotion of an American, opened its financing to public subscription. Casually, Donald noted a curiosity. The mill was importing wheat from Australia, grinding it, and throwing away the bran and other by-products. Since a sack of ground flour landed at Hong Kong cost no more than a sack of unground wheat, where was the profit?

One day, J. B. Suttor, who represented the New South Wales government at Tokyo, stopped off at Hong Kong. He had heard of Donald

[1] Companion of St. Michael and St. George, military and civil order of merit, founded by George III, in 1818.

and invited him to tiffin. Before the first course arrived, Suttor said: "I'm investing my money in one of your industries."

Genuinely interested, Donald politely asked which one, and when it became plain Suttor intended to be noncommittal, he said sharply that he hoped it wasn't the Junk Bay mill. Suttor said it was.

"Well," said Donald, "don't conclude any contracts to put money in that mill. You go right out and cancel the damn thing. If you don't, you'll lose all your money."

Suttor replied, "Oh, I think I know what I'm doing."

The storm in Donald's character blew. He threw down his napkin. "You're such a damn fool," he exploded, "that I won't have tiffin with you!" He left, but from his office he wrote Suttor a chit: "You'll excuse me for not eating with you, but you'll lose every cent in Junk Bay. Take my advice and get out."

Suttor didn't reply.

Donald's information sources were almost limitless, and through them a few days later he learned his hunch was correct. Stock was being sold by the bundles and the money pocketed by unscrupulous mill officials. Shortly thereafter, the American promoter came to him seeking publicity. Donald denied it to him but one of Hong Kong's other newspapers reported the story of the mill with lavish approval. Donald met this with a letter to the governor, giving what should have been conclusive proof to him that a swindle was afoot and that Hong Kong, since its residents had invested heavily, might be in for a financial debacle. The governor's reply was a blunt dismissal of Donald's letter. The collapse came and on the eve of it the American committed suicide. It was found that he had speculated and lost a fortune in shareholders' money on the Chicago grain market.

Later, a letter came from Suttor in Japan. He wrote:

DEAR MR. DONALD:
I have read of the death of the Junk Bay Mill man. I want to thank you, as after I left, I cancelled my arrangements. I didn't lose anything.

Others were not so fortunate. Many lost heavily.

But all was not seriousness with Donald. One of the most fascinating sides to his character was the ability to turn from probing into the most profound of community problems to things that might easily have delighted a college freshman. But he never trumped up a meaningless prank. There was always some subsurface purpose. A typical episode began one day when, passing through the lobby of the King Edward Hotel, he spied Hong Kong's superintendent of police. For months he had been chiding him editorially for his inability to check kidnaping which had become rampant in the colony. The charges were always denied.

He paused in front of the tall superintendent and said with a twinkle, "Well, how go the kidnapings?"

The superintendent gazed down on Donald, twisted the ends of his mustache irritably. He said, "Donald, you know damn well we have no kidnaping here. It just can't be done."

Donald laughed and walked on.

Later that day he was in a room of the same hotel visiting a friend, Hugh Ward, an American eccentric dancer and capable actor. Ward and Grace Palotta, a British girl, had brought a theatrical troupe from Australia to Hong Kong. While Donald and Ward were talking, an ayah entered. She was pretty and petite, black eyes and dark ivory skin.

Donald flashed a wide smile. "Hello, Princess," he called. She curtsied and withdrew.

Ward looked questioningly. "Princess?" he asked.

"Of course. Can't you see it?"

Puzzled, the actor said that he knew her only as Miss Palotta's Indian maidservant. Donald, of course, had never seen the girl before. His remark had been but a whimsey of the moment.

He said to Ward, tongue in cheek, "She's the daughter of a maharajah at Calcutta who was involved in a plot to dynamite India's viceroy. She exposed it because she was afraid her lover—an aide to the viceroy—would be killed. She had to flee."

Ward sat with his mouth and eyes wide open, looking very much like a guppy. Straight faced, Donald said, "Ward, you've got a fine story here. Its publication would give your troupe some good publicity. We could manage it by kidnaping the girl."

Ward continued to ogle him.

"I've a friend who will do it—a ship captain named Mariveles,"

Donald went on. "He's a mountain of a man with wild black whiskers all over his face. He looks like a pirate."

Donald left, located Mariveles and told him that he wanted him to kidnap a girl, outlining the scheme he had worked out on the way.

The hoax went off as Donald had planned.

Mariveles kidnaped the Indian girl as she was leaving the hotel on a prearranged errand, and while Ward raised the alarm, the melodrama was under way. Donald went down harbor where he met a sampan on which the captain was holding the girl, effected a dramatic and convincing rescue before a crowd of excited Chinese and hustled the weeping girl back to the hotel in a sedan chair. There, furious, the men of the company were on the point of hunting down the kidnaper to hang him. Donald sent a warning to Mariveles to stay aboard his ship.

Continuing with the plot, as put together by Donald, Ward himself phoned the editor of the *South China Morning Post*, George Lloyd, that a man by the name of Hugh Ward at the King Edward Hotel could supply him with details of a sensational kidnaping. When Lloyd arrived, the actor at first denied knowledge of the incident, later admitted its truth, but refused to release details since he said he had promised the story to a Mr. Donald, of the *China Mail*. At this point, Donald, listening in the next room, walked in.

Lloyd greeted him with: "Well, Donald, I hear that you have a good kidnaping story sewed up. That's not cricket, you know, since your paper already has gone to press."

Donald answered testily, "Do you suggest I supply you with stories, George. You're my opposition. Dig up your own stories."

"But," Lloyd protested, "we of the press should stick together in kicking at this rotten kidnaping business. I go to press in three hours. Your next edition is late tomorrow afternoon. The story would be stale by then."

Donald pretended to consider for awhile. "All right," he finally said, "all right. But remember to return the favor some day."

The ayah, crying and moaning, was brought in and relived the horror for Lloyd's benefit. Then Donald went back to Lloyd's office with him, and helped write the story which identified the ayah's rescuer only as "a foreigner."

After the paper had gone to press, he said: "By the way, George, expect a visit from the police superintendent when your papers hit the street in the morning. What are you going to say to him?"

Lloyd, mouth agape, stopped fumbling with a fresh batch of galley proofs.

"Well," said Donald, "I'll tell you what to say. Just say to the superintendent: Donald helped me with the story."

The next morning the superintendent dropped in on Lloyd, paper in hand, story neatly circled in red ink. He pointed to it, and eyed the *South China Morning Post*'s editor. Lloyd repeated what Donald had told him.

The British police official stood up, clapped on his hat. "Damn that Australian!" he said and stomped out.

Correspondents wired the story to other countries. In India the press branded the story an utter lie, while in Australia editorial fingers were waggled. It was said that Ward might think he was building up the princess' name to exploit, but he would find that the White Australian Policy would ban her.

The theatrical troupe never found out the truth. Lloyd never learned that he had been victimized.

Although Donald still had time for elaborate practical jokes of this kind and always would, he was drifting more and more toward persons of kindred political and sentimental spirit. He found himself fitting into the Chinese pattern. When he first began to visit the yamen at Canton, he had taken up the study of Cantonese. Sir Henry May, however, had advised against it, and had explained that he had studied Mandarin while in Peking but had found little use for it thereafter. He had added that there were more than a hundred different dialects in China. Donald had stopped his studies. Anyway, he had decided that knowledge of the language might be a deterrent. If he learned to speak it, he would be able to understand what was not meant for his ears, and the Chinese would have no conversational freedom. He made his decision clear to them. Quickly forgotten was what little he knew, and he never learned another word of Chinese. He did not even pronounce the names of his friends, or cities or towns with exactness. It lent him a quaint quality and the Chinese found him all the more enjoyable.

More than on any one thing, Donald's thoughts were on China, with a growing feeling that here was greatness, islands of it, floating unconnected, aimless. In between were seas of corruption, inefficiency, lethargy without end. These were the problems he thought about. He saw corrections for many. His exhilaration carried him frequently to Viceroy Chang's yamen where his understanding of the problem grew.

Canton was a busy hive of industry and of politics, of intrigue and happenings which stood for mystery in the eyes of the world. The heavy hand of autocratic government was everywhere. From it stemmed a widening flow of difficulties: high taxation and no benefits, few schools and fewer roads, deplorable sanitation. With the viceroy and his officials, Donald was sharply critical of the Manchus. He preached reform, a thorough housecleaning. He said he hoped they would follow his advice and recognize the evils of their times. They sat and listened, the viceroy tugging at his mustache, his peacock feathers bobbing.

One day Wen Tseng-yao, whom Donald had met with the old admiral and others on his first visit to the yamen, and whom he regarded as the most liberal and progressive of the lot, pinned him with a long and serious gaze. He said in English, "We will have a constitution and a republic one of these days." Donald stared. Was it possible that Wen was lending an ear to revolutionary talk? To the Manchu government, such talk was treason. But it was plain that Wen, a Manchu official, had decided that his remark was safe with Donald. The tutor came in, smiled a greeting and seated himself next to Wen.

Finally Wen asked, "What do you think adviser?"

Donald waited awhile before he began: "The house must topple first before the carpenter can begin to build on new foundations. But be careful who does the toppling. If it were a storm from Japan—that would be disastrous." After a pause, he went on: "When you deal with the Japanese, businessmen or diplomats, you have made a bargain no better than that with a harlot. Delight is promised, but the kiss can carry a blight."

He eyed his listeners aggressively, earnestly. With customary candor, he said: "Stay away from them, or some day their rot may eat deep into you. They're coming into China with smiles and you, like young men emerging from puberty, are itching to go to bed with them— commercially, of course. But mark what I say, you cannot do business with people who substitute guile and deceit for friendship and honesty. If you cannot see this, then you have two enemies—yourselves and them."

When Donald left, he had a feeling that his months of campaigning might be showing results. Wen's remark had been token of a new kind of confidence in their adviser. How strange it is, he thought, that this should happen to one who used to look for fires out on the highways of Sydney, and what the roundsmen euphemistically described as "dead 'uns" in the morgue.

Sometime later, in a letter to his sister, Mrs. Joseph C. Orr, of Sydney, he wrote:

Somehow, without any effort, I have managed to hold the confidence of many political factions in China. Lots of people who know China ask me how, seeing that I never learned to speak the language, and all I can tell them is that I have none of the European's superiority complex, treat confidences as confidences, play the game, and keep smiling. I must have the intuitive understanding of the Chinese character. I tell them exactly what I think of them when they are wrong, which is most of the time, and never humbug them. That is all, except that I never can be bought by them, and this they respect.

chapter

4

UNEASY DAYS FOR THE MANCHUS

A house maintained by oppression cannot long enjoy its prosperity.

❦

In Donald's visits to Canton, he heard the name of Dr. Sun Yat-sen mentioned with growing frequency. The doctor's program for reform interested him. He knew that Canton housed revolutionaries—students who had returned from abroad with respect for the Westerner's government. They were engaged in translating books on politics as a means of spreading their program among their countrymen. In secret, they met and plotted.

One day, missionary friends brought him a story of an incident that had happened in a village near Canton. A group of youthful revolutionaries had been discovered. Manchu executioners were marched to the spot, and the youths dragged into the street and beheaded. Their heads then had been suspended from high places around the village square as a warning.

Over such incidents Donald had brooded many times. The rottenness of the Peking government was evident everywhere. There was no sympathy for the cries of the people. As adviser to the viceroy, he had spoken of the inevitableness of a day of reckoning. In these instances, his advice on the necessity of considering reforms would usually be met by the typical Asiatic reluctance to face the finality of decision. He would be reminded politely: We are here only to carry out the will of Peking.

The night he heard of the latest beheading, Donald once again spent hours thinking about China's degradation. By what means might she sluice herself of her iniquities and regain the proud dignity she had once had? Would time itself be enough to educate the decadent Manchus and their Chinese cat's-paws to a better way, a more decent way of living? Apparently neither time nor the example of other nations could do it. They had had their chance and they had failed. What China needed now was a blood transfusion. She needed new life. Was Dr. Sun Yat-sen, were the revolutionaries the answer? There was no one else who offered hope, or who said it was time to throw off the leeches.

In 1908, Donald sought out the Revolutionary party in Hong Kong. He said simply that he wanted to join them, that he wanted to help, that above all he was anxious that China regenerate herself. Donald's visit surprised the Chinese. It was something that none of them had anticipated: that a foreigner, the editor of Hong Kong's leading newspaper, should offer himself as a party in a plot against the government. But they had known of him as a fighter of what was right, as an exponent of the Chinese point of view, and so they welcomed him warmly.

At this time he did not meet Dr. Sun. The leader was either in America or Britain. No one was quite sure. But Dr. Hu Han-min, Sun's confederate, gripped Donald's hand, and from that time on, he was solidly a part of the Revolutionary movement. He met with them secretly, and day after day they found themselves turning to him for explanations and advice. What was said in these meetings, he kept in the strictest confidence. The revolutionaries knew that he was continuing as adviser to the Canton government, and they were content with this for they had deep faith in his integrity.

Dr. Sun had begun revolutionary activities as early as 1894 while still a medical student at the Alice Memorial Hospital at Hong Kong. After the 1895 war with Japan, he formed a revolutionary party known as the Hing-Chung-Hui, later the Tung-Ming-Hui, forerunners to the present-day Kuomintang. The futile resistance of China had alarmed him so deeply that he had written memorials to the Throne, urging reforms. They had been tossed aside. Embittered, Sun had decided revolution was what China must have.

His party's first effort was aimed at Canton where he attempted to infiltrate his revolutionists by shipping them from Hong Kong in cement barrels. The plot was frustrated by treachery within his own ranks. Dr. Sun was forced to flee, and eventually a price of one hundred thousand pounds was put on his head.

In the days that followed, the revolutionists sought a foothold wherever they thought incipient revolt against the Manchus was manifest. Time and again, their hopes were dashed by the ignorance of the people and the superiority of the Imperial troops.

Sun gathered young Chinese into the fold, traveled the world seeking funds and members. At intervals, he returned to China, searching for opportunities to incite revolt, but each time Peking sounded the alarm and set bloodhounds on his trail. Soon he no longer could approach China; he was forced to work under foreign flags.

The quiet, dreamy doctor was the center of many an exciting drama. He himself was to tell Donald one day of a time in the heart of London, far, he believed, from Peking's sharp talons, when Manchu agents had fallen in step with him, and he had felt the points of their knives in his back. Quietly, and in what seemed impossible melodrama, they had marched him through street after street and into the Chinese Legation. There they had imprisoned him, awaiting the opportunity to transport him secretly to China for beheading. Faced with the impossibility of escape, he had dropped a note from his window to a busy street below. It was a last desperate chance and it worked. He had addressed it to his old professor at the Hong Kong medical school, Sir James Cantlie. A passer-by had found it and delivered it to Sir James who was then in London. The British Foreign Office had been notified, and Sun had been freed in time to prevent his being placed aboard a Chinese warship that had just arrived.

Overnight he sprang into prominence as a revolutionary figure in the eyes of the Chinese people and the rest of the world. By kidnaping him, the Manchus had advertised that revolution was afoot, thereby aiding, not hindering, Sun's cause. They had pointed up their own corruptness.

Donald heard one day early in 1908 that Dr. Sun had slipped into Macao, a Portuguese island off the South China coast. He knew that meant but one thing: more trouble for the Manchus. Ultimately it was to mean considerably more trouble for the Japanese, and Donald was to play a part in fomenting that trouble.

At Macao, a disreputable Japanese freighter, *Tatsu Maru* II, was loaded by Dr. Sun with arms and munitions, and headed up the Pearl River for a rendezvous with revolutionaries near Canton. Captain Woo Kwan-kien, Donald's friend of early yamen days, brought her to a halt under the guns of his gunboat, the *Bopik*. He seized the contraband, pulled down the Japanese flag, ran up the Manchu double-dragon emblem and took her into Canton. At Tokyo, a furious Japanese government demanded retribution for the humiliation.

Several days after the *Tatsu Maru* affair, Donald was at the yamen and there he found his friends nervous and confused. The old viceroy sat in his usual position at the head of the long table, his mandarin hat at a rakish angle. He said to Donald, "Adviser, we are in terrible trouble over the *Tatsu Maru* and *Bopik* incident. The Japanese have hammered the table at Peking. Now my empress has ordered me to kowtow to the Japanese flag and pay them an indemnity of twelve million dollars." He made a gesture of despair and said, "There is nothing to do but obey."

A command from Tzu Hsi, the dowager empress, an Oriental Catherine The Great, powerful, malevolent, spiteful. In 1861, she had taken up the regency for her nephew, Kuang Hsu, and for forty-seven years her shadow had been cast across the empire.

Kuang Hsu, strong neither physically nor in character, became emperor in 1875, but a reactionary element with the dowager empress as its center was in actual control. A few of the country's liberals, however, managed to gather around him, and step by step they influenced him in the matter of reforms. The central figure was his tutor, Kang Yu-wei, brilliantly progressive, scholarly, and the idol of Young China. By 1898, Kuang Hsu, under his direction, was ready to give China a new deal and what ultimately would have amounted to constitutional government.

Before the reforms could be instituted, the standpatters—the mandarins who wanted no change—complained to the dowager empress, and Kang Yu-wei, realizing that she was a roadblock to reform, suggested her disposal. The emperor agreed and called in a man he thought he could trust—General Yuan Shih-kai. Yuan, then head of China's only modernized army, was commissioned first to kill her chief adviser, then to imprison her. He weighed the pros and cons, decided it more profitable to expose the plot. The dowager empress then ordered Kuang Hsu imprisoned in the Winter Palace and took command once again, abolishing, through the aid of Yuan Shih-kai, nearly all the reforms Kuang Hsu had promulgated. Kang Yu-wei escaped, but other reformers were beheaded.

Time had diluted none of the dowager empress' arrogance or dictatorial manner. Her latest arbitrary command Donald now held in his hand. Viceroy Chang had handed it to him nervously, saying he would have to obey.

The first real opportunity had come for Donald to lash out against the moral rot caused by the Manchus. He faced his friends and said:

"You cannot humble yourselves or China like this, gentlemen. You tell the old dame you won't do it!"

"No," the viceroy protested, "never. If I did, you'd find my head in the gutter."

Donald answered sharply, "You forget there is more to China than this yamen, the concubines, your jade snuffboxes, the gold and silver, and your peacock feathers."

He ground out his cigar and rose from the long table. He walked over to Chang. "There are the people," he added.

The viceroy looked up, perplexed, uncomprehending. He asked, "Who are the people?"

Donald knew the value of words and he did not mince them. He could describe a situation so vividly that it remained in one's memory, unforgettable. "Who are the people?" he echoed and began to talk. "I'll tell you who they are! They are the sweat that runs in your rivers. They are the bones that build your mansions. They are the blood of your wine, the meat at your table. They are the quilts in winter, the fans in summer, the tea when you are thirsty. They are the laughter in despair. They are a philosophy unending, untiring, an oasis for the weary such as you."

He looked from one to another of his old friends. The viceroy's head bobbed gently, as if on a spring. Donald said, "They make men like you fat."

With exception of Wen Tseng-yao and the tutor, they could not comprehend what Donald had said. They did not know the people. They governed without a thought for them.

The viceroy said after awhile, "Well, Adviser, what do you propose?"

"Give me forty-eight hours. I'll show you who the people are."

At that time, Canton's seventy-two tradesmen's guilds, thirteen charitable institutions and the chamber of commerce were the chief influences among the masses. When the viceroy agreed somewhat skeptically to Donald's request, the newspaperman launched into a whirlwind tour of the ancient city. He called on individual guilds here, officers of groups of others there, explaining the humiliation Peking proposed, exhorting them to stir the members into energetic protest.

"You cannot permit the Manchus to force you into this shame," he declared through an interpreter. "You must rise up and speak vigorously. You will have to recognize the Manchus for what they are—vampires battening on the Chinese!"

Appearing before the chamber of commerce, he spoke for an hour. "In a war thirteen years ago," he concluded, "the Japanese sought to grind you underfoot. Now, again, they would make you feel the hard heel of their triumph. I want this body to secure two thousand signed memorials to the viceroy urging him to ignore the order of the Manchus." He hastened from one side of the city to the other. For two days, he slept little. At the end of that time, the yamen was swamped with protests.

They were but the first murmur and from them grew a rumble, louder and louder. An idea for a boycott of Japanese goods sprang up. It was quickly labeled the "*Tatsu Maru* Boycott" and it raced over South China like a typhoon. It became a violent and savage weapon. Japanese locked their doors and fled, their shops burning behind them. Chinese stores selling Japanese goods also were wrecked and fired. Agitation mounted. Here was the answer to the viceroy's question, "Who are the people?"

Donald had done an effective job, and had proved, if it was necessary, his practical value as an adviser. Japanese commercial enterprise in South China was derailed for a long time, and when Japan counted her losses, she discovered that the boycott had cost her people three hundred million yen! The outcome was that the viceroy did not kow-tow to the Japanese flag, nor did Canton pay the twelve million dollar indemnity.

Tokyo began to build a dossier on one W. H. Donald.

The fever of the boycott had just begun to cool when, in a much-publicized article, Donald exposed a new Japanese threat. With his exposure, agitation to humiliate and wreck Japan commercially in South China began again. His old friend, Captain Woo, had told him of his discovery that Japanese had sneaked into the Pratas reefs, one hundred and forty miles northeast of Hong Kong, and had stolen them from China.

When Woo arrived there he found a Japanese colony engaged in removing the highly prized fertilizer, the guano deposits of birds. He soon discovered that the Chinese had been driven off and that their possessions had been burned. The head of the Japanese colony had declared belligerently that the land belonged to them by right of dis-covery, and he pretended he was astonished to hear that anyone had ever seen the island before.

"Why," the spokesman said, "it was thrown up by a volcano just before we found it."

Woo looked at him quietly. "With ten feet of bird dung already on it?" he asked.

The Japanese grunted. He pointed to the Rising Sun flag overhead. "We stay," he said.

Woo retorted, "You people must learn to stay at home."

He left after taking photographs to prove the Japanese were in permanent residence. At first, Tokyo vigorously denied the occupation but under Donald's continuing publicity on the affair, admitted it. The "Guano Colony" was withdrawn, but not before new demonstrations against Japan had bubbled up in South China cities.

While Donald worked against one enemy of China's—Japan—the forty-one-year-old Dr. Sun worked against what to him was another—the Manchus. But he was no military leader, and his plans were always

vague and inadequate. His abortive revolt in the provinces of Kwangtung and Yunnan in 1907, the year before the *Tatsu Maru* incident,
was a good example of his early efforts. Years later, he told Donald
that his heart was nearly broken by the affair.

At Limchow where the revolt had started, the people had risen
against the Manchu magistrate who had overextended himself in the
usual and expected "squeeze" of monies. This was the sort of tyranny
and corruption of which revolution was bred, and Dr. Sun had hoped
that he might make the most of it. He had rushed a ragged band of
revolutionaries there. On street corners, at temple doors, in guild halls,
they preached a fight by the people against the Manchus.

At the time, there were four million Manchus left in the empire.
The burden of their upkeep was upon the Chinese, the Manchus
sitting in the sun, growing fat, working as neither farmers nor artisans.
They were set aside as soldiers and officials only, but as soldiers they
had merely to settle down in some city where there was a Manchu
quarter, and the pay their rank entitled them to flowed in. The grip on
the people was kept firm by a Tartar general who held the keys of
whatever city he was stationed in and commanded all troops.

Sale of office and the resultant "squeeze" constituted a long-standing
grievance. The practice was introduced in 1860 and flourished under
the dowager empress. Originally, no rank higher than a magistracy
could be purchased and then only by a person of literary attainments.
By the time of the Limchow uprising, however, conditions had degen-
erated to the point where even an illiterate could buy office if he had
sufficient money. Donald knew that his old friend, Viceroy Chang
Chen-chun, had paid half a million Chinese dollars for his Canton
post and that he had retrieved it all through "squeeze" in his first six
months in office.

At Limchow, however, the people shrugged off the pleas of the
revolutionaries to help end this type of corruption. They said they had
no dealings with the Manchus, that they only wanted to rid themselves
of a harsh magistrate. They were uninterested in Sun's dream of a
republic.

Couriers arrived from General Huang Hsin, a revolutionist planted
in the Manchu forces that were en route to quell the revolt. The rebels

were told to ready for defense, to open fire at the first glimpse of the troops. This would be the signal for General Huang to desert with some men and help repel the Manchus. The revolutionists were in a quandary. With only a few pistols among them, they were without means of defense, since the townspeople refused to supply them with arms.

Use of firecrackers was finally suggested. An idea. Perhaps the farce might do the trick. Sun's men sped through the town, talking up the efficacy of welcoming the government troops with a firecracker display. It made sense to the townspeople. Already they had given up the idea of revolt and had decided to negotiate with the Manchu force for the magistrate's removal.

One night just at dark the Imperialists appeared. Firecrackers were ignited, the people shouted and a sound arose like a small arms attack. The rumpus halted the Manchus, and General Huang and his soldiers burst into Limchow.

"Where," Huang asked, "is your army?" The revolutionists replied that they had none, that the firing was done by crackers.

Huang eyed them queerly. "You people should be home in bed!" he exclaimed. "Well, let's run. We can't fight the Manchus with fists."

In the darkness, Sun's band of impractical revolutionaries, in company with Huang Hsin's men, fled southwestward toward the French Indo-China frontier. They captured an Imperial outpost on a high hill and settled down to recuperate before launching an expedition into Yunnan Province. Pursuing Manchus were promptly forgotten and remembered only when they dashed up the hill, aided by sympathetic country folk. The revolutionists fled once more.

Dr. Sun and Dr. Hu Han-Min reached Hanoï, in Indo-China, to begin recruiting for the projected Yunnan operation. But revolutionists left behind became impatient and opened the campaign prematurely. They did well for a few days, but eventually they were pushed across into French Indo-China. It was another setback for Sun, but it was the nearest he had come up to that time to gaining a foothold.

But revolution was in their blood, and they carried the germ into the French colony. There, Sun's beaten forces joined with an old bandit leader, De Taam, who raised the flag of revolt against the

French. A war situation developed that could not be put down for a year.

The outcome of the unfortunate affair was that another country, Indo-China, slammed its doors on the Drs. Sun and Hu.

In the North, another man also watched the Manchus. He was bulky, black-mustached Yuan Shih-kai, whom Donald regarded as clever and capable yet dangerously ambitious. He had been in and out of more political plots than any man in China. In 1882, he became Imperial President of Korea and held the post until he and the Chinese were expelled by Japan in the 1895 war. As a reward for doublecrossing Emperor Kuang Hsu, the old Empress Tzu Hsi made him governor of Shantung Province. Two years later he became viceroy of the province of Chihli. Donald knew many of Yuan's close friends. He was to know Yuan himself intimately in the days to come.

Yuan had won an international popularity by ignoring the edict of the dowager empress in the 1900 Boxer Rebellion to dispose of foreigners and their interests. He pretended the edict had been falsified before it reached him. Unknown to her, instead of molesting foreigners he gave them protection. Elsewhere, however, foreign property had gone up in flames.

Late in 1908 a new uneasiness crept over Peking. The viciousness of Tzu Hsi had grown, and at the Winter Palace the deposed monarch, Kuang Hsu, lived a Roman holiday of wine, women and opium. Gradually his thin body grew frailer. Tzu Hsi and many in the court fed his weakness with a kindness that was sinister. Yuan Shih-kai, now grand councilor and head of the Manchu armies, continued his watch.

On November 14, Donald received a telegram at Hong Kong asking him to hurry to Canton. There he read alarm in the faces of the viceroy and his officials.

"The dowager empress and the emperor have suddenly died," the viceroy said, his voice trembling.

Donald was not surprised. Notorious for its iniquities, Peking, he was sure, was capable of producing any number of enigmatic or disrupting affairs. His newsman's sense told him that it was murder.

"Whoever died last," he finally said, "must have been killed. Who was it, Kuang Hsu or Tzu Hsi?"

The old man's eyes were expressionless. He wagged his big head slowly. He did not know. All that he knew was that his empress—the one who would have had him kiss the Japanese flag—was gone.

Wen Tseng-yao came in with a telegraphed Imperial announcement. He read aloud that a new emperor was on the throne, three-year-old Prince Pu Yi, nephew of Kuang Hsu. His father, Prince Chun, was to act as regent.

The old viceroy took Donald by the arm. "Adviser," he said quietly, "this is a moment of great weakness. I believe you know about such things. Will the revolutionists strike now?"

Donald looked serenely at him. The viceroy never before had even hinted that Donald might have personal knowledge of the revolutionists' plans. For a fleeting moment the Australian searched the Manchu official's face, but he saw nothing except sadness and desperation. He said: "I once suggested that we never fool each other and so, were it possible, I would not try it now. It's true that I know revolutionists and that I am in sympathy with them. But the fact is, old friend, I don't know the answer to your question. I do remember, however, an old Chinese proverb. It goes something like this: 'The past is as clear as a mirror, the future as dark as lacquer.'"

Donald went back to Hong Kong pondering the dilemma in the North. He could not escape the feeling that a crime had been committed. There he saw the first official accounts of the deaths. The Imperial Palace had announced that Tzu Hsi had died at 2:00 P.M., November 14. This had followed an announcement of a few hours before that Kuang Hsu was dead. Rumors were current that he had died two days previously.

Shortly thereafter Donald was at Penang, in the Straits Settlements. Here the brilliant tutor of Kuang Hsu, Kang Yu-wei, lived in exile, while at near-by Singapore Dr. Sun Yat-sen also was under the sanctuary of the British flag. But they were not so close politically. While they both wanted the rejuvenation of China, Kang wanted no revolution—only a housecleaning among the Manchus themselves.

Although his whereabouts were guarded, Donald sought him out to discuss the latest evidence of Peking's deterioration. With an air of secrecy, he was hustled into a carriage. The horses clopped through the handsomest residence quarter and down a lush street lined with tropical gardens, bungalows shining white, green or blue in the near-equator sun. Finally he arrived at a large, yellow palacelike house with a long, winding driveway lined with palms and banana trees.

There he met Kang—the man who ten years before had made world news. He had a finely shaped head, black hair tinged with gray, a tiny queue twisted against the crown. His mustache had the Manchu droop.

For awhile they talked of world problems and China's role in the future. Finally Donald said, "Peking says that you no longer exert influence in empire politics."

The eyes of the former power behind the throne showed fire and light. "That," he snorted, "is that scoundrel Yuan Shih-kai! He says that I am without power, does he? Well, I will see to it that he goes crashing shortly." He drummed the tips of his jade fingernail casings irritably on his teakwood desk, then said abruptly, "Yuan betrayed his emperor. He betrayed me. He was a tool of the dowager empress, and he wrecked the reforms. He is the reason why reactionaries have continued to dominate China. He is why history has been written so stupidly."

He paused, then leaned closer to Donald. He said, "Yuan killed the emperor. It is the truth. I know it and so do a few in Peking. The dowager empress died before Kuang Hsu, not after. Yuan knew that if the emperor were permitted to rule, he would lose his head for his treachery of ten years ago. I know that he paid a doctor fifty-five thousand dollars to poison the emperor."

Back at Hong Kong, Donald happened across David Fraser of the London *Times*.

"Who died first?" Donald asked.

"Don't know," said Fraser, "but I'll bet a guinea the old lady was murdered. What do you say?"

Donald laughed: "I'm no good at guessing."

History was to do no better. In the years that followed, no conclusive proof as to who died first was ever bared, nor was the strong suspicion of murder ever substantiated.

In Peking, elaborate rites had been prepared in the Forbidden City for the dowager empress and her nephew. Prince Chun, the regent, ordered a hundred days of mourning for the people, three years of it for the court. At this time, machinery was put into motion to rid the capital of the crafty Yuan Shih-kai. Under the old empress he had had too much power. Now she was gone. Prince Chun ordered him into the palace for the announced purpose of making the funeral arrangements. After that, Yuan disappeared from public view for several weeks. But he was too important a man in foreign eyes to be missing for any greater length of time. He reappeared one day with bag and baggage, headed for his birthplace and home in Hunan Province. There he settled down temporarily to a life of fishing and sour contemplation.

An Imperial edict proclaimed: "The Grand Councilor, Yuan Shih-kai, is departing because he has a sore leg."

When Donald heard about it, he checked dates. The edict had been issued just two days after Kang Yu-wei, in Penang, had told Donald that he still had influence in Peking and that Yuan's days were numbered.

5

JAMES GORDON BENNETT AND DONALD

Experience is a treasure that follows its owner everywhere.

🦋

Aт тне height of the *Tatsu Maru* case Donald had received a cable from James Gordon Bennett, publisher of the New York *Herald*. It read:

YOU ARE THE ONLY MAN WHO CAN MAKE SENSE OUT OF CHINA STOP PLEASE ACCEPT APPOINTMENT AS SOUTH CHINA CORRESPONDENT FOR NY HERALD.

Donald did, with an open go on expenses and what contemporaries considered a princely salary. Bennett, who underscored almost everything he touched with the word lavish, had become jealous of the scoops that Dr. George Morrison, also an Australian, was securing for the *Times* in London. Donald became Morrison's "opposition."

Bennett, regarded as bizarre by many, known familiarly as "The Commodore," dropped the anchor of his palatial yacht, *Lysistrata*, off steaming Singapore one day in 1908. With several dozen guests, he was on a cruise of the Far East. Anxious to know weather conditions to the north before proceeding to Hong Kong, he wired Donald.

The message caught Bennett's correspondent at edition time. Donald read:

WHAT ARE THE FOGS LIKE ON THE CHINA COAST.

He replied:

THEY ARE JUST LIKE ANY OTHER FOGS.

He heard later that Bennett had laughed and had gone boyishly from one guest to another saying, "He's a queer one, all right." Bennett messaged again:

I MEAN HOW ARE THEY.

Donald came back:

THEY ARE VERY WELL THANK YOU WHEN THEY ARE HERE BUT THERE ARE NONE HERE NOW.

The *Lysistrata* headed for Hong Kong.

It was Donald's first meeting with Bennett, and he was determined that if there was to be any jolting, he would get in the first jolt. Bennett had a flare for ribbing, sometimes with cutting abruptness. When occasion demanded, Donald, too, could chop his sentences neat and sharp.

He was on the wharf when Bennett's yacht slid into dock. Bennett hailed him, and when he came down the plank, Donald said, "Hello. Glad you're here. I want to say, first off—you may be a millionaire but you can't scare me."

"What's this?" the Commodore asked, hardly believing his ears.

"Your reputation is that you order people about," Donald smiled. "You can't do that with me. I'm an Australian. I'm declaring my independence of you."

"Good Lord!" exclaimed Bennett. "Were you born this way?"

At dinner that night, Bennett expressed his interest in matters Far Eastern. He said, "I'll tell you what we'll do. Each morning you come aboard my yacht. We'll have a conference."

Donald answered, "We'll do no such thing. I'm editor of a paper. It's just as important to me as the *Herald* is to you. You come and see me."

Bennett did. Each morning he made the long trip up Wyndham Street to the *China Mail* office. It was during one of their morning conferences that Donald explained how the world press had virtually forsaken China as a ground for interpretive writing by established correspondents. "As an editor, I'm unable to roam about at will," he said. "You bring J. K. Ohl from Manila and send him to, say, Peking, and the *Herald* will be the first newspaper with a news bureau in China." He lit a cigar and went on, "You will learn that this oldest but least understood nation writes the world's headlines. No one ever is to sleep comfortably as long as this restless giant thrashes about."

Bennett listened, and agreed. From Manila came a veteran *Herald* man—Colonel Ohl, one time of the Atlanta *Constitution*, later *Herald* man in Cuba, Japan, Korea, Manchuria, Burma and India. Except for the casual in-and-out correspondence of Dr. George Morrison for the *Times* and a Reuters man, Ohl became the only correspondent covering China on a full-time basis.

One morning Donald had just finished writing his dispatch for the *Herald* when the Commodore came in. "Well, Don," he said, "what are the bright ideas for today?" Donald's eyes idled over his desk, lighted on the *Herald* dispatch, and he said "Print this in Chinese on page one of the *Herald*." He tossed his story across to Bennett. "Great!" exclaimed Bennett. "How will we do it?"

Donald explained that he would telegraph his dispatch as usual but with instructions to take it to the Chinese consul-general for translation. The translated copy then could be taken to a printer on one of New York's Chinese newspapers who could set it in Chinese characters.

The next morning New Yorkers blinked as they picked up the *Herald*. An editor's note under the strange ideographs told readers that the *Herald*'s Hong Kong dispatch in English would be found elsewhere.

Another morning Bennett came in on the verge of gagging. He had just passed what old Hong Kong residents daintily referred to as a "honeycart"—a contrivance for collection of night-soil.

"Hell!" gasped the Commodore with his usual profanity. "How do you stand this damn stink!"

Donald laughed. "What stink?" he asked.

Bennett sputtered: "Do you mean to tell me you don't smell anything?"

"Not a thing."

Bennett looked incredulous until Donald explained that he had gradually lost his sense of smell since his arrival in China—that he could smell neither sewer nor rose. He said that he was without scientific substantiation, but he attributed his deadened smell to the fact that he smoked at least twelve cigars a day.

"Lord, what luck!" the Commodore said.

Shortly afterwards, Bennett and his party sailed for France and Donald received the following telegram from him:

NEED TWO BLACK CHOW DOGS STOP IF YOU KNOW ANYONE LEAVING FOR PARIS HAVE THEM DELIVER DOGS AT MY HOUSE STOP I'LL PAY FARE OF ALL CONCERNED.

Donald walked over to his interpreter, Li Sum-ling, with the telegram and said, "How would you like to go to Europe?"

Li's black eyes sparkled. Donald handed him the message and then wired Bennett:

LI WILL BRING YOUR CHOW DOGS.

Bennett came back:

TELL HIM TO KEEP HIS QUEUE AND WEAR HIS CHINESE GOWNS STOP WHEN HE ARRIVES IN EUROPE I'LL HAVE HIM INTERVIEWED AND HE CAN GIVE ARTICLES TO PRESS ON SITUATION IN CHINA.

One day Donald was checking proofs hurriedly at edition time when Li barged in and asked him a question concerning what he might say at Paris. Donald, annoyed, retorted:

"Oh, for heaven's sake! Ask the Commodore to publish articles advocating an alliance between China and the United States. That'll give you something to talk about." Li's queue disappeared through the doorway like a whipped puppy's tail, and Donald went on with his hurried reading. Suddenly, he looked up and called: "Oh, Li, damn it all, hustle over here!" When Li came, Donald said, "Forgive me for scolding—but that's a good idea I gave you. You follow it up. I'll give you the pros and cons. You write an article on the ship and give it to Mr. Bennett at Paris. I'll be a Dutchman if he doesn't print it!"

Li sailed, and the next Donald heard was a dispatch from Reuters dated London, stating, "The New York *Herald* is filled with articles advocating an alliance between China and America. Great space is being given editorially, in columns and interviews." Donald chuckled and dashed off a dispatch which began:

"HONG KONG—The consensus with regard to the proposed alliance between the United States and China is highly favorable. The brotherhood of the two great nations. . . ."

The following day Bennett wired Li's entire article with the message:

GREAT STUFF STOP THIS IS ELECTION YEAR AND THE HERALD IS UNINTERESTED IN MERITS OF EITHER WILLIAM HOWARD TAFT OR WILLIAM JENNINGS BRYAN STOP WE'LL MAKE CHINA ALLIANCE SUPERSEDE PRESIDENTIAL CAMPAIGN NEWS STOP YOU CAN SPEND UP TO FORTY THOUSAND DOLLARS FOR BUILD-UPS AT YOUR END.

Day after day the telegraph editor's desk on the *Herald* was swamped with voluminous dispatches from Donald. He had no knack for conciseness, and his forte was not short sentences. His stories, hardly ever under two columns in length, ran up fancy cable bills. One of his first read this way:

HONG KONG, Oct. 8, 1908—The advocacy of an alliance between the United States and China by the *Herald* has sent a thrill through the backbone of the old Celestial Empire and has perhaps done more toward a genuine awakening than any movement that has gone before.

The suggested linking of the oldest country in the Eastern World with the youngest and most vigorous in the West has fired the Chinese imagination and those who realize the vast possibilities in such a union are spreading the tidings and incidentally laying the foundation for a sound commercial connection with America, if not for a political bond, which will undoubtedly tie down for all times the erstwhile irrepressible turbulence that has ever made the Far East a source of concern to the Great Powers of the world.

The very vastness and consequent inertness of China has been the chief factor of uneasiness; her immense richness in undeveloped resources and her magnificent potentialities in commerce constitute a second; and a third, inspired by the other two, is the greed for territory and wealth displayed by all the powers except America. Already the Empire of China is sawed up into spheres of influence, and ever the powers who presume to exercise a controlling political sway within these spheres are hoping to see the day come when tenable excuse will be given for undisguised annexation.

China is saved from partition at the moment by the jealousy of the European nations, not by any particular restraining force which she herself is able to exert, and the fact is becoming more and more potent to her as time rolls on and developments assist to bring her sight into proper focus. . . .

The benefits of an alliance with America are not actually for today. Tomorrow and the years unborn will see the advantages and as nations must work rather for the future than for the present, the statesmen of the United States and China must weigh well the possible harvest to be garnered from seeds set in this season of beneficent sunshine and fructifying shower. Now is the time to plow and harrow and sow in the diplomatic farmyard. The harvest will be garnered unto seven times seven in the not too distant future.

Donald went about South China whipping up a fever for the alliance. There were official statements, expressions of the "ultimate glory" of the whole affair, photographs and fanfare. If Bennett sat in Paris mildly amused at his prank in the midst of a presidential year, Donald, conscientious, plugged hard at the alliance project. He spent the forty thousand dollars.

With the elections over, however, and Taft chosen as president, Bennett dropped the alliance as quickly as if it had burned his hand. It was never mentioned in the *Herald* again.

Li Sum-ling, in the meantime, had become a great favorite in Europe. His long black queue, his black silk gowns and silk slippers were a familiar sight in Paris. French dilettantes had whispered that he was a Chinese prince, and he became an attraction in a giddy Parisian society. The fable of Li traveled to the United States ahead of him, and when he arrived, Americans competed to act as his host. He was escorted to scenic spots, to gay parties, and everywhere people addressed him as "Your Highness." Li, the twenty-dollar-a-month translator, was in seventh heaven.

One day, however, Dr. Wu Ting-fang, Chinese minister at Washington, reached up into Li Sum-ling's lotus-strewn Elysian fields of make-believe and yanked him down. Minister Wu announced: "This man is not a prince. He is nobody."

Li returned to Hong Kong and his desk in a dusty corner of the *China Mail*. He said to Donald: "Wu Ting-fang is no friend of mine."

Old George Murray Bain was dead now, and Donald had assumed complete editorial control. He had installed the son of one of the paper's directors in a responsible position, but the time came when he found it necessary to dismiss him. Within an hour, the chairman of the board, a Mr. David Wood of the Public Works Department, stormed into Donald's office. He said that damn it all, no one was going to do this to the son of a director and that he wouldn't have it!

Donald remembered a day three or four years before and an irate Mr. Wood whose yacht he would have cut down, as certain as is the sun, if Wood had not altered course.

Now, independent as ever, Donald eyed him coldly. He said: "Mr. Wood, by the time you arrive at your office, you'll have my resignation."

When Wood got back, Donald's resignation was on his desk.

Donald went down the hill, taking with him poignant memories of two men—old Bain and George Hurd Reid. Behind was a newspaper that had come to reflect an ever-broadening picture of China. Through it, Donald had left an indelible mark on the British colony. Behind was a trail of accomplishments, notable among which was the University of Hong Kong, destined to become a great cultural center, established only after he had fought hard for it editorially. Also, he had organized the half-mile Hong Kong-Kowloon swim as an annual event and had put up a cup for the winner under the name of the *China Mail* after scoffers had said the swimming feat was impossible.

Donald opened an office on Queen's Road where he carried on his increasingly heavy correspondence for the *Herald* in addition to his metropolitan Australian papers. But pressure for his services was applied from other points. The bamboo telegraph was gradually carrying his name deeper and deeper into China, and legends, some true, some otherwise, sprang up. He was gaining a fame for wisdom, for calm, sage advice, for knowing the right word, the right action at the right time. His intuitive sense was elaborated upon, and it was said that wherever Donald appeared something important was certain to happen. Friends asserted that he could anticipate events, as he had "smelled out" the Russo-Japanese war. Requests that he be adviser to this city or that province, this office and that bureau came to him. He was offered handsome salaries. To all he replied, "I cannot now or ever accept pay for what I do for China. What I do I wish to do freely and independently, and if it is within my power to help, I will do so gladly." By letter, by conversation, he gave assistance to a confused and floundering officialdom, as he was doing for the old viceroy. But money he would not take.

Donald showed no favoritism in his unofficial role as adviser. If the cry was for help, it made no difference whether Manchu or revolutionary asked. There was only one rule: Honesty of purpose for China —and keep your money in your pocket.

On a day in the summer of 1909, a slender, cultured Chinese, Kao Erh-kim, called at Donald's office. "Peking has heard of your talents," he said. "I am here to appoint you adviser on the Delimitation Commission of the Macao boundary."

The Portuguese had settled in Macao three and a half centuries before, and thereafter they had virtually undisputed possession except for an ineffective attempt by the Dutch to oust them and one or two brushes with the Chinese. For a time, they paid ground rent annually, but in 1848 it was abolished, and in 1887 China, by treaty, recognized Portugal's jurisdiction over Macao and other near-by islands. No boundary was fixed, and the meeting that China had now called was to settle the matter.

China's desire to restrict Macao grew out of the *Tatsu Maru* gun-smuggling case at which time Portugal had charged that China had violated Macao waters in seizing the Japanese vessel. Sir Robert Hart,[1] the British director of the Chinese Imperial customs service, upheld the Portuguese claims, but his Peking superiors would not listen.

Although Donald told Mr. Kao that he knew nothing about boundaries, he accepted the appointment. Shortly, the Portuguese delegation from Lisbon arrived, headed by the mustached general, Sir Joachim Machado, K.C.M.G. The conference got under way at Hong Kong and for days it dragged through sultry weather, claims and counter-claims, gallons of tea and hot towels for sweat-drenched faces. The Portuguese maintained that Macao waters covered one hundred and twenty square miles, but, for purposes of negotiation, they offered to reduce their limits to sixty square miles. The Chinese sat obstinate, said that Macao had to be limited to two square miles and no water

---

[1] Entered customs service in 1850 as a deputy commissioner. Advanced to inspector-general in 1863, he reorganized the service practically on the lines it is now administered.

rights whatsoever. From time to time, Machado glanced wearily at Donald.

One day he came to him. He looked unhappy, frustrated. He said, "I want you to be my adviser."

Donald asked, "You ask that I ride horses traveling in opposite directions?"

"I can't understand these people. They talk in circles. Always, I have the feeling I'm walking from no place into nowhere."

"Well," replied Donald, "all right."

The negotiations continued on into autumn, Donald moving from one delegation to the other, seeking to mother two hostile views. But Mr. Kao had his hands tied. From the beginning, the people had been against negotiation. They denounced him as a traitor and threatened to assassinate him. They demanded forceful action. At Heungshan, directly across from Macao, and the birthplace of Sun Yat-sen, agitators opened a violent campaign of vituperation against Portugal. An identical situation had flared up at Canton, and once again, as it had in the boycott, the typhoon of the people raced wildly. Pamphlets and speakers spread astounding falsehoods about the Portuguese, inciting the people to a fear of a Portuguese invasion.

Watching the events, Donald thought he understood better now how unpredictable China was. He filed almost daily stories to the *Herald* on the progress of the negotiations. In one he wrote:

More than the delimitation of a frontier is involved . . . the interpretation and values of treaties are being tested, and more important still the Imperial Government of China is being asked to signify whether it really rules the populace. . . . The temper of the people may allow of an opinion as to whether China is yet ripe for the constitution which many enthusiastic and perhaps ill-advised agitators desire to have introduced immediately.

At another time, Donald apparently tried to foreshadow coming events, of which he now had intimate knowledge, by the sentence: ". . . in view of the undoubtedly important political developments that will very shortly shake the Middle Kingdom . . . it is vital to understand the present attitude of the common people with regard to foreign questions and show how the educated men of South China are prepared to regard signed treaties when they desire to serve their own purposes."

On the evening of November 12, General Machado called on Donald. He looked tired and confused.

"These people," he said, "have left me without blood, brain or energy. What'll I do?"

Donald looked sympathetically at the man he had come to admire for his honesty of effort. He said, "This land will make you sick but it is no fault of yours. Here the people have been ill for centuries and to many they are like an allergy, like goose feathers or cat's fur. I don't think I'm allergic, but you are. Go home to Portugal and be happy. Forget you ever came."

The next day the Portuguese delegation packed up and left soon afterwards. Chinese agitation quieted down almost overnight, and the Macao boundary question was never settled.

All this time, Donald had kept up his meetings with his revolutionary friends—a hotheaded, impetuous lot who stormed about in secret rendezvous shouting, "The Day, The Day! We are impatient for The Day!" At such times, Young China was a bucking stallion, and Donald found difficulty in reining it in.

From the north, the Manchus looked down with increasing alarm at an erratic and emotional South. The murmur for reforms grew louder. To meet it, the Peking government established provincial assemblies. In Peking's East City, the foundation was laid for a parliament house, but after the walls were three feet high, building ceased. The following year, in 1910, the National Assembly was established, but secret talk of "The Day" continued.

It was at this time that Donald took his one and only fling in business, with financial loss to him and his British associates. He employed an American, Dr. George Richman, of Manila's Bureau of Science, to study the possibilities of making newsprint and other paper manufactures from bamboo pulp. Richman's findings indicated that a point in French Indo-China was ideal. Donald organized a company with half British, half French capital, and himself as its managing director. Although the plant was eventually put into operation, Donald and his British partners lost heavily. To Donald's credit, however, was his anticipation of failure shortly after the venture was organized. He advised his board to transfer operations to the Philippines, but his suggestion was ignored.

In the course of the organization of the mill, he went to Europe to buy necessary machinery. He arrived late one night in Paris and sent a chit to James Gordon Bennett. The next morning at about six o'clock, Bennett's chauffeur appeared and handed Donald one of the Commodore's characteristic notes written in blue pencil: "Here is my coupé. Hurry over!" Instead, Donald scribbled at the bottom: "I'm in bed. I won't be up until nine o'clock. I'll come then." He handed it back to the shocked chauffeur.

When Donald's car pulled up in front of Bennett's avenue d'Iéna house sometime after nine, the gates swung magically open although no one was there. The house door was shut, but it, too, silently opened, and Donald walked in. Still he saw no one. Another door opened mysteriously and he walked on. Eventually, he came to Bennett's room, and there he was, standing in the doorway, grinning. Donald stopped and looked behind him, bewildered.

"Electric eye," the Commodore said laconically. "Just had it installed."

His room was covered with papers. He said, "I've done a day's work. I've been up since five." He added in sharp jest, "What's your trouble— taken to smoking opium?"

Donald snapped: "A rooster rises early and crows. Never lays an egg."

Bennett lifted his eyebrows. "I never laid an egg?"

"Come to think of it," Donald answered, "you did lay a bad one once."

"Yes?" asked Bennett, waiting.

"That job two years ago. The Sino-American alliance you courted, then jilted."

"Oh, that!" He brushed the thought aside.

Donald said, "I think I'll leave the New York *Herald*."

Bennett bristled and shouted, "What for?"

"I'm going to Shanghai."

"What are you going to do there?"

Donald knew, and Bennett might have had a hint had he remembered a line in a Donald story less than a year before: ". . . in view of the undoubtedly important political developments that will very shortly shake the Middle Kingdom. . . ." He said nothing.

Bennett looked at him searchingly for a while. "Well, you can work for the *Herald* there!"

"I don't think you can pay me enough."

Bennett asked how much he wanted, and Donald named a salary that he felt would be refused.

The Commodore waved his arms in dismissal.

"All right," he yelled, "all right. It's yours. Bugger off to Shanghai!"

chapter

6

RANDOM REVOLUTION

When the oil has burned dry,
the lamp goes out.

W̲ʜ̲ᴇ̲ɴ̲ Donald arrived in Shanghai in early spring, 1911, he lost no time in seeking out revolutionists. He had been advised that at the park of Mr. Chang Hsu-ho he would make his first contacts.

As he jogged along toward the park, Shanghai's majestic panorama unfolded. From the Bund that flanked the noisy, sluggish Whangpoo River—strewn with ships as if they had been spilled from a cornucopia—Nanking Road knifed through the hubbub of Shanghai's commercial heart until it blunted itself against the fierce confusion of a big crosstown artery, Thibet Road. Thereafter, it changed its name and complexion and, being Bubbling Well Road, rolled sedately as a stream past the racecourse, past high-walled, iron-gated residences and into what was then country. Two miles from Thibet Road it halted where Bubbling Well itself bubbled merrily in the center of the street. Along it came carriages, bells tinkling, their proud Chinese occupants followed at respectful distance by servants on ponies. Here and there, careening around rickshas, wheelbarrows and oxcarts, a foreigner in motor car with brazen horn. Donald passed through this medley of East and West, this incongruous jumble in the richest, most colorful city in the Far East.

He alighted at Mr. Chang's park. It was cool and inviting, a retreat for Chinese elite. Here, young swains courted maids without benefit of parental supervision. Here, also, revolutionists met, sometimes in secret, sometimes in the open to harangue audiences on the aims of Dr. Sun.

66

He had come to Shanghai for one purpose: revolution. Here was the machinery comparatively safe from Peking's agents. Even before he had left for Europe, he had, working with the revolutionists, trying to instill caution in them, helped set the day for the uprising against the Manchus. It was to have taken place in April, but the revolutionary express had been derailed at Canton earlier in the year. Overzealous converts under the spell of revolutionary whips had revolted prematurely and had been wiped out. It was another setback for Dr. Sun, who was somewhere in the United States collecting funds, giving vague promises to his benefactors, who ranged from Chinese laundrymen on New York's Mott Street to Japanese tailors in San Francisco.

Donald met his confederates, and as they talked he sensed that the quality of unrest as he had known it in South China was different. On the surface, the program against the Manchus appeared the same, but was something missing? The intangibleness of the thought bothered him. After awhile, he walked down to Charlie Soong's printing shop, on Shantung Road, where the high echelon in the underground often met.

Soong, the father of six children whose names one day were to be prominent in China's history, had been educated in religious colleges in the United States. He had returned to China to engage in religious work but, after an unfortunate incident with a dictatorial-minded associate, he had turned his religious zeal toward the much-needed industrialization of China. Before the close of the nineteenth century he had become a fast friend of Dr. Sun Yat-sen, and his home in Shanghai was often the intense little doctor's refuge.

After awhile, Sun came to be regarded as a member of the household by the Soong children: the boys, Tse-ven, who years later was to be China's premier; Tse-liang and Tse-an, destined to have roles in China's economy; and the girls, Ai-ling, who was to become Madame H. H. Kung; Ching-ling, the future Madame Sun Yat-sen; and Mei-ling, who was to marry Generalissimo Chiang Kai-shek. Himself now only a humble print shop proprietor, Charlie never dreamed that he had founded a Soong dynasty as powerful as many a Chinese dynasty in the past.

It was shortly after he met Sun that he set up his publishing house, and out of its front door came Bibles and other religious literature. From the back went revolutionary pamphlets and printed tirades against the Manchus. In addition, he had the task of trying to keep unbroken the link between his wandering doctor friend and "The Day."

Charlie was genial and hearty. He hailed Donald when he came through the door:

"Well! How's Australia's gift to confusion to the enemy!"

Donald laughed and sat down, after talking a few minutes with Ai-ling, a pretty, shy girl with intense black eyes. The year before, at twenty, she had returned from school in America. Now, besides teaching English, she was assisting her father in revolutionary activities. Mei-ling, about twelve, and eighteen-year-old Ching-ling were still in schools in America.

For awhile they talked quietly of the failure at Canton earlier in the year, of the rashness that made military organization difficult, of plans to stir up the people. Soong mentioned that there was pressure to explode the rebellion late in October. Donald was doubtful and stressed as he always did, the need for unity and organization. The Canton affair had pointed up a sad absence of cohesion. He asked his oft-repeated question:

"After the job against the Manchus is done, what then? You people have dodged the matter of government. Government is big and should be an efficient business. It must be more than a dream and a hope. You must have men trained and capable who will fill it with democracy."

One of the Chinese waved his hand delicately. "Oh," he said, "those are practical matters. I suppose someone is looking after the details."

Soong looked distressed.

Donald sat thoughtful. After awhile he said, "Government is no more or no less than a man's home. It is as easy as that—with the right people in it. There are rules, but not many. There is kindliness, appreciation, give and take. And, if it is a good home, it is also rich in imagination and accomplishment."

Through the window he could see on the streets below a swarm of humanity, unanimated, tired, pathetic. He went on, "It may take something more than we have to arouse passion in bodies that have become sodden clay. What do we have to offer such people? A dream is not enough, nor is it enough that we have brash young steers who act like Australian bushmen in town for a Saturday night drunk."

Soong nodded and Donald added, "What we are doing lacks spark. It lacks wind to sweep it along. It lacks a fire to burn into the people. There are four hundred million weighed down by the sorrows of centuries. They have been plagued by wars. They have given life and received only poverty and serfdom in return. Famines and floods have made them stoop while disease and pestilence gnawed at them. They have kneeled in supplication to a heaven only of corruption and lassitude."

Famine and flood. Dread words. Their ugliness was being written once again on the map of Central China. Famine had begun in the spring. Floods now had greatly accentuated it. They were engulfing a people who were asked to think of their political future. But what is the future of a man neck deep in swirling, muddy waters? It is true, perhaps, that a hungry people fight, but could it be true of a starving, emaciated people who, with bellies bloated from grass and roots, drop in the streets to writhe and groan?

Swelling river waters had brought disaster. The Yangtze, which snakes several thousand miles deep into China, had risen, swept away embankment after embankment and had inundated every province from Ichang to the sea. Cities and villages were wiped out, and drownings went into the hundreds of thousands. Millions were sent scurrying to the hills where they lived like animals, squatting unprotected under torrential downpours. They died by thousands from disease.

By September, flood waters were still high. Marooned on the hills, the millions sat and stared at the wastes. In areas near Shanghai, desperate bands were marching over the countryside, pillaging and burning shops and buildings. Adequate relief had not come from the government at Peking, and at Shanghai Mr. Amos P. Wilder,[1] the American consul-general, headed a famine committee while foreign firms were forced to give assistance. Famines had swept the country in

[1] Father of Thornton Wilder, American author and playwright.

1887 and in 1906-7, as they had countless times in centuries past and China had promised to take substantial preventive steps. She never did. The suffering had shocked the world, and each time foreign nations had sent relief funds, but officials had considered them merely fair game for plunder.

While the Yangtze Valley swam under an ocean of filth, Donald traveled upcountry to report for the *Herald* on the destruction and destitution. At Nanking the flood waters had started to recede. There he found his old friend, Viceroy Chang Chen-chun, who now was the high potentate over the populous provinces of Kiangsu and Kiangsi. It was a damp but joyous reunion. All around the viceregal yamen— one-time palace of Taiping kings[2]—the flood waters flowed, lapping against his wall, but the viceroy, older and feebler, was content that his fading vision blotted out the unhappy sight.

"Well, Adviser," he asked, "what do you think of the state of things now?"

Donald smiled. "If I were you, I'd keep my trunk packed," he said.

"Ah, but everything is receding."

"Old friend," Donald replied, "unhappily for you, that is the sad truth."

He headed into the city. So deep were the waters, a sampan carried him into the customhouse. Here the coolie, whose business it was to clean up the offices and courtyard, was up to his waist sweeping the top of the water, but Donald saw nothing to sweep. He thought: Will nothing ever change? How great will persuasian have to be to uproot old customs?

Before he returned to Shanghai, he surveyed thousands of square miles of inundated lands.

Corruption was rolling over the country with a squalor like that of the floods. On land, in provinces to the west and south, Peking sought honestly and almost futilely to stamp out opium growing in order to live up to its agreements with Britain and India of several years before.

[2] Fomented the Taiping Rebellion, a revolt against the Manchus, 1850-64. It started as an obscure religious (Christian) movement and spread rapidly. The Ever Victorious Army, first under the American, General Frederick Townsend Ward, later under the Britisher, General Charles "Chinese" Gordon, subdued it.

Imperial troops dashed from one section to another, lopping off poppy farmers' heads, carrying them about on skewers as a warning. On the sea, pirates roamed in junks, forcing coastwise vessels to install armor plating, hire armed guards. The Pacific Mail Line's steamer, *Asia*, en route from Hong Kong to the United States in late spring had piled up on rocks south of Shanghai. Before passengers or valuables could be removed, hundreds of junks had appeared and thousands of pirates had swarmed over her like ants around a lump of sugar. They had stripped her of a rich silk cargo and every other movable article. Dramatic stories by Donald and pictures of the disaster boomed *Herald* sales in New York and Paris. Elsewhere on the sea, both foreigners and Chinese engaged in the lucrative business of smuggling coolies into America and Australia.

Shanghai, where foreigners were the "untouchables" in their extra-territorial privileges, and Chinese could find partial sanctuary from the Manchus, was a receptacle for human residue. Scandal after scandal jarred the city that had become the financial and commercial axis of the Orient. A former Manchu official of Shanghai borrowed more than two million American dollars from British, German, French, Belgian, Dutch, Japanese and Russian banks, supposedly to bulwark wobbling native banks. Not long afterwards, he packed his belongings along with the bankers' cash and disappeared.

This was but one echo of the collapse of the great rubber boom of 1910. The frenzied rush for rubber shares, the wild flotation in Shang-hai of rubber company after rubber company—forty-five in all—was now beginning to produce other echoes. Men, once substantial, lost fortunes and reputations. There were falsifications of books, embezzle-ments, crafty and dishonest manipulations, and, as was inevitable, suicides. Chinese and foreigner alike had piled up fortunes on paper in an intoxication of get-rich-quick. The collapse submerged them in colossal debts. A British magistrate peered from under the muddle of extraterritorial entanglements the chaos had brought and opined: "Com-mercial morality is at a very low ebb."

So frantically eager were the Chinese to build fortunes overnight that even the directors of the Szechwan Railway Company bankrupted it by plunging company funds into bogus rubber estates. Other provincial railways were in a similarly critical position. Money had been lost in a variety of speculations.

Peking took what seemed the only logical step: It ordered the nationalization of railways which, when effected, would result in the abolition of each province's control of its own lines. This meant the business of the provincial roads would have to be wound up, thereby exposing the tremendous corruption. From the start, it was plain the directors would not be able to give an accounting. They would not be able to justify their huge expenditures of company receipts.

But there might be a way out. If a fire could be ignited among the people against Peking and its orders, the provincial railroaders could hide behind the ensuing smoke. Quickly, they convinced the populace that the Manchus were trying to usurp the rights of the people to run their own railways, that the Manchus would make everyone a slave. The cry grew and grew, and turmoil set in. Where Dr. Sun and his rabidly patriotic disciples had failed to capture the imagination of the people, the respected wealthy railway directors and other capitalists, who by one means or another were linked to the people's economy, were successful.

It was then that Donald felt he understood why he had sensed a difference in the character of the unrest in Central China as against that in the South. It was in the incentive. The push toward revolution was coming not so much from the bottom as from the top. It came more from capitalists who wanted to safeguard the source of their easy wealth from Peking interlopers than from the people.

Peking had borrowed money from foreign powers to finance its operation of a national railway system, and this, too, became a matter which the provinces seized upon in their anti-Manchu clamor, demanding cancellation of the loans. But in this, sympathetic elements in the Revolutionary party met immediate resistance from Donald. He would not associate himself with anything that might bring discredit to China or to a commitment by its government. Working quietly and inconspicuously, he placed speakers in meetings to resist the cancel-the-loan trend. Meetings were boisterous affairs, pro-Manchu and anti-Manchu cliques clashing along with divided elements among the revolutionists themselves.

The Peking government was on trial. It had entered its most anxious days. China boiled with unrest and hatreds. There was bad temper everywhere.

Still no date had been set for the revolution. Then, on October 9, 1911, just as twilight settled over the sprawling city of Hankow which looked bleakly across the still-swollen Yangtze to Wuchang, men gathered in a rain-washed mansion in the Russian Concession. It was rebel headquarters. They sat down in a barren room on the top floor to discuss, as they had for nights on end, the business of revolution, the business of dispatching the Manchus into a hell of obscurity. In the basement below, men with greater technical knowledge were at work on the technical side of the problem. They were making bombs.

In the conference room, Huang Hsin—who had dashed into Limchow four years before to find rebels using firecrackers instead of arms, and who had led the unsuccessful Canton uprising earlier in the year—spoke. Donald was not present but he heard the details later. Huang said, "We should be ready by the end of the month."

A slight, sharp-eyed youth protested: "But we lack army and arms. We are only a handful." He added reverently, "Our great leader—Dr. Sun—what has he to say?"

Huang answered quickly, "Dr. Sun? We don't know where he is. But never fear, we are on the verge of being ready."

A few minutes later, an ear-splitting explosion shook the house violently and broke windows across the street. One of their bombs had exploded accidentally. Several buildings away, a German butcher was about to close his shop. Frightened, he telephoned the police. Before they arrived, Huang and his men had departed. They knew police would find their elaborate bomb factory. It was night now, and they hurried across the river to Wuchang, leaving behind in their haste the seal of the "republic" and a roster of all conspirators.

At Wuchang, the word was whispered that rebellion was inescapable, and in the gray light of morning the rebels took the long dangerous step from which there would be no return. They shot the Manchu garrison sentries and marched into the quarters of the commanding officer, Colonel Li Yuan-hung. Colonel Li, regarded as weak, undetermined, uninspired, had fought in the 1895 war against Japan. He had expected to be made the Tartar general in the province but Hupeh's viceroy had appointed another, reportedly souring the colonel. Thus, when the rebels burst in on him, it took little to convince him that he should bring his garrison under the revolutionary banner.

He was elevated to the rank of general and took immediate command of the rebel forces. The city gates were closed and a hunt for the Manchus began. Chinese had always believed that no Manchu could count to ten, and all suspects who were unable to reach this figure were summarily decapitated in a wild orgy of slaughter.

Rebel artillery blasted through streets, and for a short period Manchu gunboats answered, then became silent either through lack of shells or defection of crews. To the surprise of everyone, the first assault was over as quickly as it had begun. The viceroy, assisted, oddly enough, by General Li Yuan-hung, fled sans dignity to a waiting Japanese gunboat. Li, who but a few hours before had been a Manchu officer, discarded his military clothes, slipped into a gown and became president of a provisional government, with Huang Hsin as vice-president.

The war to end two and a half centuries of Manchu rule was on in earnest. Peking began to move its armies with General Tuan Chi-jui at their head.

The suddenness of the coup at Wuchang caught the leaders at Shanghai unprepared. Headquarters had been set up on Avenue Road at the house of Dr. Wu Ting-fang, former minister to the United States, who, after returning to China, had become sympathetic to the revolutionary cause. When Donald arrived there, he found an incoherent uproar. Dr. Wu was striding up and down his living room, hands behind back, muttering. Other than the general idea that the Manchus must be ousted, there were no workable plans. The revolution had been born in a dream. Until now it had remained beautiful and visionary, undisturbed by practical matters. Worst of all, no one had heard from Dr. Sun Yat-sen.

Donald took charge immediately. He directed the telegraphing to the provinces, urging them to declare independence from the Manchus, but, above all, to do nothing toward setting up new governments. Of the men at headquarters, Dr. Wu was the most seasoned. At one time he had been in the inner circle of the Manchu court, and he was known equally well in America and Britain. Donald knew that Wu was his man. It was of no consequence to the machinery at Shanghai that Li Yuan-hung had been set up as a provisional president at Wuchang. Donald saw to it that the little man who once had practiced law in Hong Kong was persuaded to become the working head of the revolution. Dr. Wu took the title of minister for foreign affairs.

Wen Tseng-yao became vice-minister. He had husbanded republican ideals from the time he and Donald became fast friends at the Canton yamen, and when the revolution offered the opportunity for expression, the curiously irascible, jocular Wen deserted the old viceroy. Assisting them was a brilliant newcomer, Dr. Wang Chung-hui[3] who was singular in his deep interest in the common man. But thirty-six-year-old Donald, of Lithgow, Sydney and points north, was the dynamo. The organization and unity that he had begged for in the past had not materialized. He set about to shape it the best he could. He became without so asking, without being so designated, the real rebel minister for foreign affairs!

Dr. Wu fretted badly as the revolt gained impetus and there was no news of the man who had spent so much time in attempting to foment trouble—trouble that in the end was instigated largely by the discontent of provincial capitalists. The *status quo* in railway graft had been a big spark plug.

Each morning when Donald appeared at Dr. Wu's office, he found unhappy confederates. Wu would wail, "Where in the devil is this fellow, Sun Yat-sen? He said he started this revolution. Well, if he did, where is he?" He placed a standing order that cables were to be sent every day until Sun was located, and had replied.

Provinces were reporting to Shanghai their discard of Manchu rule, but the rebels still had nothing substantial to offer for substitute government. Responsibilities mounted. They irked Dr. Wu, but always at hand was Donald, directing, advising, pointing out the path to follow. Step by step, some semblance of organization developed. Rebel men, some capable, some not, were taking over important posts. The job of chief of staff at Hangchow was given to a young officer, Chiang Kai-shek, who once had heard Sun preach in Japan. He had fled a

---

[3] Yale graduate, translator of the German Civil Code into English, coeditor of the *Journal of the American Bar Association*, progressed to England, was then called to Bar of Inner Temple.

Japanese military school at the first word of revolution—a technical desertion from Nippon's army. Before Chiang moved on to Hangchow, he and Donald struck up an acquaintanceship that was to be at its height when China herself, aided by them, reached her pinnacle.

Soon after the start of the revolution, Donald moved to take care of diplomatic matters. From the beginning, he had stressed the importance of no overt act toward foreigners, and he found ready rebel acceptance. Lives, property, churches and colleges were given scrupulous protection. All of this provided the framework for the scheme he had in mind.

The problem was to secure a powerful confidant, to invite some nation to share rebel secrets. If it could be done, there would be prestige and there might be support if complications developed. For instance, a greedy nation, such as Japan, might take advantage of the turmoil.

Whom should he approach? Britain or the United States? And would they accept if asked into rebel confidence? Donald walked to the Bund and along Garden Park. Inside, he could hear a British regimental band playing "England Forever." For nearly an hour he paced the broad street. The question: Should he cross Garden Bridge at which he now stood to Mr. Wilder and the American Consulate General, or should he cross the street to Mr. Everard Fraser and the British Consulate General? Finally came the decision: It would be the nation whose name stood for the greatest influence in the Far East.

Donald, the Australian correspondent for an American newspaper, stepped through a confusion of traffic, and a sentry clicked to attention as he entered the grounds of a bit of England.

He had never met Mr. Fraser, although he remembered being repeatedly invited to do so when he first called on the old viceroy at Canton. There had been the matter of an appointment which he had ignored.

When Donald walked into his office now, the Britisher laid aside his work and said cordially, "Well, Mr. Donald, I suppose you have come about the revolution."

Donald said, "Oh, and how did you know?"

Fraser laughed. "Didn't you know that you're getting famous?" he asked.

Donald sketched roughly the plan the revolutionists were beginning to evolve and their willingness to take Mr. Fraser and the British government into their confidence. They were offering him certain exclusive information on their decisions, programs as soon as they were made, and they would keep him constantly informed of what movements were in the offing.

A flicker of what Donald took for skepticism passed over the consul-general's face.

Donald said, "Mr. Fraser, I don't want to argue with you, but this revolution is to succeed. I need not point out that foreknowledge of what is happening will be of tremendous value to your government. Of all nations, Britain has the largest commercial stake in China. There are long, hard years ahead. It's a good thing to have good friends."

Donald went on, Fraser studying him intently, "This is not a question of asking for recognition yet, but a situation only in which Britain is invited into the conference rooms of men who seek justice."

Fraser asked for details, received them, then agreed to Donald's proposal. He walked with Donald to the door and asked, "By the way, when does your Dr. Sun arrive?"

Donald chewed his cigar. He said, "I don't know."

The next day, as had been arranged, Donald brought in his rebel troupe for further discussions: Dr. Wu, Wen Tseng-yao, Dr. Wang Chung-hui, Yu Ya-ching and Dr. C. T. Wang. The latter, president of the Chinese Y.M.C.A., was a graduate of Yale, like Wang Chung-hui, and had become a "name" in America.

The group discussed with Fraser essentially what had been talked about the day before, but as they prepared to depart, Donald stopped at the door.

"Mr. Fraser," he said, "there's one thing I didn't tell you yesterday." Fraser waited.

"I didn't tell you that in case the Japanese attempt to jump into this arena, we expect the British to pull them out."

Fraser laughed a bit uncertainly.

In the days that followed, Donald kept him informed of all developments and he, in turn, transmitted the information to Sir John Jordan, the British minister at Peking. Sir John relayed it to the Foreign Office at London. Donald, the unofficial foreign minister, also interpreted for Mr. Wilder and other consuls the background to the bewildering chaotic picture.

The flame of revolt licked up the Yangtze Valley. New converts streamed to the cause, and because badges for them had not arrived and white arm bands denoting "rebel" did not stay put, the cutting of the queues was ordered. The pigtail-less head became the badge of revolt. This was the last step in disrespect for the Manchus. With it, there could be no delaying of allegiance to revolution. Still, it was not easy, for the Chinese had cherished his queue nearly as much as he had his family.

The Manchus began to grovel as their empire shrank in all directions. Towns, cities and provinces went over to the Republicans—the name by which rebels now referred to themselves. Peking offered concession after concession and began to deal out reforms as a dealer might flip out a draw poker hand. Few paid attention to what they promised.

Donald was in the office of a Chinese newspaper when a new edict arrived from Peking. There were other rebel partisans with him. The editor came in with a telegram in figure code—the only means by which Chinese characters can be telegraphed. He began to decode, shouting in derision as he went along.

"It's written, I suppose, by the little emperor who cannot write," Donald said drily.

They all laughed. The editor said that it was proclaimed as such. He began to read:

"I have employed too many nobles in political positions. Much of the people's money has been taken, but nothing to benefit the people has been achieved. . . . The soldiers and the people are innocent. If they return to their allegiance, I will excuse the past. . . ."

Dr. Wu had come in and stood listening. He said: "They are saying: 'Gentlemen, enter—we did not see you outside before. We apologize for our negligence.'"

The editor went on, quoting the three-foot-tall emperor, "All these things are my own fault. Hereby, I announce to the world that I swear to reform and with our soldiers and people carry out the constitution faithfully, modifying legislation, developing the interests of the people and abolishing their hardships. . . ."

Wen Tseng-yao began to stride the floor. He stopped in front of Donald.

"These Manchus think we are fools," he shouted. "They think that by an eleventh hour confession to squeezing and robbing, they are telling us something new. They are like the criminal when the police catch him. They think that by wailing, by blubbering out a tearful admission of guilt, we will pat them on the head, tell them we are sorry, and let them go back and play in their gold-inlaid temples."

A new voice spoke up. It was that of Wen Shih-tsen, the tutor who, when Donald visited the yamen at Canton eight years before, had been the first to ask, with some aloofness, if he had secured an appointment from Mr. Fraser. Wen, like many other young Chinese, had been soured by the decadence of the Manchus. But with the intellectual ambidexterity common among his people, he went on working with the old viceroy even while serving the revolutionists. In Nanking, he was Donald's "eye" and kept him apprised of what went on in the Manchu inner circle.[4]

Now he said: "We have stuck a sword up the little boy's rear end."

In Shanghai, newspaper correspondents faced the task of winnowing the truth from the bushels of conflicting news. Battles seemed to be fought for the possession of telegraph stations. When, by a fortunate maneuver, Republicans captured such a station, the world immediately was invited to consider the spectacle of some thousands of Imperialists lying stiff and stark, with faces "upturned to the frowning sky," as General "Chinese" Gordon had once pictured a battlefield. Half an hour later, the rebel operator would be ousted, and paeans of Imperial triumph would thrill the wires. The world would hear that the rebels had been "beaten and baffled, backward reeled and are flying across the horizon in a state of pitiable disorganization." Shanghai's foreigners said it was a Chinese puzzle. But Carl Crow, a sharp, young reporter for an American-styled daily newspaper, the *China Press*, knew it was not a puzzle to one man.

"Donald," Crow was to say, "was the only foreigner in Shanghai who had the remotest idea of what the revolt in China was all about."[5]

[4] Became a Japanese puppet in 1932 and was made mayor of Tientsin.
[5] Carl Crow in *China Takes Her Place* (1944).

7

RECONNAISSANCE AT PURPLE MOUNTAIN

To beat a tiger one must
have a brother's help.

❦

Hankow's native city of half a million persons had gone up in smoke. Earlier Republican successes had been wiped out, and reinforced Imperial armies had rushed in on October 27 to set a match to homes and buildings, temples, missions, hospitals and utilities. Like an insect hill stirred, thousands of Chinese ran screaming from flames, from bursting shells and falling buildings. Immense clouds of smoke totally obscured the sun, and the roar of the inferno could be heard for miles. The death toll was appalling. It was uncalled for, and it fanned a new and fiercer hate against the Manchus.

As the bulk of China slipped from under Peking's grasp and into a confusion of politics, Republican armies gathered in the creaking, gray little Yangtze river port of Chinkiang—forty miles below Nanking. Nanking was the last citadel of the Manchus, and its capture might close the war.

One of the major problems, and one that gave concern to Donald and leaders at Shanghai, was to keep this allied army free of barks and snarls within its ranks. Men from provinces far apart met almost as foreigners, speaking different dialects, carrying traditional prejudices. Cantonese thought Fukienese poltroons, while Chekiang soldiers infuriated others with boasts of their own superiority. It was a condition of mind that existed from southern China to Mongolia.

A few weeks before, Hanyang, the strongest position in Republican hands because of its large arsenal, had fallen into the Imperialist grip as the result of a ridiculous teahouse argument between comrade rebels. Hunanese and Hupeh soldiers had drifted into a furious debate over who was doing the most fighting, and it had continued on into the camp. Finally, the Hunanese, sulking, had packed up and withdrawn from their defense of the arsenal. Delighted, Imperialists had walked in and reoccupied the munitions-packed buildings.

Through the turmoil, the Chinese soldier appeared an odd, casual, forlorn fellow. No large crowds gathered in the streets, as they might in London or New York, to roar themselves hoarse at Celestial Tommy Atkins. He went his way without public petting, with only passing, disinterested glances. He loped to the front along roadways, chewing on peanuts, his tranquillity undisturbed by the diapason of battle. When he arrived, he would wander onto the field, stand a few minutes, look around, unsling his rifle—usually wrapped in a white rag—fire a haphazard shot without adjustment of sights, then sit down. Whether rebel or Manchu, his cannon was fired recklessly, often missing the mark by a quarter mile or more. Generally without concept of national patriotism, he owed his allegiance only to the man who saw that he was fed and clothed—his commander. His courage often stemmed from the fact that he was ignorant of the effect of an exploding shell.

When the war first flared up in the Yangtze Valley, wily, fifty-one-year-old Yuan Shih-kai was summoned from his enforced retirement to Peking to save the Manchu regime. Before accepting the offices of premier and general of the armies, Yuan had queried the American-educated Tong Shao-yi, holder of Peking's purse strings. He was assured there was enough money to continue, and shortly his train rolled into Peking station. Wearing a yellow jacket—insignia of highest rank—he alighted and gave only curt attention to luxuriously gowned Manchu welcomers. In elegant theatrics, he walked briskly the length of the platform to show that the "sore leg," for which he had been dismissed three years before, was in excellent working order.

But Yuan found the Peking treasury virtually bare. Tong Shao-yi's negotiations to milk a heavy loan from the Paris Bourse had failed. At the same time, Donald had suggested that the Republicans request Andrew Carnegie to influence financiers elsewhere not to jeopardize future international relations by helping Peking. Carnegie had complied and Donald had cut another notch in his rebel gunstock.

The day came when Tong advised Yuan that the cash bowl was about empty.

"Well," Yuan is said to have replied, "the old saying is that with money man is a dragon, without it he's a worm. It looks as if you're the worm."

Yuan led no armies. No money, no fight, he had said and he had meant it. He stayed in the capital, premier in a government that had shrunk from dragon to worm.

While the armies were assembling at Chinkiang, Donald made numerous trips to Nanking to advise rebels of their part in the coming siege of the city. He set agents at work to win over loyal troops, but in this he failed. They would not desert his old viceroy friend.

Imperial General Chang Hsun, illiterate and brutal, subordinate to the viceroy and the Tartar general, seized command of Nanking while Donald was there. He had once been a stableman, a Mafoo, and had been raised to generalship by the old dowager empress when he fled with her in the Boxer Rebellion. Now, under the pretense of protecting the two officials, he locked them up and unloosed a nightmare of terror. Since white still was one of the badges of the rebels, the Mafoo General beheaded everyone who had a white handkerchief, also every man who had no queue. Donald departed hurriedly for Shanghai.

There he found a new commotion at Republican headquarters. Rebel forces had swollen to a considerable size at Chinkiang, but they were not moving. It was imperative that Nanking be taken. The revolution had sunk deep into November, but day followed day in which there was no report on rebel movement. Then came the explanation. The customary intrigue for power was afoot. General Hsu Ko-ching, generalissimo of the forces picked to attack Nanking, was a victim of jealousy. The Chinkiang military governor, General Ling, wanted to be generalissimo and, failing, was obstructing Hsu. Ling's action caused Hsu to face a near-mutinous condition among his own troops who were impatient to charge on Nanking.

When Donald heard about it, he caught the next train for Chinkiang.

Along the low, flat Yangtze Valley, the floods had gone and in their place was snow dirtied by rains. From the train window, he could see it weighing heavy on the thin trees, while the farmers' ancestral grave mounds, piled with slush, were more grotesque than ever. Nature had caught the spirit of man's ugliness.

The mess, the tangle, the confusion.

The train lumbered past desolate little groups of men and women, their faces gaunt, expressionless. The sky, looking down on it all, was gray. Petrie had said that China was a tired and broken old house with its rump over the mud.

The train rolled on, past an emaciated old man hungrily eating lice from his infested jacket. What wretchedness everywhere! The mottle of gore and fury, deceits and plots. He, himself, a few days before had engaged in one in which the hope was to take Nanking without a battle. Officers of the Mafoo General had been offered a large sum to decapitate him, then surrender the city. The bribe had been insufficient, and the scheme had failed. Now there was the problem of General Ling, vain, selfish, unruly.

The train pulled into Chinkiang station.

From the car's vestibule, Donald saw a big man, broad and burly, stomping up and down in the snow, gazing eagerly at train windows. He had a youngish face, with blue eyes, and hair only slightly but plainly prematurely gray.

When Donald stepped down, the man singled him out from the crowd of detraining Chinese. He rushed up and pumped his hand.

"I'm Roy Scott Anderson," he said, half shouting. "I heard you were coming, and I've been waiting for you."

Anderson, an American, manager of the Standard Oil Company's Chinkiang office, had been born in China. His father, a missionary, was president of Soochow University, near Shanghai. Rare in that he spoke seven or eight Chinese dialects, Anderson's acquaintanceship with Chinese ranged the length and breadth of the country. He was respected for his complete honesty and his easygoing affable nature. Friends considered him brilliant.

He went on breathlessly. "I want to join up. Got my finger in it a bit, anyway. Two rebel generals are hiding in my house now. My wife doesn't like it." He explained that the generals were Hsu and his chief of staff, Ku Chong-shin, who had taken refuge there from Ling's hatchet men.

They left the station and walked down the road.

"What do you think of the revolutionists?" Donald asked.

"Not much," Anderson said. "I think these people will make a mess of any substitute government."

"Then why do you want to join up?"

"I want to see China rid of the Manchus. They're a rotten crowd."

"Well," said Donald, "that's good enough for me." He explained that he had hurried to Chinkiang to straighten out the rebellious General Ling. Would Anderson like to come along? Anderson would be delighted!

The American, towering, and Donald, square shouldered, determined, marched into Ling's headquarters. After a short, pithy summary of the situation confronting the Republicans and their determination to tolerate no defections, Donald ended up with a sharp rebuke of the recalcitrant Chinese.

Ling laid down a long, thin pipe and eyed him evilly.

"Your hold up of your armies," Donald said forcefully, "your obstruction of Hsu is interfering with this blasted war. You are ordered to march with Hsu tonight."

They left without another word.

It was late night now, and it was raining. Little rivers ran from Donald's hat as he stood for a moment before leaving to catch a Shanghai-bound train. Anderson asked, "Will Dr. Sun be coming soon?"

Donald turned up his coat collar against the pelting rain. "Nobody knows," he said, and a strange rebel figure, he hurried down the dark road.

The train was late. He sat before a fire in the stationmaster's office. After awhile, tired, he laid his head against an iron safe and went to sleep. About 3:00 A.M. a Chinese shook him, thrust a note into his hand and disappeared. By the still flickering light of the coals, he read: "Come to my office at once. Hell's a-popping. Roy."

Half asleep, Donald stumbled out into the rain and down a road deep in slush. He could hear rifles firing and bullets whining overhead.

At the Standard Oil office, he saw a large pyramid of cases. A man, legs dangling, sat quietly on its peak.

"Hello, there, what's this?" he asked Anderson.

"Oh," the American answered, "that's the money of Generalissimo Hsu."

"Who's the bloke?"

"He's the treasurer."

"Did he bring it?"

"I guess so."

"How much is there?"

"I don't know—maybe two or three million."

"Where's the generalissimo?"

Anderson looked from the window to the river.

"He's out there somewhere. I think he's on a rebel gunboat. Maybe you heard the shooting. Ling's men chased him out of my house about an hour ago. Now, what do we do?"

"Well," replied Donald, "we will go and find the generalissimo."

They found him aboard the gunboat and brought him ashore.

"Now, Admiral," Donald said smiling warmly at Anderson, "we will straighten out this bloody mess."

"Admiral?" Anderson asked surprised.

"That's you. I watched you walking down the deck of that gunboat with that roly-poly gait of yours. You're 'The Admiral' from now on."

Anderson laughed and they set off to find the key men in the Republican machinery. Together they decided that if Ling refused further to co-operate, he was to be liquidated in the usual Chinese fashion. Then once again Donald and Anderson marched into the headquarters of General Ling.

The room reeked with opium. Donald confronted the sallow man. In the strongest terms, he told Ling that he would either move his troops or the Republicans would see to it that he lost no time in joining his ancestors.

Ling's face was stony.

Donald added: "Do I make myself clear?"

"Yes," answered General Ling.

They returned to Generalissimo Hsu and found him nervous and distraught. The news that Ling was now agreeable seemed no tonic. He told Donald that the advance on Nanking could not be made.

"Why?" demanded Donald, straining to maintain his patience.

Hsu looked embarrassed. He said with customary verbal detour, that his officers believed the roadbed to Nanking had been mined and their impatience to be under way had undergone a wilting.

Donald sat chewing a cigar as Hsu detailed his woes, then suddenly he felt the same inexplicable urge that he had felt at big moments in the past.

He jumped to his feet. He said: "Your rail line is clear. I'll prove there are no mines under the tracks." Anderson catapulted his two hundred fifty pounds after him.

"I'm going to get a locomotive," Donald said. "I'll run the damn thing right up to Nanking's front door."

With Anderson, he entered the rail station and the office of Mr. Pope, the general manager of the Shanghai-Nanking Railway.

"I want a locomotive," Donald said, as if he were buying a ticket.

Pope raised his heavy eyebrows, adjusted his glasses. He had heard of Donald.

"What for, laddie?" he burred.

"We're looking for bombs—the kind that go under railway tracks."

Pope adjusted his glasses once more. "Bombs?" he asked matter-of-factly. "Someone's been putting bombs under my tracks, laddie?" He studied the idea for awhile. Donald and Anderson exchanged grins.

"Well," Pope said fussily, "You'll have to sign a chit for it. Locomotives cost money, you know."

Donald signed, and the two friends walked over to where the engine, big, black and belching, sat on a siding. Neither knew which handle to pull, but Anderson, speaking Chinese, rounded up several war-frightened mechanics, learned a few rudiments. Then with a snort and a scream, the engine took off, Anderson at the throttle. Donald braced himself. He said:

"All right, Admiral, tallyho! Watch me for signals. If trouble's ahead, I'll raise my arm. Hope you can find the brakes."

They roared down the tracks toward Nanking and strategic Purple

Mountain. Hand on throttle, the American leaned awkwardly from the cab window, scrutinizing shoulders of the roadbed. Donald fixed his eyes on the track ahead.

Mile after mile raced by. They saw only the quiet countryside and then, rounding a curve, suddenly there were objects on the track. Donald's arm went up, and Anderson struggled to bring the engine to a grinding, jerky stop. When Donald jumped down and ran ahead, he found push cars loaded with rice. Farmers were readying them to be rolled into Nanking to feed General Chang Hsun's defenders. Donald ordered them lifted from the tracks and reported to Anderson that from now on the rails were safe. His hunch had been right. If the rice cars were to be pushed into Nanking, it was plain the road was not mined. Once again they charged ahead, this time to seek out the city's defenses.

They began to climb into the Purple Mountain foothills, coughing and echoing through steep embankments. Finally they swept past a knoll—and there was Nanking in the shadow of Purple Mountain, grim, bristling. They were in the Manchu camp and under the mountain's ridge when Donald looked up and saw the gleaming barrel of one big gun, then four more. Anderson saw them, too, and screamed the locomotive to a stop.

"They won't shoot," Donald shouted, his confidence springing, as it often did, out of nowhere. "They're more surprised than we are."

"Uh-huh," Anderson muttered. He gave the engine a full dose of steam and they hurtled down the tracks in reverse, homeward bound. Donald was rocked back on the coal, and he sat there laughing as Anderson crouched low, intent upon his job.

Roaring into Chinkiang, Anderson tooted the whistle in signal of victory. The Australian and the American had done what no rebel officer had wanted to do. They had taken a big chance to prove that the line was safe. Hsu was greatly impressed by the report that advance was possible and that no guns would be encountered before Purple Mountain. Outlining a plan for attack, Donald quickly persuaded Hsu to commence operations. General Ling was commanded into action. Donald stressed that the key to Nanking's capture was Purple Mountain and that the army should detrain at its base, Yao-hwa-men, opposite the city's East Gate.

That night the trains were loaded with Ling's soldiers, and bugles blasted all over the place. Anderson wondered if, as at Jericho, they hoped to blow down Nanking's thick walls. The campaign was off to a picturesque start. There were salutes, clicking heels and barked commands. Thinly clad troops, carrying umbrellas and muzzle-loading rifles were crammed into dirty cars. Sandwiched in were the indispensables of any Chinese army—the executioners with their broad swords and the little boy molders of bullets. The awkward cannon rumbled aboard, and the procession began. Donald and Anderson were among the last to jump on for the forty-mile journey.

The train rolled noisily down the tracks for five miles, then halted. Commands filled the air, the troops swarmed off and began to set up field guns although Nanking was still thirty-five miles away.

"Oh gawd!" Anderson exclaimed. "Are these rascals going to sit on their behinds here!"

"We'll see about this," Donald said, and they shouldered their way to the private coach where General Ling sat with his officers. When Donald spoke, he continued to suck on his long pipe, eyes half closed. This was the end of the line! Still sulking, he was not going to charge on Nanking.

Surrounded by troops loyal to Ling, Donald was powerless. He and Anderson left in disgust. Anderson, taking some liberty with Shakespeare, said, "I'd like to hoist that fellow with his own petard!"

Back at Chinkiang once more, they told Generalissimo Hsu of Ling's trickery and insubordination. Donald was determined that there was to be no more stalling. He had checked at the railway yards and found adequate rolling stock. The same plan that had been given to Ling was handed Ku, and the preparations were speeded once more. Before Donald left headquarters, Hsu said, "By the way, Adviser, isn't there a Dr. Sun connected with the revolution? Where is he?"

"I haven't heard," Donald replied.

He hurried to Anderson's house for a change of clothes and found a telegram awaiting him. It was from James Gordon Bennett, and it read:

HOW IS IT YOU DIDN'T TAKE THAT RIDE WITH KENNEDY TO PURPLE MOUNTAIN STOP KENNEDY SCOOPED YOU ON GOOD STORY.

For a moment Donald was puzzled, then he remembered. When he and Anderson had returned from their excursion under the guns of Purple Mountain, he had written out the details and had them at hand when J. Russell Kennedy, of the Associated Press, stopped by at Anderson's house. Kennedy was one of several correspondents who were following the revolution on a hit-and-miss basis. The world press generally regarded the revolution as "just another Chinese revolt." But Donald applied himself as assiduously to his newspapering as he did his revolution. The *Herald* was the only newspaper outside his Australian string which gave its readers an accurate, intelligent account of the war.

Kennedy was only a nodding acquaintance, as were most of the correspondents with whom Donald came in contact. He made a point of avoiding them because, as he told Anderson, "I know too much about this revolution. I don't want to pretend I don't know when the lads ask questions." Much of what Donald knew was confidential, and he never betrayed a confidence. Few understood the real reason why he shunned them. He had come to live by two of his favorite sayings: He travels fastest who travels alone and he travels fastest who travels dry. He had learned from his yachting days in Hong Kong that in emergencies men always turn to the man who doesn't drink. To the newcomer who would hail the Australian with a hearty "You must have a drink with me!" Donald's smiling answer would come as a jolt: "There's only one person who can say I must drink. That's me, and I'm not saying it."

The evening Kennedy had dropped in, Donald had planned to file a story in his usual impersonal style on the Purple Mountain escapade. However, in a hurry to board Ling's troop train, he generously gave his notes to the A.P. man, cautioning him to use them only as a basis for information. Apparently Kennedy had done otherwise.

When Anderson came in, Donald showed him the Bennett telegram. Anderson was furious. He said it was a dirty shame and declared, "From now on, the Republican army has a censor, and I am it!"

Donald was pleased at Anderson's show of comradeship. "How did you become censor?" he laughed.

"I just appointed myself!" Anderson boomed, and he sat down, wrote out his own appointment, then signed it. Thereafter, no copy cleared a rebel area without Anderson's signature.

The point of censorship settled, Donald and Anderson, bathed and refreshed, headed for the railroad. Ku's troop trains were rattling out of Chinkiang, bound for Purple Mountain and the most important battle of the war. Anderson and Donald climbed aboard, and they rolled past the camped army of General Ling. General Ku looked bleakly at it.

"I know this fellow Ling," he said. "We'll do the fighting but when it's all over, I'll wager he'll ride into Nanking as a little tin hero."

Toward evening, they arrived at Yao-hwa-men and set up camp. A house for headquarters was found, and Donald and Anderson lay down on a wide Chinese bed, exhausted after forty-eight hours of virtually nonstop activity. At first too tired to sleep, they listened to the sounds of an army bedding down. In the distance they could hear an advancing flotilla of wheelbarrows—essential to a Chinese army— all squeaking in stentorian and beautifully dissimilar tones. The heavier the load, the louder the song. Unless a barrow would sing a song as it rolled along, it was no good to the coolie. Donald had known an American who failed dismally when he tried to market a new barrow sans squeak. Through the windows, the two men could see the flotilla coming in, each barrow perfectly balanced, piled high with ammunition and provender and not an item out of place. Many a time they had seen them mount a ledge of stone a foot high, then flounder to the hub in ruts, to emerge with only a few encouraging grunts of the sweating coolie.

Finally pianissimo came to the night's concerto of barrows and voices. Donald and Anderson fell asleep.

Through the night, the rumor mill, without which no army is complete, ground a grist of fantasies—a wine for Chinese blood. The lowliest, dullest clod is often transported for the moment into Olympian realms on the wings of rumor. It is the vehicle for the drama in which he finds solace for his weary, prosaic life. But high and low lend an ear, and for each the rumor often is better to fondle than the truth. As the night wore on, rebel officers would burst into headquarters wildly enthusiastic to report the latest development heard via bamboo telegraph. Each time, Anderson would shake Donald and repeat their stories. He would shout, "They have broken through the gates . . . they have entered Nanking . . . the city is on fire!" But Donald understood his revolutionary army better than Anderson. Although at times fool-hardy, he knew they would make no attempt to crack Nanking until Purple Mountain's guns had been silenced. He would mumble, "I don't believe it . . . don't wake me" over and over.

As a final touch, Anderson aroused Donald and told him there were two Japanese correspondents waiting for him.

"They want to cover a war," Anderson explained.

Donald half rose and looked at them as one might sight down a gun barrel. Seven years before he had sat on his rump in Japan for nearly a year hoping day after day to cover a war. He never did, and all the time Japanese newspaper men streamed to and from war zones almost at will. Here now was the sort of Roland for the Oliver Japan had once meted out!

He waved them aside. "Throw them out," he told Anderson.

Anderson didn't hesitate or question. He seized each by the scruff of the neck, shoved them out the door and ordered Chinese armed attendants to hustle them aboard a train for Shanghai.

When he returned, Donald said: "Look—some of us have had our fill of these people. They're poison. They have deep hates, and no good can come of such things. They are emotional and unpredictable. They are a land of psychopaths in a sea of melancholia." Donald had dressed and was in the bathroom. Anderson could hear him sputtering in a basin of water. The sputtering stopped, and Donald called out, "The Japanese correspondents—from now on, every time we meet up with them, out they go."

That was the law thereafter for Anderson and Donald, and they never wavered from it. In the days that followed, Japanese bounced and bounced hard. The first instance was on a Shanghai-bound train. They had just begun to move when Anderson sighted a Japanese correspond-ent several seats ahead. He looked at Donald, and Donald nodded. Together they arose, picked him up and carried him to the door. Donald opened it.

They watched him roll down a hillside.

The dossier in Tokyo on "W. H. Donald" grew thicker, and near it in the same drawer appeared a new folder labeled "Roy Scott Ander-son."

chapter

8

THE SIEGE OF NANKING

*There is no wall through
which the wind cannot pass.*

⁂

THE tempo of the war at last was to be stepped up. Donald and
Anderson were about to race through one of the most exciting, one of
the most significant episodes the two would have in what was to be a
long career in master-minding Chinese civil wars.

When Donald emerged from the bathroom shortly after the Japanese
correspondents had been expelled from the Yao-hwa-men headquarters,
he found Anderson and several Chinese officers in the kitchen preparing a Chinese breakfast from a scant larder. They were making a gruel
from rice, and they had set out on the table some dried fish and cured
eggs.

"Whipped up some breakfast," Anderson announced. "Sit down."

Donald looked blankly at the fare. "Never eat the stuff," he said.

"What!" exclaimed Anderson to whom Chinese food was more
familiar than ham and eggs.

"I've never eaten Chinese food in my life," Donald explained. "I
don't know why, but when I look at it, my stomach turns somersaults."

"Good heavens," Anderson said, "and you've been in China more
than eight years!" With deftness, he gripped an aged, slightly bluish
egg between his chopsticks, and as he bit off a chunk, he said, "Well,
how are you going to eat? We're not in Chinkiang or Shanghai, you
know."

The Australian pointed out good humoredly that theoretically he and
Anderson were not enemies of the Manchus and that he proposed to

walk through the gates, buy some supplies and return. Anderson gulped down the rest of his egg and they headed for East Gate. As they walked, Donald explained that he had a personally trained cook travel with him whenever it was possible.

As the two approached, Manchu troops standing stiffly before the gate and along the wall watched in some puzzlement, but none the less alertly. Donald and Anderson found the gate intact, solid as ever. The rumors of the night before had been only rumors. Rebel troops plainly had made no attack upon it.

"You'll have to do the talking," Donald said. "I don't speak a word of the blasted language, you know. Never wanted to eavesdrop on these people."

Anderson spoke to the sentries. There was no trouble. They were waved on under the arch. "If they only knew who they had invited in," Anderson muttered.

They stopped for a moment and surveyed the wall. Built of stone, it was a monstrous thing, rising sixty feet in the air, and thirty to forty feet thick. It was backed by high, wide earth embankments.

"The old fellows who built it," Anderson said, "must have been cautious beggars."

The purchases were quickly made, and they returned to headquarters where Donald ate a breakfast of fresh eggs, kippers, tea and biscuits.

Generalissimo Hsu had arrived in a private coach, and he came in and talked while Donald ate.

"You'll have to take Purple Mountain first," Donald said. "You know that, don't you?"

Hsu admitted that its capture was essential. "But," he said, "it will be difficult. I believe there are guns all along the top of it. They'll blow us back down the hill."

"There aren't any guns at the top," Donald said.

Hsu shrugged. "Who can say?" he said.

"I'll be able to say," Donald replied. "I'll walk up and over the top of the damn thing."

General Ku came in, and Donald asked him about the adequacy of his artillery. Ku said that his weapons were mainly three-inch pieces and none too many.

"Well, we'll have to do something about that," Donald said. He asked Anderson to telegraph the arsenal at Shanghai on the matter, and he himself left to begin the scaling of the 2000-foot precipitous Purple Mountain.

He had set himself to an arduous, backbreaking task. Purple Mountain had a lift of one foot in two, and it was jagged and rocky in one place, a tangle of undergrowth or thick with bamboo in another. He ripped his trousers and skinned his knees and tore his fingernails. All the while his eyes were pinned on the mountain's crest—where Hsu feared strong fortifications. The morning wore on, and hunger began to jab and knuckle him. At a deserted farm he stopped, pulled up a cabbage and ate it.

Rested, he pushed on, inching nearer the bony back of the mountain, aware that if his hunch were wrong, the crack of big and small rifles might break the almost ominous quiet at any moment. A few pheasants whirred out of a thicket and overhead several geese honked, but he saw no man, he saw no gun. There was one last sheer boulder—and he was at the top, looking down at no fort but at a near-by weather-beaten temple. Several priests with shaven heads dozed in the doorway.

When Donald walked up, they opened their eyes slowly and gazed at him quietly and politely. By sign, he made known he was thirsty and hungry. One arose softly, glided into the temple and returned with a bowl of dirty-looking tea and two boiled duck eggs. Ordinarily, Donald could not have stomached either, but, famished, he gulped them down. Bowing his thanks, he began his descent.

It was late afternoon, and far below on the railway side of the mountain he could see what looked like a thin lead pencil. It was the Generalissimo's train, parked on a siding. He hurried, for the November night was creeping in swiftly, and he had no appetite for being caught by darkness on the mountain's steep trails. Suddenly, behind a parapet several hundred feet below, he saw two faces peering up. Rifles cracked. Two bullets chirped by and struck a rock. Donald stopped and watched his two assailants who, for reasons he could never explain, fired no more.

It was dark when he climbed aboard the generalissimo's coach. The first compartment was empty, and he went in, lay down on a berth and within minutes was sound asleep. When he awakened, it was morning, and through the car window he saw with a start a wide expanse of slowly moving yellow water. There was no mountain.

A boy came in and set down a pot of tea and a dish of watermelon seeds. Donald demanded irritably: "Boy, what fashion I come this side?"

"Fat man all same Buddha bring you here," the boy answered. "I think mebbe he name b'long Anderson." He poured Donald's tea, talking all the while.

"Last night much trouble," he went on. "Manchu soldiers find G'issimo at he headquarters and G'issimo makee run fast here." The boy was describing Generalissimo Hsu's flight with appropriate gestures and ran up and down in front of Donald with short, mincing steps. "By and by, Manchus begin shoot big guns this side and evvabuddy plenty fear. Just then big engine makee chop-chop down tracks, stop mebbe one minute, then makee push very hard." He demonstrated by pushing against a small table how they were propelled to safety. "Evvabuddy looksee out window and see Master Anderson inside engine. He laugh: 'Ho-ho-ho, evvabuddy!'"

Donald still glared irately at the boy. It did not occur to him that he should feel grateful. He had been hauled away from his pet baby—the revolution. He could run no war, he could cover no war on a siding fifty miles or more from Nanking. Why hadn't he been awakened in the midst of the excitement?

"Master, s'pose bomb come," the boy answered, and with his finger described the arch of a shell through the air until it landed on Donald's nose, "more better you sleep!"

"You are the biggest fool that ever walked," Donald snorted, slipped a five-dollar note in the boy's hand and left. Passing the next compartment, he heard voices and looked in. The generalissimo and his staff were all there around a table lined with empty and half-empty beer bottles. In the distance guns were booming. He closed the door softly and hurried away. The bombardment grew louder. Rebels had occupied Tiger Mountain just beyond Nanking and were engaged in a gun duel with the Purple Mountain fort.

A locomotive was a short distance ahead, and when Donald climbed in, he found Anderson asleep. The American had planned to rouse him early but, exhausted, had slept late.

"A fine thing, Admiral!" Donald called. "Why didn't you wake me up last night?"

Anderson laughed, handed Donald a shovel, and indicated the coal pile. Almost immediately they took off for Yao-hwa-men.

That evening, after Donald had made his report, they sat on a railway truck discussing affairs in the tortured land over which a gloomy dusk was now falling. Donald had asked Anderson his opinion on China.

"Well," Anderson answered, "as you know, I've lived here a long time, and I like it. Wouldn't stay if I didn't. However, there's a lot wrong with it, and, therefore, I think the revolution has its good points. It ought to scrape a lot of scales and a lot of filth from the old dragon. But I'm not placing any bets that it's the whole answer. After all, I realize as well as you do what gave the revolt its final shove. Out of all the millions here, how many are there who understand the meaning of the better life Dr. Sun's disciples have preached about?"

Anderson paused, and they both listened to the labored grunts of a train somewhere in the distance. After awhile, he said:

"The people don't really know what democracy means. They're merely prattling a tune that has all the sour notes of *status quo*. When the revolution is won, I wonder whether the people will have won. I wonder if the only thing gained won't be protection for railway and other moneyed interests."

Donald said nothing. He gazed down the long track that advanced eastward into the dusk. "Here they come," he said. "Here come the guns you ordered yesterday morning."

When the engine with two flatcars drew near, Donald waved it to a halt. They walked over and found each car held a 4.7 cannon.

Anderson looked expectantly at Donald. "What are you going to do with them?" he asked.

"Oh, we're going to take them down and set them up in front of Taiping Gate," Donald answered. "When the time comes, you and I are going to blow the damn gate down."

"We are?" Anderson asked, controlling his amusement.

The only reply was a swift, serious glance. Quickly, Donald began to give directions. Another railway flatcar was filled with heavy beams, and by late that night the guns had been unloaded almost directly in front of Taiping Gate and were sitting solidly on planks behind the railway embankment. In the darkness, Donald and Anderson stood looking appreciatively at the two monsters and the growing pile of ammunition coolies were removing from the cars. Donald asked:

"Do you know how to shoot these things?"

"Haven't the slightest idea."

The absurdity of the situation struck them both, and they sat down on the rails and laughed, the sound doubtlessly perplexing the Manchu guards patrolling the walls a few hundred yards away.

"Well, no matter," Donald said, "the coolie who came with the guns knows something about them, and I learned how to shoot a mortar a long time ago. Anyway, the wall is big and the gate is big. We'd have a hard time not hitting one or the other."

For an hour or so they studied the mechanism with the coolie's help, and finally Donald said, "You stand by the guns until we are ready. Tie an extra length of line to the lanyards and crawl down into a hollow. Fire from down there. You won't get hurt that way if the damn things blow up."

He gave Anderson the details of the plan. Rebel forces had begun a vicious attack on the east side near the tombs of the Ming emperors and were pushing Manchu troops back into the city. The next day General Ku's army was to begin the ascent of Purple Mountain, following the trail blazed by Donald. They were to swarm to the top and then charge, bayonets fixed, down upon the fort where Donald and Anderson had seen the five heavy guns on their first trip by locomotive. Donald would be with them, and when the fort was cleared, he would creep to a position somewhere above Anderson and his guns to direct the attack on the gate.

With Donald leading the way, the ascent was begun on the morning of November 30. Small buglers perched on knolls, blowing vigorously and happily, encouraged the long lines extending to the plains below. White flags carried by anxious, breathless soldiers fluttered nearer and nearer the top and by midafternoon it was reached amid tremendous cheers. Looking back, Donald saw men laden with heavy gear hastening upward under continuous fire from the five big Loyalist guns on the ridge. But a dip in the mountain sheltered the climbers, and shells whined overhead to explode harmlessly half a mile beyond. From the city a bombardment began with rifle and shrapnel joining in. Nothing stopped Ku's men, however, and at the top Donald led a party to a ledge and peered down on the fort below. They saw that the floor had been whitewashed, apparently by revolutionaries within the Manchu ranks. It meant that when night came, the fort would be plainly marked as a target.

The rebels now were crouching behind the crest, and the crackle of rifles started, interspersed with the thunder of three-inchers, while from the tops of the walls and from within the city guns flashed angrily upward. Throughout the night the roar of battle went unabated, the rebels raking in particular the ridge below, which had been marked for bayonet charge at dawn.

Satisfied that the rebels were firmly entrenched, Donald—a Jack-of-all-trades with many a job to do—slipped away and began an agonizing descent. The only correspondent covering the action, he had a story for the world, and he had a telegraph station to find. The railway depot near Taiping Gate was in rebel hands, and a telegrapher was sitting in the dark before his instrument when Donald came in. By candle light and by pencil he wrote a 2000-word dispatch for the *Herald* and Australian papers which began:

OUTSIDE NANKING, Dec. 1. (1911)—A city and a mountain are in a life-and-death struggle this morning. Shells are singing high over a purple peak to the plains on the far side, shrapnel is bursting high and distant, rifle bullets are falling short and few among the Chinese rebels are dying.

The Manchu fighters below, however, are in a desperate plight, revolutionists' guns being centered on the smaller targets of a white-washed fort and bulky walls, whilst the defenders have the whole mountain to shoot at, with no certainty of being able to shoot anyone. But they are holding on tenaciously.

On the mountain, men could be seen earlier kneeling behind rocks, shifting here and there to get aim, and as night came down flashes of the rifles showed they were holding their positions. In the fort, the flashes of light tell a different story. Dead men can be seen lying about the guns. . . .

Donald hurried from the station to where Anderson stood guard over the big guns, arranged a code of signals for firing, then wormed his way back up the mountain. Dawn was beginning to break when he arrived at the crest, and with General Ku he looked down on the ridge which had been battered ceaselessly during the night. What they saw made it clear there was no need to storm the fortification with bayonet. Manchu soldiers lay sprawled everywhere, dead.

With the strategic mountain completely in their hands, Ku's men, Donald with them, clambered down to the fort, mounted their own guns where the broken Manchu guns had been and resumed the bombardment of Nanking. The high, thick walls were alive with blue-turbaned Manchu troops, and rebel shells splashed among them with growing accuracy. The all-out battle for the ancient city was on.

Donald made his way quickly down the slopes until he was overlooking Anderson's position. Standing on a ledge in full view of the wall, he waved a greeting, and Anderson raised a hand in salute. The Australian swept the scene with glasses, then focused on the gate. A large number of Manchu troops had clustered around one of the towers, and Donald felt it opportune to fire. As prearranged, he dropped his white handkerchief, then watched Anderson direct the loading, jump into a shallow ravine and jerk the lanyard. One gun coughed, but against the gate nothing crashed. Inside the city wall, however, smoke enveloped what he knew instantly was North Star Temple. The roof sagged, then plunged downward. Anderson had missed the gate, missed the wall, and had sent his shell into the city.

Donald had heard that it was in this temple the Mafoo General had imprisoned his friend, Viceroy Chang Chen-chun, and the Tartar general. A moment later, a familiar figure assisted by several others departed hurriedly. It was the old fellow being led to safety. He breathed a short prayer for him, then motioned to Anderson to lower his range on the other gun. But it, too, sent a shell over the wall, and a great cloud of smoke and dust arose from a narrow street. Donald signaled Anderson to lower the guns still further. Anderson went about it, shaking his head, puzzled that he could have missed a thing as big as the Nanking Wall.

Gunners on the wall now unloosed a fusillade at Donald, and he ran and jumped for the nearest shelter. It was a trench filled with corpses, victims of rebel guns the night before. It was shallow, and he was forced to press against torn, dismembered bodies. There was a foul stench. Rats had begun their work. When he emerged, he saw a Chinese climb out of another hole dripping. The refuge he had flung himself into was an abandoned cesspool.

But attention was directed away from Donald. On the dull, green plain below white flags fluttered in the trenches of Taiping days. Thousands of black spots creeping with them ever closer toward the gray, grim walls of Nanking moved as pins on a map—from mound to mound, trench to trench. Volleys of shots from behind the embattlements would stay the advance temporarily, but it continued until the black spots and the white flags were within five hundred yards of the walls. Everywhere the sound of fury went on. Batteries above Donald growled, and crashes came from many a new position. Rebels were on Purple, Tiger and Stern mountains, and from slopes of adjacent Gupde Mountain Republican guns were just beginning to roar. Loyalists were frantic. They scurried back and forth on the walls, watching the white flags, watching the mountains. Surrounded on three sides, the city faced a desperate situation.

Anderson was looking up and then Donald saw what he had seen. Scores of Loyalists were crawling cautiously one by one along the wall's top toward positions in the gate tower. Donald watched until they were in, signaling directions to Anderson all the while. Then he dropped his handkerchief, and Anderson fired almost simultaneously. One shell crashed into the roof with a clatter of tiles, the second fell on the roadway. Before the smoke could clear from the gate entrance, men were fleeing in all directions, down the embankments and along the road within the city. A group of rebel riflemen who had taken up positions near Donald watched the operation with high excitement. As Anderson fired again, two men ran from the damaged gate tower and were felled by the explosion. A loud cheer went up from the Donald-Anderson gallery. But a moment later it gave way to laughter. Both the men jumped up as one man, sped down the embankment and across the country without stopping or looking back.

Donald waved enthusiastically, then indicated to Anderson to direct his cannon point-blank at the gate. Both guns barked, and when Anderson looked up from his hollow, the Australian signaled that each had cut through dead center on the gate.

It was late afternoon now, and the first hint of dusk had appeared when a large American flag emerged from the East Gate. Under it was a white horse, and on the white horse was a man in a silk hat and a frock coat. Donald called out for all guns to cease firing. General Ku came down from the ridge and with other Chinese officers and Donald advanced to meet the envoys. The man on the white horse turned out to be Mr. Gilbert, American vice-consul at Nanking.

After formal greetings, Gilbert said he bore an offer from General Chang Hsun to surrender the city at seven o'clock the next morning if Chang and his personal army were permitted to escape across the Yangtze. Donald and Ku agreed it was a small price to pay for Nanking and the end, perhaps, of war. But the party of rebel officers had swollen larger as the conferring went on, and differences of opinion developed over the merits of permitting the Mafoo General to escape. Arguers said he was a bloodthirsty ruffian, and they meant to have his head at any cost. The conference ended in a squabble among the Chinese, and Gilbert put on his silk hat, mounted his white horse and rode back to report failure.

Donald walked over to Anderson as Purple Mountain's artillery spat once more. Anderson looked up inquisitively, and Donald explained that hotheads had derailed a peace offer. Anderson eased slowly down onto a shell casing, his big, boyish face cupped in his hands.

"Oh, Lord," he sighed. "Sometimes I get so damn sick."

That night at rebel headquarters on the ridge, Donald helped cool down the radical elements. After a stormy session, agreement was reached to accept the surrender at 7:00 A.M., and the decision was communicated to Nanking defenders.

An exchange of fire kept up all night, but in the morning shortly after six o'clock it ceased as a train with three or four cars snorted past Purple Mountain and halted at the station nearest Taiping Gate. Standing with Ku, Donald watched the train with some astonishment.

"Wonder who these blighters are," he said.

"Ten to one, it's our old friend General Ling," Ku replied wryly. "He must have heard they're surrendering."

Donald saw through binoculars about two hundred ragged troops straggle from the cars and march behind a leader toward the gate. It was Ling, all right, wearing a bowler hat and a military overcoat.

"The beggar means to accept the surrender himself!" Donald exclaimed.

"Let him," Ku said disgustedly. "I told you he'd pull a trick like this. If he wants to be military governor here, well, all right. As for me, I'm tired. I just want to go to sleep."

Donald left Ku and made his way to the gate. There he took up a position as observer to the parley, which Gilbert had joined, accompanied by representatives of several European powers. It developed that the Mafoo General had fled northward the night before, taking with him the pick of his army, the viceroy and the Tartar general. A General Chao surrendered the city.

Bugles blew. The battered gates swung open. Nanking had fallen. The empire of the Manchus had all but crashed.

The only correspondent to witness the surrender, Donald photographed the historic scene for the *Herald* and Australian papers, then hurried through the gates to the telegraph office. One of the first to march in, he had not gone far when Anderson overtook him. Together they walked through bloody streets, past bodies decapitated in the wild, nightmarish hours before the city fell. The rest of the rebels swarmed down from the mountains and fanned out through the city, looting and drinking all afternoon and evening.

One of the prize spoils was the discovery of the Mafoo General's No. 1 concubine, overlooked in his haste to flee. She was a pretty wench, petite and shapely, with big, almond eyes and red, sensual lips. Officers and men, who had not enjoyed the enforced celibacy in the days outside Nanking's gates, clamored to buy her at auction. But wiser heads, one of which was Donald's, agitated to keep her, arguing she might bring a high price in some eventual bargaining. The opportunity came even before Donald left Nanking. The Mafoo, who was more accomplished in a boudoir than on a battlefield, sent word he was willing to pay heavily for his lost lady. He did. It was arranged to trade the pretty little thing for an assortment of locomotives and much-needed cargo and passenger cars he had taken.

With Anderson, Donald walked to the train for Shanghai. Above the city white flags whipped vigorously in a December wind, and the shouts of soldiers and people banged against the skies. They gazed fondly, almost possessively, at the silent wall, the old buildings, the excited streams of humanity.

"Well, Don, looks like old Doc Sun may have his chance at bat, after all," Anderson said.

"When he does, Admiral," Donald answered, "he ought to tie two red ribbons on those cannons of yours."

chapter

9

THE ARRIVAL OF DR. SUN

One generation opens the road upon
which another generation travels.

A<small>FTER</small> leaving Anderson at Chinkiang, Donald returned to Shanghai to be met by jubilant Republican friends. They shook his hand and plied him with questions about Nanking—the city they had marked for the new capital of China. Donald gave them a resume of the city's capitulation as he was whisked from North Station toward headquarters to discuss the forthcoming peace conference.

Dr. Wang Chung-hui, the brilliant young lawyer, said, "Everyone is saying that you just about captured Nanking singlehandedly."

Donald laughed and denied it vigorously, but Wang's remark dated the birth of a legend that was to grow.

Following the conversation between himself and Wang, Donald asked: "Where's Dr. Sun?"

Dr. Wu arched his eyebrows and looked at Donald blankly. "Dr. Sun? Who's Dr. Sun? I don't believe I know him."

In mid-December, a scant two weeks after Nanking fell, Tong Shao-yi arrived at Shanghai from Peking in the full panoply of Manchu extravagance. He had been dispatched by Premier Yuan Shih-kai to gain the most favorable armistice terms possible while Yuan sparred for time to find support for a limited monarchy. Yuan felt he had some basis for negotiation. He still had control of a large, well-equipped Loyalist army.

Tong swept into the city elaborately gowned and with a retinue of fifty men accomplished in Western sciences with whom he hoped to impress the Republicans. A year before this he would have awed all Chinese and sent them genuflecting. But his arrival was like something out of the long dead past. A feeling for simplicity had been born, and almost overnight old-style officialism had been shoved into a limbo of relics. Tong met only a sullen scorn. Instead of heads bobbing respectfully, there was a queueless populace, caps undoffed, gaping at him. He was the only one to bow and scrape as he made his way along the wharf from his steamer.

Donald and Vice Foreign Minister Wen Tseng-yao sat across the street in the Palace Hotel dining room and, facing the Bund, watched Dr. Wu Ting-fang provide a cursory welcome. Wu pointed to a waiting motorcar, then hurriedly left in another one himself.

"What's Ajax[1] want with that army!" Wen scowled at the colorful parade of men who trailed behind Tong. "It's just like him to come here and flaunt extravagance in our faces."

Donald smiled. Less than a year before, Wen, then junior resident commissioner to Tibet, had traveled from Lhasa with a cortege of three hundred men. Now the spirit of the new era had engulfed him. Scorning motorcar and carriage, he went about unostentatiously in a ricksha as self-inflicted punishment for once having been a gourmand at the Manchu table.

Tong Shao-yi and his peace mission had left the river front now, coolies in their wake picking up half-smoked cigarette butts. Wen set down a cup of tea. "It's good," he said companionably, "to be among real people. I mean people with a purpose. I think of my life as a mandarin as nothing more than bones rattling in dry skin."[2]

"I remember you as a fellow who had a purpose, all right," Donald replied. "You just didn't have anyone to tie the loose ends for you."

Wen nodded reflectively. "I think you're remembering the time at the old yamen when I said we were heading for a republic." He smiled and went on, "But you are wrong, my friend. I had no purpose. People with a purpose are fighters. I was content until a few months ago with

[1] Tong Shao-yi's nickname. Suspected of pro-Japanese activities, he was assassinated in Shanghai in 1940.

[2] Dissatisfied with the Kuomintang, Wen Tseng-yao became a Japanese puppet in the 1937-45 Sino-Japanese War.

a dream." He pointed to crowds of Chinese shuffling along Nanking Road. "That's the trouble with too many of my people," he said. "They're content with dreams. It has always been enough to wrap themselves in a thin rice sack on a cold winter's night, dream of warmth and wealth, and be content in the morning with the rice sack."

Donald sawed a muffin in two. "Do you think we have won?" he asked.

"You can answer that better than I."

"Well, I think we have licked the Manchus. But winning—that's something else."

The peace conference between Tong Shao-yi and the revolutionaries opened at the Town Hall and ended after two sessions. Tong was astute enough to know that the Manchus were finished, the attitude at Shanghai being the last big convincer. He had come down from Peking by rail to Hankow and on this leg of the trip had passed through territory in which the double-dragon flag of the Manchus still flew. Leaving Hankow by steamer, however, he saw only areas completely under rebel control and a people vigorous in their antipathy for Manchu government. At Shanghai, the grim faces of the "new order" told him a story of the feelings of the millions who lived in the lands to the south.

Tong was no Manchu but a southerner, a Cantonese, and the revolutionaries he faced across the conference table were Cantonese. Donald and the other rebels had anticipated a battle of wits between Dr. Wu Ting-fang and the sharp, eloquent Tong, and held some fears as to just how well Wu might fare. The first session was given to discussion between subordinates as to procedure. At the second session, the revolutionists invited Tong to speak first, in order to provide them with an opportunity to pull his arguments to pieces. But Tong refused, and sat like a stony statue into the face of which a lighted cigar had been inserted. Finally Dr. Wu arose, delivered a short summary of the causes of the war, then said:

"The land is rotting. There is hunger, death and starvation. There is unemployment and poverty. There are inefficiencies and misdeeds everywhere."

Smoke curled up from the cigar in the statue in front of him.

"Let us not argue about it. The Manchus are responsible. They have failed after more than two hundred and fifty years as our conquerors."

He stopped and gazed at Tong for some time.

"I am a Cantonese," he said "You are a Cantonese. All the delegates along my side of the table are Cantonese. We are all Cantonese." He was silent for a moment, but he did not take his eyes from Tong. "I repeat," he said softly, "that I am Cantonese and you are Cantonese and we are all Cantonese."

He signaled for Tong to rise. Tong did and Wu sat down.

Tong removed his cigar. He said, "I agree with everything you say," and sat down.

Dignity was forgotten. The rebels stood up and whooped. Tong had been won over. The difficulties of the moment were at an end. Next day Yuan Shih-kai publicly dismissed Tong, wiring him secretly, however, to negotiate with Dr. Wu no longer on a basis to save the Manchus nor to speak on their behalf, but only to secure the best possible peace. Work began on an abdication treaty, the drafts flying back and forth between Shanghai and Peking as they were studied, altered and studied again. Donald checked each carefully, mindful of the Machiavellianism of Yuan.

It was the afternoon the peace conference ended that the first word of the whereabouts of Dr. Sun was received. On the way to revolutionary headquarters, Donald had picked up a copy of the British afternoon paper, and there he saw a story datelined Singapore. At Dr. Wu's house he found most of his old confederates, and he announced solemnly, a suspicion of a smile lighting his face, that the public print carried an interesting item. He pointed to a paragraph near the bottom of the page, and Dr. Wu read aloud: "Dr. Sun Yat-sen has arrived in Singapore, en route to Shanghai, with some American generals."

Everyone sat or stood as if slightly frozen. Wen Tseng-yao broke the silence. "American generals?" he bellowed. "What in the hell do we want with American generals?"

The room buzzed with speculation. How did the generals manage to leave their duties in the United States Army? How did they contrive to come with Dr. Sun? Was the United States sending its general staff? What was Sun up to now? What could they do with generals with the war over? While they talked, Donald quietly called Mr. Wilder at the American Consulate General. But Mr. Wilder had not heard Sun was on his way to China, nor did he know anything about American generals in the company of the revolutionary leader.

Dr. Sun arrived on Christmas Day. It was bleak and chilly, and a wet wind whipped up the Whangpoo and beat against him as he stepped ashore. No one knew he was arriving, and there was no welcome, no public display, no huzzas. He hired a motorcar and went to a house in the French Concession.

At Wu's house, Christmas had not interrupted work. Dr. Wu, Donald, and others were laboring over one of the last big chores of war— the abdication document.

Donald was near the phone when it rang. A voice announced the presence of Dr. Sun in Shanghai. Donald repeated the news, and there was a flurry behind him. An appointment was arranged, and when Dr. Wu went to call on Dr. Sun, Donald and Wen Tseng-yao were with him. This was to be the trio's first meeting with the great, round-eyed doctor.

At the house, they were shown into a drawing room where Dr. Sun and a strange-looking, small, humpbacked man were waiting before a bilious fire in an unimpressive grate. Introductions were made solemnly. The visitors stared, for the deformed man had been introduced as General Homer Lea.[3]

So this was the "American generals!"

Wen Tseng-yao scowled, bit his lip, and looked out of the window. Dr. Wu mumbled something in Chinese. Both ignored the "General." The silence was awkward. At last Donald said, rubbing his hands and indicating the weak flicker in the hearth, "Well, let's warm ourselves by this brisk little fire."

Dr. Sun sat at one side of the fireplace and Homer Lea at the other. The three guests ranged themselves in front of the tiny flame. Dr. Wu

[3] Lea had been in China on a previous occasion and had been an officer in a Chinese army. In 1901 he had attempted to free Emperor Kuang Hsu. Later he traveled with the exiled tutor, Kang Yu-wei. Author of several books, his *Valor of Ignorance*, written shortly after the turn of the century, published by Harper & Brothers, showed how the Japanese could successfully invade the United States. He died in 1912 soon after leaving China.

seemed to have nothing to say. Wen obviously was annoyed. Chinese do not like deformed people in any circumstance, but for the leader of the revolution to have allied himself with a dwarf was, in their minds, beyond belief or excuse. The silence settled down again, and each sat inspecting with showy casualness such things as his fingernails, his watch or the bric-a-brac on the mantlepiece.

Again Donald sought to animate the little group. "Doctor," he said, "the question now is what form of government China will take." He looked straight at Dr. Sun who returned the gaze with wide-eyed politeness. Donald went on, "The Manchus are finished, but the shape and substance of government to replace them has never been decided."

"We'll have a republic," Sun answered and offered no more.

Silence crept in like the fog once again. It was so intense that it seemed to ache, and Donald marveled that neither Wu nor Wen cried out in pain. The flame in the fireplace nodded once, twice, then died. A heavy, wet snow began to fall outside, and a new chill came over the room. Donald knew that he could expect no help from either of his friends who, aware he sought their eyes, stared ahead, unblinking.

He asked, "Who will be the first president?"

"There he is!" came in a queer, altisonant voice from behind Donald. It was the first time they had heard Homer Lea speak. It was like the sound of wind or a cock crowing at dawn. Wen hid his chin in his jacket, his eyes glaring. Donald turned slowly and saw the "General" pointing at Sun. Lea began to pace up and down, head bent forward, hands clasped behind back. At each about-face, he would perform it in brisk military fashion with click of heels.

Somewhere out in the hall a grandfather clock chimed three.

After awhile Donald said, "What of Yuan Shih-kai?"

"Yuan Shih-kai?" screamed the "General," "Why, I'll drive him across the Gobi Desert!"

Wu and Wen sat tight.

"Oh?" Donald asked. "Will he wait until you walk up and whack him? He has an army, you know."

"So have we! So have we!" Homer exclaimed shrilly.

Like the two Chinese visitors, Donald folded his hands across his vest front and said no more.

Shortly, the three callers arose, made formal good-bys and departed.

Wen waited until he was inside Wu's motorcar before he exploded. "I don't understand it. I don't understand it. It doesn't seem possible that a man such as Sun could have been the leader of the Revolutionary party all these years. How is it he's able to associate with this man!" Wen continued to seethe and Wu sat in icy silence.

Donald, too, was silent. He was wondering, as he was often to wonder later, even after he came to know the little doctor intimately and to love him, what it was in Sun that had enabled him to gather and hold such a huge and devout following. What quality in him had made him, in spite of his successive failures, a symbol of hope to desperate millions? Whatever that quality was, Donald reflected, it had not been evident that afternoon.

At headquarters a burst of indignant talk met Wen Tseng-yao's heated revelation of Sun's disregard for Chinese superstitions. For hours, they talked of nothing else. Donald sat reading a newspaper while they fumed. He could hear them pounding a table and striding up and down in the best Chinese portrayal of indignation. Finally one of them came to him and declared no one must ever know Sun had brought a dwarf with him in the guise of an American general and that Homer Lea should be returned to America.

Donald rose, folded his paper and put on his hat. "I'm going home to bed," he said.

The next day the answer to the oft-repeated question: "Where's Dr. Sun?" was learned. Sun himself told Donald that when the step to change dynasties was taken, he was in California. He heard of the outbreak on October 10, through newspapers. Later he received one of Dr. Wu's telegrams from Shanghai headquarters. He could not read it because it was in code, and his code was in Texas. To Texas he traveled, and in time he decoded the message as well as others that had followed it.

Donald remarked: "I remember those messages sent day after day. We never did hear from you."

"Didn't you, now?" Sun said slowly as if trying hard to remember. "It seems to me I answered. I'll ask General Lea about it some time."

Sun went on to explain that he had collected Homer Lea, who was then training a few Chinese troops in America, and how they returned leisurely to China via Europe and Suez.

"I'm awfully sorry that I didn't get to see the war and everything," Sun added. "I even missed the peace conference."

Donald laughed. For a moment he had a fleeting picture of Anderson sweating behind the guns; of Generalissimo Hsu who had no conception of what republicanism meant, but fighting, nonetheless; of filth and muck and blood spewed everywhere. It was a montage, with faces here and there asking, "Where's the doctor?"

In the next few days the two held long conversations on the economic, political and social problems facing China. A man of vigorous health and vigorous principles, Donald had vigorous plans for China. He pointed to the obvious ills and offered suggestions as to how they might be remedied. Sun had known of Donald for many years, of his deep interest in China, of his zest for getting at the heart of things. Listening intently as Donald spoke with bluntness, his big eyes were dreamy and owllike. Here were two men as different as oil and water who were going to mix well together. Donald was practical where Sun was visionary, realistic where Sun was idealistic, sagacious and shrewd where Sun was temperamental and a dreamer. In the efforts at reconstruction in the days ahead, this young Australian was to stand close by the side of Sun who, in matters with an earthy flavor, was exceedingly childlike. He was to guide him and talk to him like a Dutch uncle.

For the people, there was magic in the name of Sun Yat-sen, and his long years as titular head of the Kuomintang party made him the obvious choice for president. Revolutionary leaders, their initial resentment quieted, made plans for him to go to Nanking. There, on January 1, 1912, he was installed as provisional president of the Republic of China. Homer Lea was left in Shanghai.

Dr. Sun took up residence in the old yamen vacated by Viceroy Chang Chen-chun. It was to become the scene of great activity, of tremendous going and coming. The whole machinery of a republic had to be initiated, for it had been decided that a republic was the only way out of the national chaos. A suggestion had come from Peking that the six-year-old Manchu emperor, Pu Yi, should marry a Chinese girl, be given a Chinese name, and carry on under a limited monarchy similar to the British system. But Republicans uttered a vigorous no to any further carrying of the Manchu burden.

Donald attended the inauguration at Nanking, filed his stories on the momentous occasion, then returned to Shanghai. The next day was bitter cold, and Donald, alone in the Republican headquarters where there seldom was any heat, was pacing up and down to keep warm when Wang Chung-hui burst in. He was excited and breathless.

"I've been looking all over for you!" he shouted. "You must write a manifesto for the President. It has to be done at once!"

At that moment, Wen Tseng-yao ran in, also excited. "Dr. Sun just phoned. He says he needs a statement for the world on why the Manchus had to be overthrown and something about the policies of the new government."

Donald sat down before a typewriter and began writing, but the air was so cold his fingers were soon stiff and numb. Wen and Wang stomped up and down, and in a while Donald joined them. Dr. Wu was not at home, and he had left a stove cold and without coal. Now and then Donald would return to the typewriter, write a few lines and rejoin the pacers. The two Chinese would take turns removing their hands from their pockets to check and read over documents in the safe.

Evening wore into night, and gradually the first public proclamation which would be made by the new government took shape. Donald would toss up an idea, listen as his two friends reacted, then beat it into a carefully worded sentence. When the first draft was finished, Wen went out and came back with a pot of hot tea. They penciled in alterations, and Donald began to write again, the other two calling suggestions from wherever their pacing had led them. Donald would either accept or reject. Just before 6:00 A.M., the fourth and final draft was complete. They phoned Dr. C. T. Wang and told him he would have to hurry to Nanking and take the manifesto to Dr. Sun.

After Dr. Wang had left, Donald discovered that religion had been omitted, and prepared a wire to him to insert, "and insure religious toleration" at the end of the sixth paragraph on page four. The paragraph then read: "We will remodel our laws; revise our civil, criminal, and commercial and mining codes; reform our finances; abolish restrictions to trade and commerce; and insure religious toleration."

Wen called to Donald as he was leaving for the telegraph office: "Don, it might be a good idea to ask C. T. to make the old doc sign it right away and then hustle it over to the consuls of the powers. You know how the doc is. He might forget about it." Donald added the suggestion, and at Nanking Dr. Wang followed the instructions.

The document was signed without even the change of a comma, and on January 5 copies went to all the consuls for transmission to their home governments.

Around the globe, presidents and kings read what the newborn Republic of China had to say—from the typewriter of a young Australian newspaperman with a big nose and an easy smile.

10

THE DONALD WARNING

*A man without determination
is but an untempered sword.*

✺

On the afternoon the provisional and still-unrecognized Republic of China issued the "Donald Manifesto," word reached Shanghai that Japan's minister to China, Baron M. Ijuin, had offered military support to the Manchus, who had not yet abdicated, in return for widespread privileges in China. Donald was at work in his office on Szechuen Road when an excited little band of rebels burst in and asked what was to be done.

"If Japan steps in, we're finished!" Dr. Wang Chung-hui pointed out. "We couldn't win against their army and navy. It would be suicide." The others agreed that they were facing one of the most critical periods in the revolution.

Donald laid aside a dispatch he had just written for the *Herald.* "Well," he said, "we'll see what can be done about those people."

Making a quick decision, he outlined what he proposed to do, and when the rebels left, he pounded out a telegram, stuffed it in his pocket and walked over to the British Consulate General several blocks away. It was about dusk, and Mr. Everard Fraser was taking his usual evening stroll, pausing occasionally to watch the congestion of sampan and junk traffic in the broad Soochow Creek just beyond the northern edge of his consulate grounds.

Fraser greeted Donald warmly. "Ah," he said, "the revolutionist! I'm delighted to see you."

Donald grinned, then said seriously:

"I'm here to put Britain to a test."

"Are you now? Well, then, have a go at it. You know, all sorts of people have been doing it to us for centuries."

The cumbersome river traffic had untangled, the wild, angry shouts of the coolies and their families had died out, and where only a moment before had been confusion that seemed to defy solution, now was complete serenity. The correspondent and the consul stood absorbed not in a scene upon a creek alone but in a picture eternally China.

Donald said, "At our first meeting we arranged for Britain to enter the complete confidence of the rebels. I hope since then everything has worked out to your satisfaction?"

"Entirely," Fraser agreed.

"We have become good partners?"

"You might say that."

They were walking now along a path under trees at the rear of the consulate. "You will recall," the Australian said, "that after we made our arrangement, I said we would expect Britain to pull Japan out if she ever stepped into this arena."

Fraser halted and gazed at Donald for a moment.

"Yes," he said slowly, "I remember your saying that."

They resumed their walk. Fraser asked, "Well?"

Donald handed him the telegram he had written. "I'd like you to send a copy of this to the British minister at Peking—to Sir John Jordan for transmission to London."

Fraser took it and read:

MINISTER FOR FOREIGN AFFAIRS TOKYO JAPAN

YOUR CONSULS WITH THE CONSULS OF ALL OTHER POWERS HAVE EXPRESSED THE HOPE THAT HOSTILITIES WILL CEASE AND PEACE BE RESTORED IN CHINA STOP WE NOW LEARN THAT YOUR MINISTER IN PEKING IS NEGOTIATING WITH THE MANCHUS TO SUSTAIN THEM ON THE THRONE STOP THE REPUBLICAN GOVERNMENT TAKES STRONGEST EXCEPTION AND WARNS UNLESS JAPAN PUBLICLY REPUDIATES THIS POLICY HOSTILITIES WILL BE RESUMED AND FULL RESPONSIBILITY WILL REST UPON THE SHOULDERS OF JAPAN.

The Britisher scratched his head.

"It's a bit strong, isn't it?" he asked.

"It has to be."

"Will the rebels send it?"

There were no "ifs," "buts" or "maybes" in Donald's vocabulary. He had the sort of vanity that sits confidently on the shoulders of the great. "They will send it," he answered.

Fraser studied it for awhile, then took a pencil that protruded from Donald's pocket and added at the end "and all consequences whatsoever." He poked the pencil back into Donald's pocket, tapped it briskly, and looked amused.

"All right," he said, "all right. I'll send my copy to Sir John Jordan tonight."

Donald hurried to Republican headquarters. He set the telegram before Dr. Wu. The foreign minister scanned it, and his face reddened.

"I can't send this!" he objected. "Damn it all, this will produce war!"

The "bad weather" signals for Donald broke out. "You make me sick, Wu!" he said violently. "If it were not for the country's good, I wouldn't talk to you at all." He rose and began to pace the floor. "There are times when you and a million like you need starch, and I'm the lad to put it into you."

"Humbug!" said Wu.

"Any damn fool can see what the Japanese are up to!" Donald turned suddenly. "This could be the end of all we fought for. With the power of Japan behind them, the Manchus could crush us even now." He stopped at the window and looked down at two big Sikh police standing with bayonets fixed at Wu's gate.

"You'll need thousands of those fellows to save your head if Japan ever backs the Manchus," he said, and turned and glared at Wu. The foreign minister's face was no longer flushed. It was white and waxlike. He stared at Donald who now stood over him.

"What I propose is dangerous, but how much better we will sleep, whether in bed or in our graves, if we go down fighting. We have the alternative: Take a gamble or be kicked out."

For nearly two hours Donald sought to reason with Dr. Wu, but the little Chinese lawyer sat impassive, repeating over and over, "No, no, it will mean war with Japan." Finally Donald went into the next room where Dr. Wang Chung-hui and Wen Tseng-yao awaited the outcome.

They agreed to go into Wu's office on the pretense of looking for a book, and when Donald said, "You must send it," to step in and support him.

Returning, Donald renewed his buffeting of Wu who kept changing his position to escape the breeze of words. By the time Wang and Wen entered, Donald had Wu in the center of the room at a small table. At the agreed juncture, Wen stepped up and said casually, "Oh, we agree with Mr. Donald." Both Wang and Wen then joined in, arguing strongly for Donald, but Wu sat dourly, like a bird in a cage. Suddenly he lifted his face to Wen and demanded:

"Do you think I'm a simpleton?"

"I think you're a damn sight worse," Wen snapped. "I think you're a jackass."

Dr. Wang stepped around from behind the broad-backed Wen. "Dr. Wu," he said a little timidly, "I think you have a monolithic mind."

"I have a what!" demanded Wu.

Donald reached into a bookshelf, pulled out a dictionary and handed it to Wu.

It was nearly midnight before the climax came. Wu had grown tired, and his face was drawn. With his eyes, Donald motioned Wen to the desk where the foreign minister kept his seal of office, a big and bulky stamp. Wen tiptoed back with it, set it on the telegram and tried to grab Wu's hand to force him to make the stamp. But Wu jerked away, snatched at the seal and with a loud oath slammed it down on the telegram, and it was signed.

After that, they sat and waited, the Chinese perhaps a little more anxiously than Donald. What was going on in the realm of the frock coat, the striped trousers, among the gentlemen who called each other "Your Excellency?" What sort of a stew was brewing in London and Tokyo foreign offices? Would the rebel order to "Keep off the Grass" unchain Japan's military who continued to lust for slices of China?

Four days later, a Reuters dispatch came out of Tokyo: "The Japanese government have decided to remain neutral in China." In two days, Reuters carried the following story: "London—The British government have decided to adopt a policy of neutrality in the present China affair.'"

What had happened to yank Japan from the China scene? What fluttering had gone on in the higher echelons, and what had been said across this mahogany desk and what had been said across that? Had the Japanese government, mindful that its overseas trade could not prosper in a chaotic China, been deterred by the rebels' sharp warning? Had the British ambassador in Tokyo said to the Japanese foreign minister: "See here, old boy, my government cannot countenance you fellows playing hob with China at this time."

Donald asked no questions. He never knew just what had happened in the palaces at Tokyo and London. He was content with the result. Japan had publicly dealt itself out of the play for spoils in China and support of the Manchus. Britain's neutrality declaration was tantamount to telling the world that it had abandoned the Manchu regime, and that was followed by an offer to act as mediator.

But the world had not yet heard the end of the affair. In the press, a storm was blowing. Behind the storm, oddly enough, was J. K. Ohl, the man James Gordon Bennett had sent to Peking on the advice of Donald. There Ohl had fallen under the spell of the Manchus and had been in their camp, fighting their battle in the *Herald* while Donald supported the revolutionists both on the battlefield and in his stories to the same paper.

There was no indication of how Bennett himself stood on the China crisis until his Paris and New York editions spoke editorially the day after Britain announced her position, and then it was plain that Ohl, not Donald, had influenced him. Under the heading, "England again Backing the Wrong Horse," the Paris edition proclaimed:

As regards China, England seems to be, in Lord Salisbury's telling phrase, "backing the wrong horse." The maintenance of the Chinese Empire, said Lord Charles Beresford a few years ago, is essential for the protection of Anglo-Saxon interests. Since that opinion was expressed, nothing has happened to invalidate it. The downfall of the Empire means the breakup of China. . . . Though the republican idea is accepted in certain southern provinces, others, Yunnan for example, reject it entirely; Mongolia and Tibet and Chinese Turkestan mean to remain monarchist or become independent, and all the provinces north of the Yangtze still cling to the monarchical regime. It is evident, then, that a Republic of China is a material impossibility. . . . A disintegrated China means general anarchy and foreign intervention, the destruction of Chinese independence and the domination of Asia by Japan and Russia. Is that what England is working for? . . . A special cable dispatch from the *Herald's* Peking bureau reports a growing conviction that Britain and Japan are united in the desire to split China into a "North" and a "South."

The New York edition made similar comment.

Japan was the first to bristle under the blast. The Osaka *Asahi* retorted: "Rashness and self contradicting characterized the *Herald's* article and its Peking correspondent. . . . The charge that England and Japan are following a policy of obstruction is untrue, as is also the assertion that England is opposing the Imperialists." The *Japan Times*, echoing the opinions of its government masters, growled: "The *Herald* is laboring under a profound mistake. The dissemination of such unfounded suspicions wrongs all parties concerned. It is sheer wrongheadedness to blame England for acting as mediator." The *Japan Times* added it regretted that the *Herald* credited certain Peking reports (Ohl's) and was "led into making suggestions apparently intended to sow seeds of discord between Japan and England." The American-owned *Japan Advertiser* reprimanded the *Herald* for lack of common sense.

The *Herald* lashed back:

The horror expressed by the Japanese press over the *Herald's* editorial fixing the responsibility for the present situation in China primarily on England and Japan smacks of the mock turtle variety. One thing is certain—the *Herald's* editorials and its cables from Peking have resulted in turning the full light of the entire world upon the position taken by Great Britain and her press in favoring the unpractical revolutionaries and therefore directly contributing toward the breakup of China which must follow a republic or series of republics. . . .

In China, the Peking *Daily News*, unofficial organ of the Manchu government, attributed England's coming forward in the role of mediator to a desire to protect her vast commercial interests in the Yangtze Valley, but remarked, "The time for her coming forward was rather inopportune and furnished just cause for suspicion."

Ohl kept up his barrage on behalf of the Manchus. In the midst of the crisis, Russia told Peking bluntly she meant to assume a protectorship over Mongolia, which had just announced its secession from China, and Ohl seized upon the event to cable:

. . . THIS BRINGS CHINA FACE TO FACE WITH THE SPECTRE OF PARTITION STOP IT IS A LOGICAL CONSEQUENCE TO BRITISH ACTION IN AIDING THE REVOLUTIONISTS STOP BUT FOR THIS BRITISH ACTION THERE IS NO QUESTION THAT THE INTERNAL SITUATION WOULD HAVE BEEN SOLVED PROBABLY PEACEFULLY A MONTH OR MORE AGO.

But Donald took no part in the furore, and in a while it winded itself. The revolutionists' ground was firm now that the "Donald Warning" had caused Tokyo to adopt a hands-off policy and had encouraged England to show outwardly its moral support for the rebels. All that remained was for the Manchus to quit a throne to which they clung only precariously.

At Nanking Dr. Sun was struggling to form a cabinet and build a government. Donald came home one night to find an urgent telegram from the little doctor:

PLEASE USE ALL POWERS AT YOUR COMMAND TO CONVINCE DR. WANG CHUNG-HUI HE MUST ACCEPT POST AS MINISTER OF JUSTICE STOP CHINA NEEDS HIM.

Donald knew that Wang had been dodging the offer for some time, probably because he had already built a lucrative law practice in Shanghai. He telephoned Wang, and the next evening the young lawyer appeared at Donald's flat for dinner.

They discussed politics and the matter of the empty justice portfolio for a while, then Donald twitted him with: "When are you going to get married, Wang?"

Wang inserted a cigarette into a long holder and said, "Find me a wife and I'll take the job as minister of justice."

Donald smiled and asked for his specifications.

Wang inhaled deeply, then blew the smoke slowly toward the ceiling. He was putting together his thoughts as precisely as he might prepare a law case.

"Well, first, she must be modern educated. She must be pretty. She must speak English and, say, French or German."

More smoke wafted ceilingward.

"What is of utmost importance," he went on, "is that I must see her firsthand. To inspect her—with propriety, of course—before I marry her. We're in a new China now. The grab bag days of matrimony are not for me."

Donald had not been prepared for Wang's radical approach to the orthodox marriage customs in China. He said, "My friend, the custom —if not good, still ancient—is that you don't inspect the bride until the niceties of nuptials are over. You're not supposed to be fiddling around with her beforehand."

"I don't want to fiddle," he said. "I just want to look." He shrugged. "Anyway, those are my terms."

Donald's boy came in with a second cup of tea which, in Chinese custom, is a neat and agreeable reminder to the guest that the evening is at an end. Donald walked with Wang to the door, told him to be on hand the next afternoon at four to meet a pretty girl, and his visitor, laughing, went down the stairs.

Donald had in mind the daughter of Wen Tseng-yao, Constance,[1] vivacious and petite. A good conversationalist, she spoke English perfectly, was educated in the Chinese classics, and more than measured up to the specifications of the unconventional Dr. Wang. Donald invited her to tea the next afternoon.

When she arrived, she greeted him with, "Hello, Uncle Don. I have a funny feeling that you're up to some sort of game." When Wang arrived, Donald introduced them, then excused himself, leaving the young man to stare at her and to choke out a red-faced acknowledgment. He was still looking at her as if he were seeing a walking, talking dream when Donald returned. She was pattering brightly, but the lawyer, who had been so glib the day before, fumbled with his hat and gulped. Several times he shot imploring glances at his host.

Donald thought: Good heavens, this rascal really has buck fever.

After a while she announced she had an engagement and left. In a moment or two, Wang stumbled to his feet, groped for the doorknob

[1] She later became a doctor with the Seventh-Day Adventists in Shanghai.

and somehow or other got out after giving Donald a bewildered look.

Four or five mornings later, Wen Tseng-yao burst in on Donald.

"What do you think? What do you think?" he said angrily. "This rice pot Wang wants to marry my daughter! Do you think I'd let Constance marry a fellow who prattles about social justice just to hear himself talk?" It was plain that Wen had accepted Wang as a colleague in revolution only.

Donald eyed him uneasily, wondering where he stood in the affair. Then, thinking of the still-vacant ministry, he said, "You could be making a mistake, you know."

"Bah!" snorted Wen and stomped out. He didn't learn until years later that Donald had been the middleman.

Wang's first frustration had kindled his fervor for marriage, and he insisted that Donald find him a wife, noting that the justice portfolio was still unfilled. He kept up his pestering until a tired Donald put a stop to it. Then, one day, Wang came to him again. He had another prospect—the niece of Chen Chi-mei, one of the revolutionary generals.

Donald asked, "Well, what's your problem this time?"

Wang reddened. "I've never seen her. I've got to have a look at her."

"Good God!" Donald said, his annoyance mixed with mirth. "Wang, you're a worm!"

That night, however, he secretly arranged for the girl to sit in her room with the lights on at a certain time. Feeling like a fool, he helped the young man climb up on a box and gaze in for several minutes. Trembling with excitement, Wang climbed down and breathed:

"That's fine. That's fine. She'll do."

Sometime later, Donald received a wedding invitation, and he attended the ceremony, content that the new government at last was to have a minister of justice.[2]

The government at Nanking had begun to resemble the orderliness of a school grounds at recess, and Donald went there at Sun's request to comb out the tangles. There he found a scroll awaited him, the

---

[2] Several years afterwards, Mrs. Wang Chung-hui died. Later, when Wang met Donald, he exclaimed: "You've got to find me a wife!" Donald retorted: "Oh, go to hell!"

President presenting it at a solemn ceremony. It was a foot wide, a foot and a half long, and it stated simply that Donald had been appointed foreign secretary and advocate of the Republican government of China, noting that he was a man "calm and careful, experienced in foreign affairs, who has rendered signal service in Nanking and Chinkiang."

Dr. Sun had become the center of a hubbub. His day was filled with listening in on discussions of important matters, with interviewing thousands of job-seekers of all kinds. Every day the trains disgorged new hordes, among them scores of Japanese who settled down in the yamen as if by right. They brought their bedding, their cooking and eating paraphernalia and milled and wandered about like herds of sheep.

One day, after he had pushed his way down what had been immaculate and quiet halls under his old viceroy friend, Donald walked into Dr. Sun's office and asked somewhat irritably just who the shoddy citizenry belonged to.

Dr. Sun appeared embarrassed. "The Chinese have come for jobs," he explained. "I made a mistake. When I was collecting funds in America and elsewhere, I promised that all who gave would be provided for when we got rid of the Manchus. I had to get money. I had to promise something. Now they have come to collect." He toyed awhile with a writing brush, then said apologetically: "I never thought the Manchus would be thrown out of Nanking so quickly or so easily. I feel a little ashamed."

"Who are the Japanese?"

"I don't know," Sun answered, looking worried. "There are two or three friends who helped me sell the republic idea to Chinese abroad. But I never saw the others before."

Donald asked if Sun couldn't flush them out of the government palace and make it plain they were unwanted.

Sun looked at him unhappily. "I just can't do it," he said. "I just can't do it."

Donald sensed something bordering on revolt over Dr. Sun's squatters. That day he buttonholed Generalissimo Hsu with: "Why don't you people go down and clean out the yamen?" Within the hour, Hsu's troops marched into the old Taiping Palace and with bayonets prodded hundreds into the street, bedclothes, bird cages and all, and herded them in the direction of the railway depot. When Donald returned to the yamen later in the day, he found the courtyards and halls solemn once more, and only a handful of soldiers standing briskly at attention.

While Nanking was preoccupied with the headache of government, Homer Lea slipped into the city and, ill, went to bed. No one saw or heard of him for days. When he was well enough for visitors, Donald called to find him frailer, seemingly smaller than ever before. But his eyes burned brightly and there was a new treble in his strange voice. For a time he talked spiritedly, and then looking out of his window where he could see rows of ancestral grave mounds, he said morosely:

"China is graves. They are all about us. Look at them. Graves, graves, graves." The "General" flung his arm in a wide arc. Then his mood changed. With a bony, crooked finger he reached out and tapped Donald on the head.

"Mark me," he wheezed, "we're going to have trouble with those Russian fellows. They're asking for a protectorate over Mongolia now. But that's not all. You just wait and see. They're the sort who have a destiny. There's always someone at some time or another on the march to conquer the world. They're that kind of people!"

Donald rose to go, but Lea gripped him tightly by the arm.

"Buy me a big horse in Shanghai," he begged. "I must have a big horse—as big as you can get. And a big sword. I'll need them. The Russians are up to no good."

Shortly afterwards, under pressure of such men as Wen Tseng-yao and others who feared his presence might bring misfortune to the new government, the "General," who had been disdained even by the American Consulate at Nanking, was encouraged to leave China.

Day by day, the situation at Nanking grew a little more hectic, the people in government a little more harried. There was vast intrigue for office and for jobs, by parties and by cliques. There was incompetency, inefficiency and, as a bad odor lingers, some of the decay for which the Manchus had been blamed. There was the question of the make-up of ministries and bureaus and the pressing need to complete the ousting of the Manchus. The abdication treaty had not yet been signed.

For Donald, there was much writing of statements and official proclamations. Seldom were he and his colleagues in bed before two or three o'clock in the morning, and they were up by seven. His social life, which in the years up to now had been very meager and select, all but vanished. There was little time for small talk over teacups. What energies there were to spare were used for political maneuvering. He told Anderson one day: "I've pulled enough strings to tie this blasted country together." For all this, Donald would not accept remuneration from the Chinese. He clung religiously to his old code: Keep your money in your pocket. Frugal where he himself was concerned, generous with others, this descendant of the Scots held money as unimportant and was content to let his newspaper salaries take care of all his needs. Above all, he valued his independence. He wanted no binding ties. He wanted to come and go as he pleased. If Donald ever bragged, it was about this one thing.

Against a backdrop of turmoil, Dr. Sun stood quiet and uninflammable. A dreamer for many years, it was difficult to influence him to act decisively now that he might implement his old dreams. Donald talked to him on all manner of subjects, urging action on this or that problem. He soon found, however, that the way to make Sun father responsibility was to do the job himself, then get his approval. But he could not untangle all the problems. Platoons of secretaries, departments and bureaus waited in vain for instructions, for signatures on matters of importance. Waiting rooms were filled with callers of every kind, and there was a constant holdup of affairs.

But Sun's thoughts were always earnestly and honestly on the welfare of China. He made valiant efforts to grapple with the monstrous difficulties that confronted the land. One day Donald found him poring over some yellowed charts. He looked up, eyes shining, and exclaimed:

"I think I have a solution to the silt-shifting problem in the Yangtze."

Donald asked what he proposed.

Sun ran a pudgy finger along a chart. "I'd build a stone wall from Hankow to the sea," he said. "The river would then wash the silt along the wall, and silt banks wouldn't form."

Donald stirred uneasily. "From Hankow to the sea is six hundred miles," he said gently. "Between Hankow and Nanking the river at floodtime rises from twenty to forty feet or more. That means your wall would have to be more than forty feet high and about as long as from

London to Berlin. What you propose is quite a project, Mr. President."

Sun looked surprised, then laughed heartily. "So it would be," he said. "So it would be."

One by one, a few competents trickled into the government, and the little President became more and more released for the decorative essentials, for reception of visitors, for listening to the thousands of persons who wanted to sell themselves or an idea. But even in this there were problems. He fell easily for the urgings of the spellbinder. The bringers of rosy promises, the founders of questionable schemes, concession-hunters, inventors of all manner of panaceas found welcome and were promised help. Dr. Sun seemed unable to distinguish the honest man from the charlatan, the good idea from the bad. Whenever Donald found time, he would take up a post as "front man," screening out the panhandlers and tinhorns.

Among the interviewers who came were newspapermen. The name of Dr. Sun made headlines throughout the world now, particularly in the United States and Britain where he had carried on so much of his missionary work. At a press conference one day, a correspondent asked the President whether he was a socialist. Sun turned to Donald. "Am I?" he inquired.

Donald answered promptly, "You are everything that is required as a nationalist."

Late one day, after a last caller had straggled out, Donald dropped in on Sun.

"Mr. President, I thought I'd call a matter of some importance to your attention. Our treasury has blessed little money. I think you should look forward to the day when you might obtain a foreign loan. You'll have to wait, of course, until this government is recognized."

"Oh," said Dr. Sun, "we won't need a loan. I have a better scheme, Don."

Donald braced himself.

"We have many mints," the President explained, his face radiant. "We can make all the money we need."

Donald kept his face expressionless. "Where will you get your bullion?" he asked. "Where will you get the reserves for your paper money?"

"Bullion? We would melt down our silver teapots!"

He sat thoughtful. After a while he said, "You know, it might be possible to do away with such things as bullion. It's an expensive matter buying silver, copper, lead or nickel."

Donald thought: O Lord, what now!

"I've been thinking," Sun went on, "that we might use our paper money and save the expense of metals. We could print all we needed, and when it was worn out, we could print some more." He paused, and it was evident the idea was maturing.

"By George!" Sun exclaimed. "We could be the richest nation in the world that way!"

The year had advanced into February. One day Yuan Shih-kai sent word to Nanking: "If I could be elected president within forty-eight hours, I would force the Manchus to sign the abdication treaty."

Republicans went into hurried consultation, Donald with them. There was no question but that Yuan was nothing more than a militarist yet strength had to be master. He controlled a real army, and while he may not have known it, the rebels knew their ill-shod forces could not march against it. Scattered opposition to Yuan's proposal was met by Donald's admonition that they would bring on civil war and again would spend years attempting to secure political control if Yuan was ignored.

Agreement was finally reached to accept Yuan as president, and on February 12, tiny Pu Yi was lifted down from the Dragon Throne, and the reign of the Manchus was at an end.

It was a gala day at Nanking. Flags and banners flew everywhere. Dr. Sun, Donald and high officials of the government drove outside the city wall to the Ming Tombs where the last of the Chinese rulers was interred. The road, over which giant arches had been set, was lined with fifteen thousand troops. The great tomb, with its crumbling altar, had been swept for the first time in several centuries and was bedecked with scrolls and greenery. Amid the piles of fallen brickwork, the pointed-chinned face of the last monarch peered from a big painting down upon a solemn band of his descendants.

Donald walked up the steps with Dr. Sun who was pale with emotion. The little doctor made a spectacular obeisance at the foot of the painting, then sank to his knees, head bowed.

"O Spirit of the Mings," he said softly, "China at last has been wrested from the usurping Manchus. We are once again under command of the Chinese race."

The next day, Sun and his cabinet resigned on the condition that Nanking be kept as the seat of government in order, they hoped, that the republic might escape the corroding, stagnant atmosphere of the old capital. The National Assembly which had been convened several weeks before, accepted the resignations but neglected, however, to observe the stipulation, voting the honor to Peking. The yamen burst into a furore (like the world coming to an end, Donald cabled the *Herald*) and the military breathed dire threats. The assemblymen were rounded up, their error pointed out, and they trooped back to rectify the mistake. The following day, Yuan was elected president with the provision that Sun and his cabinet stay on until Yuan came to Nanking.

That was all officially for Dr. Sun Yat-sen—forty-four days as the young republic's president. Twenty years of scheming and dreaming and puff!—it was all over. Yuan, the one-time arch enemy of reform and liberalism, was in the driver's seat. But Sun stayed on at the yamen, awaiting Yuan's arrival.

In a few days, a revolutionary mission, headed by Tong Shao-yi, now a full-fledged Republican, went to Peking to escort Yuan to Nanking. But they had not reckoned with Yuan's own ideas, the ideas of his military, or with the foreign powers who had expensive legations in Peking. The northerner still had in his blood a lust for the traditional glories of the Manchus, the pomp and circumstance, the ornate dress, the mandarin hats and buttons, the peacock feathers, the splash of color and the spangle. Nanking, on the other hand, was conspicuously decayed, down at the heel, dirty and woebegone.

When Tong petitioned Yuan, the old warrior threw up his hands and is said to have complained: "My army would not permit the removal of the capital."

Tong then pressed his insistence with Yuan's officers and was met by an explosion that hourly erupted more violently. Before nightfall a mutiny was under way. It was finally quelled, but the Nanking mission had no heart to negotiate further.

That night was February 28. Donald was in the yamen at Nanking talking to Dr. Sun when a secretary brought in a telegraphed report on the mutiny and the failure of the mission.

Sun handed the message to Donald.

"I told you he was a tough one," Donald said. "He's as full of tricks as a magician."

The little doctor snapped his fingers. "Yuan is nothing but a paper tiger."

"Well, what are you going to do?"

"I'm going to march my army to Peking."

"There's an inch of snow beyond the Yangtze, and the farther north you go, the colder it is. Your troops have little to eat and less to wear." Donald paused to let the words sink in, then went on, "And, incidentally, what about finance?"

"Finance?" cried Dr. Sun, nettled. "Finance is the last thing I think of."

No move was made against Peking, however. The determination of Yuan, the "Paper Tiger," to stay there was not challenged again, and by April the Nanking government had traveled to Peking. There the republic was established amid the remnants of Manchu splendor.

Donald returned to Shanghai and made ready to journey to Peking where he was to take over the *Herald* bureau. J. K. Ohl was leaving China, never knowing that the British policy against which he had battered his protests and those of the Manchus had had its genesis in the sharp, calculating mind of his colleague to the south. Before Donald left, he ran into Anderson and they spent an evening discussing the state of affairs in the nation. It was a session between two men who without a doubt knew their subject matter better than any other foreigner or any Chinese. Both had had deep, rich experiences, and they saw objectively, without prejudice, without favoritism. Donald was depressed and unhappy. He had hoped for so much from the revolution, and what he found was so little. There were new bosses for the fleshpots but no improvements—merely a modernization of "squeeze" methods. Dr. Sun seemed to have purposely blinded himself to practices that nullified reform and repudiated the undertakings set forth in the "Donald Manifesto." The lack of honesty, the undercover plunder in the provinces were in diametric opposition to the old arguments for the overthrow of the Manchus.

Donald dwelt on the political corruption that still existed, on inexcusable derelictions, on all sorts of venal customs, and told Anderson he could not bring himself to write about them. He could not publicly whip his friends, most of whom held high government offices.

"If I lend myself to a campaign of newspaper exposés," he explained, "it might contribute more than any one thing to the undermining of this young republic. Perhaps it's best that I've said nothing. The heavy type and the black ink is no cure-all. It's not the only road to justice. Time has a way of bringing wisdom, of healing faults."

"Yes, that can be true," Anderson agreed. "But when a sore festers and stinks, can time alone fix it?"

"No. Time must have its midwives and its nursemaids, like machinery must have its oil. Time must have its elbow grease, its sweat, its heartaches and, I suppose, blood sometimes." Donald lit a cigar, paused reflectively, and Anderson was content to watch him.

"There's a hard road ahead, but I've got elbow grease for it," Donald said and added, "I think my job is to work for change and keep my mouth shut."

Before he left Shanghai, two letters had arrived, both from Dr. Sun. The first read:

NANKING, CHINA
March 21, 1912

MR. W. H. DONALD
SHANGHAI
DEAR MR. DONALD:

The country is now in unity, and the great work is completed successfully. Recalling the past, I am very much obliged and appreciate that you have done your utmost to make our doctrines known to the wide world and bring the revolution to success. Especially during the Nanking war you went back and forth between Nanking and Shanghai with the sole object to give every possible help to the populace and military.

Now I take the opportunity to express my deep gratitude and hearty thanks.

I am,
Yours very truly,
(signed) SUN YAT-SEN
President

Enclosed was a specially made gold medal, bearing the names of Dr. Sun and Donald. A short citation with it eulogized the Australian's part in the revolution.

The second letter stated:

NANKING, CHINA
March 21, 1912

MR. W. H. DONALD
SHANGHAI
DEAR SIR:

Dr. Wang Chung-hui has handed to me your letter of February 27th, expressing your earnest wish to write a book on the Revolution under the auspices of the Republican Government and asking permission to use the original documents pertaining thereto in the possession of the Government.

As this is a very laudable undertaking, I take pleasure to grant your request, authorizing you to write a book on the Chinese Revolution to be published under the auspices of the Republican Government with free access to all the original documents pertaining thereto in the possession of the Government.

I am,
Yours very truly,
(signed) SUN YAT-SEN
President

P.S. This authority is granted on condition that the manuscripts will be submitted to, and approved by Dr. Wang Chung-hui.

Later, Sun referred to the proposed book. "Don," he asked, "did you ever write your book on the revolution?"

Donald looked straight into Sun's eyes. "Yes," he said, "I did."

"Did you now? I can't remember seeing it."

"It had only ten words."

"Ten words? What were they?"

Donald's expression did not change.

"They were," he said, " 'The revolution succeeded in spite of those who led it.' "

THE STRUGGLE FOR POWER

*A faithful friend is
like hands and feet.*

President Yuan Shih-kai settled the question of what to do with the retired Dr. Sun by giving him the elaborate title of "Director for Construction of all Railways in China," with a salary of thirty thousand Chinese dollars a month. It was intended as a sop, but the intense little doctor took his appointment seriously.

He arrived in Peking from Nanking one day with Mrs. Sun, in addition to a sizable crowd he referred to as his staff, and moved into the Waichiaopu (Foreign Affairs) building. Again, there was a daily rush of foreigners and Chinese to unloose grandiose ideas, to see what might be milked from him. As before, Donald was at hand, sifting out those who might lead him astray. He never quite understood what it was in Sun that commanded his protective instinct, but there it was, hovering belligerently whenever he caught the wrong gleam in a caller's eye.

Anderson, who had been moved to the Peking office of Standard Oil, had remarked one day, "Don, you may have tied into what could be a thankless task—this Dutch uncle to old Doc Sun."

Donald had answered, "If I give up what you call playing Dutch uncle, China might be hurt. Doc's known as the Father of the Revolution. He has the respect of the man-in-the-street in China and elsewhere. We just can't let him do anything to arouse unfavorable attention while the country is struggling to get on its feet."

Sun's need for a safeguard against his own utterances or whims was to crop up many a time in the days ahead. So, while he concerned himself with his magnificent and impractical dreams, Donald carried on the variously important minor chores which fell to him as practical handy man to the revolution and self-appointed protector of Sun.

For instance, a Frenchman, H. H. Spielman, who later organized the highly successful International Savings Society, at Shanghai, had begun to interest Sun in starting a bank. Sun, believing he had a flair for finance, was already seeing himself as a bank president when Donald drafted a polite dismissal to Spielman and had Sun sign and dispatch it. Again, passing through the anteroom one day, he saw a familiar face. It was that of Sir Francis Taylor Piggott, regarded in England as a legal scholar and eminent Orientalist. He had been chief justice in Hong Kong in Donald's days there, and Donald had appraised him somewhat differently.

"What's that fellow out there want?" he demanded of Sun.

"Oh, I'm thinking of having him advise me on my legal problems. He's been after the post for some time."

"Chase him away," said Donald.

"Why?"

"He has a Hong Kong mind."

Sun reluctantly broke off further talks with Sir Francis.

Before he set himself to what plainly was a monstrous task—the building of railways in a rugged and impoverished land—Sun decided on a triumphal tour of the country where the existing railways could carry him. A long train was placed at his disposal, and he headed for the northern provinces. It was a tour elegant. The reception room was the ornate and comfortably appointed saloon car of the late dowager empress. There were two dining cars, several other saloon cars and many sleepers. Donald and Dr. Wang Chung-hui went with him, along with an assortment of others, including his wife; Ai-ling Soong, his shy, pretty secretary; a large number of beautiful Chinese women; his bodyguard and his staff.

Throughout the nights as the train passed small stations, bugles blared a welcome and a farewell, and since sleep was difficult, the guests took to mingling to while away long hours. From behind the sleepers' green curtains voices not always familiar to a particular berth sometimes were heard, and once a secretary told how he had observed with almost overpowering astonishment a dainty, jeweled hand drooping carelessly from a berth he was certain was occupied by a rough, barrel-chested revolutionary general.

At the large cities, the train stopped, Dr. Sun got off, met the dignitaries and occasionally had tiffin and made a speech. Donald noticed that at such affairs Sun insisted he sit beside him. When he pointed out that the provincials doubtlessly coveted the seat of honor next to the great revolutionary leader, Sun countered:

"No, I want to sit near you. I can't talk to these upcountry fellows."

There was something in what he said—the difficulty of conversing in dialects a shade different every hundred miles. But Donald guessed the motive was quite different. He suspected Sun feared some unappreciative citizen might pay his disrespects with a bomb. If so, Sun may have figured that, in the fleeting moment before the bomb was hurled, the thrower would catch sight of Donald, a foreigner, and pause to reflect on international complications. Whatever the reason, he had to sit next to the doctor most of the time.

As the train rumbled through villages of whitewashed mud houses, through grassy plains and over warty heights, Donald sought to interest Sun in the problems of his land. He discussed the cities in which they had tarried, and the ones to come, laying stress on the economic backwardness, an inescapable picture. Sun would sit with fixed, wide-eyed attention, hands clasped across his front as the correspondent talked of the necessity for reforms in official and private affairs, of the need for development of a countrywide movement to help a people desperately in need of help—a people to whom revolution should have meant a change but had not.

Often Ai-ling would take a chair near them, make notes as Donald talked and smiled encouragingly. Sun would transfer his quiet, expressionless gaze from Donald to her, and there he would keep it, not an eyelash flickering. Donald would go on talking of how industries would have to be started to produce necessities from raw materials, how mining must be begun first, and, overall, the need for highways to link people and cities and industries. He underscored everything that meant progress.

"I'm certain," Sun said one day, "you think more about China than you do your newspaper work. Why do you worry so much about us?"

"Damn it all, I sometimes wonder," Donald answered, a little wearily. "I sometimes wonder whether it has just become a habit."

In his speeches, Sun often emphasized the points Donald had drummed into him. But what he said for the most part fell on deaf ears. Provincial officials were uninterested in uplift or national welfare. They were interested in how to make a dollar, dishonest or otherwise. Bored by Sun's lectures, they were happy to see him and his bulky entourage under way.

At the beginning of the rail junket, the custom had developed for Donald to be called at 7:00 A.M. The first time it happened without warning. Dr. Wang Chung-hui, looking sleepy, shook him. "Doc wants you," he yawned.

Donald dressed quickly and hurried to the dowager's car to find Sun sitting on a side seat. A large map of China was on the wall opposite him. A tea table held a bowl of water, a packet of cotton wool, a Chinese writing brush and an ink slab. Intent on what he was doing, the ex-President did not notice Donald enter and join him in peering at the map. It was being covered by ink lines from one city to another. Donald coughed politely.

"Oh," said Dr. Sun, looking up, his cheeks puffy as a cherub's, "I want you to help me with this railway map."

Donald sat down as Sun explained the lines.

"I propose to build two hundred thousand li[1] of railways in ten years," he declared. "I'm marking them on this map. You see the thick lines running from one provincial capital to another? Well, they will be trunk lines. The others are laterals and less important connections."

Donald said, "Yes, yes," as the doctor talked animatedly.

"Tsk, tsk!" Sun would say, and he would take a piece of cotton, dip it in water, wipe out a crooked line and mark a straight one in its place. This went on every morning for days, the little railway builder sitting before his map, making a new line here, straightening this one, straightening that one. He was wrapped in his dreams, the pulse-thumping, the blood-tingling kind. At last, all the capitals were linked by trunk

[1] About thirty three thousand miles.

lines, all the prefectural cities connected by smaller lines and there were branches in all directions, like a banyan tree. It was an amazing production. The doctor with a deft stroke built a hundred miles of rails in one place, a thousand in another.

Donald thought: This man is a dreamer beyond belief!

But Dr. Sun believed his dreams.

Donald said nothing for days. He was worried by Sun's newest effort, since he had received numerous requests from foreign correspondents for interviews with Dr. Sun at the big railway junction of Fengtai. Something had to be done, for he knew what the result would be if they ever laid hands on the doctor's fantastic map. He pondered the matter of approach and it was not until they were nearing Fengtai that he reached a decision.

The train was due at the city within an hour when he joined Sun in the big reception car. He lighted a cigar, said offhand:

"I wouldn't show your railway map to the correspondents. You would be giving away your own special ideas."

"Oh, no," Sun answered affably, "I don't mind. I want people to know about them. My map will save China."

The train whistled and the silence that followed was broken only by the click of wheels. Through the broad windows, Donald watched the countryside, mean, disheveled, pathetic. Fengtai was less than twenty-five miles away. He cleared his throat, began again:

"A few days ago you said you'd build two hundred thousand li in ten years. That might not be possible. It would take a lot of money, for one thing, and, for another, I don't think you'll have that many miles built in thirty years."[2]

"It is very simple. We shall get all the money we want. I'll build some of the lines with British capital, some with American, some with German, some with Japanese, and so on."

Donald answered sharply: "Don't you know the Manchus tried to do the same thing? They tried to nationalize the railways and operate them on foreign capital. They got instead a railway revolt."

The little doctor made a clucking sound and looked out of the

[2] Thirty years later, China, including lines built before 1912, had roughly 75,000 li of railways in operation.

window. Donald took another tack. Sun had drawn a line westward from Szechwan Province, around the northern side of the Himalayan Mountains to the western limits of Tibet, then around the north of that country, entering China again through Kansu Province. The line had been drawn without regard for precipices or valleys, mountains or glaciers, forests or deserts, rivers or lakes.

For a moment Donald debated inwardly the merits of pricking this dream of rail empire. Then he said gently:

"Doctor, that line circling Tibet can never be built. You can build it with brush and ink—and that's all. Some of the passes over which your railway would run are fifteen thousand feet high."

Sun arched his eyebrows. "There are roads, aren't there," he said more as a statement of fact than a question.

"Not roads, Doctor. Just narrow, rough trails. They go spiraling up into the sky. They're steep, so steep a strong yak can hardly climb them."

"Where there's a road, a railway can be built," Sun answered softly, plainly dismissing the subject.

Donald rose. Sun was being as untractable as he had ever known him. Here was the sort of stubbornness that had made him cling tenaciously for years to his idea of revolution.

"Doctor," Donald said, "we're about to enter Fengtai. There will be people to greet you, and correspondents will come aboard. Perhaps it would be a good idea if we strolled to the rear platform."

"Fine, fine," Sun agreed, and added, "a little fresh air might blow away your cobwebs."

On the platform, Donald excused himself, and Sun did not see him again until he was seating correspondents in the reception car.

Joshing and small talk from the newsmen was met amiably by Sun, then he announced, "Gentlemen, I have something I think may interest you." He turned to face his map, but it was not there. Perplexed, he asked: "Don, have you seen my map?"

Donald looked quickly to the door leading between the two cars, then rose. A secretary entered and approached Dr. Sun. "Gentlemen," Donald began, "Dr. Sun Yat-sen is working on a railway plan. His map would have explained it. I'm sure—" At this point, the secretary stooped and whispered in Sun's ear. The doctor looked worried and said, "I don't understand, but if it's true, we must be moving on." To the correspondents he announced: "I'm sorry, gentlemen, but the engineer has received reports of the danger of a bandit attack. He says that he must start the train at once."

Newsmen made polite but hurried good-bys and, sensing a better story, piled off. The train was under way within a minute or two. A few hours later Sun's map miraculously turned up, and by the time Shanghai was reached, he was once again absorbed with putting his dreams onto paper.

At the big metropolis, he established his main railway construction office, and on his staff were such men as Dr. Wang Chung-hui and Ai-ling's father, Charles Soong. Soong now was treasurer for his old friend.

Although Donald was stationed permanently in Peking, he made monthly trips to Shanghai. He had succumbed to repeated requests from a tall, lanky American, George Bronson Rea, to take over the editorship of the *Far Eastern Review*, owned and published by Rea at Shanghai. The *Review* was a highly respected publication devoted to industrial engineering and construction subjects as well as to matters of general concern in the Orient. Donald prepared his material at Peking, and his trips to Shanghai each month were to put the magazine to press.

It was during one of these that he questioned Sun's right to negotiate loans to build his railways. Sun admitted his only authority was in a piece of paper signed by Yuan Shih-kai. Donald pointed to the immensity of the folly.

"You should have Parliament give you a charter to negotiate loans. Now you have nothing."

Sun looked surprised.

Donald explained that the time to act was now, since the Kuomintang—Sun's party—held a majority in Parliament but he wondered how long that majority would last under Yuan.

Sun asked Donald if he would write him a charter, and, undeterred by the novelty of the request, he did, patterning it after copies he was fortunate to find of charters Britain had issued the old East India Company and the Rhodesian Company. The charter read that Dr. Sun should have control not only of construction of future railways, but also all future transportation developments, including "dirigible airships and airplanes."

Dr. Sun liked the charter, but he had no regard for the future of the airplane. He deleted the reference to such things, saying, "They'll never be able to carry anything but air."

Parliament passed the charter, and Sun was equipped legally for his dream. But he faced a mountain of rough going. The old resentment against nationalization of railways, the Sunday punch behind the revolution, still would not countenance foreign rail loans. In the move to upset the Dragon Throne, the people had been steeled to fight what Sun was now asking. Little vents of heat spurted here and there in the provinces.

Sun signed but one contract—the sole product of his scheme to make the maps of China and Tibet prunelike under cross-wrinkles of tracks. Donald negotiated it for him, it being referred to later as a brilliant piece of work although it came to nought. George Pauling and Company, of London, were the contractors. They surveyed the area, but while they were preparing plans, World War I broke out and the project was dropped, never to be resumed.

While the champagne of railway dreams bubbled in his head, the high blood pressure of romance also pounded within the quiet, dignified little doctor. In Shanghai one day, he gazed intently across the desk at Donald after the sweetly timid Ai-ling had passed through his office and whispered that he wanted to marry her. Donald advised him to sublimate his desire, since he was already married, but Sun said that he proposed to divorce his present wife.

"Ai-ling's Charlie Soong's daughter," Donald pointed out. "Charlie has been your best friend. Without him, you'd have been in the soup many a time. And as for Ai-ling and the rest of the children, you've been their uncle. They've been almost like your children."

"I know it," Dr. Sun said. "I know it. But I want to marry her just the same."

Sun insisted that Donald accompany him that night to Soong's house where he intended to petition the father to permit the marriage. Donald reluctantly agreed, warning Sun, however, that he had no intention of supporting him in his highly unorthodox mission.

Soong met Sun's request as if the little doctor had struck him a stupefying blow. The color drained from his cheeks, and he looked haggardly at the man by whose side he had stood for nearly twenty years. After a while he said:

"Yat-sen, I am a Christian man. All the time, I thought you were, too. I did not bring up my children to live in the sort of looseness you propose. I will not accustom myself to people who trifle with marriage. We are a Christian family and, Lord willing, we will go on that way."

Sun, confused and embarrassed, looked from Soong to Donald, but Donald offered no help. Charlie rose and faced a window.

"I want you to go, Yat-sen," he said quietly. "I want you to go, and I never want you to come back. My door is closed to you forever."

Shortly afterward, Ching-ling, Soong's second daughter, returned from America. A girl of porcelane beauty, she, like Ai-ling, was a graduate of Wesleyan College, in Georgia. Her sister no longer was Dr. Sun's secretary, and Ching-ling, bright eyed, clever, ambitious, insisted her job was with the Father of the Revolution. Soong, still despairing, did not protest. Sun soon transferred his love to Ching-ling, and for him the pretty twenty-year-old girl developed a hero worship that was to go beyond his grave.

While Sun wrestled with railways and romance, Yuan Shih-kai's government breathed heavily under the diseases prevalent for centuries in Chinese governments—indolence, corruption, incompetence. Added to these distresses was a new one—poverty—common to the people of China, but seldom to government. In Peking, the foreigner, always the great opportunist, watched and waited. Weakened and floundering, China now offered an opportunity for aggrandizement almost as ideal as during the opium wars in the middle of the nineteenth century, as during the 1890's when Britain, France, Germany and Russia participated in land grabs from Port Arthur to South China. The opium wars had brought control of the lucrative Chinese customs to the British, which had resulted in an exceedingly low export and import tariff for at least thirteen nations who wanted to use China as a market. The wars and additional incidents had also opened up seventeen treaty ports where foreigners could operate unhampered by Chinese sovereignty.

In the spring of 1913, diplomats and bankers met in the sanctuary of Peking's Legation Quarter and developed the Great Scheme—the International Consortium. The banks of major Powers, with the consent and encouragement of their respective governments, were a part of what was then history's greatest pooling of international wealth. Two Powers, however, were conspicuously missing. The first was the United States, President Woodrow Wilson refusing endorsement to what obviously was the sort of conniving Washington had repeatedly frowned on in the Far East. The other was Japan, purposely excluded by the Consortium.

China's salt administration, a producer of monthly revenues as bountiful as those of the customs, was to be the plum for the Consortium. The scheme was to loan China a colossal sum (colossal for China and the times), secure it on the salt revenues, and place a foreign inspector-general in control. But the plot had a more insidious motive. Foreign "advisers" were to be impressed into multiple Chinese bureaus. There, through the delicately padded night stick of diplomacy, they would police and superintend a variety of functions, and handcuff Chinese economy a little tighter to foreign requirements.

The loan was to be twenty-five million pounds sterling, a debt staggering to the crippled nation. Sun and his Kuomintang raised a howl of protest, but Yuan, eager for wealth, eager to build himself a potent army, paid no attention, listening only to the Consortium's whispers that the loan would save China from imminent financial crisis.

When word of the undercover negotiations leaked out, Donald was furious—furious at what was a flagrant disregard for Chinese sovereignty, for Chinese dignity, furious at a scheme that plainly would depress China deeper into a political and economic morass. The Consortium would retrieve its principal and interest at usurious rates and China would be prostrate for countless years. Donald favored financial aid for China, but he knew Yuan and the leeches about him would fritter it away with only a small per cent going for any betterment.

Less than twelve hours before the so-called Reconstruction Loan was to be signed, Donald and Dr. C. T. Wang,[3] a Kuomintang member of

[3] Later minister of foreign affairs, subsequently Chinese ambassador at Washington.

Parliament and vice-president of the Senate, called on a Mr. Hillier. He was manager of the Hong Kong and Shanghai Bank in Peking, a British corporation and one of the Consortium's members. Donald sought to influence the Britisher to halt the loan and, failing, he warned that a day of reckoning was inescapable for those who employed questionable financial methods. Since he never tossed a meaningless phrase into the air, it is not surprising that years later, when the chance came, he wrote finis to the Consortium.

After he and Dr. Wang left Hillier's office, they set crowds of paid demonstrators into action. Anti-Consortium banners were paraded up and down before the banks. The mob jeered, howled, and made impassioned speeches. The tricks Donald had learned from the *Tatsu Maru* boycott were employed, and he and Dr. Wang stood by watching a protest they knew would have no result other than to record protest.

The contract was signed in secret in the early hours of the next morning, but when the Kuomintang-dominated Parliament met later in the day, it turned down the loan. However, neither Yuan nor the bankers paid heed.

Again revolution brewed, then spilled over the weary land. The Kuomintang could not restrain its furious hate of the dictator-minded Yuan who in turn, waited for the day to crush Sun's party. Intrigue, plotting, scheming gripped the country from the brightest tearoom to the darkest cellar. Donald, always the cautious schoolmaster, never rash when a steady hand was needed, begged Dr. Sun to keep aloof from those who had revolution and unrest in their blood. He urged patience and the need to give constitutional methods a reasonable period to succeed.

"I cannot," Sun said one day, his big eyes brimmed with tears. "They're demanding I go along with them. They went with me when I asked years ago."

In June, 1913, shortly after Yuan and the Consortium had made their bargain, Yuan dismissed three provincial governors who had protested his action. He had first taken the precaution of strengthening his army and of placing troops where he thought they would do the most good. In July, the southern provinces declared independence of the northern president, and the second revolution—the first in what was to be a long series of civil wars—began. But Yuan, using a sizable portion of his Consortium money, quickly crushed the revolt, and when it was ended, Dr. Sun was finished once more in China.

Dr. Sun fled to the sanctuary of Japan. Among others who hurried with him to escape the talons of the vengeful Yuan was a man who had played truant from a Japanese military school to join the 1911 revolution, Chiang Kai-shek, and Charlie Soong and his family. Soong's youngest daughter, fourteen-year-old Mei-ling, was in America and had just entered Wellesley College, while "T.V.," the oldest son, was at Harvard.

In Japan, romance came to a head for Ching-ling and Ai-ling. One day Dr. Sun, now divorced, married Ching-ling in a quiet ceremony. How much Soong's attitude toward Sun softened has never been clearly established. Perhaps it relaxed sufficiently to permit the marriage; on the other hand, Ching-ling was more headstrong, more impulsive than her sister. Because of this, she may not have listened to parental refusal.

Ai-ling found her love in another refugee, a chubby, round-faced man, Dr. H. H. Kung, the seventy-fifth direct descendant of Confucius. They, too, were married in Japan. Kung, a member of a rich banking family in Shansi Province, had played a minor, although not unspectacular role in Chinese politics. As a youth, he had joined in a plot to assassinate the dowager empress, only to have the plan disrupted by the Boxer uprising.

Out of Japan, however, came talk that was disturbing to Sun's friends. He was reported listening to a new scheme in Japan's old game of "divide and rule" in China. Tokyo was said to be ready to back him in a new revolt either in China proper or in Manchuria. Donald heard the stories. He was undecided on what to believe. The little doctor had gambled for a long time. He might gamble again.

At Peking, Yuan pressed his authoritarian plans. He announced that he had just discovered the Kuomintang party was a rebel organization, responsible a few months before for several "crimes." A solemn edict came from the old Manchu Temple of Heaven on November 5: "I am compelled to withdraw parliamentary badges from all Kuomintang members, and I declare the Kuomintang an illegal organization."

This, in effect, was a dissolution of Parliament. Yuan's action left only a minority, a number insufficient for a quorum, and thus the squat, bulletheaded man became absolute dictator. The edict had been timed opportunely, for Yuan had had picked parliamentarians dawdling over the writing of a constitution.[4] They had just completed the clause concerning the election of president, and he had had it written in a manner not only to protect his tenure indefinitely but also to enable him to select his successor.

When Donald returned to his combination flat and office in the Legation Quarter the evening of the edict, he learned of Yuan's sudden action in a note from Dr. C. T. Wang. The hastily written message stated that the dictator was arresting all Kuomintang members and that Wang, their parliamentary leader, was marked for execution. What was to be done?

Donald telephoned Wang—the man who had forsaken the presidency of a Y.M.C.A. for revolution and politics.

"Yuan's gunmen are outside my house," Wang reported. "They haven't tried to enter yet. I think they're waiting until dark."

Donald answered quickly: "Destroy all your important papers, C.T. I'll call you back later." Within a few minutes, Wang's phone rang again, and Donald instructed him to disguise himself as an old lady, to wear the familiar black headband common to elderly women, and allow himself to be led unsteadily by servants to his carriage. He was to drive to the Methodist Mission, enter the front door, hurry out the back and slip up a street to the Legation Quarter to Donald's office.

It was late night before Wang arrived, perfectly disguised even to the croaking tone of his voice. The first lap of flight to safety had been run.

Commanding servants to stand guard, Donald hurried down the street to the American Legation where he felt co-operation might be obtained. At least he had no Consortium enemies there. Edward Thomas Williams,[5] who was acting American minister pending the

[4] Thirty-four years later, in 1947, China adopted its first constitution.
[5] Educator and diplomat. After holding a number of posts in the Far East, he became chief of division of Far Eastern Affairs (1914-18) and professor of Oriental Languages and Literature at the University of California (1918-27).

arrival of a new envoy, did not appear pleased at being disturbed at so late an hour by the breathless Donald. But the Australian waited on no ceremony. He said bluntly that if Yuan attempted to have Wang arrested at his office, he would barricade his doors and windows and open fire.

"Now," Donald declared, and he meant it, "are we going to have the Legation Quarter turned topsy-turvy with a gun fight, or aren't we?"

When Donald left, he felt that the necessary pressure would be applied, and that behind it would be the prestige of the Quarter's top-flight diplomats.

Before the sun was up, he and C.T., still made up as a senile old crone, were on the train for Tientsin and safety.

12

PEKING INTERIM

*The older ginger and cinnamon become,
the more pungent is their flavor.*

T̲ʜ̲ᴇ̲ day had been hot, but now it was beginning to cool. Donald left the telegraph office after filing a story for the *Herald* and in his usual brisk manner walked to an intersection where he bought a copy of the Peking and Tientsin *Times*. Bold type in the ordinarily conservative *Times* proclaimed a dramatic event in Europe, and he slowed down, reading as he walked, his ricksha man trailing patiently behind. The *Times* announced:

TROUBLE IN THE BALKANS
Austria Declares War on Serbia!

It was July 29, 1914. He read avidly, convinced that this last in a series of Balkan explosions would unchain anxious, well-prepared war machines everywhere in Europe. He wondered how deeply Asia would be affected when the big war flared, and, dwelling on this thought, he entered Legation Street a few blocks from his home.

Of a sudden, he felt a strange ripple in his body, and, struck by its strangeness, he halted as a momentary flush leaped to his cheeks. He rolled up the paper, stuffed it in his coat pocket and resumed his walk, thinking no more of the incident. At his door, his amah met him with a motherly, you-seem-tired look, and she hobbled over to a big easy chair, patted it expectantly. When Donald sat down, she hurriedly brought him his slippers and turned on the electric fan. After that, she shuffled in with a glass of cool lime juice. He returned to his paper, and then again came the strange flush. This time it stayed. But Donald, a man who never had been sick a day in his life, paid no attention and went on with his reading.

At six o'clock, his face felt as if a flame were licking around it, and by seven the heat had increased. Then he took his temperature and the thermometer read 104. He called in his amah to say he wished no dinner, and telephoned a German physician.

"You say your temperature is 104?" the doctor asked half incredulously, as if he were reluctant to believe a man in such condition would be on his feet telephoning. "Well, take some aspirins and go to bed. Have me called if you feel worse."

But Donald did not call him that night, and for the next five hours he rolled and tossed in his bed. In the light of his table lamp the walls and ceiling seemed to run and melt into each other, and chairs and tables and pictures would appear far away, then near.

At midnight, the amah came in with a glass of milk. She stopped in wide-eyed amazement at the foot of his bed.

"Oh, master!" she cried and set her tray down with shaking hands. "What ting happen! You no b'long same man!"

Donald rose weakly to a sitting position and stared through a lifting fog. The fever had gone, and now he felt only damp and unsteady. But what was the poor old woman jibbering about? Her bewildered eyes were fixed on his head.

"Master, you no b'long same man," she cried again. "Hair he all turn white. You b'long all same old man."

Donald reached out for the milk.

"Don't talk nonsense," he said.

"True," she answered, verging on a sob, "I speak true." And she ran and fetched a mirror.

Donald looked at himself. It was a different man than the one whose reflection he had seen while shaving that morning. The amah was right. What had been rich, brown hair now was streaked with white. He eyed himself carefully, head on, profile, at a distance and close up. He said to himself: Let's see, I was just thirty-nine last month. He handed the mirror back to the old woman.

"Oh, damn!" he muttered.

In the morning, the doctor called at the house. He sat tapping his teeth with a thermometer, looking at Donald queerly.

"I don't know what caused your fever or what caused you to lose the color in your hair. One thing I'm sure of, however. It wasn't from worry. You're the only man I know who doesn't worry." At the door he stopped. "You know," he said, still eying Donald oddly, "there may be some good in this bit of ill wind. You look exceedingly distinguished now. The Chinese will think of you more than ever as a sage." He clapped on his hat. "Good-by, Confucius," he called. "I'll send you my bill."

Yet the strangeness of the episode was that as much as ten years later, even his closest friends were not aware that it had happened. They knew him as a constant user of aromatic hair oils but over and above that there never was a suspicion that Donald had compensated for the change in his hair. It was apparent that at thirty-nine he was not inclined toward a Confucian appearance.

Several days after his illness, Europe burst into flame like a series of chain explosions. Germany had declared war against a Russia that had failed to heed Kaiser Wilhelm's warnings and Czar Nicholas had advanced his troops into East Prussia. Germany had swept into Luxemburg, Belgium and France, and the French, followed by the British, had struck back.

In the Far East, Japan, the opportunist, did not wait long to decide her course. First, Germany had been one of the Powers who had made her relinquish the territorial loot gained in the 1895 war with China, and had added insult to injury a few years later by participating in the big Asia land grabs, pressuring from China what Japan herself coveted —Shantung's Kiaochow Peninsula and its important port, Tsingtao. Second was the decade-old Anglo-Japanese military alliance, and four days after Britain entered the European war, Japan sought to make use of it. Coincident with her warships appearing threateningly off Tsingtao, Japan suggested London might invite her to attack Germans in China. But Britain wanted no sword-bearing interloper in any part of what she considered her special trade domain and replied politely that the situation could be handled nicely without Japan.

Japan was not to be so easily brushed off. In a few days she demanded that Germany forfeit Kiaochow. At this juncture, China momentarily considered war on Germany to retrieve the area herself—which she might have done with ease, since Yuan's army was sufficient to overcome the negligible German defenses. But Japan anticipated the possibility and acted. On August 23, she declared war on Germany and, under the banner of returning Kiaochow to China, struck. In short order, she seized all former German holdings—railways in particular—and moved far beyond the territory which had been controlled by Berlin. The British sent in a contingent of troops to assist, but the Japanese kept their unwanted allies in a subservient position, and sent little spearheads in all directions under the pretense of military necessity. Within a month, Japan had fastened a tight grip on an important area in China.

A gloom settled over Peking. Japan, the old enemy, was on the march —ostensibly against a foe, Germany, but actually against a neutral neighbor, China. Where would she stop? Donald was plagued by this concern. He knew Japan. On his way home one evening, he stopped off at the American Legation, a stately, colonial residence at the head of Legation Street. The present minister, Dr. Paul S. Reinsch, had arrived late in 1913 to take over from the acting minister, Williams. Donald always found Reinsch eager to talk, anxious to acquire knowledge of the ever-growing tangle of China.

The American was reading a copy of a communication to Japan's Foreign Office in which Washington noted with satisfaction Tokyo's pledge that it was seeking no territorial aggrandizement in China.

"I think we may be getting a little too excited about Japan," Dr. Reinsch said. "People have a habit of building straw men for the bloodcurdling fun of knocking them over."

Donald answered without hesitation. "Never think of Japan as a straw man. Think of her as evil and sinister, and you'll never make the mistake of being caught off guard. And this Shantung affair— we've not heard the end of it. This is the beginning of another effort to clamp her claws on China."

Reinsch conceded that Donald was an older hand in the Far East and promised that he would follow his advice to keep an eye alert for future developments.

Japan consolidated her position in the former German area, and in time Germany's Pacific Micronesia—the Marshalls, the Carolines, the Marianas and Palaus—fell into her lap.

With the war in Europe, the Far East almost overnight lost its importance as a news source. The press of the world was concerned with the most terrific struggle of all times. Donald realized this, and with the complete honesty that characterized all his work, he resigned as New York *Herald* correspondent and recommended that his bureau be closed. What had been the best service on Oriental affairs to the American public came to an end. Simultaneously, he relinquished his Australian papers for the same reason.

Not long after, however, the *Times*, of London, felt that it needed another man to watch over what to the British was a tense situation in China. Donald was named Peking correspondent. David Fraser whom he had first met during the Russo-Japanese War, was still the *Times* man in China, but he roamed for the most part between various points in Asia. Donald was to be a permanent fixture for the *Times* at the former seat of the old Dragon Throne. This he combined with the editorship of the *Far Eastern Review*.

To correspondents in China, Donald, with the shrewd eyes and the easy smile—the sometimes brutally frank Donald—had become a sort of oracle. He knew the causes and reason behind any event, and he had an uncanny sense for anticipating happenings. From the beginning of the revolution, he had been a major-domo for newsmen, helping where he could, keeping always out of sight when he knew he was without license to break confidence. He held a peculiar, indefinable position, unofficial yet indescribably official, and that air, that something continued to hover about him. In the old days, correspondents had gone to him more than to the little doctor for news, and they still did. Perhaps it was his particular brand of honesty, a simple yes-or-no attitude toward truth as he saw it, that accounted for his unusual position.

In Peking, *laissez faire* was routine for the run-of-the-mill reporter. He spent his days at the fashionable clubs and hotels over Scotch and sodas, or he dawdled at the legations courting the favors of secretaries, and, when he could, the daughters and even the wives of the diplomats.

In the main, he was content with routine handouts on the foreign point of view. But when an explanation was needed of behind-scenes affairs in the curious tumble of politics, he sought out Donald who was the only man holding the confidence, the complete trust of the Chinese. Donald, himself, rarely called on the legations for either news or information. He worked always in the inner circle of Chinese politics, and, because of this, the day was to come when he would make startling news time and again for the legations themselves.

Many of his government friends were companions of revolutionary days, and some were men he had known in the Manchu regime who, by the simple process of shearing their queues, had become Republicans. He came to know Yuan Shih-kai well, and they had many a long and friendly talk together. Despite the President's flagrant reactionary qualities, Donald respected him for a certain magnetic power and, above all, for his knack for tidy, precise organization. But Yuan had the unilateral mind of a dictator; he was without concept of social problems or understanding of democracy. He sought to run the country according to his own likes and with offices top heavy with old-style officials. Often Donald would hammer at him on the urgency of employing a greater number of foreign-educated Chinese in positions of responsibility.

In the several years they knew each other familiarly, Yuan never addressed Donald by name, preferring to use as a title a reminder of the Australian's connection with the revolution. One day after Donald had pointed out the need for a transfusion of young blood into his government, Yuan remarked:

"Old southern Republican, I have a young man in my government, Dr. V. K. Wellington Koo.[1] He's my counselor in the Foreign Office."

Yuan thought a single young man ample as a representative of Young China.

Of all the men in the capital, Chow Tzu-chi, the minister of finance, was Donald's favorite. "Old Joe," as he was familiarly known because

[1] Statesman and diplomat. A graduate of Columbia University, Koo's career has carried him from a variety of important posts in China to delegate at many significant conferences, such as Versailles and the Washington Disarmament and ambassador to Power nations. He is now ambassador to the United States.

the pronunciation of his family name resembled that of "Joe," had been consul in New York under the Manchu regime, later governor of Shantung. He was kindly, capable, perhaps the sharpest in an era of decadent Chinese politicians. He had a good sense of humor and was cynical about politics. The two became close friends, and Old Joe, who stuttered when excited, was taught by the Australian to say "bloody" in what Donald called "stuttorial eloquence."

He would tell Donald all the political gossip of the day, explain the intrigues and unfold the possible direction of events. Of himself, Old Joe once said: "The other ministers think I'm a fool. They tell me everything, or they don't bother about my listening."

But Donald never considered his friend a fool. He knew that few things ever escaped his attention. He was to see this truth emphasized shortly as Japan began one of history's biggest blackmail schemes.

13

JAPAN'S TWENTY-ONE DEMANDS

*A dragon stranded in shallow water
furnishes bait for the shrimps.*

WORLD War I had blustered over the map of Europe for five months when Japan confirmed the suspicions Donald had voiced to Dr. Reinsch and sought once more to garrote an economically weak and politically confused China. It was January 18, 1915. Cleverly and stealthily she reached for dominance over her neighbor with her notorious Twenty-one Demands.

Japan had hoped to conceal her move from the world. But Donald, with his faculty for rattling diplomatic dovecots, was at hand. The leak came in the strange manner which typified his movements behind the Chinese curtain.

China had withdrawn Japan's right to occupation in Shantung, and that very night, Mr. Eki Hioki, the Japanese minister to Peking, appeared at the Temple of Heaven to confront a sleepy president. Mr. Hioki, whose clipped phrases sounded like Morse code, read off Japan's "grievances," pounded the table and left a sinister-looking document watermarked with dreadnoughts and machine guns.

Donald was in Shanghai putting the February issue of the *Far Eastern Review* to press, when an urgent telegram arrived from Finance Minister Chow Tzu-chi. It read:

PLEASE RETURN IMMEDIATELY STOP MATTERS OF GRAVE CONCERN TO ALLIES HAPPENING HERE.

When the evening express from Shanghai rolled into the Peking station, Donald stepped off into what were to become four exciting months in Chinese history. Roy Anderson met him, and, clutching his arm, walked him through the shuffling crowds away from the tumult of the station. They threaded their way in and out of reeking swarms under the massive Hatamen Arch and down the road which spilled toward the heart of the city.

It was a bitter cold night. The wind, marrow freezing as it is in a Peking winter, pitted them with sand. Anderson said, "Hioki has inserted the dagger."

"Oh?"

Anderson went on, "It seems to be serious, but I can't find out how far it goes. The Chinese won't talk. All I can learn is that Japan is trying to step on everyone's toes—China's most of all."

They hailed two rickshas and began to bob and thump over the rough streets toward the Hotel de Pekin. Slits of light winked through the cracks in the long, wooden shutters which now were beginning to blacken out fronts of shops, marking the end of the business day. From behind them came the clack and clatter of mah-jongg tiles and the occasional wail of a child. In the street, men and women, sniffling and hawking, hunched in their heavily quilted jackets, and a mangy camel drooled at the curb. "Wang bah t'an!"[1] an oxcart driver flung at a drove of ricksha coolies ambling about him like birds about to fly.

Donald and Anderson strode into the hotel and sat in a secluded corner for a few minutes in rapid conversation. When Donald became impatient and rose to go, Anderson checked him with: "I've a list of 'must' appointments for you." First was Dr. Reinsch. Then there was Old Joe, and at least six other cabinet ministers.

"I'll find out everything," Donald said and hurried off.

At the American Legation the usually calm and conservative minister was visibly alarmed.

"The worst sort of blackmail has begun," Dr. Reinsch announced.

"I'm not surprised," Donald answered quietly.

The minister unfolded what little he knew of the Tokyo plot, explaining that the Japanese were maintaining an airtight secrecy. Obviously, they had shut Chinese mouths by threats of serious consequence if even so much as a hint leaked to the outside world.

[1] "Son of a turtle egg!"

Dr. Reinsch had been pacing his library. He stopped in front of the stocky Australian. "You're the only man I know," he said, "who might be able to find the truth of this ugly business. Don, for God's sake, find out what these damn people are up to!"

Donald rubbed out his cigar. "I'll see you later," he said.

When he entered the capacious house of Chow Tzu-chi, at the eastern end of Tsungpu Hutung, the finance minister's usual good humor had fled. He tried to speak but only stuttered in his excitement.

"We're in a b-b-b-bloody mess," he blurted out.

Donald hooked his arm, and they walked out through the compound to Old Joe's favorite place, his fish pond. Often Donald had found him sitting by it, meditating, watching the carp dart in and out among the lilies.

Old Joe tossed a pebble into the water. "Before you left for Shanghai," he said, "I told you something desperate was under way. Now I cannot tell you what it is. All I can say is that the Japanese are demanding certain things. If more is said, Tokyo might back Dr. Sun in a revolt against this government."

For awhile they sat watching bubbles rise to the pond's surface. Then Chow said, "Don, what are we to do?"

The situation was unique. One of the greatest international plots in history had begun, and the victim dared not speak for fear of further humiliation. But, if the Allies were to be informed of the impending coup, the truth had to be found out.

Donald said, "Old Joe, I don't want you to tell me what the demands are. I don't want anyone else to. But I have an idea how to get them."

Chow said nothing. He drew a fan from the wide sleeves of his gown.

"I'll write down all the demands I believe Japan capable of making with regard to Manchuria and China," Donald explained. "Joe, you'll strike out with pencil anything that's not correct. If I omit any, perhaps you might be able to suggest something that will make me think of them. Then I'll take the paper to other members of the government and go through the same process. In time, I'll have the tenor of the demands. After that, I can expose them through the *Times* in London. No one need ever know my source."

A carp swam in a dizzy circle around a lily pad. "I know how he feels," Old Joe said.

Donald began to write. The minister picked up a pencil, reached over, crossed out several points and asked, "In what place are munitions made?" Donald wrote down "arsenals." Control of arsenals was one of the demands. So it went, Donald setting down every possible proposal he knew Japan might make, Chow striking out some, leaving others. Control of certain railways was also among the demands as well as control of mining, police and army.

In the days that followed, the correspondent made the rounds of cabinet members until he had a long list shaped and reshaped.

Shortly, he was able to cable the *Times*, sending out the first alarm of the threatened fire in Asia. But no indignant protest roared out of the British capital. Donald waited and wondered. So important was his information, he felt that the *Times* must be displaying it prominently.

From time to time, he dropped in to see the British minister, Sir John Jordan, but more often his steps led him to the near-by American Legation and Dr. Reinsch. He urged upon each the strongest possible reports to their home governments, but Sir John, cautious, almost imperturbable, was not to be budged. He would say, "I have nothing official. I have only rumors." Donald's early days in Hong Kong had taught him patience. The British official mind, stickler for orthodoxy, was not new to him. On the other hand, Dr. Reinsch, keen and sensitive, kept the state department fully informed on new developments gathered by Donald. The American press, however, slumbered on since no American correspondent had wind of the biggest story in Asia. Further, no word flashed out of London to bare Japan's infamy. What had happened to Donald's exposé?

One day in February he called on the American minister and found him reading a letter from President Wilson. "Listen to this," Dr. Reinsch said, and read:

I have had the feeling that any direct advice to China, or direct intervention on her behalf in the present negotiations would really do her more harm than good inasmuch as it would very likely provoke the jealousy and excite the hostility of Japan, which would be first manifested against China herself. . . . For the present, I am watching the situation very carefully indeed, ready to step in at any point where it is wise to do so.

Donald said skeptically, "It looks as though China will swim alone."

Dr. Reinsch folded the letter. "The war in Europe is a nasty business," he said.

The time came when the Chinese ministers would say no more. They only sat and stared when Donald talked. Mr. Hioki was pounding the table with new vigor, reiterating his insistence that China accept the Twenty-one Demands, emphasizing his order that China keep them secret. Soon, however, some inkling of what was going on trickled to Peking streets, and over teacups diplomats' wives would ask, "Do you know what those horrid little people are up to now?"

One day in his new headquarters, a dusty, little office in the old Russo-Asiatic Bank building, Donald was writing a dispatch to the *Times* when Frederick Moore walked in. Moore was Peking bureau manager for Associated Press. He said jestingly that he supposed Donald was up to his usual tricks and carrying the demands around in his hip pocket. Donald laughed and hauled the typed dispatch from his machine, handing it to Moore.

Moore whistled. "Is this correct?"

Donald nodded. "They may be even worse."

Moore begged Donald for a copy, and Donald agreed, provided he would not divulge his source. That evening the A.P. man sent his dispatch, and the next morning came the first reaction. Moore tossed the telegram dejectedly on the Australian's desk. It was signed by Melville Stone, head of the Associated Press, and read:

BARON CHINDA [Japanese ambassador to Washington] CATEGORICALLY DENIES YOUR DISPATCH STOP SEND SOURCE OF YOUR INFORMATION STOP DISPATCH HELD UP PENDING RECEIPT.

Moore said, "Don, I can't wire them that you're the source. I can't double-cross you, so what in the hell will I do?"

Swearing Moore to secrecy again, Donald sent him to Chow Tzuchi and to the Foreign Office's counselor, Dr. Wellington Koo. He was to ask but one question: Does my message understate or overstate the demands?

By noon Moore was back, full of fight. He roared that he'd show the "pro-Japanese" Stone[2] something, then wired his inability to name his source and pointed out that his first dispatch was an understatement.

Stone replied, obviously irritated: "I won't publish your stories until you wire me the source." Again Moore refused. No further reply came for some time, and then it came with a shock. A new A.P. man named Smith arrived. Moore had been dismissed without a word.[3]

As Donald heard it, the "inside" on the story in America was even more exasperating. Baron Chinda had telephoned from Washington to Stone at New York. "If you release this story," the Japanese diplomat had warned, "it will mean war!" Chinda had been indefinite as to whom war would be against, but Stone, perhaps seeing himself as a Goliath warding off catastrophe, sent a hasty "Kill" to his newsroom.

Tokyo, its frustration growing, continued to press its negotiations in secret, trying all the while to chisel out the clue to the leak it now knew existed. Several tricks were attempted, one being somewhat more carefully planned than the others. The first secretary of the Japanese Legation, the very bland Mr. Funatsu, invited Finance Minister Chow to dinner for a discussion of Chinese art. As Chow, the lone guest, walked into the dining room with his host, he thought: What's this little dwarf up to?

While the Japanese talked glibly and expertly of tapestries, pottery making, block printing and stone carving, Old Joe smiled and nodded his gray head approvingly, waiting patiently for Funatsu to tear off his mask. Finally the Chinese said, "Now I must be going."

But Funatsu answered quickly, "Oh, please not. Let us go back to the drawing room."

Chow noticed that a large map of the world had been hung there in their absence. The Japanese bowed, smiled, and walked up to it.

"I want you to notice," he said, "how much land is occupied by the foreign powers who are now fighting each other in Europe and how much more is occupied by the yellow races. All the way from Japan through China, Indo-China, Malaysia, Dutch East Indies, Burma,

---

[2] Previous to the episode, Stone had visited Japan where he had been decorated.

[3] Later Moore went to work for the Japanese. Prior to the outbreak of World War II he was attached to their embassy at Washington, D. C.

India, Afghanistan, Arabia, Africa, Palestine, Syria, Mesopotamia, Persia and Turkey, the land is inhabited by non-whites." Funatsu's eyes glittered. "It is inhabited by Asiatics, indeed," he said triumphantly.

Chow's face was expressionless. It might have been Buddha himself contemplating the little diplomat.

"Now," Funatsu continued, "the reason Japan has put in its demands—"

Chow did not move a muscle. "What demands, Mr. Funatsu?" he asked quietly.

Funatsu bowed ever so slightly, rubbing his hands. "You know what ones," he hissed.

"No. I don't understand you."

"Why, you're a member of the cabinet—you must know!"

The Chinese minister spread his fan. He waved it a few times under his chin, then folded it. "Ah, yes, but they do not tell me everything."

Funatsu stared incredulously. He tapped a cigarette. "Well," he said after a pause, "no matter." He turned to the map. "I want to tell you that Japan put in the demands to help China, not to harm her. Japan thinks the Asiatics should be amalgamated into one co-operative whole to combat the white race.[4] The first blow in this direction will be made through China. China cannot, after all, offer to give Japan what we want. The demands are to make it easier—to give her the excuse of bending to force." He rubbed out a half-smoked cigarette, then went on: "What we suggest is good strategy. It is plain you need someone to run your country. We propose to do that for you. If Britain and America thought China was inviting us to be its guide, they would apply pressure to prevent you. But when Japan demands—ah, that is a different matter. They can screech their heads off, and Japan will not give a fig for what they say."

Funatsu swung from the map, advanced a step toward Chow and shot out almost angrily, "Are you not weary of the domineering attitude of the white ministers in your capital? They do not pound the table in Tokyo. They would be sent home if they did."

A bit breathless, the Japanese paused. "The Germans will win the

[4] This was an early expression of what became Japan's Co-Prosperity Sphere, a program which was put into full speed in China in the decade between 1930 and 1940.

war," he continued. "The democracies will be defeated with Germany bled white. Such a condition will advance our holy program. You see what it means, do you not? It means that the Asiatics combined will then be masters of their fate and of the world. We will kick all foreigners out of China and the Far East—"

Chow showed interest. "How long," he interrupted, "will that take?"

"About seven years."

"Oh, what will the foreign powers be doing in those seven years while you are shoving out their nationals?"

But before the question could be answered, Chow said, "I'm sorry. I must be going."

He went to Donald's house to tell him in detail how he had parried with Funatsu.

"B-b-by golly!" he exclaimed. "I wasn't going to let that b-b-b-bloody b-b-b-bastard catch me."

Some time after Moore had received his curt telegram from Stone, Donald was at the Hotel de Pekin and happened across William Giles, correspondent for the Chicago *Daily News*. Giles, like other correspondents, regarded the Australian as a better source of news than any legation office or government ministry. He said, "How serious is this thing the Japs are up to, Don?"

"It's bad, Bill, and I'm afraid I've been bogged down by London on my stuff. The A.P. has mucked up Moore. If you want a go at the story, here's your chance."

Donald gave him a copy of his own summary of the demands, cautioning him, as he had Moore, to keep his source secret. The Chicago *Daily News* published Giles' story, unexpurgated. It was a world scoop. Donald was as jubilant as Giles, though giving away a hard-won story is rare in the dog-eat-dog code of newspapermen.

Immediately, however, Japanese ambassadors in world capitals rose to give vigorous and effective denials. As a result, the next day Donald received a wire from the *Times*:

CAREFULLY VERIFY ALL INFORMATION WITH REGARD TO JAPAN STOP HAVE REASON TO BELIEVE EVERYTHING FROM PEKING WILLFULLY DISTORTED.

It was signed by Wickham Steed, foreign editor of the *Times*.

With this and Moore's telegram from the Associated Press demanding proof of the Japanese action, Donald went to Chow Tzu-chi. "Look, Old Joe," he said, "you're in the soup and you know it. If I'm to help, I must get my hands on an official translation of the demands."

Chow rose and walked to the window. He watched the republic's rainbow flag flap indolently, then hang listless atop a near-by building.

Donald went on, "Japanese envoys abroad have obviously been told to deny all information that goes out of China. Japan thinks she has sewed up the whole world. Damn it all, are we going to let her get away with it? We've got to break through. We've got to get the official translation to Sir John and Dr. Reinsch."

Chow turned. "B-b-b-but," he said nervously, "it can't be done. These p-p-p-people are in a position to b-b-b-blow us up. They're getting troops ready in the North. Mr. Hioki told us today their fleet is headed this way."

The windy Donald subsided into a gentle, persuasive Donald. He leaned back in his chair.

"There's a day to be born, Old Joe, and a day to die," he said. "Here China is again, not ready for either, dangling somewhere between the two, neither dead nor alive, hanging on by its fingertips. Too often, China bleats when it's in trouble. You people stand docilely like sheep, hopeful, prayerful that some kind shepherd will ward off the shearer. But we're up against a situation in which bleating will do us no good. I remember an old naval captain telling me that when great issues are at stake, great risks are called for."

Chow made no comment, and Donald then said he had thought of a way to secure the translation without directing suspicion against anyone. Never a man to make things unnecessarily difficult, he outlined a plan as simple as it was brazen. It was to center around Dr. George Morrison,[5] President Yuan's official political adviser. If successful,

[5] Author of *An Australian in China* which covered his own exploits. Dr. Morrison, one-time court physician in Morocco, came to China shortly before 1900 and once performed the remarkable feat of walking from Rangoon to Shanghai. He traveled in South China as correspondent for the London *Times*, and it was in this period that James Gordon Bennett picked Donald as "opposition." In 1912, Morrison took up his post with the Chinese government. He died in 1920.

Donald's scheme would produce the official document which the British and American ministers had been awaiting.

The next day, Donald called on Dr. Morrison.

"George," he said, "I've come to tell you about a plan—"

"I know," Morrison interrupted, "I've been talking with Mr. Chow."

"Well?" Donald asked with an amused smile.

"It's risky business," Morrison said flatly. He rose and looked strangely at Donald. "Would you excuse me? I have to go into the library for a moment."

Donald tensed. Would the scheme work out as outlined to Old Joe?

While he watched, Morrison straightened a number of papers on his desk. Had his hand stayed longer on those in the center? Not a movement escaped Donald. He fumbled for a cigar, and then the Yuan Shih-kai adviser walked past him without a glance and out of the office.

This was it. This was Donald's chance. He stepped toward the desk. As he did, a door squeaked open behind him. He stopped short, then turned. A white-gowned Chinese boy armed with teapot and cup had entered. Donald relaxed, smiled and waited for him to leave, but the boy lingered. "Look," Donald said desperately, "hurry out and get me a cigar." When the boy left, he quickly snatched up the papers which Morrison had seemed to indicate.

Footsteps in the hall. Hastily he stuffed the papers inside his coat. Morrison entered.

"Sorry, old boy," he said, "that I kept you waiting."

"That's all right, George. I'll be running along, anyway."

Their eyes met just before Donald closed the door.

He hurried toward his office. He was anxious to scan the papers. Were they the right ones? Did he at last have a bona fide translation of the Twenty-One Demands? Crossing a street, he ran into Anderson who changed his course and began to walk beside him.

"The talk is," Anderson said, "that President Yuan is in cahoots with the Japanese." Donald answered that he didn't believe it, that whatever Yuan's shortcomings, they didn't go that far.

"Well, do you think Sun would be a partner in the Japanese threat to start a revolt in China?" Anderson asked.

"I don't know," Donald replied. "How does anyone know what Sun will do? After the revolution, his first big hate was Russia. Then suddenly he became rabidly anti-Japanese. Now he's besieged by Japanese generals and industrialists. They're telling him they can make him the head man in Manchuria, president once more of China and high potentate of this and that."

They walked on, Donald thinking of the papers he carried, debating whether to divulge to Anderson, with whom he had shared so many secrets, the fact that he had just stolen a state document. But as he was about to speak, the Standard Oil man said, "I must leave you here," and strode off.

At his desk, Donald opened the document. Before him was the translation. Morrison had played the game. A quick reading showed he had been correct on nearly all points, although he had understated the viciousness. With the speed his long newspaper experience had brought him, he wrote another telegram for the *Times* in which he underscored the gravity of the situation. He followed it with a private wire to the foreign editor:

SIR JOHN JORDAN NOW WILL CONFIRM THAT THE GREATEST CARE HAS BEEN TAKEN TO VERIFY ALL INFORMATION STOP JAPAN WILLFULLY DENYING EXISTENCE OF DEMANDS STOP IF THOSE DENIALS ACCEPTED BY GREAT BRITAIN THE GREATEST INJURY WILL BE DONE TO A COUNTRY WHOSE INDEPENDENCE SHE HAS GUARANTEED.

As soon as his dispatch was filed, he went to see Dr. Reinsch and Sir John. To each he said, "Here they are!" The American minister gripped his hand. "It took a fellow like you to do it," he said. The Britisher grunted, "Good work, lad."

The story was broken wide open. Giles' dispatch had carried a top banner in the Chicago paper, but now Peking correspondents would make headlines in every country. Reinsch and Jordan had wired their respective governments and on this basis the Chinese consented to release the full text of the demands for publication. Smashed was Japan's suffocation of the world press and of Chinese officialdom.

Weeks later Donald learned how the *Times* had rendered a disservice to British readers. Wickham Steed explained in a letter why Donald's initial cables had not been published.

We did not doubt them [he apologized], but as you were the only one reporting the demands, we thought it in the interest of the Allies not to publish them pending further developments. When your first dispatch arrived, I personally visited our Foreign Office. They said they had nothing but rumors. I then went to the Japanese Ambassador here. I asked him about the demands. He denied them. When I told him our Mr. Donald was a careful correspondent and would not report make-believe, he admitted that perhaps there was some truth in the demands concerning Manchuria but that there could be none in those with regard to China. I cut out the portions which the Japanese Ambassador assured me could not exist and published the remainder. The German press seized upon these to draw attention to a rift in the Allied front. When your second long wire arrived, I again went to the Foreign Office. They told me it was correct, that they had received a wire from Sir John Jordan to this effect. The Japanese Ambassador still denied the existence of the demands as stated in your dispatch.

Donald was not soon to forget the incident. The *Times* had chosen to believe the representative of a country whose policy eternally was to sweep the dirt from its front door to concealment in the rear rather than a man held in the highest esteem in British and American journalistic circles. He walked to the Finance Ministry and sailed the letter at Old Joe.

"B-b-better go out and sit by the fish pond," Chow said sympathetically.

As matters stood now, China was confronted with imminent strangulation. The tentacles that reached out from Tokyo were as encompassing as any one nation had ever sent out against another. With the exception of a section of the Fifth Group, the demands were economic. They were obviously intended to procure for Japan mineral and other resources and to hold China as a preferred field for investment of Nipponese capital and the marketing of their goods. What Japan demanded was rankest imperialism.

The Fifth and final group aimed its feelers at China's main arteries. Tokyo insisted that Japanese advisers be installed in all political, financial and military institutions, and that even the police be under Sino-Japanese control. Further, Japan demanded the right to disseminate Japanese religious propaganda.

Japan continued her pressure. With exception of a strong protest from the United States, there were no remonstrances from the Allies. The possibility of American punitive action as suggested in Wilson's letter to Reinsch never materialized.

Once when Donald dropped in on Chow Tzu-chi, he found him more than a little depressed. "The rottenness of everything makes me ill," he groaned. He walked to an open window and spat. "Do you know what this Hioki said yesterday? That d-d-damn little d-d-dwarf said that when there's a fire in a jewelry shop, neighbors cannot be expected to refrain from helping themselves!"

Donald replied, "It's damnable. Our exposure of the demands has not been enough. The Allies are up to their necks with Germany. Japan knows she can grab anything in China and no one is to say no. She realizes that this is the golden opportunity, and you can bet that she will try to make the most of it."

It was May 1 when China offered Japan an unnecessarily submissive counter proposal—against Donald's advice. However, the Chinese had become panicky. Nipponese troops were on the move in the North and the Imperial Navy prowled off the China coast. The Japanese now realized that the Chinese could be pushed far beyond what they had hoped for, and, on May 7, they countered with an ultimatum insisting upon acceptance of the original text.

Late in the afternoon of May 9, Donald received a chit from the Chinese Foreign Office asking him to come at once. He found the minister, Mr. Lu Tseng-tsiang[6] at his desk, nervously thumbing papers. The vice-minister, Mr. Tsao Ju-lin, said, "The forty-eight hours those people have given us is up at ten tonight. We must give an answer or face war. We are in no position to fight, but we have arrived at no conclusion." He shot a look at Donald. "Mr. Donald," he asked, "what is to be done?"

[6] Lu Tseng-tsiang, supposedly disillusioned by the deplorable state of Chinese politics, later became a Trappist monk in Belgium.

Mr. Lu stopped fumbling with his papers. "We should have listened to you on the first reply we sent those people," he said.

Donald nodded. He said, "I'll have the answer in your hands by tonight."

He walked thoughtfully toward his office. The sultriness of May was everywhere. Heat waves sent up little odoriferous billows of brisk, penetrating horse manure, of drying fish, and the heavy, damp fragrance of steamed rice. Over all hung the sharp, nauseating smell of rancid peanut oil from portable curbside cookeries where it boiled and smoked.

At the Russo-Asiatic Bank building he bought a newspaper, and as he mounted the steps, he read the warning that Japan's ultimatum was to expire at ten o'clock that night. War, it seemed, was imminent. Japanese residents in Peking were asked to stand ready to evacuate while Japan's reservists in Mukden had been ordered to their stations. The Japanese fleet was ready for action.

Ugly and mean, the drama was nearing the last act. The usual hubbub and garrulousness of the crowds on the packed streets below seemed to have faded almost to a whisper. Only the news vendors were shrill and raucous. Ricksha pullers padded by swiftly and silently.

It was seven o'clock when he began his writing of the "Donald Reply." The watch hands soon enough would be at ten. What he was doing hurt him. His words were to all but prostrate China before Japan. Of the five groups, Donald knew that four would have to be accepted. He wrote accordingly. There were changes, then it was done, polished in the Donald manner, ready for the sharp scrutiny he knew Mr. Obata, obstinate and aggressive counselor of the Japanese Legation, would give it.

It was nearly nine o'clock when he headed not for the Foreign Office but for the quarters of Dr. Reinsch. There the minister said, "Don, I hear the Chinese are to answer the ultimatum within an hour."

Donald drew a paper from his coat pocket.

"Yes," he replied. "I dropped in because I knew you'd be interested." He laid his reply in front of Reinsch.

Reinsch found it simple and brief. When he reached the salient point, he read aloud: "Upon the understanding that all outstanding questions are hereby settled, China accepts the first four groups of the Demands."

"And the Fifth Group?" Dr. Reinsch handed the paper back to Donald.

"It's an impossible situation. The only thing that can be done, and I've tried to do it, is to safeguard China from acceptance of that group. If it is ever rammed through, China will lose its life."

The fine, sensitive face of Dr. Reinsch clouded. He said: "Damn!"

Donald left, his thoughts wrapped in the night's shameful drama. When he discovered his steps were leading him toward the British Legation, he stopped, shrugged and altered his course. It was half an hour until ten. Before him loomed the Chinese Foreign Office. It was a sad Donald who hesitated a moment, then mounted the stairs.

The Foreign Office was in confusion. Secretaries and clerks rushed in and out of rooms, gathered in small groups to talk excitedly. Donald saw no one that could give either calm or intelligent consideration to the situation. Foreign Minister Lu was waiting for him.

"Oh," exclaimed Mr. Lu, speaking like a machine gun. "You have it? You have it? Where is it? Where is it?"

Donald set the reply before him. "If I were you, I'd get it to the Japanese Legation before ten," he said quietly. "Don't invite any more trouble. There's enough now."

"Yes, yes," Mr. Lu said, and rushed from the room.

Donald paused a moment, surveyed the disorder and then walked out.

He went to the hospital of a German physician, Dr. Dipper, and to the room where Dr. Wellington Koo lay ill. He said, "The Foreign Office is in a panic. Will you please get up and go over."

Koo stared at Donald through sick eyes. "I cannot," he answered. "I'm ill."

"So is China." Donald said, "if you don't go, they'll make a mess of things, and we'll have the Japanese on our necks before morning."

Koo rose slowly. "I'll go," he said. "Damn it all, I'll go."

Donald headed for home. He had ahead of him the job of writing for the *Times* how China was folding up before the greatest single diplomatic coup of the century. He felt sure that the editor would engage in no emasculation this time.

The following morning he returned to the hospital to see Dr. Koo. The counselor did not look at Donald nor return his greeting. He pulled the covers over his head.

"I can't talk to you," he said bitterly. "I'm too ashamed." He added that he had resigned. Donald urged him to tell what had happened the night before, and throwing back the bed covers, Koo sat up. He said that when he had arrived at the Foreign Office the previous night, he had asked to see Donald's reply, but it had already left. The minister said that they had sent it to Mr. Obata to see if it was all right.

Koo had jumped up and begun to stride about the office, exploding like a string of Chinese firecrackers.

He had shouted. "They send you an ultimatum and you ask them please to draw up your reply? You people call yourselves diplomats! Why, you are nothing but stupid fools! This is why we are eating Japanese dirt—because China has too many people who cannot see beyond their rice bowls. They live for today, not for the tomorrows. They are children with no perspective. They do not stand upon their two feet and say that they are men, nor when they fail, do they have bad dreams. There is always the opium house, the singsong girl, the feasts, or the retreat to the mountain to live in seclusion amid the luxury of ill-gotten gains."

Koo had then sat down and asked for paper. "I will write my resignation and be done with you!"[7]

As Koo had finished, a Foreign Office subofficial had returned with the Donald reply. Minister Lu had stared at it. So had Koo who had pointed to Chinese characters lettered along the margin. "What's this?" he had demanded.

The man had answered weakly, "Oh, Mr. Obata read it and then he took up his brush. He said to me, 'You have forgotten Group Five.' He inserted, 'and reserves the Fifth Group for future consideration.'"

Koo had thrown down the paper and stomped out.

After he left, the reply was rewritten in Chinese, but overlooked was the deletion of the words "upon the understanding that all out-

[7] Dr. Koo withdrew his resignation a few days later.

standing questions are hereby settled." It was sent to the Japanese Legation with this inconsistency. Donald's phrase had been written obviously to cover the Fifth Group and to prevent it from becoming a serious factor again. In the years that followed, however, Japan raised the question several times, but it was never pressed, and China maintained control of her military and police agencies. In this respect, Donald had outmaneuvered the Japanese once more.

The events of the past four months in which Donald had been enmeshed did not disillusion him. They formed merely an episode and served to underscore the enigma of Chinese politics, a matter of which he was always fully conscious.

A few days after the reply had been sent to the Japanese, the Australian met Sir Richard Dane on Legation Street. Sir Richard was director-general of the Chinese salt administration and had been brought up from a similar post in India at the time of the Consortium.

"Er-r-r," he said, "I made a mistake last night. I was over at Doc Morrison's for dinner. We were talking about the reply to the ultimatum. I said to Morrison, 'I suppose you wrote that.' Morrison told me that they had people at the Foreign Office who could do that. 'No,' said I, 'there is a foreign hand showing all over that document.' But Morrison said that he had nothing to do in any way with the negotiations nor did he know who wrote it."

Sir Richard pinned Donald with an amused gaze. "Who wrote it?" he asked.

Donald, who had made a career of admitting nothing, said, "I wonder."

But in Tokyo the war and foreign ministries once again took from their drawers a fattening dossier.

chapter

14

MOMENTARY MONARCHY

He who rides the tiger finds it difficult to dismount.

BY LATE summer, 1915, China was heading into another crisis. The emergency through which the government had just passed had highlighted its impotency, and some saw this as the impotency of a republic. Although republicanism's opponents—the Monarchists—had kept silent under the iron dictatorship of Yuan, they had remained a live faction. There was a continued deep yearning for the old trappings, the splendor of the royal court, the easy life of those who fed from it. It was inevitable that this feeling would eventually crystallize into action, as it did, but probably the chief catalytic agent was a chance remark made by Donald one hot afternoon in August.

He and Anderson, in Anderson's Ford, were in search of fugitive currents of air, before appearing at a dinner for chief members of Yuan Shih-kai's cabinet. The Ford horned and poked its way through crowds of lazy dogs and people the heat seemed to have paraffined into wax museum figures—standing, drooping, sprawling.

Since Anderson had the front seat stacked with sample cans of Standard's best oil, Donald was sitting in the rear, his cane dangling over the side. Occasionally, he flicked it at one of the mongrels or tapped another on the buttocks. He smiled at dirty-faced children and waved whenever he caught sight of an acquaintance. He was humming the refrains of a London music hall favorite, which related how one J. W. MacHonochie had a monarchy all of his own.

It turned out that Mr. MacHonochie had drifted into the Caroline

Islands and married a buxom queen. Anderson boomed in with his cello bass, and they harmonized well until Donald suddenly broke off to remark that in his opinion, the republic, under Yuan, was a bloody failure.

Anderson grunted in agreement.

There was silence for awhile, then Donald said, "Admiral, what's wrong with a monarchy?"

"Nothing," answered Anderson, who had disliked the Manchus but who, like many older Chinese, had come to feel that while a monarchy might not be good for some, it was good for China.

Having provoked an argument, Donald immediately reversed his stand and contended with vigor that a monarchy was harmful and a republic was China's only salvation. As they wound in and out of a labyrinth of alleys and roads, the two argued heatedly, and the argument had not ended when they arrived at the dinner. It was to be carried on by others month after month, gathering momentum until Yuan was made emperor.

At the dinner, Donald sat next to Chow Tzu-chi and across from Liang Shih-yi, the so-called political boss of Peking, referred to by Chinese as the "God of Wealth." It was a seventy-five course dinner, and the bowls of shark's fin soup, Peking duck, sweet and sour pork, lobster, chicken, fish and rice, interspersed by pewter pots of warm Shaoshing wine, passed up by Donald only, came in endlessly. Bones were ejected recklessly about the floor and table. More courses, then steaming towels for sticky hands and faces, and more warm wine and more courses.

The hum of voices let up momentarily, and Anderson said in a clear, loud voice, "Gentlemen, Mr. Donald and myself, prior to coming to this dinner, engaged for several hours in an argument. We were arguing whether a republic or a monarchy is better for China."

Quiet was immediate. Everyone stopped and looked intently first at Anderson, then at Donald. Donald, whose meticulousness and fastidious regard for his health never permitted use of unclean-looking towels, wiped his mouth with a handkerchief. He had been eating a rare steak and boiled potatoes, cooked especially for him. He pocketed the handkerchief and smiled.

"That is so," he said. "I contend that the republic must be upheld. Mr. Anderson says a monarchy will be better in the long run."

The table burst into talk. It was as if the idea had been welled up inside of them for too long, and now it leaped at the chance for an airing. Each perhaps had cherished the thought but had been afraid to speak lest he find his neighbor or colleague unsympathetic. But two foreigners broaching the subject—that was different. Except for one, they backed Anderson. A monarchy, they said, was what China must return to. The exception was Liang Shih-yi who sat scowling into an empty teacup. Donald alone defended the republic. The others explored monarchical benefits, touched on the force of long habit on the people and analyzed the failure of the republic. For awhile, Donald fought back, enumerating the crimes of monarchy. Then suddenly the pragmatism of the conversation bored him, and with his faculty for detaching himself from people and things, he turned to his dinner and paid no further attention.

As quickly as a shift in wind, the whole atmosphere of the discussion changed. Voices were lowered. Donald heard the minister of commerce say, "The South, I mean the revolutionaries, is beaten and broken."

That woke up Donald. He pushed back his plate and eyed the speakers with new interest.

"Gentlemen," he said, "you cannot restore the monarchy. The South will not let you. It will revolt."

There was a moment of dead silence. Liang Shih-yi looked earnestly at Donald but said nothing. Then a barrage of voices barked out that the South could not fight, would not fight, and would accept any form of government imposed by Peking.

Donald shoved back his chair and stood up. He smiled. "Well," he said, "do as you please. But I warn you: Put forward the monarchy idea, and I will see to it that the South fights you!"

The dinner broke up in a hubbub of voices.

The next evening when Donald returned home, his boy said, "Master, Mister Chow Tzu-chi wantchee see you flen."

"All right, I'll go."

"No, no. Mister Chow no wantchee you—only flen."

Donald called Anderson, and, later, just as he was finishing dinner, the American stopped by after having visited Old Joe. He slid down into a chair, ill at ease. When he looked up, he saw Donald was watching him.

"I suppose I might as well tell you the whole story," said Anderson. "I know I can't hoodwink you."

He picked up a fork and tried to balance it crossways on his forefinger. He said that he figured Donald would be as surprised as he was to hear that their friends were going ahead with plans for a monarchy.

"They want me to convert you," he said, looking straight at Donald. "They want me to hold you off from going to the South. You've frightened the life out of them."

"Well?" demanded Donald. "Are you going to convert me?"

Anderson stood up, his massive frame towering over Donald. "It wouldn't do you any harm if I did," he said. "I'd like to rub out of you some of this rubbish about republics and democracies being the only answer for these people. You know, there are people besides yourself who have ideas on what's good for this country."

Donald bristled. Capable of self-criticism and laughter at himself, he extended the privilege to no one else. Those who dared faced a volcanic temper. "Start a monarchy," he threatened, "and I'll guarantee China will be in flames within a year."

Anderson began to walk up and down the room, digging his foot into a luxuriant sofa at one end, rapping his knuckles on the wall at the other.

"You're a damn visionary," he said. "A fellow can go off the deep end building beautiful pictures and then trying to fit people and things into them. It doesn't always work out that way. Some are born to rule, others to be ruled. The Chinese are happiest when ruled. Why? Because they're uninterested in ruling themselves. The family's the thing. To them, republicanism with all its personal responsibilities, with all its obligations of citizenship, its duties, its lofty purposes and goals is for those who like it."

"Nonsense!" Donald said. "You were born in this country, and like others who have grown up on a diet of amahs and *laissez-faire*, you're too close to the forest to see the trees." He rose and walked up to

Anderson. For a moment, they stood glaring at each other, then Donald said, "I'll back my judgment against all of you! There'll be civil war. Write that in your diary!"

Anderson stood angrily over him. He was infuriated with Donald's seemingly extravagant conceit and bullish stubbornness. For several seconds, neither spoke. Then Donald laughed. "If they ever get their monarchy," he said, "maybe they'll make you a duke or a lord. You'd look good in a yellow jacket and a red-plumed hat, covered with beads and sweet-smelling stuff!"

Anderson's face relaxed, and they left the room the best of friends.

A few days later, a dinner of cabinet members was held at the estate of one of Peking's most prominent bankers, and again the conversation centered on the monarchical idea. Distressed, Donald wandered to a pavilion where supple Chinese women in sleek, flattering gowns explored with delicious little giggles the novelty of embrace via the newest vogue—Western dancing. While he was gone, the men, in a smoke-filled room in the house, decided on how monarchy was to be restored. Since it would mean revolution to put the Manchus back on the throne, the simplest way out was to convert Yuan Shih-kai into an emperor.

At the time, few, if any, of the leaders of the South were in Peking. They had fled several years before when Yuan collapsed Parliament and made life uncomfortable for Kuomintang members. Donald pondered his course, finally deciding to await further developments. So far, nothing was known publicly of what struck him as a coup against the people, and he hoped that the heat for monarchy, as so often happened in the tempestuousness of Chinese politics, would simmer down.

A few days later, Anderson and Donald were strolling in the Legation Quarter discussing the fervor behind the movement when Anderson suggested they call on Professor Frank Johnson Goodnow,[1] an American and legal adviser to Yuan Shih-kai. They found Goodnow only hazily familiar with the plot. Donald detailed its background, and Anderson put in a bit spicily:

[1] Before Goodnow's appointment to the Chinese government, he was professor of administrative law at Columbia University. On his return from China, he was president of Johns Hopkins University until 1929.

"Donald started the whole thing, and now he's trying to squirm out of it."

Goodnow laughed heartily. "Shall I make a study of the situation and send it on to the President?" he asked.

"By all means," Anderson inserted quickly.

"Any recommendation short of a republic would be a disservice," Donald said firmly.

When Goodnow's memorandum reached Yuan's hands, the pro-monarchy clique went into a spasm of joy and came out in the open with their intentions. Goodnow had taken the theoretical view that the monarchical form was better suited to the traditions and actual political developments of the Chinese. The clique bowdlerized this to fit their plans.

Yuan, with great political astuteness, remained in the background, taking no apparent part in the campaign. He said only: "I will do whatever the people want." The Monarchists claimed that telegrams were flowing in from all parts of the country demanding that Yuan ascend the Dragon Throne, but Donald knew that the majority of the "urgings" were manufactured in Peking. The only newspaper Yuan read was printed in the palace grounds. It contained material calculated to excite him into accepting the robes of emperor. Other Peking papers debated the republic versus monarchy proposition animatedly, but the country at large seemed blissfully unaware of the significance of the movement. Although Donald was concerned by the quiet, he told Anderson he stood by his convictions the South would fight.

Shortly after the memorandum appeared, Donald invited Anderson to accompany him on a call on General Tsai Ao, one of the revolution's southern generals, young but able. He had moved to Peking recently, and Yuan, fearing him, had given him a sinecure in the form of chief of the national cadastral survey.

At his house, Anderson had to listen to a long discussion between Donald and Tsai in which the word "revolt" cropped up many times.

That night Donald received a phone call. It was from the general who told him that Yuan's operatives had been observed loitering near his house not long after Donald had left. Donald gave some quick instructions to his boy and then they hurried away. Neither returned until the early hours.

It had been August when Donald started the monarchy argument. Now it was mid-December. At this time, and after a unanimous vote by a convention of district delegates at Peking, Yuan, in a private and lavish ceremony, ascended the throne in the great throne room in the Forbidden City. A system of royalty was set up. Friends of Yuan's became barons, dukes and earls. For himself, he took the title "Emperor Hung Hsien."

It was whispered that the *fait accompli* was to be proclaimed on January 1, 1916. However, the serenity of the kingmakers was suddenly blasted one morning by a telegram to Yuan Shih-kai and his followers. The late afternoon Peking newspapers carried the story. Anderson burst in on Donald breathless, shaking a powdery snow from his huge frame in the manner of a Newfoundland dog. "Listen to this!" he exclaimed and read:

YUNNANFU, Dec. 20. General Tsai Ao, backed by the Governor of Yunnan Province, today directed the following order at the so-called Emperor-Designate: "Off the throne by December 25, or Southern troops will march north!"

Anderson looked puzzled. He reread the item several times before he said:

"I thought Tsai Ao was here."

"Obviously not," Donald said.

"Well?"

"I warned you and everyone else the South would fight."

"Uh-huh."

"I smuggled him out one night in a laundry basket. Later I bargained with a boatman to carry him away. How he got to Yunnan was his business."

Anderson threw down his paper with exaggerated force. "I'll be a son of a sea cook!" he bellowed.

Yuan ignored General Tsai's demand, and the northern march began. The typhoon of the South was under way, and it became evident there would be no stopping it short of Yuan's death or flight. Disaster loomed unless the pomp-hungry officialdom could be brought to their senses. Peking, however, viewed the threat sufficiently only to postpone the official promulgation of the monarchy.

One day Donald and Chow, who had been lukewarm on the movement from the start, called on the political boss, Liang Shih-yi. They found him in his garden, and the three walked the paths together over tiny half-moon bridges, around ponds and through bamboo groves that stood stiffly at attention.

"The whole affair is out of hand," Liang said. "We can do nothing to persuade Yuan. He's in the hands of reckless Monarchists."

Donald insisted that Yuan be told that revolt against him was widespread, but the two Chinese said it would be useless for he believed only what he read in the palace newspaper.

"I damn well will tell the old coot!" Donald exploded. Liang and Chow exchanged glances, and the next day—a day early in March— Donald found a summons to the palace awaiting him when he returned home at noon. It said simply that the emperor would see him and Anderson at three o'clock that afternoon.

Yuan Shih-kai had taken up his residence in the foreign-style part of the palace built by the dowager empress. When they arrived amidst the splendor of red and gold buildings, they were met by Admiral Tsai Tin-kan, Yuan's "front" man.

As Donald shook hands with him, he asked, "Well, Admiral, is the emperor interviewing me or am I interviewing him?"

The admiral laughed, then his handsome face grew serious. "I understand, Mr. Donald," he said in his precise English, "that you are—er— let us say you are to talk essentials. But please don't tell anyone I helped make these arrangements. The Monarchist crowd would kill me."

Donald promised, and as Tsai ushered them into a large room, he whispered to Donald, "I hope you can get Yuan to quit the throne. We're in trouble, and he's the only one who doesn't know it."

They sat down at a long table, Donald on the right next to Admiral Tsai and opposite Anderson, who was to interpret. They had not long to wait. At the far end of the room a door opened. The admiral sprang to his feet. Donald and Anderson followed. Squat, bulletheaded Yuan,

"Emperor of China," entered. As he walked across the long, polished hall, Donald watched him closely, and suddenly—the "hunch." He could not define it—but there it was, a strong whisper, the "telegraph" punching out something which evaded translation. Yuan advanced. His stumpy, fat body was bent, his short-cropped hair was gray. What had been a round and pleasant face was white and shrunken.

He shook the hand of the Australian. "How is the southern Republican?" he asked in a weak effort at congeniality. Donald smiled and introduced Anderson. There was an entire absence of regal ceremony.

They sat down. And then the "message" cleared up. Looking at Yuan, Donald knew that the man was dying.

Donald launched into a rapid summary of the depressing conditions that faced the nation. The only man in China who could tell everybody what he thought and get away with it, he declared that seventeen of the twenty-two provinces in China proper had turned against Yuan, and more could be expected to. Peking itself might shortly be threatened, and the end of it all would be the creation of a number of autonomous states, a turning back of the clock to a hodgepodge of individual feudalistic rule.

Yuan looked up at a wall clock, and then his almost too-bright eyes burned into Donald. "Not seventeen, just seven provinces that show signs of being unhappy," he remarked dryly. "I read it in the palace paper this morning."

"Your paper prints nonsense," Donald said boldly, and as he said it he noticed Admiral Tsai stir uneasily. But Yuan looked only at Donald, his eyes this time quietly searching the correspondent. Donald went on, "This country is falling apart. You cannot allow this to happen. Your bones would not rest easy with those of your ancestors." Yuan smiled weakly at this, then the troubled, tired look clouded his face. Donald talked on about the need to stop the war, the need to wipe chaos from the land, the need to return to a state in which the people might prosper, the need to quit the damnable business of periodically killing each other.

Yuan seemed to have wilted. He slouched forward in his chair, his forearms resting on the table.

"There is only one way out of this trouble," Donald said. "You must abdicate. You must stop this make-believe."

Yuan said, "I am tired." He rose. The three men jumped to their feet, and the man who had been responsible for toppling Kuang Hsu from his throne many years before, the man who had forced Sun from the presidency shuffled wearily across the hall and out the door.

Donald, Anderson with him, went directly from the palace to both Sir John Jordan and Dr. Reinsch, told them of the interview and of his certainty that Yuan was dying. Sir John, a firm believer in Yuan's grip upon life as well as upon China, said he thought Donald was talking twaddle. The American minister was equally skeptical. After that, Donald tried to get in touch with southern agents in Peking to tell them not to worry about Yuan any longer, but they all had slipped away to join their advancing armies.

Three days after the Donald-Anderson visit, on March 21, Yuan issued a mandate canceling the monarchy and restoring the republic. Once again, Yuan was just "Mr. President."

But Donald was not impressed by Yuan's action. He argued that a return to republicanism was not enough, and he told Liang Shih-yi that fighting would go on until Yuan quit the government altogether. The old dictator was *persona non grata* with Young China, particularly those in the South, Donald emphasized. His abolition of the Kuomintang and suppression of Parliament which precipitated the 1913 revolt and sent Dr. Sun scurrying to Japan had not been forgiven. The chance to rout Yuan was at hand, and the South could not be expected to hesitate.

April and part of May went by in smokiness and warfare, and the country ached like a mouthful of bad teeth. Then one day Liang telephoned Donald, and the correspondent hurried to his house.

"Yuan will resign and leave Peking," Liang announced. "He wants you to arrange with the British minister for accommodation at either of the two British colonies—Weihaiwei or Hong Kong."

Sir John reportedly had just been unsuccessful in petitioning for a transfer from his China post, and when Donald entered his office, he was irascible and testy.

"Donald," he said, "you irritate me. I'm getting damn tired of hearing the stupid statement that Yuan is about to retire. He is the most important man in China. He cannot resign and he will not resign." The Britisher glared at Donald, the colonial, through bushy eyebrows.

"The Japanese are offering sanctuary to Yuan," Donald shouted back. "They promise him royal honors. That's smart diplomacy. But you, as always, are fogbound, squatting more on the Thames, peering up at Whitehall. God damn it, sir! Can't you see what this will mean to British interests if you refuse Yuan a haven in at least Weihaiwei—the Weihaiwei Britain stole from China!"

Sir John reared up from his chair, and his voice was hoarse. "Blast it all!" he bellowed. "They have not officially asked me for sanctuary. And, furthermore, you can get the hell out of here, Donald!"

Smarting, Donald strode down Legation Street, turned in at the gate of Dr. Reinsch and marched into his library.

The American minister looked up. "What's the matter?" he asked, puzzled by Donald's solemn face.

Donald did not sit down. He stood feet apart. "I'd like three or four of your marines. I want three or four who are good shots."

"What for?"

"To go to the palace. We've got to get Yuan Shih-kai out. That's the only way the blasted war can be ended. We've got to get him out, and we've got to get him to safety. The British have refused all help." Donald walked up to the minister's desk. "Now," he asked, "what do you say?"

Reinsch looked at the Australian queerly. "I've heard stories of some of your escapades, Don," he said slowly, "but I never thought you'd ask me to help kidnap a president."

"No such thing," Donald said seriously. "Yuan wants to resign. He needs only an escort and a place of refuge."

Dr. Reinsch stood up. "Will the marines have to shoot?" he asked.

Donald now was walking quickly up and down the room. "I hope not," he replied. "We'll take the car to the side door. If any of Yuan's guards get wind of what's up, they might try to stop the car. But we won't stop. That might cause them to shoot, and we'd have to defend ourselves."

Reinsch hesitated a moment, then he said, "All right. When do you want them?"

"I'll let you know. And—can we have a guard to go with a train to Tientsin?"

"I think so."

"Then, how about a cruiser to take Yuan from that port?"

"I'll have to wire Washington on that." Dr. Reinsch pushed a bell, and when a secretary entered, he dictated a dispatch to Washington.

The next morning Donald called at the legation, and the minister handed him a telegram that read:

IF YUAN SHIH-KAI RETIRES TREAT HIM AS A DISTINGUISED GENTLEMAN STOP GIVE HIM PROTECTION STOP WIRE ADMIRAL MURDOCK IN REGARD TO CRUISER.

The armies of the South continued their drive northward, and the unrest in Peking was intensifying. The cancellation of the monarchy seemed to increase rather than allay anxieties. Each day Donald went to Liang Shih-yi to exchange information, hoping there would be word for him that Yuan was ready to leave the capital.

Near the end of May, Donald received an urgent message from Liang and he sped over to the old Chinese, thinking that at last the time had arrived. Liang said bluntly: "Yuan has changed his mind." But, as he read dismay in the Australian's face, he added, "He will go, nonetheless. He has decided, however, he wants no foreign protection. Now he wants an absolute guarantee of safe conduct by the South."

Donald, startled, dropped into a chair.

"I can understand your surprise," Liang went on. "But if we want to get rid of him, we'll have to humor him. He is primarily concerned with protection for his family and ancestral tombs. That is something the Americans cannot give him. He wants you to go to Shanghai to negotiate these terms with the southern leaders."

Donald got up and walked slowly from the house.

He made reservations on the 8:00 P.M. train for Shanghai and then went home to pack. Anderson came in.

"Where to, Gulliver?" he asked.

Donald explained. Anderson sank down onto the bed.

"Oh, no," he groaned. "Oh, for Pete's sake, no!"

Donald went on with his packing. After awhile Anderson said: "You're a blockhead for going. We're sitting on a keg of dynamite here. The whole thing could blow up at any minute. Anyway, every time you leave, you know doggone well something always happens."

Donald snapped his bag shut. "It's seven forty-five," he said and shouted to his boy: "Tell the chauffeur to bring the car." As he started for the door, the boy came running in from the rear with a telegram. Donald tore it open and read:

COME TO SHANGHAI AT ONCE STOP WE NEED YOUR ADVICE.

It was signed by two of the southern leaders, Dr. Wang Chung-hui and Dr. C. T. Wang.

When Donald arrived at Shanghai, he checked in at the Astor House and telephoned Dr. Wang Chung-hui. The lawyer for whom he once had tried to arrange a marriage hurried over with the man he had whisked out of Peking dressed as an old crone. They invited him to a conference which was under way at the moment.

"Who's there?" Donald asked.

"Doc Sun has sneaked in from Japan, and there are a few of the old boys and some of our newer friends," Dr. C. T. Wang explained.

"Who are the new friends?"

"Oh, they're Chinputang[2] members."

"I won't go. I'm not inclined to rub elbows with rascals."

C. T. asked what he meant, and Donald replied, "I can't change my spots as quickly as you. Remember the time Yuan wanted to murder you, and I got you out in the nick of time? It so happens that one of the men now at your conference was minister of interior then. He told me he didn't give a damn if you were shot!"

C. T. shrugged. "The past is past," he said. "We're good friends now."

Donald drummed a table and looked out of the window. "I will not go," he said.

When they saw they could not break through his stubbornness, Dr.

[2] Self-styled Progressive party, they aided Yuan Shih-kai when he dissolved Parliament in 1913, but now amalgamated with the Kuomintang to oust Yuan.

Wang Chung-hui told him that the conference was anxious that he mediate to bring about the retirement of Yuan. Donald listened with interest. He had not yet mentioned why he had come to Shanghai. After awhile, he said:

"That may be difficult. Just how far will the South go to get rid of Yuan? Will they give him safe conduct out of the country? Will they protect his family and his tombs?"

His friends smiled. "Poof!" C. T. said. "That's easy."

"Go back to the conference and bring me that assurance in writing. After that, I'll see what can be done."

They returned with the promise, and Donald, chuckling at his speedy success, wired Peking. By the following morning he had a reply stating that if a few more points were adjusted, Yuan would announce his resignation two days later, on Monday, June 6. That night the southern delegation met in Donald's room, and he drafted and dispatched the telegram that was to bring about Yuan's resignation.

Monday came, but no message arrived to announce that Yuan had stepped down. In the afternoon Dr. Wang Chung-hui and others came to Donald's room and began to talk angrily. C. T. Wang was certain that Yuan had double-crossed them.

Donald sat quietly looking out across the city in which he had made so much history. Just ahead was the British Consulate General and down the street to the left was the American. Somewhere not too far from the banks of Soochow Creek to the west was Dr. Wu Ting-fang's house where the heart of revolution had ticked. Smoke was pouring from hundreds of roadside charcoal burners, blending with summer's dusk. He did not take his eyes from the city when he spoke.

"Yuan hasn't double-crossed you," he said. "Yuan is dead."

They stopped their pacing and their talking and looked at Donald. He did not turn, and for awhile no one said anything.

"Dead?" C. T. echoed. "He can't be. He's just treacherous, that's all."

Half an hour later, the telephone rang. It was a telegram for Donald from Peking. It read:

YUAN SHIH-KAI DIED THIS AFTERNOON.

chapter

15

OIL THAT RUFFLED THE WATERS

*If one word does not succeed,
ten thousand are of no avail.*

YUAN Shih-kai had been dead for three months, and the effervescence of history had tossed the Kuomintang back into the government. Donald had returned from his conference with Dr. Wang Chung-hui and Dr. C. T. Wang in Shanghai in June with strong stipulations. Changes in government were in order or the South would go on fighting. With rival political parties he bargained shrewdly but fairly. The outcome was that Li Yuan-hung, the Manchu general who at the beginning of the 1911 outbreak had switched sides, was accepted as president and under him the Peiyang military party's man, Tuan Chi-jui, formerly a top-ranking Manchu general, as premier. In the cabinet reshuffle, Donald prevailed upon Tuan to install Dr. Chen Chin-tao, China's most able mathematician and a Kuomintang man, as finance minister, while Old Joe moved on to minister of commerce, agriculture and industry. C. T. Wang returned to the post from which he once had been driven—vice-president of the senate.

A new problem, however, was ruffling the fringes of the new serenity that had come to Peking. Strangely enough, oil was doing a stirring, not a calming. Donald's part in the forthcoming events heavily underlined his influence with the Chinese government and illustrated how far his reputation had penetrated beyond China.

Several years before, through a temporary agreement with the Chinese government, the Standard Oil Company of New York had begun a search for oil. Instead of transporting it thousands of miles,

Standard had hoped to find on the spot oil for the lamps of China. Accordingly, two prominent American geologists had been sent to survey China, and they had found seepages in Shensi Province, west of Peking. There they had bored experimentally. Drills, miles of pipe and other cumbersome equipment were carried in with great difficulty.

The temporary agreement had called forth charges of bribery from the Chinese press. Now Standard was pressing for a long-time contract not only for Shensi but for the exploitation of all China. To handle the negotiations, the Chinese set up in Peking an oil development board, staffed by a small army of government hangers-on—not one of whom was an oil expert. From the beginning, Standard had run into a mound of trouble, of delay and confusion, of stalling and innuendoes concerning the peculiar pecuniary relationship that should exist between negotiators. Chow Tzu-chi, under whose ministry the negotiations were proceeding, stratosphered himself above the greedy scramble at his feet. The trouble lay in his oil board, honeycombed with the usual band of unscrupulous.

Anderson was one of the negotiators for Standard, and he acted as liaison between the Chinese and his Peking office. But the cold wind of disapproval was blowing daily down the collar of the blue-eyed giant. He would stand for no deal that was not clean or straightforward. His honesty was brewing only a sourness. He had a strong feeling that fellow negotiators were engaged in extracurricular talks to which he was uninvited.

There was an undercurrent: Get rid of Anderson.

Anderson's patience had begun to thin.

When Donald entered his office one morning in September, a stoutish man who was sitting by his desk jumped up.

"My name is Higgins," he said, and handed Donald a card from Dr. Reinsch. The card stated that Higgins was a nice fellow and would Donald please assist him.

Mr. Higgins unrolled a wall map of China.

"What my map lacks," he said, "is the location of railways. I'm going to do some traveling."

"Oh?" Donald asked.

"Quite," replied Mr. Higgins. "I'm a student of China. I'm making some studies to write a thesis on Chinese geology."

Donald had taken the map and was studying it. Certain peculiar marks interested him. After awhile he said, "I can give you a copy of a railway map. I've just drawn it for the *Far Eastern Review*—a magazine which I edit."

Higgins took the map, looked at it and said: "I would like the projected railways."

"Oh," Donald said matter-of-factly, "you want to know if a railway is going to be built by the French through the Shensi oil fields or if a railway is projected to run near any other so-called oil field."

Mr. Higgins blushed. He protested that Mr. Donald was in error.

A few minutes later he left but returned in the afternoon. "I've come," he explained, "to tell you I lied this morning. It has been bothering me. I think you're a man to whom I can tell the truth."

He handed Donald a letter from a firm of solicitors of London Wall, London, instructing Higgins to proceed to Peking and report all he could learn about oil in China.

Mr. Higgins shrugged. "That's all I know about my employers," he said. "I'm a geologist, not a student. I came here from Korea." He tilted his bulk slightly forward and added, "I'm anxious to know how you knew I was concerned with oil, not railways."

"That wasn't difficult. Your map of China is the only one I've ever seen with oil indications marked on it."

Donald generously gave Higgins his file on oil, cautioned him not to ask him anything about the negotiations between Standard and the Chinese. Higgins agreed, and Donald did not see him again for several months.

When Anderson came in that night, Donald was in his study sitting quietly by his phonograph listening to Caruso's recording of "O Sole Mio," his favorite. In his Tsungpu Hutung home, close to that of Old Joe's, he had gathered about him the accouterments of a gentleman bachelor. He had the finest collection of recorded classical music of anyone in Peking, and his library of first editions was the envy of book collectors. His house was a solid brick structure with roof garden, ruled over by a fierce little matriarch, his amah, gray, toothless, and charged with a demoniacal fervor for propriety and "evvating proper for mastah." It was a refuge largely for those who knew and could talk about China. But he was not entirely without female companionship, for then and always he had a distinct attraction for women.

Donald waited until the Caruso record was finished, then he smiled at Anderson and said, "Well, Admiral?"

Anderson, who had slumped into a chair, announced that he was going to New York to see if he could find support from his home office to put negotiations back on a basis that he could stomach.

Within a few days he left. Then, one night early in November, he walked in on Donald and slumped once more into a chair.

"The stinkers," he said, "the goddam stinkers."

He explained that he had resigned immediately upon his arrival at New York, providing for himself the freedom with which to air his opinion on negotiators and negotiations. However, the directors had shrugged off his report, suggesting that he return and carry on. Anderson had put on his hat and had headed for the door. Whereupon, they had begun to bargain. They had argued that the fate of American interests in the Far East might hang on as slender a thread as the collapse of the negotiations. If Standard was out of China, Britain, Japan or even Russia might step in.

Anderson told Donald that at last he had said wearily that he would go back under certain conditions. They had agreed, he said, and he had returned to China only to find they had not met his conditions.

"Now I'm through with Standard Oil once and for all," Anderson declared grimly, "and I'm damn glad I'm out."

Donald sat quietly as Anderson related the story, and when he finished, he said, "Good lad."

That night he happened across Old Joe.

"Anderson's resigned from Standard," Donald said.

Chow half closed his eyes and nodded slowly. Then he said, "Oh," and changed the subject.

On the following day Old Joe showed his first interest in the oil talks and had a meeting called at which he was present. Joy Everall, who had replaced Anderson, represented Standard.

Old Joe took his seat at the head of the long table. He bowed to everyone, then pinned Everall with a serene gaze. He asked, "Do you represent the Standard Oil Company?"

Everall replied that he did.

"Will you show me your credentials," Old Joe said softly.

Everall, flustered, replied that he had left the telegraphed authority at his hotel.

Old Joe stood up. "In that case," he said, "we will adjourn for two weeks. Please bring it to the next meeting." With puffs of cigar smoke trailing behind him, Chow walked sedately from the conference room.

Delay was what Standard was most anxious to avoid. In the field, they had expensive men working and their overhead was running into big figures. At the end of the fortnight Chow again took a seat at the meeting. Everall produced the telegram empowering him to act. Chow read it carefully, cigar smoke billowing about him, then handed it back to Everall.

"Does this paper give you authority to sign, say, this afternoon, any document upon which we might agree?" the minister asked with an air of innocence.

Everall replied that it didn't.

"Well," said Chow, "what we require is a director—someone with power to sign. Please wire New York to send such a man. Until he comes, there will be no more meetings."

Mr. E. W. Bemis, a senior director, hurried to China. When he arrived in Shanghai, Dr. Reinsch was requested by telegram to inform Chow that Standard wished to speed up the negotiations and to arrange an immediate meeting. Reinsch called on Old Joe.

"When will Mr. Bemis arrive?" the Chinese asked.

Dr. Reinsch replied that he was due the following day.

"Ah," said Old Joe, "then I'll push things along as fast as I can. We will have a meeting, let us say, two weeks from the time he arrives."

For two weeks, Bemis sat at his hotel, furious but helpless. One day he met Anderson.

"Confound it!" he swore. "What can I do to get these people to talk?"

Anderson glowered down at him. "I no longer work for Standard," he said.

A few days later, Everall saw Anderson at the Hotel de Pekin.

"How's Donald?" he asked.

"All right," Anderson replied.

"Well, if he ever wants to be a paid negotiator, he has a job with us."

"I'd give anything to be present if you will say that to him personally," Anderson said and walked off.

On the appointed day, the talks resumed, and they continued for several weeks. Bemis, confident of success, arranged for a large dinner to celebrate the end of negotiations. At last the final day of the conference was set with the banquet scheduled for that night. Bemis and his Peking office were joyous. They gathered at the old yamen for the last time and engaged in good-natured banter awaiting the arrival of the Chinese, but Chow and his board did not appear. An uneasy feeling began to limp around the table. Finally Old Joe's secretary entered and stopped at Chow's chair.

"Gentlemen," he announced, "I have been instructed to inform you the Chinese government cannot comply with the requirements of the Standard Oil Company."

That was the end of the talks. The banquet was canceled. Mr. Bemis left that night for Shanghai and New York. In a short time, Standard's geologists were sent home. So were the drillers and all the others who had been working in Shensi.

Shortly after Mr. Bemis left, the counselor for the British Legation, Ronald Maclay, called on Donald. He came right to the point. "Mr. Donald," he said, lighting his pipe, "I wonder if the Chinese will reopen negotiations on the basis of the old agreement made before 1900. That agreement was for development of mining and other resources in Szechwan Province."

Donald smiled. "You mean—will I find out?" he asked.

"Quite."

Donald looked intently at him. "Why do you come to me?"

"First off, because you're British, and what's more important: these people will talk to you."

"Hold on," Donald answered, "I'm not British. I'm Australian."

"What's the difference?"

"You'd know if you were a colonial living in Hong Kong."

Maclay relighted his pipe. "Blood's thicker than the water between us," he said.

Donald was amused. "Britishers can be a rum bunch, you know," he said. "England is like a tight shoe. It pinches up its people sometimes in the queerest places."

"You mean we've got corns?" Maclay asked.

Donald laughed. "I suppose," he said meditatively, "that if two flags were before me—one British and, say, the other American—and someone put a gun to my head and commanded: 'Pick one!'—well, I suppose I'd pick the British." He stood up. "All right," he added, "I'll see Mr. Chow Tzu-chi for you."

Old Joe shoved a box of cigars across his desk at Donald. "Our old agreement with the British over Szechwan has lapsed," he said. But Donald pointed out that the Chinese government had never signified its attitude, and since it was a good thing to have foreign powers investing in China, perhaps a basis for negotiation could be found. Old Joe was thoughtful. "Perhaps," he said.

The British Legation opened exploratory talks immediately, and in London a powerful syndicate was set up to carry out development work when and if an agreement was reached. Through Maclay, Donald learned who the members were.

Higgins, who had kept from sight during Standard's negotiations, dropped in on Donald at about this time.

"I know whom you're working for," Donald told him. "You're working for Lord Cowdray, the president of S. Pearson and Son."[1]

"Good," answered Higgins. "That's tophole. I'm glad to know."

"Slow there," Donald cut in. "Not so good."

Higgins looked puzzled.

"The other members of the syndicate," said Donald, "are the Central Mines of South Africa and the British and Chinese Corporation.[2] The syndicate, like Standard, will fail in its efforts. It will fail as long as the British and Chinese Corporation has anything to do with the negotiations. Why? Because there's a man named Sidney Mayers at its head.

[1] Leading company in the Pearson Syndicate, rival in many parts of the world of the Standard Oil Company.

[2] Makers of loans for Chinese railways, the corporation had been active at the time Dr. Sun Yat-sen was planning his railways.

That's enough. You write Lord Cowdray and tell him that. Tell him a man who knows told you. Tell him Mr. Doolittle said it."

Still puzzled, Higgins inquired: "Who's Doolittle?"

"I'm Doolittle," said Donald.

Higgins asked no further questions either on Mayers or about the B. & C.C. He sent off his letter as Donald had suggested.

Nevertheless, formal negotiations for the British opened under the leadership of Mr. Mayers, and, characteristically, they dragged on phlegmatically. Donald had spoken to no one concerning his knowledge of the talks, but one day at the Peking Club—frequented rarely by Donald—a Mr. Wheeler buttonholed him. Wheeler was mining adviser to the Ministry of Commerce, Agriculture and Industry, at the head of which was Old Joe.

"I say," he asked, "could you do something to push these negotiations?"

"What negotiations?" Donald asked.

"Oh, come now—the ones for Szechwan. They're at a deadlock, I can't understand it."

"Why ask me? You're a paid official adviser to the ministry."

Wheeler colored slightly. "I know it," he said, "but I can't unlock these people's heads, walk in and browse around to find out if something is ticking, or isn't." He added warmly, "You could ask Chow for a copy of the agreement, read it over and say whether you think it fair."

"I don't poke my nose into other people's business," Donald said.

Wheeler sparred. "But," he protested, "I think the terms are fair. I believe the agreement can be executed. All that is needed is someone to build a fire under Mr. Chow."

Donald stepped around him. "I can do nothing," he said and walked off.

The talks crept along. Wheeler badgered him again. Although Donald reiterated that he preferred to mind his own business, nevertheless, he asked the minister one night how the negotiations were going. The Chinese replied they were at a standstill because the terms were too stringent.

Donald could not explain to himself why he did it since he believed, as he had told Higgins, that the negotiations were doomed to failure.

However, he began a persuasion of Old Joe. He talked about the cost of developing new ground, especially like that in distant Szechwan and spoke of the encouragement given in Australia and other countries to promote the finding of gold and precious metals. He even produced the mining laws of Australia, the Philippines, Canada and South Africa, pointing out their flexibility and liberalness. Chow smiled. He was not impressed.

"Supposing I handle the negotiations?" Donald hazarded. "Would the Chinese accept the terms?"

Chow replied, "Tomorrow morning at ten o'clock."

"Well, I'm not going to," Donald laughed. "But you should do something. Now, will you send the British proposal to me. Let me give an opinion as to whether the terms are in China's interest."

The next morning Donald was handed a copy of the British terms. He began to read and stopped when he saw the name "Sidney Mayers." He recalled, as he had had occasion to several times in the past but now more forcibly, an unpleasant encounter he had had with Mr. Mayers. The Britisher had shown a marked lack of gratitude for assistance given in the days following the 1911 revolution. Donald said to himself: Why should I put millions of sterling into the pockets of such people.

He tossed the document into a desk drawer. He did not read it.

That evening Donald saw the old minister and was asked if he had received the papers. Replying that he had, he immediately began to talk about other things. Chow asked no further questions, but when he met Donald the following evening, he inquired if Donald had read the proposals. The Australian said he hadn't.

"Our last meeting with the British is set for tomorrow," Chow said.

"That's all right," Donald answered.

When he called on Chow the next night, the minister said, "I've ended negotiations with the British over Szechwan."

The two old friends stood looking quietly at each other. Donald reached in his pocket. "Have a cigar," he said.

In the morning Mr. C. S. Lindsay, a Canadian mining expert and a member of the British delegation, called on him. He said that he could not understand why the negotiations had suddenly collapsed and asked if Donald thought the Chinese might renegotiate if the terms were modified. Donald did not answer. He opened his desk drawer, extracted the British proposal and handed it and a letter asking for his opinion to his caller. Lindsay appeared baffled, then looked questioningly at Donald.

"If it will comfort you any," the Australian said, "I'll tell you I haven't read it."

When Lindsay finished reading the letter, he asked what it meant.

Donald answered that it meant that if he had read the proposals and had thought them acceptable to China and had said so, the agreement probably would have been signed. Looking even more baffled, Lindsay asked why he hadn't read them, and Donald, leaning back in his chair, said he would tell him a story.

Gifted with a retentive, anecdotal mind, he never forgot anything. He could recall the very hour at which incidents happened in bygone years. He could remember, for instance, that he had begun the climb up Purple Mountain at 9:20 A.M. and that he had completed his descent at 6:32 in the evening. His repertoire of stories and memories had grown steadily year by year, and he had come to be regarded as a raconteur without peer. Further, he insisted upon completing any story he started.

"Well," he began, "you probably know that most international politics in China are bound up in railway loans and agreements. You've heard of the old days when the Battle of the Concessions raged. How the French persuaded the Chinese government to give them a series of railways to build. How the British also acquired a group of lines, and how the Germans got some, and even the United States acquired an interest."

Lindsay was listening eagerly.

"The British lines included the one now existing from Pukow on the Yangtze River to the border of Shantung Province," Donald went on. "Beyond, it was German. The British were given the right to build a connecting link from Pukow to Sinyang on the Peking-Hankow Railway, which is French built. But in 1905, by secret agreement, the British and Chinese Corporation—the organization that floated the loans and looked after British railway interests—gave to French interests certain rights with regard to personnel on the line and the sale of materials for its construction."

Lindsay put in, "Sounds like a hell of a way to look after British interests. Why give the gravy to the French?"

Donald nodded, then explained how George Bronson Rea, publisher of the magazine of which Donald was editor, came into possession of the secret 1905 agreement, but Donald had opposed its publication. He could not believe in its accuracy, since the gifts to the French were so contrary to British policy in China.

"The time came," Donald continued, "when the British wished to construct this line. It was necessary for the Chinese Parliament to pass a bill for this purpose. But the bill got stuck in committee, and British diplomacy could not move it. The B. & C.C. man, this same Mayers, asked me what could be done about it. I appealed to the vice-president of the Senate, Dr. C. T. Wang, and he promised its passage within a few days."

"Well," Lindsay inserted, "Mr. Mayers must have been grateful."

Donald eyed the Canadian for a moment, then went on: "At about this time, the significance of the B. & C.C. agreement with the French began to impress me. I had to talk to someone about it, so I went to Sir John Jordan. I told him that the Pukow-Sinyang rail agreement would shortly be passed by Parliament. I said that he'd better prepare himself for the French putting in for their rights under the 1905 agreement."

Donald said Sir John asked what agreement, and he answered the one that gave the French the right to build a railway for the British.

"Rubbish!" the British minister had retorted. "There's no such agreement. I'd know about it if there were."

Donald said that he had shrugged and replied he only hoped to prepare him for the French minister who would come pounding at his door.

"It's impossible!" Sir John had insisted.

"I told him I'd bring the agreement the next day," Donald told Lindsay, "and bring it I did—the one Rea had dug up."

Sir John had looked it over and handed it back to Donald with the comment that there was no such agreement, but as Donald rose to go, the minister had blurted out: "Goddam those B. & C.C. people!"

Lindsay sat wide eyed as Donald continued to unwind his story.

Mayers was just leaving the Peking Club one night as Donald was passing, he told Lindsay, and Donald had fallen into step with him. Forgetting the railway agreement and thinking only of political developments, Donald had remarked that things had been happening in Peking.

Mayers had exploded: "Yes, I hear that some damn puppy dog has been sticking his nose into things that don't concern him."

Donald had felt the blow. At the next street intersection, he took a silent, oblique turn. Mayers strode on, head in air.

Donald said he went to his office and then called Rea. He said: "You can print that 1905 agreement now. Every word of it is true."

After that he had written Mayers informing him that he was withdrawing any further editorial support of B. & C.C. and detailing how in the past he personally had persuaded Dr. Sun to favor B. & C.C. in railway contracts. Mayers had answered with what was an unsuccessful attempt to rewin Donald's support. Finally Dr. Morrison had intervened on his behalf, but Donald had told him: "Go back and tell Mayers that the puppy dog he referred to has a bite like a bulldog."

Donald paused, and Lindsay eyed the man who had scuttled his hopes and those of his British colleagues.

"Well," he said, "I can hardly blame you. But you cost us more than thirty thousand pounds in initial expenditure alone. And who can say how many millions in hoped-for profits."

Donald rose, walking about the room slowly as he talked. "No," he said, "my refusal to act did not cost you anything. What caused the loss was the appointment of Mayers as negotiator. He is known as Pontifical Sidney among foreigners, and this attitude has inflamed the Chinese. He is a table-thumper, and they were determined never to conclude any agreement with him. That is why I told your Mr. Higgins long before the negotiations opened to write Lord Cowdray that Britain would fail."

He stopped before Lindsay. "During the negotiations," he said, "I never had to say one derogatory word to the Chinese. I never spoke about the talks unless it was to persuade them to act. But when the onus of whether they should do something or nothing was placed on my shoulders, I decided to say nothing at all and let the Chinese carry on as they desired. The result was collapse."

Lindsay smiled weakly. "They fell with a thud, all right," he said.

Donald went on, "One of the troubles is that the British, like all foreign negotiators in China, always demand the maximum, hoping to secure it by influence or diplomatic pressure. In this case, diplomatic pressure had failed, and they were trying to use my influence."

He resumed his walking, chin in hand. "They would have had it, no doubt," he said, "had Mayers been more gracious. I would have given it because I want to see British and American investments made in China on a mutually beneficial basis."

Lindsay shook hands with Donald, and in a few days sailed for home. So did all the others, with one exception. The exception was Higgins, and he came to see Donald one day, waving a cable. "I'm the lone survivor," he said. "They want me to go to London. I wonder why I've been picked."

"Oh, that's easy," Donald replied. "They're bursting with curiosity. They want to ask you who Mr. Doolittle is. They want to find out how he knew the negotiations would fail even before they started."

Higgins set off for London, and some time later Donald went to Japan, staying in the house of an old friend, E. W. Frazar, at Nikko. Frazar was in Yokohama, and one day he wired Donald:

HIGGINS IS HERE FROM LONDON STOP HE IS HEADING FOR NIKKO TO SEE YOU.

Under the giant cryptomeria trees of Nikko, Donald strolled with Higgins. The stoutish little man told him that he had been right, that London had wanted to know about "Mr. Doolittle." They walked on past solemn temples, Donald thinking all the time how curious it was for him to come all the way to Japan to thank him for nothing. But cautiously Higgins unfolded the purpose of his visit.

"I am asked by London to find out what you will want to reopen negotiations for the British and Chinese Corporation."

Donald halted, a smile tickling the corners of his mouth. "Three times the salary of Mayers," he said, "and ten times his interest in B. & C.C."

Higgins shrugged resignedly. "That means, knowing you, that you'll not do anything," he said.

They threaded their way back through the forest of cryptomerias.

16

HISTORY AND HISTRIONICS

If there is no wind,
the trees don't move.

Ｆᴏʀ China, 1917 brimmed with history and histrionics. The high point was a spectacular breaking out from the cocoon of nearly five thousand years to enter world politics for the first time and to join in the World War. The decision was momentous, just as any sudden departing from ancient policy is epochal. In this, Donald became a spearhead in what his friend, Samuel G. Blythe[1] dubbed the "Flying Wedge" that prodded China into the realization that it was a part of a general scheme and not the old Middle Kingdom, complacent and content, self-sufficient and unique.

With the opening of unrestricted submarine warfare by Germany, President Wilson moved to congeal neutral world opinion against the Kaiser Wilhelm government. On February 3, he severed diplomatic relations with Berlin and simultaneously denounced its submarine policy.

On the afternoon of February 4, Dr. Reinsch received the news together with a note for the Chinese government. The note asked China, with other neutrals, to support the United States by protesting Germany's underseas warfare. The American minister immediately called Donald on whom he relied to decipher prevailing Chinese sentiment. Further, Donald long had been an open advocate of positive action on the side of the Allies. It had been he who had urged Yuan Shih-kai, at the outbreak of the conflict in 1914, to declare war on

[1] A writer for the *Saturday Evening Post*, Blythe was in Peking early in 1917.

Germany and seize what Japan later took—the rich concessions in Shantung. His efforts, however, had been blocked by Sir John Jordan who, with incredible shortsightedness, advised China against it, remarking that the war was to last but a few months.

Reinsch told Donald, "I think we'll have to work fast for two reasons. One, to be effective, a quick support of the American policy is necessary. Two, we must beat the Chinese reactionaries and Germans here to the punch."

"We have a job on our hands," Donald answered. "A simple protest might be considered routine by some nations. But for these people it's earth shaking, you know."

Dr. Reinsch said that he realized it and hurried to deliver the American note to President Li Yuan-hung. Before he returned, Donald had organized the so-called Flying Wedge. He called Anderson first, and together they picked the men they believed would be most effective. Dr. John C. Ferguson, an American who had been an adviser and educator in China for thirty years, accepted the challenge, as did Dr. George Morrison, still an adviser in the Chinese government. The American writers, Blythe and Charles Stevenson Smith, agreed to fit into the Wedge. Dr. Reinsch, Anderson and Donald completed the unique little band.

That night they plotted a course of action that was to whirlwind over six days—six stirring days in Chinese history.

The first question was the point of attack—Parliament or cabinet. China once more was chaotic politically. Dissension had arisen over the writing of the constitution which had been suspended by Yuan Shih-kai in 1913. Parliament was not admitting the President's authority, while the cabinet refused to recognize any responsibility to Parliament. Li was at odds with both parties.

Donald, with his intimate knowledge of hard and soft spots in the government, charted the campaign. Dr. Reinsch was to tackle the premier, Tuan Chi-jui, who was known to be both pro-Japanese and pro-German, yet indolent in matters political. Dr. Ferguson and Dr. Morrison were delegated to work on President Li, who regarded himself as a student of military matters and was reputed to be convinced Germany would win. Donald was to concentrate on the Young China element in Parliament since he alone held their complete confidence. Anderson and Blythe were to assist him in the assault upon the cabinet which held a mixture of Young China progressives and reactionaries. Smith was to co-operate generally with all sections of the group.

The next day, Monday, the Wedge went into action.

Disappointments bobbed up everywhere. Li told Morrison and Ferguson he saw no reason why China should follow America. He said China must adhere to her neutrality. A canvass showed that the premier was not to be moved, that the bulk of the cabinet was opposed, mostly on the grounds of precedent but some of them because they shared the view of the President. There was one brilliant exception—Dr. Chen Chin-tao, a Yale graduate and the man Donald had engineered into the minister of finance post. He saw the situation at once and the possibilities in it. This first small crack for the Wedge was widened later in the day when the American-educated Dr. C. C. Wu, of the Foreign Office, joined Dr. Chen. He was the son of the old rebel, Dr. Wu Ting-fang, who was again minister for foreign affairs but was ill at the time.

That night, the little band held a council of war. The seemingly bleak situation was weighed, and Donald's opinion that their salvation lay in the co-operation of Young China was subscribed to by the others. It was plain now that the burden had been shifted to Donald.

The plotting of strategy began. He was in the thick of what he relished. Since his early days with the old viceroy, he had worked to make China an entity among nations, a factor in world politics. Now the first great opportunity was at hand. With Dr. Reinsch and himself leading the discussion, they tested the needles they hoped would wake a sleeping giant who wanted only to sleep.

Donald then began to line up Young China and to impress upon them the deep significance of world co-operation. His old friends, Dr. C. T. Wang, the Senate whip, and Dr. Wang Chung-hui, now regarded as China's leading jurist, were pressed into action. They saw the importance of China in world affairs and promised an intensive campaign of their own.

All day Tuesday the Wedge and its Young China backers worked swiftly for advantage. Hour after hour Peking resounded with speeches to timid Chinese, urging and forcing, begging and cajoling. It was a hard, two-fisted battle. Blythe summed up the day's work with: "He who dallied was a dastard! He who doubted was roundly damned!"

By Wednesday morning the Chinese section in the Wedge had widened. The magic phrase, "Donald is behind it," had spread. For Young China, this had become a guarantee that the nation's welfare was being safeguarded. But new stumbling blocks cropped up. Arguments rose over what Japan, even though one of the Allies, might do in retaliation. The older generals, confident Germany would win, and the opposition in the cabinet, influenced by Japan, whispered that what Donald and the Americans were asking was not merely to denounce German sub attacks but to declare war. Angered, the generals threatened revolt.

A cabinet meeting showed that the majority was still opposed. Further, President Li was making his opposition felt, and Premier Tuan remained unenthusiastic. Shifty, he awaited the outcome, spending his days, as was his custom, at chess.

There was no letup to the campaign, and the list of sympathetic Young China adherents grew more imposing. As forces behind the Wedge strengthened, however, Germans in Peking, caught napping, mustered for the fight. But they made a poor guess. Believing the attempt to get action against them would be made through Parliament, they concentrated on the elder statesmen among the 700-odd members and ignored the cabinet. As soon as Donald and Dr. Reinsch noted this, they gave the impression that they were working exclusively among parliamentarians, and the Wedge then tripled its efforts with the cabinet.

The foreign diplomatic corps, as well as Chinese officialdom, was boiling by Wednesday night. The heat was increased as men who might help were pulled from bed at all hours and argued or pounded, as was necessary, into service. Young China was busy haranguing its own borderline members. Both the President and the premier were seen several times but they evidenced no change in attitude. Some time before midnight the cabinet met again. A hint of promise emerged. One or two ministers joined the valiant Drs. Chen and Wu in declaring that China should follow the lead of the United States. Prior to the meeting, Anderson and Donald had called on all diplomatic repre-

sentatives of the Allies asking that they tell the Chinese their partnership would be welcomed. Since there was no time to receive instructions
from their home governments, the diplomats had done so unofficially.

There were further bright spots by Thursday morning. Reports from
the Young China section were reassuring. The Germans had not discovered the drive on the cabinet and were confining their lobbying to
Parliament. The premier finally announced that he was open to conviction but the President was still firm.

A third meeting of the cabinet at which Blythe, Anderson and
Donald were present was called in the afternoon when the inevitable
offer of the Chinese to temporize came forward. The cabinet wanted
to know if it could issue some statement to please the United States
but refrain from a formal protest to Germany. Blythe nudged Donald,
and Anderson nodded encouragement. Donald rose, outlined clearly
what was proposed, what the benefits to China would be. He talked
for nearly an hour, with Anderson interpreting, brittlely at first, then,
as he noted continued equivocation, stormily.

"Don't attempt to compromise," he said. "It won't work. You'll have
to go the distance, otherwise you need not start. If some day you'd be
regarded as a power, as a nation that speaks with dignity, the time to
begin is now!"

Premier Tuan stirred, said shrewdly, "What you suggest is no better
than walking up and kicking an old and unoffending friend."

"In world diplomacy," Donald retorted, "that is not reason enough
to sit quietly by. When a crime is being committed, when a murderer's
loose, the world citizen cannot stand mouth agape. Conscience tells
him that suddenly he has become a policeman." Donald looked at Dr.
Chen who smiled approvingly, and the Australian went on: "True,
none of your ships have been sunk because you have no ships, but
there are Chinese crews aboard every manner of vessel in world trade.
Their lives are being lost. Doesn't that mean anything to you?"

Tuan puffed on a cigarette.

"We're not asking you to declare war," Donald continued. "Neither
do we ask that you break diplomatic relations. We ask only that you
denounce murder on the seas."

The most prominent of the opposition addressed Donald. The fear of Japan was still strong. He was anxious over the "old enemy's" attitude.

"Ah," Donald answered, "mark these words. You have Japan by the throat, and you do not know it. Japan is one of the Allies. Your act will align you with the Allies. Japan can do nothing but applaud."

The meeting ended in a mutter of voices.

The Wedge continued to gain, picking up recruits in influential quarters. It was apparent now that the opposition of the President was negligible. It was apparent, too, that Dr. C. T. Wang had won parliamentary sentiment despite the efforts and money of the Germans. Scouts reported that more of the cabinet had changed their opinions since Donald's onslaught, the body being divided about equally. But the older generals were repeating their threats of revolt with new vigor. Toward the end of the day, a delegation of them called on the premier and several members of the cabinet.

That put the situation squarely up to the Flying Wedge. The now tired little band of Americans, Australians and Chinese was convinced that if the stern old militarists could be offset, victory might be had. Certain factors were in their favor: Half of the cabinet behind them, and opposition here and there weakening. The logic of the Wedge's demand was beginning to seep through.

They held council, counted their credits and debits. The conclusion was that they were on the verge of success. The decision: The old generals were not to stop them.

Working with the Wedge were certain of the younger generals, largely from the South, who had been efficient figures in the 1911, 1913 and 1916 revolts. Among them, General Niu Yung-chien was the most forceful. Donald had known him from Purple Mountain days. Niu was on hand as the Wedge conferred.

"Do you intend to allow these older generals to prevent this great step by China?" Donald asked Niu. "Do you intend to lose this opportunity because a few political soldiers lack wit and patriotism— because they are playing paltry politics? You have it in your power to get this essential declaration. Will you help?"

Niu agreed enthusiastically, and asked what Donald proposed.

"Well," said Donald, "it's easy. You can go to the premier and the cabinet. You can tell those jellyfish that if they don't accept this heaven-sent opportunity to put China into world affairs, you and your armies will install a government that has sufficient intelligence to do it."

Within the hour, Niu led a delegation of generals in full uniform to a series of calls upon wavering government members. The dreaded typhoon of the South was threatening again. Donald heard later that they promised revolution "before the next sun sets" if the government failed to stand by the United States. He knew his South and he knew they meant it.

The next day, the Wedge found that it had won. The cabinet had come around rather precipitately. The premier capitulated whole-heartedly; the President somewhat less spiritedly. The suddenness of the coup left Peking's Germans slightly dazed. In lobbying with Parliament, they had been unaware that they were backing the wrong horse all the time. The act, as agreed upon, was solely in the province of the cabinet.

The rest was formality. It remained only for the writing of the notes, one to Washington, the other to Berlin, and in this the Wedge was happy to oblige, Donald in particular. By now, he was an old hand at writing China's enunciations. The note to Washington advised that China stood with the United States against Germany's blockade. In the note to Berlin, the hope was expressed that Germany's threat of unre-stricted submarine war would not be carried out, but it warned should China's protest fail, a breaking of diplomatic relations would follow.

The tornado of six days was at an end. On Friday night, February 9, the notes were made public.

China had emerged from the Middle Kingdom.

Hardly had China's policy been proclaimed, however, when a rumble came out of Kiangsu Province where General Feng Kuo-chang held concurrently the posts of provincial governor and vice-president of the republic. The Wedge, with a sinking feeling, realized it had made a blunder. General Feng, powerful because he commanded the support of most of China's provinces, had not been consulted.

Donald scooped up Blythe and they hurried the five hundred miles to Nanking. In the Bridge Hotel there, Donald saw a wall map of

Europe, and as he stood looking at it, an idea was born. Not many minutes later, he laid the map in front of bald, slender, musical-voiced General Feng. Standing interestedly by was Feng's corps of German advisers. Forewarned of the purpose of the Australian's visit, they eyed him with challenging amusement.

Donald fished a silver dollar from his pocket and placed it over the Central Powers, leaving the rest of the world exposed.

"As a military man," he inquired, "would you rather be fighting with the Powers under that dollar, or would you have the remainder of the world to draw upon?"

Feng looked up at his advisers. "This is not the sort of map you showed me," he said.

Donald put in, "No doubt they didn't. They probably showed you one of their newer models where they have stretched out temporarily into Belgium and France."

The general saw the point. He turned to his advisers and accused them of misleading him. They denied it and a heated discussion followed with Donald pointing out why the crash of the Austro-German Empire was inescapable. Finally Feng said to Donald:

"All right, you have my vote for any action in concert with the Allies."

Blythe continued on to New York. Donald returned to Peking. But China's protest, like that of other neutrals, failed to influence Germany. Early in March, Donald began discussing China's next step, the breaking off of diplomatic relations with Berlin.

He pointed out first that this would gain for China a seat at the peace conference and obviate the need of Japan's representing her—as wily Tokyo diplomats were anxious to do. Second, it was the opportunity for Young China to sweep away the archaic, corrupt governing class. Third, China would then be in a position to repudiate the German and Austrian shares of the Boxer indemnity amounting to several million dollars a year. China could seize German ships in Chinese ports and have a fleet for postwar use. Also, China would be in a better position to remove Japan from Shantung Province after the war and block German re-entry.

The cabinet did not ponder long this time. On March 13, it handed the German minister his passport, severing diplomatic relations. China had made good in its first effort in world affairs. It had backed its warning with action. Cheers came from all over the world, except from Germany and Austria, and, as Donald had predicted, the loudest came from Japan.

Three weeks after China broke with Germany, the United States entered the conflict, and Donald began to talk of the efficacy of an outright war declaration. His purpose was twofold. First, he hoped it might produce a more united home front. Second, he realized that the declaration would not turn China into a world battlefield, but, on the contrary, into a reservoir from which the Allies might draw, thus strengthening China's global position. The time was to come when she would follow his advice, but first she was to witness once more a war within her own borders.

Donald was faced by a growing deterioration in government. His friend, Finance Minister Chen, too scrupulously honest for provincial governors, had been jailed on trumped-up charges. The ministry of communications was in charge of an underling. The minister of education, who also acted as interior minister, was seriously ill. Several Kuomintang members had lost prestige with their own party. As to a war declaration, the President said he was willing if Parliament would approve, while the premier took the attitude that the move would be made whether or not Parliament was willing. He threatened to dissolve it if it balked.

On a day in late May, 1917, the rupture came. President Li dismissed Tuan after their differences became irreconcilable. Whereupon, the ex-premier packed up and journeyed to near-by Tientsin, announcing that he was through with politics forever.

A new paralysis crept over Peking. Since the jail held Dr. Chen and sick beds held others, the capital was without financial or military leaders. An immediate reaction sprang from the provinces. Military governors threw their support behind the ousted premier, declared Li's act illegal and retaliated by choking off Peking's needed supplies. The prospect of privation was faced. Tuan, however, remained aloof from the movement.

A few days after the premier's dismissal, Donald called on Li, and from the President's office he hurried to Anderson's house. The American read concern in his friend's face.

"Well," he asked wearily, "what now?"

"Brace yourself," Donald answered. "The President isn't going to pick a new premier. Guess what."

Anderson refused to guess, and Donald continued, "He's going to bring in the old Mafoo general to settle the new revolt. It means that the old bandit will be premier in fact if not in name."

Anderson exploded. General Chang Hsun, the dowager empress' former stableman, a war lord unschooled in affairs of government! The American recalled his butchering habits, the time he had unloosed a reign of terror while they were outside Nanking's walls in the 1911 revolution. Still sympathetic to the Manchus under whom he had gained his power, he adhered to Manchu customs, as did all of his soldiers, refusing to either cut his own queue or permit queueless Chinese in the territory where he held autocratic rule.

Discussing the new problem, Donald and Anderson headed for the train to Tientsin. They agreed that Tuan alone, a good military man if nothing else, might save the government from being managed by an untutored rascal. At Tientsin they heard that the Mafoo general was also there, and Donald elected to call on him first.

Chang Hsun, although illiterate, spoke a fair brand of pidgin English, and when he opened the door, he exclaimed, pointing at Donald, "Here's that damnfool rebel again!" He laughed heartily at his own joke, and led them into the house.

Donald grinned, "I remember the first time you called me that."

Anderson looked interested, and Donald explained that it had happened in 1912, shortly after he had bargained the Mafoo's prize concubine against needed rolling stock. He had been on his way to Peking and had stopped off in Shantung to call on Chang Hsun, who was then living in a railway car. As Donald had neared it, the Mafoo had thrown open a window and shouted, "I know you! I know you! You're a damn rebel. I saw you outside Taiping Gate fooling with some guns." Donald said that he had expected a volley of shots, but instead the General had invited him in.

The Mafoo smiled in recollection, apparently unaware that Anderson had actually pulled the lanyards. Then Donald asked:

"Well, General, still paying your troops by the old means?"

"How's that?" Anderson inquired.

"The general is unique," said Donald. "He's got something like fourteen thousand troops, and he pays them off through poker. The officers play with the men and win their money. After that, the general and his wife play with the officers, and they win it all back. It's like a merry-go-round."

Anderson brought the conversation into the present. He asked what Chang Hsun thought of the republic after five years—the republic he had fought to hold off.

The Mafoo spat. "Ugh," he said, "all these people put me in mind of a gardener who tries to grow his cabbage with its roots up in the air. They're like people who want to get to the ceiling without anything to climb on." He paused, stroked his black, drooping mustache, squinted and added ominously, "The republic is like a porcelain shop. In the village, the old shop did all the business. Then came a new shop with some bright, cheap ware. In time, it all broke, and the people went back to the old shop."

Donald asked, "Oh, you think the emperor will be back on the throne?"

"Yes, he will," Chang answered belligerently. "I'll put him there."

The two friends made polite good-bys and then called on Tuan Chi-jui. They found him playing solitaire. He waved them leisurely to chairs.

"We've just talked to Chang Hsun," Donald began.

Tuan set a red jack on a black queen. "Yes?" he asked.

Donald studied Tuan for a while. Then he said, "We've come to ask you to return to Peking. We believe you're the only man to save a bad situation. If you don't, I'm afraid there's going to be a terrible collapse."

Tuan flipped up an ace. "There's only one thing that will make me return," he said, "and that is if anyone is foolish enough to put the boy emperor back on the throne. I'll fight whoever tries that."

"Well," said Donald, "we may expect you soon, then."

He and Anderson returned to Peking and several days later, on the night of June 29, two men, strangers to Peking for some time, arrived. One came in stealthily. He was Kang Yu-wei, the exile, long an advocate of a constitutional monarchy, the brilliant tutor of Emperor Kuang

Hsu, who had fled to Penang nineteen years before in the Dowager Empress-Yuan Shih-kai coup. Donald had interviewed him there in 1908. The other arrived in a sweep of glory. He was the Mafoo General, riding on streets spread with yellow earth—the badge of monarchy—and preceded by his fierce, mounted troops. That night the two met secretly.

Chang Hsun spent his first two days unsuccessfully in efforts to form a cabinet. The second night, July 1, he gave an elaborate dinner, attended by the upper crust of Chinese officialdom and their friends. Donald and Anderson were present. The dinner wore on through unending gourmet's delights and gallons of warm rice wine. Sometime after midnight, a red-faced, glassy-eyed official pinned the Mafoo general with something that resembled a leer.

"General," he said, a bit thickly, "you can't form a cabinet and you know it."

The Mafoo's big ears reddened. "I damn well could form one if the Manchus were here," he said. "I'd set one up in fifteen minutes."

"But," the taunter replied, "the Manchus aren't here."

A silence had come over the room when Chang Hsun made his first utterance. Now all eyes were on him.

He pushed back his chair and rose slowly. He emptied his wine cup. "Well," he declared loudly, "I'll fix that!" He motioned to several men, and then left the room.

Among those who followed him were the army chief of staff, the head of the gendarmery and the police chief. He commanded them to obtain from President Li a memorial asking for re-establishment of the monarchy. They obeyed, placed the President in protective custody, and the Republic of China came to an end. Then, with his troops, Chang Hsun headed for the Imperial City where the old Manchu royal family still lived. It was after 3:00 A.M. when he prostrated himself before the eleven-year-old ex-emperor, informing him that the entire nation demanded his return. He took the frightened Pu Yi to the great throne room. There, the Mafoo enthroned him in the presence of his retainers and members of the Imperial family who had been summoned from their beds.

The next day Peking woke to find the yellow dragon flag flying everywhere. Republican banners had been hauled down, and a wave of high excitement swept the city where the Manchus once had ruled for two hundred and fifty years. Before many hours, the story of the coup was out. Kang Yu-wei, the shrewd old plotter, had master-minded it. After his secret meeting with Chang Hsun two nights before, he had written the edicts, named a new set of nobility and charted a new course for an old empire.

But it was all over in ten days. That first morning, July 2, Tuan Chi-jui heard the news at Tientsin. He buttoned on his tunic, picked up his sword and drove to where the Eighth Division was encamped. Its officers readily turned over command to him and he marched swiftly on Peking, as he had promised. On July 12, the old Mafoo raised the white flag, and the monarchy was over. Tuan resumed his post as premier, and Li returned to the presidency. Little Pu Yi removed his imperial robes and went home to play.

Status quo returned to Peking, but not for long.

The movement for a war declaration was under way again, backed principally by provincial leaders. But Parliament, on whom the declaration depended, could not come to a decision. The militarists, headed by Tuan Chi-jui, applied increasing pressure and when this failed, they dissolved Parliament by force. With most of the parliamentarians scurrying irately to the South, the war lords then ousted the President, who had opposed them. Vice-President General Feng was installed, and on August 14, 1917, China took the big step and entered the war. Under British supervision, she began to send labor battalions to the Western Front. On the home front, she struck out with unprecedented resoluteness. She was displaying boldly her sovereignty. She seized German properties and commercial enterprises as well as German ships in her harbors.

China, the giant, at last had begun to yawn and to rub its eyes. It was beginning to peer beyond its own perimeter, beyond the short horizon.

chapter

17

THE GIANT STRETCHES

*Even a Buddha will get angry if
slapped in the face often enough*

THE BIG yawn toward an awakening which had begun in 1917 was
continuing. The old revolutionary spirit was stirring, and old forces
were reforming and reshaping, again under the banner of Sun Yat-sen.
Few men in history had had the persistency, the strength of purpose of
the indefatigable doctor. The little fighter's dreams, although often
detoured by their impracticality, had but one goal—the betterment of
China. He had begun his fight in the early 1890's. He was still at it.
Since his exile in 1913, he had not been idle. He had slipped back
into Shanghai late in 1915 and begun spadework for the constitutional
government that Yuan Shih-kai had destroyed. Yuan's death in 1916
opened the door for further activity, and in 1917, he and Madame
Sun went to Canton—the incubator of revolution. There, he established a provisional military government for South China with himself
as generalissimo, and later he was elected president by the rump
parliament that had gathered in the South after Tuan Chi-jui had
dissolved it prior to the 1917 war declaration.

In contrast to Donald's efforts in the North, he vigorously opposed
China's entry into the war. He insisted on first things first: A working
government for China. But his voice was lost in the war cry that swept
the country.

Before the year 1917 was at an end, the inevitable cliques of the
ambitious and the opportunists had fomented trouble and had wrested
control of the independent government from Sun. Disgusted, he re-

turned to Shanghai where he spent the next two years either assembling or having others assemble for him books which bore his name.

During this period, Donald devoted himself to his journalistic work and to Chinese factions, whether "ins" or "outs," whenever the opportunity to help China was presented. Shrewd in his premeditated advice, he was equally clever, often audaciously so, when a situation called for impromptu action. His genius for extemporaneous solutions of impossible problems was well illustrated by an incident that occurred in 1919 and that those concerned in never forgot. At that time he was interested in a proposed engineering project at Hong Kong. En route south, he visited Dr. Sun at Shanghai, where he read over some of the doctor's manuscripts, then continued on to Hong Kong and up the Pearl River to Canton. The military government that Sun had set up there was still functioning, with the old rebel, Dr. Wu Ting-fang, acting as foreign minister. When Donald walked into his office, Wu jumped up.

"God has brought you here!" he exclaimed.

"No such thing," Donald laughed. "I paid my way on railways and steamers."

"Well, you've come in time to help us," Wu announced. He explained that his little government was having trouble with the British colonial administration at Hong Kong. He had run up against the customary aloofness. They would not reply to communications and refused either to recognize or talk with any of his envoys.

"Worse than that," the little lawyer lamented, "they have some of our gunboats. They won't release them, and we need them badly. You must get them for us, Don."

Donald sat down at a typewriter. "That's easy," he said and asked for a telegraph form and several sheets of official paper. Wu stood by perplexedly as he typed a letter to the big New York firm of Stone and Webster, railroad and general contractors. Donald wrote, tongue in cheek, that negotiations he had been carrying on for them with the Canton military government for construction of a railway running out of Canton had been concluded and that Dr. Wu had decided to award them the contract. He then wrote out a telegram in similar phraseology.

When he finished, he said that he was going to take them to Mr. Montague Ede, at Hong Kong.

Wu studied him. "Ede?" he asked.

"Ede," Donald replied. "The head of the British combine, the Cassel Concession."

"Oh," said Dr. Wu, "the people that Peking gave a railway and mine development monopoly to in this province several years ago."

"That's right," Donald answered. "An agreement which your military government never got around to ratifying. Well, when Ede sees these communications I've written to his rivals, why, you'll get your gunboats quick enough. You'll get a lot of other matters settled—and you can lay a bet on that!"

As Donald entered Ede's office at Hong Kong the next day, Ede greeted him with:

"Merciful heavens—did God send you here?"

Donald remarked that he had heard a similar phrase at Canton the day before.

"Have you been at Canton!" the Britisher exclaimed. "God love you, that's just where I want you to go for me."

"Why do you want me to go to Canton?" Donald asked.

"The Cassel Concession is becoming a dead letter. Sun's out and Wu will do nothing. You're the only one who can help us."

Donald took the letter and telegram from his pocket and handed the telegram to Ede. "I was just on my way to send this."

Ede read it. "My God!" he yelled. "What's this?"

"Oh," Donald answered leisurely, "just a little business the American firm has been doing. When they get this wire, they'll send out a man and railway construction will go ahead."

Ede was agitated. He began to pace the floor.

"But," he blurted out after awhile, "that railway is the principal one under the Cassel Concession!"

"Is it?" Donald asked innocently. "That's too bad. If it is built by Americans, the British will lose it, won't they?" Donald joined Ede in his pacing, seemingly buried in deep thought. Then he halted and said magnanimously, "I'll tell you what I'll do. You have influence with the governor. You can take this telegram to him and tell him that if he sends his secretary, Mr. Fletcher, to Canton to settle a few questions and releases Canton's gunboats, I'll tear up this wire and letter. I must have an answer by three o'clock this afternoon, and Fletcher will have to go by tonight's boat. Otherwise, I'll not be able to convince Dr. Wu that he should cancel this arrangement."

Ede hurried off to see the governor, and before three he reported to Donald that the entire matter had been arranged. Donald tore up the telegram and letter and then wired Wu that all was well.

The next morning, he left for Peking, and shortly after he arrived there, two letters came from Dr. Wu. The first read:

CANTON, 25th April, 1919

DEAR MR. DONALD,

I, Ting-fang, the Minister of Foreign Affairs, deem the responsibility of this post to be rather exceedingly heavy. It is a great necessity for me to seek the assistance of the greatest brains of the age to bring China to a state of peace and prosperity. I have the honor to learn that you have come from an advanced nation and are interested in Chinese politics. Hereby, I request your Honor to be our Adviser and give us every possible assistance.

(Signed) WU TING-FANG

Donald's face lighted as he read it. His old friend had an odd way of tendering his honors. No one reading the letter would have guessed that eight years before they, without Dr. Sun, had run a revolution almost singlehandedly. Interested in Chinese politics, was he? Donald laughed and tore open the second letter.

In it, Wu told how Fletcher, accompanied by the British consul at Canton, had called on him and straightened out all points which the Hong Kong government previously had chosen to ignore. But Wu wound up by asking Donald to accomplish a matter which in the long history of British and other foreign relations with China had been beyond even bare consideration. Wu wanted a portion of the customs revenues diverted to the rebel Canton government!

Here was a difficult assignment, yet Donald had asked for it. The idea was born that day he had talked with Wu in Canton. Always the iconoclast, Donald was unconcerned with tradition.

Regarded as security for foreign loans, the monies of the customs had been held beyond the touch of any Chinese faction. Donald had heard the same old argument since he had landed in Hong Kong sixteen years before. When he called upon conservative, mild-tempered Sir Francis Aglen, the capable inspector-general for Chinese customs, he knew he was up against a system that countenanced no changes.

The Australian began by impressing upon the Britisher that times were changing in China. New ideas were being launched among a people to whom a gradual enlightenment was coming.

"Mark this, Sir Francis," Donald cautioned. "It will not be many years before China sets up an independence that will jar the old die-hards." The inspector listened attentively, returning Donald's steady gaze.

Donald continued, elaborating on how the followers of Dr. Sun would become paramount in time, for the growing generation would make them so. The time was to come when China would unite, would finish with civil wars and would begin a life of substantial quality and progress. He pointed out that the Canton government and Dr. Sun had claims for consideration, for they had opened the door for the changes and, since they would develop them, it might be prudent for the customs to assist. Otherwise, the end might be disastrous.

"Is it possible that you're suggesting that someday the customs might be piecemealed if I don't concur?" the Britisher asked, the thought plainly distasteful. "Is it possible that factions here and there might set up governments and run their own customs, paying no tributes to us?"

"Precisely," said Donald. "In this particular case, your refusal might incite the Cantonese to boycott the customs and establish their own collection bureau."

Sir Francis studied the thought for awhile, asked more questions, found ready and convincing answers, then finally agreed to recommend strongly that Donald's request be granted by the Powers.

Donald once more had paved the way for a breakup in the old order, but not without further struggle. The Powers had become accustomed to the smooth working of the customs, and, consequently, Britain and the United States made a show of force by landing troops at Canton. But Donald's backbone was stiff and so was Wu's, and with Aglen's support a compromise eventually was wrested from the

Powers. The rebel government at Canton received a share of the revenues collected in the area which it dominated—the rich provinces of Kwangtung and Kwangsi.

Dr. Sun was given credit for the victory, and his prestige among Chinese was heightened. Donald was content to see the honors go to his old friend whose sincerity and honesty were finding a widening appreciation.

In 1920 Sun was able to regain control of the southern government, and he and his wife returned to make plans for a northern expedition to unite all China. However, a revolt by one of his generals collapsed the expedition and in 1922 once more the Suns fled. With them went their stanchest lieutenant and secretary, Chiang Kai-shek. In Sun's long years of exile, Chiang had stood by him, planning and plotting, stirring up occasional and always abortive revolts.

From the north, Donald watched Sun's ups and downs, and from time to time he would send his old friend and many of his former revolutionary confederates advice and encouragement.

An inveterate letter writer, Donald's letters to his friends were filled with his observations and conclusions on Asiatic affairs, such as those currently upsetting China. His friends found his remarks clear, sound and picturesque. One recipient of such letters was Harold Hochschild who in 1921 had met Donald through Roy Anderson. They had become close friends before Hochschild left Peking. Donald wrote him at this time:

... The "great statesman" Sun Yat-sen is, to use an American colloquialism, "up against it." He is now not even liked by his fellow townsmen. The merchants have even shown hatred of him and his works, and the poor chap has left the city "to lead an army against the North." Sun is always leading an army against the North, but somehow it never seems to get very far on the way. He is now beset with many difficulties. He has no money and his followers are gradually falling away from him. It is high time that someone went to his assistance ... and poor old Sun is hanging midway between humiliation and utter and absolute collapse. ...

The peace conference that had followed the end of the World War failed to provide the fair play for which Donald had hoped. For China, the cards had been stacked. In payment for Japan's dubious assistance,

England, France and Italy had secretly agreed to recognize Japan's occupation of Shantung—the province China had hoped to regain—and to mandate to her all former German islands in the Pacific. Further, Japan said flatly she would refuse to enter the League of Nations if the promise was not kept, and President Wilson, anxious for the success of his dream, joined in the Versailles agreement. China's contribution in the war from a military standpoint, of course, had been relatively insignificant. Her labor troops had performed splendidly in trench digging, in barracks building in Europe, but there China's help on the battlefield had ended. However, she had rendered one service from which the Allies were to profit for many years to come. She had destroyed German and Austrian commercial interests within her borders, and the trade-hungry business houses of the United States, Great Britain, France and Italy had leaped into the gap.

Since she herself went without reward,[1] it is understandable why China's first excursion into world affairs left her perplexed and angry. Yet, from this indignation sprang the first signs of a solidifying national opinion.

When it became apparent that the Versailles conference was to ignore China's rights, Donald encouraged Young China leaders into vigorous demonstrations. These, however, were not of the terrorist variety engaged in by immature students, which gripped many sections of the country. China's delegates took notice and refused to sign the treaty.

A further factor in China's firm stand was a barrage of telegrams received by her delegation. In this, Donald showed how he could brush with humor the seriousness of his quiet, anonymous tutelage. He inspired nearly a hundred per cent of the telegraphed protests, and the manner in which he did it tempered his anger with a chuckle. George Bronson Rea, publisher of the *Far Eastern Review*, was in

---

[1] At the Washington Conference in 1922, China received her only reward—a doubtful one. She was given only what was originally hers, with a few minor exceptions. The nine Powers in conference at Washington pledged to respect China's independence and territorial integrity, and gradually to surrender their rights and privileges. Sufficient pressure was exerted on Japan to cause her to meet with China in a separate conference and negotiate the surrender of Shantung, keeping for herself a few mining concessions.

Versailles attending the peace conference. Donald had gone to Shanghai where the entire publication duties rested with him.

Under his editorship the *Review* had become an influential organ and because it had fought militantly for industrial, economic and social progress, the Chinese held it in high esteem. Rea had always concurred with him in his stand, but shortly after Rea's arrival at Versailles, Donald began receiving articles from him with a tenor never before used in the *Review*. They were strictly pro-Japanese, and in China what was pro-Japanese was, and always had been, anti-Chinese. Donald read the first one and tossed it aside. Others that followed beat with equal subtleness the drums for Japanese expansion in China. The whisper came back that Rea was listening to Japanese propaganda and was actually in their pay.[2]

While Rea listened, Donald, halfway around the world, made Young China's outcry heard—at Rea's expense. From leagues and guilds, from political and commercial associations came expressions of outrage. Years later, Rea, in his book, *The Case for Manchukuo*, referred to Donald as the cleverest propagandist to come to the Far East and told how the Australian had financed the flood of strong yet futile complaints. But Donald had paid for every telegram out of Rea's bank account.

Early in 1920, when Rea returned to Shanghai, Donald walked out with the same boldness, the same independence that sent him down the hill from the old *China Mail* many years before. He did it neatly and with point. When Rea and the *Review's* readers throughout Asia opened the current issue, they found in a bold-faced box on page one why Editor Donald was departing. Donald had written that the *Review's* publisher was pro-Japanese. He said that he took great pleasure in cleaning out his desk, putting on his hat and coat, and closing the door behind him.

Donald's part in encouraging China into the war might have put his reputation as a wise counselor in balance momentarily but, if so,

[2] The *Review* maintained a pro-Japanese policy throughout the twenties and thirties. Rea left it, however, in 1932 to become adviser to the Japanese puppet government in Manchukuo. In 1933, he pleaded the puppet state's case before the League of Nations. En route home to Manchuria, he died aboard ship.

his prestige was not to dangle long. There were some grumbles against him, but his prompt and forthright leaving of the *Review* restored in Chinese eyes what face he might have lost. His action, however, had not been taken for that purpose, for his bluntness was the antithesis of the urbanity of the East. He regarded face as rank pretense and hypocrisy, and he railed against it as one of the reasons for China's inefficiencies. There was another reason why the high regard for him continued. China's social students were beginning to conclude that the war effort had won a victory in one respect. It had made China take notice of the rest of the world. Having noticed, China was to struggle within herself for a better life.

The national opinion that was forming had begun to express itself through general dissatisfaction, in widespread strikes and anti-Japanese boycotts. The lowly laborer, the man-in-the-street, encouraged by young orators, halted his work. At the time, Donald saw the workers' attitude as a healthy sign. It contained the ingredients of a great national consciousness which, in time, he thought, might be capable of insisting upon better government and more wholesome practices.

Yet, the new era was to give rise to a "mad hatter" student movement, unmarked by the calm dignity for which Donald had worked. What was happening was the plug-in for the start of a strange renaissance.

The first blush of a national anger had come during the war, with Japan and the United States as its focal point. It had been aimed at the Lansing-Ishii agreement in which the United States, for reasons never fully explained, said that she recognized that Japan had "special interests in China, particularly in the part to which her possessions are contiguous." Dr. Reinsch, who had spent much energy in efforts to baffle Japan in her inroads on China, had not been told that Secretary Lansing and Japanese Foreign Minister Ishii were engaged in an exchange of notes. He had been further embarrassed when, either by accident or intent, he had learned of the agreement from the Japanese minister at Peking.

Shortly thereafter, the veteran American diplomat, humbled and perhaps more than a little cynical over American foreign policy, resigned on the pretense of ill-health and went home to America. He saw a job there. America needed an awakening. An indifferent public opinion had caused a repeated neglect of China, and he wanted America itself to quell, before it grew, a few spurts of anti-Americanism in China. When he left, two old friends, Chow Tzu-chi and Donald, accompanied him as far as Tientsin. The trio, as far as China was concerned, had had parallel purposes and now with one of them humiliated, the other two felt the hurt deeply.

For Young China, the first target in the unrest that followed the peace conference was the Anfu[3] Clique, backed by Japanese money. With customary craftiness, Tokyo had given China 320,000,000 yen ($160,000,000) under the guise of loans for railway, mining and industrial expansion. These were known as the Nishihara Loans and had been made during the war. They were never repaid. Actually, most of the money went into the Anfu Clique to promote pro-Japanese sentiment and to oust President Feng and elect a pro-Japanese president, Hsu Shih-chang, referred to derogatorily by Young China as "Old Susie."

Japan's continuous effort to keep China weakened served to sharpen Donald's watchfulness against all foreign designs aimed at the republic's finance and economy. There was no question now but that China was at her lowest ebb financially. After deductions from customs and salt receipts to cover foreign loan repayments, the revenue available to China for administrative purposes was far below the $128,000,000 Peking was spending each year. It was plain that China needed money, but China, stung once by the Consortium which Donald had opposed at the time of Yuan Shih-kai, was not seeking it at any price. However, the same group, led by a new member, America, flush with war money, was attempting to float a new loan.

The big entrepreneurs were retrieving their principal and interest in the first loan through the revenues of China's rich salt administration. Now they were up to a new scheme. Secretly, they hoped for a monopoly on all Chinese borrowings. This fact was carefully guarded, but, nonetheless, the Chinese had strong suspicions regarding the

[3] The name was formed from the "An" in Anhwei, the province of the army clique, and the "Fu" in Fukien, the province from which the navy drew most of its admirals.

Consortium's intentions. No high official in the awakening times of 1921 leaned toward giving any organization a monopoly.

Ever since the bankers had resumed their overtures in the late teens, Donald had waited patiently for an opportunity for some opening through which he might upset them. At the time of the 1913 loan, which he had accurately forecast would be used for Yuan's war chest, he had warned the British banker, Mr. Hillier, that a day of reckoning would come. Now the reckoning was at hand.

By 1921, grizzled, old Chow Tzu-chi, a master at stalling, had become the central target for the bankers. He was finance minister once more and one day when Donald was in his office, a secretary brought in a handful of cards.

"You have callers, Old Joe," Donald said. "I'll go."

But the minister motioned him to stay, and, assuming the visitors to be the usual swarm of Chinese after favors, Donald lazed away time discussing inconsequentials. When he left, he was surprised to find the waiting room crowded with foreigners, all of them members of the Consortium.

That evening he saw Old Joe and asked what the bankers had wanted.

"Oh, just what they always want—recognition of the Consortium," Chow said with a shrug. Donald replied that since it was plain the government wanted to shake off the leeches, as he called them, it could be done easily. He asked whether the Consortium had mentioned wanting a monopoly or wanting the land tax as security. Chow said the matters had not been brought up.

The next morning Donald typed a brief, to-the-point letter. It read:

DEAR SIRS:

Pursuant to your conversation of yesterday afternoon, I wish to place it on record that I will not be a party to fastening a financial monopoly upon China or do anything to hypothecate the land tax as security for loans.

He left a place for Chow's signature.

That afternoon Old Joe forwarded the letter, and Donald promptly tipped off Rodney Gilbert,[4] an old friend and reporter for the British-

[4] Now "Heptisax" of the New York *Herald Tribune*.

owned *North China Daily News* at Shanghai. He also gave the story to William Giles who, at Donald's instigation, had exposed the Twenty-one Demands in 1915 in the Chicago *Daily News.* Now he was correspondent for the influential Peking and Tientsin *Times.* As he had with Gilbert, he cautioned Giles to keep the source secret.

Chow's letter infuriated the bankers. The land tax or monopoly had never been mentioned to him! Immediately they began to discuss how to drive the finance minister from office. Their indignation mounted with the publication of the letter in the two leading British papers in China. For the next three or four days they argued, drafted and re-drafted replies. Cables went out to world capitals. Back came a flood of instructions and suggestions. The powerful bankers were out to eliminate an opponent. That opponent was Chow, with Donald in the shadows.

One night, I. Hodoroff, correspondent for the Russian Tass, the Soviet News Agency, phoned and said a bit breathlessly that he was worried over Donald's welfare. He said that the bankers were blaming Donald for the letter and were threatening privately to drive him from Peking. Donald laughed. Later that night, Giles called to report essentially the same story.

After advices from home offices had been sifted, the Consortium dispatched its reply to Chow. Nervously, they waited for an answer, but no acknowledgment came. On the fourth day, Donald dropped in on Old Joe and asked about the bankers' reply.

"I don't know," Chow remarked. "I haven't read it."

What a contrast to the Consortium's agitation! The letter had lain on his desk for four days, half buried in routine papers.

"For heaven's sake!" Donald said. "Send it to me. I'll draft an answer."

Old Joe lighted a cigar. "Why bother?" he said.

But that night the Consortium's letter arrived at Donald's house. He found that the bankers had gone to great lengths to say that they had not, at their meeting with the minister, mentioned a monopoly or the land tax. They said many other things, but Donald seized upon the first two assertions for his reply. He wrote, leaving a place for Chow's signature:

Dear Sirs:

The people of China will be grateful for your assurances that the Consortium, as I gather from the tenor of your letter to me, has no desire to impose a financial monopoly on China and does not wish the land tax as security for any loan that may be made. The people of China will appreciate this declaration so much that I will, with your approval, be glad to give the widest publicity to your letter.

That was the end. Donald's reply through Chow and the exposure in the press paralyzed the Consortium, and it went out of business. His warning to Mr. Hillier, eight years before, had been made good.

chapter

18

THE WAR LORDS

Man's life is like a candle in the wind,
or like the frost upon the tiles.

EVEN as China pivoted off an old course, Donald himself turned toward a new phase in a career that already was without parallel in the Orient. The new phase was to integrate the journalist even deeper with the history of China.

After he left the *Far Eastern Review*, he went with Anderson to Vladivostok. There they carried on negotiations for the Sinclair Oil Company with the then independent Far Eastern Republic which had been formed after the World War out of several former Russian provinces. On his return to Peking late in 1920, Donald prepared to quit the reactionary capital for the more liberal Shanghai. Reluctant to lose his advice, government officials offered him any one of a number of positions if he would stay, but he refused. In his seventeen years in China, he had never been a paid government official. He did not want to be one now, despite his strong desire to help.

One day shortly before he was to leave, wily old Chow Tzu-chi telephoned.

"Don," he said, "I've put through a plan that is something you've always wanted. You've been talking about the need for a statistical bureau. Here's your chance. I've arranged for the customs to earmark twenty thousand Chinese dollars for you each month. You'll have complete freedom to do what you wish with the money. The main thing is that we want you to stay in Peking."

Donald knew now that he would not leave. For years he had urged the Chinese to develop more and more statistical material. There was a dearth of available information. There were no records fathomable by the inquisitive, there was no down-to-earth data, no library of facts. Those who sought information had to find it for themselves, by tours, by guessing, by hit-and-miss.

Donald had tried to fill in the gap as editor of the *Review*. His leaving had not lessened his obsession with his objective. He had become convinced that China's salvation lay in economic modernization. Here, as Old Joe said, was the opportunity.

He accepted, and organized the Bureau of Economic Information, with himself as director. As such, he became a government official. Within a few weeks, the bureau began to hum with activity. Donald gathered about him a cosmopolitan staff. George E. Sokolsky,[1] a shrewd American, was the first recruit, followed by H. B. Elliston[2] a sharp young editor who had quit a Shanghai British-style newspaper after he found that it was supported by Japanese money. There were Chinese on the staff as well as a number of attractive and well-educated Eurasian girls. Step by step, they proceeded to shed light on unknown China in the form of statistical supplements, memoranda, weekly bulletins, books and a monthly journal Elliston established. The great organizational abilities of Donald now were in use, and the staff responded, as might a push button, to his direction.

Months rolled by, and Chow Tzu-chi watched in amazement. Talking to Roy Anderson one day, he remarked, smiling, "I give this damn fool Donald twenty thousand dollars a month and what does he do! I had intended it mainly as a reward for his many years of service to China. But I should have known better. Instead of spending it on himself as any good Chinese might have done, he actually sets up a bureau and is paying all salaries and operational costs. He has no personal ambition whatsoever."

From the time he started the bureau until he handed it over eight years later to a Chinese government that had burst up from the south, the gathering and disseminating of economic information, the making sense out of China for Chinese and foreigner alike, became a passion.

[1] Top-ranking American columnist.
[2] Editor, the Washington *Post*.

He put in long, busy hours at his office, inviting Chinese who dropped in to discuss matters other than economic to see him at home at night. There, up to the early hours, he wrote his newspaper dispatches. But before that, more often than not, he had spent hours counseling China's politicians and military-politicos. In these talks, he usually hewed close to one line: Cultivate a frame of mind to counteract China's multitude of political and social mistakes.

Throughout the years, the pattern of his social life had changed little. Under Peking's exhilarating influence, he had relaxed a little, but in the main the smug patter of the socialite, the Londoner-who-never-left-London continued to bore him. When Sir Miles Lampson,[3] after an absence of a few years, returned to China with his wife to assume the post of British minister, Lady Lampson said to Donald, "Now, let me see, what is there peculiar about you?"

"Have a look!" Donald smiled.

She studied him in amusement. "Oh, I know," she said. "You never go out to dinner. Now, will you go to dinner with us?"

He answered frankly, "Dear Lady, I will not go to an ordinary social dinner because it is a waste of time. I have no time to waste. But if you want me to come to dinner and there is somebody who wants to talk about China, then you tell me and I'll come. Otherwise, please don't ask because I won't."

As H. B. Elliston was later to write: "Few things happened in the China of the twenties—the so-called war lord era—that he had no hand in." Most of the episodes, too many to enumerate except for major ones, had to do with what Elliston aptly called "China's eternal triangle—two generals fighting whose plans were upset by the treachery of a third." In this period of in-again-out-again governments, Donald maintained his bureau in the face of several efforts to close it. When he finally gave it up, he did so with no regrets, for the bureau, despite Donald's best efforts, had stumbled against the customary great wall of petty politics and jealousies.

It was during these troublesome times, in November, 1921, that Lord Northcliffe, publisher of the London *Times*, arrived in Peking on a round-the-world trip. David Fraser was there at the time, and

[3] Became British high commissioner in Egypt, now Lord Killcarn.

the aggressive, ebullient man whom conservative British thought erratic, descended on both Fraser and Donald to learn about China, he told them, "in less than a fortnight."

Right off, he asked Donald to arrange an interview with President Hsu Shih-chang and the premier, a strange, uncommunicative little fellow named Chin Yun-peng. Donald accommodated, and as he and Northcliffe were motoring to the premier's after having called on "Old Susie," Donald asked the translator why he hadn't translated what the President had said.

Northcliffe looked surprised. "How do you know what the President said?" he asked. "You don't speak Chinese."

Donald smiled noncommittally, said nothing about having written beforehand the President's statement to Northcliffe.

Premier Chin was small and roundish with one crossed eye. He had a unique way of encouraging it back into focus—he smoked a cigarette in a holder that actually touched the toes of his shoes. When he looked at it and then looked at a caller, both eyes were in focus. Gradually, however, the eye would become errant again. Chin would look at the cigarette and then look up. But, in time, the eye would wander off obliquely, and the whole process had to be repeated.

Northcliffe waited until the premier had the eye in plumb before he said magnanimously, "Now, Mr. Premier, what can England do for China?"

Chin's eye slipped off, and he gazed for some time at the smoke of his cigarette curling about his toes. When he looked up, he said, "Lend us money." His eye crossed again. Later, Donald, laughing, related the story to Anderson, telling how those three cryptic words were all that Northcliffe ever got out of the premier.

The night before the publisher left, he had dinner at Anderson's house with Donald, Fraser and Elliston. In the course of conversation, he remarked that Fraser was planning to return to London and asked Donald to take over Fraser's position.

Donald's resentment over certain policies of the *Times* burst out. In years past, he had hoped for the opportunity that now was present. He said bluntly:

"Not on your life. I'm not going to act for the *Times* anymore. The *Times* is not an independent paper. It caters to Japan."

The publisher of London's illustrious Thunderer, which had always prided itself on its independence, was not prepared for the jolt. He demanded, "What do you mean?"

Donald explained that he had received several telegrams in 1915 during the time of the Twenty-one Demands, all of which indicated a pro-Japanese influence. Several years later he had flashed a story on Japan's intentions in the matter of the Nishihara Loans. But the dispatch was not printed. Instead, someone on the *Times* had cabled him, "Why attack an ally?"

Northcliffe, a man of action, shouted for a cable form and wrote out a message to Wickham Steed, who had risen to be editor, ordering him to fire whoever had rebuked Donald.

Donald went on to "lay down the law," as he put it, and the publisher listened attentively. Telling him in detail how the Anglo-Japanese Alliance was harmful to China in that it encouraged Japan, Donald insisted that the great influence of the paper be used to break the alliance. Further, for England's sake, the policy of the *Times* on the Far East should be altered. China's newly developing national patriotism henceforth would be more sensitive about just who were China's enemies and who were China's friends. The republic which England at one time had encouraged must be given a chance. Britain would have to understand that an awakening was at hand and that this awakening would have to be aided and abetted, not smothered.

In the end, Northcliffe said, "All right, all right," and asked Donald to write all the editorials on Far Eastern policy and cable them to London. Donald declined, and later when Anderson inquired why, he grinned: "I've got too much sense to do a lot of things."

Nevertheless, Donald believed that that night marked the beginning of the change in the policy of the *Times*. Although Northcliffe died shortly after his return to England, the *Times* began editorial pressure against the alliance that culminated in London's renunciation of it.

The war lord era, which extended from the time of Yuan Shih-kai's death in 1916 through 1927, was typical of the eruptions that China periodically subjected herself to. John Gunther, who came many years afterwards to survey the scene where turbulent warlordism had reigned, left with two unanswered questions. If the Chinese are pacifists, why did they have so many civil wars? If they were reasonable, why did they let war lords flourish?

The war lords who governed a single province or group of provinces, ruled despotically in defiance of Peking. They were armed political bosses, fighting among themselves and singly or in concert against the prevailing central government. When any faction seemed near to complete victory, Japan supported its opponents in order to prolong civil discord and keep China weak.

History was repeating itself in a normal way. The war lords were a modern counterpart of the fierce khans who centuries before had swept out of the North. The fall of every dynasty in the long history of China had been followed by a generation or more of civil war. What was happening now was the product of the Manchus' collapse and the wobbliness of its successor—the Republican government.

In the early twenties, Marshal Wu Pei-fu, Marshal Chang Tso-lin, General Feng Yu-hsiang and General Tsao Kun each cut blazing careers by fire and sword across China. Donald knew them all as friends. He met them in their military camps, in their offices when they had them, or in his home. But in none of them did he see any hope for China's salvation, and while he gave counsel when they asked, he found it impossible to take their programs seriously.

Chang Tso-lin, Manchuria's war lord, was one of the most powerful, a man whose finely chiseled features and delicate hands belied his ruthlessness. He had started as a guerrilla chieftain in the North and had been employed by Tokyo in the Russo-Japanese War to harass the Russians. Many believed him pro-Japanese, but Donald was certain that Chang was playing a clever game, milking what he could from them.

Tsao Kun was less colorful, but gargantuan six-foot four-inch Feng Yu-hsiang, known widely as the "Christian general," was one of Asia's most picturesque hell-raisers. Before each battle, he exhorted his troops with sermons, and they marched into the fray singing, "Onward Christian Soldiers."

With Wu Pei-fu, a carouser and heavy drinker, Donald, the tee-totaler, early struck up a unique friendship. Wu, with slightly reddish hair and light brown eyes, was a curious combination of scholar and warrior. Perhaps the least unselfish of those who fought for power, he made numerous but always fruitless efforts to stabilize China. Donald knew him as a man with many a strange notion, and Bertrand Russell, the British writer-economist, found this true in matters relating to battle. Noting that it was bad manners in China to attack an adversary in wet weather, Russell told how Wu did it and won a victory. The beaten general complained of the breach of etiquette. Wu went back to the position he had held before the battle and fought all over again on a sunny day!

Warlording got under way in earnest in 1920. In this year, Wu, Chang and Tsao marched into the capital to collect tribute from a Peking treasury already on the verge of collapse. They left only after President Hsu handed over nine million dollars which they divided among themselves. Before leaving, however, they performed one valu-able service. Guided by a national opinion that was being directed at the corrupt and pro-Japanese Anfu Clique, they drove it underground and jerked Tuan Chi-jui from the premiership. Tuan and the clique escaped in the usual Chinese manner—through the one city gate which adversaries always conveniently left open for this purpose.

Thus, for a time, Japanese agitation and maneuvering in influential circles was lessened.

Chang Tso-lin returned to his capital, Mukden, from where he set forth in 1922 to take over affairs in Peking. He met no resistance from "Old Susie," who was content to be a figurehead president, but from Wu's provincial capital came an order to Chang to dismiss his military rule. Chang ignored Wu, and civil war broke out.

As in other struggles in the war lord era, there was the *opéra bouffe* touch. Pekingites, Donald and Anderson among them, would drive out to watch a fierce cannonading in which the objective seemed more to outdo each other in noise than to inflict casualties.

One day, as Wu pushed closer, Donald, with customary casualness, walked through Chang's trenches and beyond into no man's land. He had decided to write an on-the-spot account for the *Times*. As he neared the Western Hills, Chang's forces were creeping up on Wu, while Wu's army was stealing toward Chang, with the hills as a screen.

Suddenly, the front flared into action, Donald's position became untenable and he withdrew quickly in the direction of an ancient temple that he had rented and made over into a home at Hengshan, in the former hunting park of Manchu royalty. He came upon a sunken road and noticing a number of stones in a line, he bent over to find they were holding down a telephone wire. It was too much for Donald. He picked it up and walked until it broke. In that instant, Chang's communications with his advancing front line were severed. Then he pulled until it broke once more and, winding up several hundred feet of wire, he tucked it in his raincoat sleeve and resumed his journey.

It was not long until he saw an officer galloping toward him. Donald halted and the officer drew up and began to sputter breathlessly in Chinese. When he finished, Donald used two of the several Chinese expressions he knew. He said, having recognized the officer as a Chang man: "Chang is *ding hao*" (very good) and "Wu is *bu hao*" (no good). The rider grinned and, with the inexplicableness of the East, rode off with no further interest in him.

When he reached his temple a few hours later, Donald put the wire into service on an electric bell.

That night, Chang's flank was turned, and he fell back hurriedly. He was still retreating the next morning. Wu began pursuit by train and Donald and Anderson boarded it at Fengtai station.

Wu greeted them warmly. "As you can see," he said, "I'm making short work of the old tufei. But I'm not sure yet whether it's a trick. The old bandit's line crumpled too fast to suit me."

Donald laughed and told how he had broken Chang's communications the night before. It was clear then to Wu why Chang had suddenly backtracked. He laughed and promised to visit Donald's temple to inspect his electric bell.

The train sped along for several stations until some of Wu's advance officers flagged it to a stop and reported that Chang's artillery was blocking the way at the next station.

"If his guns are really there," said Wu, "the old bandit will shoot our whiskers off if we try to go through."

Donald looked at Anderson. "Well, Admiral," he asked, "how about it?"

Perhaps Anderson, too, was thinking of that day in 1911 when they had charged a locomotive down the tracks toward Purple Mountain in search of guns. He stood up, and he and Donald went to see to the unhitching of the engine. But this time as they rattled away, they were only passengers. Two Chinese, an engineer and a fireman, did the work.

They pulled into the station and had just moved beyond when they saw the artillery pointed menacingly at them. The engineer braked his locomotive, and two of Chang's officers walked over, saw Anderson and Donald looking down at them and then turned and walked off, presumably to headquarters. On Donald's signal, the engineer backed off swiftly. No shots were fired. When they returned, Wu abandoned any thought of pushing on that day. But the next morning, Chang had withdrawn, and Wu's train moved on to Tientsin and to the Central Railway Station. There, they were told that two trains of troops belonging to Chang Tso-lin were at Tientsin's East Station but without locomotives for their retreat northward.

Donald looked for what, in the war game of capture or be captured, would be the normal and expected conduct of the victor. "Now you have a chance to take them prisoner," he told Wu.

"No," the marshal answered, "we don't want to capture the old tufei's army. We'll send them locomotives and let them go home."

Donald protested that Wu was saving them for another war, then studied the war lord with amusement. He knew his China and his Chinese enough to know that Wu was thinking of face, more important at times than rice for a hungry stomach. Wu was gambling against the time when he and his army might be in a similar fix. If and when he ever showed his posterior in retreat, Chang might be considerate of his face. Two years later Chang repaid the courtesy. He defeated Wu near Peking and accommodated with transportation for the marshal and his army.

Under the impact of war, the government of President Hsu Shih-chang wobbled, clung on only precariously. Several nights after the Tientsin affair, Anderson and Donald called on Chow Tzu-chi, now premier. While they talked, the phone rang, and when Chow returned, he was pale and nervous. "You know what that d-d-damn old d-d-drunk wants?" he stuttered in his excitement.

"What damn old drunk?" Donald asked.

"Wu P-P-Pei-fu," said Old Joe. "He's d-d-drunk up at P-P-Paotingfu. His aide says he's running around in his underwear. Anyway, he wants the three of us to go over to the p-p-palace and kick 'Old Susie' out."

"That's all right," said Donald. "He's pro-Japanese."

"B-B-But," Chow groaned, "that would make me p-p-president!"

"Fine," said Donald. "Let's go."

Sometime before midnight, the trio located President Hsu, but it was not until seven in the morning that he was properly convinced it was for his own welfare and that of China's to leave. They told him how Wu, in pyrotechnical language, had threatened to throw him out bodily if he did not depart peacefully.

Chow was sworn in immediately as acting president. When it was all over, Donald shook Old Joe's hand and said, "Congratulations, Mr. President!"

Chow grimaced. "Don't call me that b-b-bloody thing!" he said.

Marshal Wu settled down as overlord of the Peking government and, within the scope of his ability, sought to unite China. Convinced that Li Yuan-hung would be the most acceptable to all factions, Wu recalled him to the presidency. Chow Tzu-chi was happy to retire. Wu reconvened the old Parliament, and quiet came to Peking again for a few months.

Li lasted until September of the following year, 1923, when he was driven out by palace intrigues. At this time, General Tsao Kun, a supporter of Wu's, took over the presidency in what Donald regarded as the most dishonest election in the short history of China's republic. It was a practical lesson in the quick road to supremacy for the dictators of the Western world that were to follow. Donald knew that the war lord bought every single vote in the Parliament of more than seven hundred members. Wu, however, continued as the real power.

In September, 1924, Wu was unable to maintain peace, and a new civil war flared up north of Peking and in the Yangtze Valley. Donald was in the midst of it as an observer, a ready counselor to the participants, but more often than not just a good listener. He described the brewing storm to friends in the United States, Mr. and Mrs. N. Peter Rathvon. On October 1, he wrote from Peking:

. . . I had a talk with Wu Pei-fu the other day. He looks better than I have ever seen him. His eyes are clear, skin fresh and fit-looking, and no evidence of Shaoshing wine. . . . He is full of confidence, perhaps the valor of ignorance. He is to remove Parliament and have a new election, re-organize the administration, build more roads and railways, give peace and security to the people, make this and that. Great dreams are in the head of Wu for the consumption of those whose assistance, moral or practical, he now requires. But he believes it all.

They (Wu and Chang Tso-lin) are both going at it in a style different from the old Chinese methods. Now we have large forces being deployed, trench mortars, airplanes, gas and what not. A lot of hot air, too, and much fighting on paper. Each of the myriad of war lords writes manifestoes, and read separately each one is convincing. The Chinese are good at that kind of thing. . . .

By the end of the month the war had thrown up a characteristic Chinese picture and Donald wrote:

Now that the music of guns is in the air, and the city gates are closed, the wires cut, and food supplies are short, it seems like old times. Before, I felt lonely without the hullabaloo of alleged war. Now that the sounds are all about us and the Chinese people are rushing hither and hence and yon with their bales and boxes, looking for some place to deposit them safe from looters, things look amazingly better.

We are in stirring times. The Christian general, Feng Yu-hsiang, mistaking Judas for Christ, turned on his patron and erstwhile friend, Wu Pei-fu, while the latter was being jammed in a nasty corner (fighing Chang Tso-lin) at Shanhaikwan, and has just about pushed him out of business as a war lord. My old amah the other day said: "Mastah, I blong Chlistian. Feng Yu-hsiang also blong Chlistian." "Yes," I replied, "a peach!" She continued, "Before he go fight for Wu Pei-fu, now he run back Peking, fight against Wu Pei-fu. Mastah, this Chlist pidgin no blong ploper."

Feng told me a few days ago (I saw him at his headquarters to the north of the city) that he was a real patriot and was for peace and the safety of the people. . . . His henchman (C. T. Wang) told me this morning that they were bound to win and that it was only a matter of days when the flight or suicide of Wu would be chronicled. It is, of course, impossible to say whether the claim of the Feng aide is right or not, but this can be said: The Christian converts have shown up rottenly and are as treacherous as no pagan could be. . . . When Wu bobbed up in Peking a few days after Feng's defection, no one was more surprised than the amiable Feng. Wu was directed to go to Chinese Turkestan or Kansu as Wastelands commissioner. Wu replied that since he was not capable of holding such a position, he thought that Feng ought to be appointed commissioner while he would be glad to act as No. 2. . . .

Feng assumed the political boss-ship of the government and invited Sun Yat-sen, president of the rival southern government, to confer with him in the North. Ailing in health now, but anxious to complete his dream of organization and peace, Sun arrived at the end of December, 1924. The trip had been a strenuous one since he had spent more than a month in speechmaking along the way. Shortly after he arrived, the little doctor collapsed. He was taken to the Rockefeller Hospital of the Peking Union Medical College where doctors discovered that he was dying of cancer of the liver.

For Donald, sad days were ahead. He was the recluse with a thousand friends, but only a handful were close. Now death was to step in to whittle down the number of the select few.

In February, 1925, Chow Tzu-chi returned to Peking after an extended tour in southern Asia. At Hong Kong, a British doctor had discovered an abscess in his groin and advised that it be lanced immediately, but instead Old Joe had continued his trip north.

The day he arrived was cold and raw. His two old friends were at the station to meet him. Donald was dressed warmly, but Anderson, as indifferent as Donald was particular, was without even a light overcoat. Donald warned him about his carelessness.

Finding Chow gravely ill, they had P.U.M.C. doctors lance the abscess immediately, but in a few days the old fellow grew worse. It was then that Donald found that Chow's No. 1 concubine, who dominated his household, had persuaded him to forego foreign treatment in favor of native herb doctors. Donald reprimanded the concubine and once more brought in the Rockefeller specialists. That night, he returned to his hunting park temple and phoned Anderson to learn that he was confined to his bed with a cold and fever. In the early hours of the next morning, Donald was advised that Old Joe wanted to see him. He arrived in the city just as the big wall gates were being swung open. At the house the concubine met him before he reached Chow's room. She announced sourly that the "Master" desired to dismiss the foreign doctors but wanted Donald's permission.

When Donald walked in, his old friend smiled weakly. "Don," he said, "I'm in the hands of Buddha."

"Do you believe in Buddha?"

Standing by his bed, Donald waited for the answer. "Yes," Chow said slowly, "I do."

"All right," Donald whispered. "I'll go out to the Sleeping Buddha Temple and have a service said for you."

Donald, the man whose religion defied a label, went. Buddhist, Christian or Confucian, no matter, he respected the religion of others. When missionaries would ask him to say grace, he would answer quietly, with a hardly perceptible twinkle, "I always say silent grace."

When he returned to Chow, he brought a box of cigars with him, and the two old friends who together had witnessed China's ups and downs for more than a decade sat and smoked and only occasionally did they exchange a few words. At last, when Donald rose to go, Chow whispered faintly, "You take the cigars, Don. I don't think I'll want any more."

Not many hours later, Old Joe died. Donald learned of it the next morning from Chow's nephew. He said that after Donald left, the concubine had persuaded the family to telegraph priests in a temple in Shantung Province for instructions. She had said there was a spirit there which could heal those whom doctors could not help. The priests replied that the spirit would come to Peking and that a table should be laid with a clean cloth. A crystal bowl filled with water would have to be placed in its center, and the family was to group around until they saw something drop into it. This they had done and when the concubine announced that the "something" had fallen, they followed out the priests' instructions and forced Old Joe to drink all the water. He had died a few minutes later.

That day, Donald called on Anderson to tell him of Chow's death.

As he arrived, he met him walking out of the door, wrapped in a big blanket. The American was pale and haggard.

"Pneumonia," he whispered. "I'm going to the French Hospital.

Donald accompanied him there, and then hearing that Sun was in a sinking condition, he hurried to P.U.M.C. He found the little man holding on grimly, and after chatting awhile, he promised to call the following day. In the morning—the morning of March 12, 1925—he telephoned Sun's hospital only to find that he had been moved to the home of Dr. Wellington Koo. Sun was dying. Hurriedly, he checked by phone at the French Hospital. Anderson had been asking for him. Doctors held out little hope.

Donald stood for a moment in reflection. Two friends were slipping away. For fourteen years, Anderson had been with him, helping mastermind civil wars, assisting in the never-ending tangle of politics. They had ·been the go-betweens for the war lords who could always trust them but could not trust each other. There was the picture, too, of Sun, kind, patient, humble, standing with General Homer Lea before a weak and flickering fire on a damp December day. There was Nanking and the memory of Sun and himself grappling with the mountainous problems of the young republic.

His two old friends were now on deathbeds only a short distance apart. Sun would have grouped about him friends and anguished members of his family. And at Anderson's bed? Perhaps no one. Perhaps the hospital might not have had time to inform friends. He hurried to Anderson.

There was no boyish smile now. Donald saw a face that had suddenly grown old, as tired and as weary as those of the people among whom Anderson had always lived. Anderson said, "Don, I'm finished. I can't live. I know it."

Donald forced a smile. "Admiral, do you mean to tell me you're giving up before old Doc Sun?" he asked. "Why, the doc is still alive and you say you're passing out? Nonsense!"

Anderson was quiet for awhile. Then he said, "I hate to go. I hate to go. Everything is so unfinished." His breathing was hard. Then he went on, "We've failed, Don. We were never able to do what we tried to in this country." Donald sat beside his bed, nodding in agreement.

Shortly, Anderson's breathing became labored. Donald called in a doctor who made an effort to bleed him. It was a race against time to relieve pressure on Anderson's lungs. Through fading eyes, the sick man watched the struggle. The blood was sluggish. It appeared almost congealed. Anderson moaned, "That finishes me." He lost consciousness and died within minutes.

For awhile, Donald stood by the bed, tears running down his cheeks, and then he walked slowly away, out of the hospital and to the home of Dr. Koo. There he found a number of Sun's close friends, his wife, his daughter and son, Sun Fo, standing in hushed silence around the bed. The little doctor's face was tired. The one-time pudgy fingers were thin and bony. He was breathing his last.

An hour after Anderson died, the spirit of the man who was to become China's patron saint hurried after him.[4]

[4] Sun's memory was perpetuated by an elaborate mausoleum, reached by tiers of glittering-white steps, high on Purple Mountain where in 1911 the decisive battle for Nanking was fought. The honor grew partially out of the Kuomintang's realization of its great political value. For Anderson, foreign and Chinese friends subscribed for the erection of a monument at his grave in Peking.

chapter

19

TRIUMPH BY CHIANG

*Though the left hand conquer the right,
what advantage is gained?*

⁂

THE summer of 1925 marked the beginning of a new confusion in China, of intrigues, procrastination by the Powers against the inevitability of change, and a war of ideologies—the end of which even now cannot be measured.

There were several factors in the confusion. Communism, with its glib slogans and intoxicating effects, had come, inflaming China's old ailment, erraticism. Sun Yat-sen was dead, and the work he had tried to do was unfinished. According to Russia, jealous of the century and a half of British, French and American hegemony in China, China's revolution had yet to come. The second generation of revolutionaries was left Sun's will which commanded China to awaken and align herself in a common struggle with those who treated her as an equal and to attend to the abolition of all unequal treaties. Sun asked the people to dedicate themselves to national reconstruction and to his Three Principles of the People.[1] Wang Ching-wei, one of the early members of the Kuomintang and a participant in the 1911 revolution, was given credit by some for the writing of the will but others held that the hand of Donald could be detected.

Inherited, too, was a spreading hero worship for Dr. Sun. Yet, more significant than anything else, was the largess of communistic influence he bequeathed to China. In the year before he died, he had faced his

[1] Nationalism, Democracy and Livelihood.

238

southern faction toward the left and toward Russia.[2] Even then, however, he had made an effort to persuade Western nations, through the United States, to send advisers to educate Chinese in legislative reform. Failing, he had embraced Russian ideals more than ever. Because Russia who, like China, had ended her monarchy with a revolution, had gained unity through a one-party government, Sun believed China might do the same thing.

He had sent to Russia for Michael Borodin, a clever Soviet political strategist, to help in the reorganization of the Kuomintang along Soviet lines. Borodin had arrived with spectacular ideas, together with funds fed through the Soviet Embassy. He was followed by numerous Russian military advisers among whom was General Galen who became a technical expert for the army being trained by Chiang Kai-shek. At about this time, Chiang, who was president of the Whampoa Military Academy, left for Moscow to study Russian military methods.

As a symbol of friendship, Russia had renounced its extraterritorial rights handed down from czarist days. New credit was given to Sun for this, and his and the prestige of Soviet Russia continued in ascent. Borodin capitalized on it with a whirlwind campaign of "political education" among students principally, and from north to south cries echoed "Down with the Imperialists!" "Down with the British!" and "Down with unequal treaties!" In Peking, twenty thousand students marched in demonstrations. It was champagne for Russian Marxists and heady business for Chinese agitators. Each of the demonstrators was given twenty cents, so whether they were sentimentally in accord or not, it was profitable.

As the wind of Russian propaganda increased, the windows of capital began to rattle in the big cities. At Shanghai, a strike took place at several Japanese mills, and students took up the cudgel. On May 30, a British police sergeant ordered a crowd of student demonstrators

[2] However, the orientation of Dr. Sun's party toward the Marxist doctrine would have been far more complete if it had not been for Sun's reading of a little-known volume, by a Russian-born New York dentist, Maurice William, entitled *The Social Interpretation of History*. Dr. William, an ex-Marxist himself, argued so persuasively against Marxism that Dr. Sun was influenced to abandon his favorable attitude toward communism in the later lectures of a series delivered in Canton and Peking just prior to his death.

fired on, killing and wounding a number. The city retaliated with a general strike. At Canton, the infamy was added to when British and French troops fired at strike sympathizers—and more students died. The clamor of the abolition of extraterritoriality, of inequalities grew, and the China coast blazed with hatred for the foreigner.

Communism's supporters passed over no opportunities to discredit the Westerner. Missionaries were singled out early as special targets. Throughout cities in South and Central China posters appeared bearing such inscriptions as: "Christ was British because he was born in Jerusalem, and Palestine is a British Protectorate." Commenting on the posters, Donald wrote to a friend: "How will the American missionaries and others who claim some acquaintance with Him feel about that?"

From the North, he looked on skeptically. A respecter of democracy, he had little respect for the Soviet oligarchal government. He wanted changes, but he did not want to see them accomplished through violence. He wanted China to dispose of her problems with calm, dignity and intelligence. But it was plain that the changes were not to come that way.

His mounting distaste for the situation was expressed in a letter to his American friends, the Rathvons, on July 7, 1925:

We are still in the throes of the student movement. Strikes of workmen go on at Shanghai, Hankow and Hong Kong. Agitators are thriving on the proceeds of subscriptions, but the workers are getting tired of pulling their belts in. They are the ones who are losing, while the merchant classes are getting into bad financial troubles, and many will go bankrupt. It is curious that men have not the courage to tell the schoolboys to go to the devil. The boys by yelling and by threatening to kill, burn, destroy are dominating everything—even the officials. Never did such an extraordinary condition of things exist. It can only exist in a country where courage has oozed out completely and where no real man exists with the capacity to direct the mob to a sane understanding of things.

War is wanted with Great Britain. The curious thing is that the Chinese believe they could fight anyone and defeat them. The valor of ignorance, of course. It is pathetic to a degree. There is so much misdirected energy and enthusiasm, and misdirection is so easy, that one despairs of anything worth while ever arising out of it all. The foreign nations will have to revise their notions, nevertheless, that is certain, and maybe they will do so. We have

been drifting along for years with certain ideas of privileges remaining un-
altered until we have come to accept them as unalterable. The time has
really come when a change must be made. . . .

The disorderliness grew. The Powers, as a man who might look up
quickly at the bang of a door, took heed. They acted to meet the
demands of China, voiced first at the Versailles conference. There, she
had asked for a consideration of the unequal treaties but she had been
out of order, for the request was beyond the province of the peace
conference.

China had requested full sovereignty. She defined it as (1) control
over the public finances, both as to the raising of funds and as to their
expenditure, and (2) unquestioned authority over the people and
property within her jurisdiction. In these two matters, China was conspicuously limited. The fiscal limitations under which she labored
were severe. She was without the right to decide tariffs either to secure
revenue or to protect native industries. By treaty, first with Britain
following the Opium War, but made universal by the most-favored-
nation clauses, China had entered into unilateral agreements to charge
no more than five per cent ad valorem on exports and imports. The
sacrifice of this authority had not brought her reciprocal advantages.
Goods from China were charged any amount the importing country
desired. China's customs, as well as salt revenues, collected under the
supervision of foreign inspectors-general, were applied first to the retirement of foreign loans which, by 1925, had mounted to more than a
billion United States dollars. Therefore, only the surplus from these
two lucrative sources was available to the government.

The second matter in which China was deficient was her lack of
jurisdiction over most foreigners within her borders. Their extraterritorial privileges barred the way. Many saw these privileges as harmful to Chinese dignity and sovereignty. Yet for Chinese capital, which
sought refuge from warlordism, banditry and fantastic taxation, for
foreigners who wanted protection from like evils, for politicians who
would escape the assassin, for scalawags, foreign and Chinese, extraterritoriality was a cool bench in a shady park. It gave to such cities
as Shanghai, Tientsin and smaller areas the opportunity to erect unmo-
lested fine schools and hospitals, modern buildings and shops, livable

residental areas where honest effort at sanitation was made. From such environment, Chinese could not help but benefit. While Donald did not share the average foreigner's opinion on the right of the foreigner to operate his own courts, police, armed militia, military and naval forces, neither did he favor the precipitate action Communists and antiforeign elements now were demanding. He knew that China, so often impatient where patience was needed, would have to walk slowly and cautiously, even as he knew that the Powers would sooner or later retreat in identical fashion.

Now the Powers met the present clamor by calling a conference at Peking to study customs revisions in addition to the question of granting China complete tariff autonomy. The conference was set for October, 1925, and was to be followed by a meeting of the Powers[3] to consider renunciation of their extraterritorial privileges.

Members of the various commissions to the two conferences began to gather early for preliminary study. Among the first was the American delegate, Silas H. Strawn, a sharp, capable Chicago lawyer, and his wife. Like many another visiting notable, Strawn held a letter of introduction to Donald. They became fast friends, and in the conferences that were to follow, Strawn time and again was to draw upon Donald's knowledge of China's problems.

The fury of China's masses had mounted. Donald felt a deep concern for what he knew would be the inevitable Chinese vengeance if conciliatory steps were not taken by the Powers. At dinner one night, he was seated next to the chairman of the British commission. He remarked that disagreeable events were on their way but could be avoided if the British government would take certain steps.

"If not," Donald warned, "the Chinese will strike back with a vicious boycott on all your goods."

The Britisher looked at Donald with a lack of warmth and remarked that his observations did not support such a view. But Donald's tenacity when he was certain of his own rightness was not brushed aside so easily. The next morning he wrote the chairman a letter pointing out

[3] Treaty rights were held by Belgium, Brazil, Denmark, France, Great Britain, Italy, Japan, The Netherlands, Norway, Peru, Portugal, Spain, Switzerland and the United States.

that if London would say to China, "We are willing not only to inquire into but also to talk frankly with you about unequal treaties," the storm that was gathering against the British, encouraged by the Russians, would cease. Later, in reply, Donald was invited to the British Legation where he was confronted by the entire British commission. He explained in detail his certainty that Britain faced a disastrous blow to her trade in China.

The British imperialistic mind, comfortable in the rightness of benevolent autocracy, weighed the thought. After awhile the chairman suggested that the problem might dissolve if nothing at all was done.

Donald blazed: "If you do nothing, then the inevitable will happen! Britain cannot help but lose politically!"

He went home, irritated, but he did not give up. He addressed another letter to the commission, repeating that calamity was certain if the British failed to yield—that concessions would be lost as well as prestige and trade. The commission once again ignored the warning.

Before the customs conference could convene, the typhoon of anti-British sentiment rolled across China leaving an almost iron-tight boycott in its wake. It lasted fifteen months. More than a million Chinese dollars was lost every day in Hong Kong alone, and London was forced to extend a credit of three million pounds to save merchants from collapse. By early August, only twenty per cent of British trade in Shanghai remained, and bit by bit it, too, disappeared. Russian agitators and their Chinese cat's-paws were in an orgy of delight. In the months ahead, violence and threats of violence were to cause Britain to relinquish her concessions at Hankow, Kiukiang, Amoy and in a number of other cities. Donald had been right.

Years later, in recounting the stormy period in a letter to a friend, he wrote, "One of the features of the British attitude in China always was that they never could be told anything by anyone on the outside. They were never ready to learn and, as usual, they bundered on to many disastrous climaxes."

He went on to cite another example in the myopia of British diplomacy. The fifteen-month-old boycott had hardly ended when, in September, 1926, the British gunboat *Cockshafer* came under fire of Chinese shore batteries while rescuing several Britishers trapped on a steamer at the Yangtze port of Wanhsien. The *Cockshafer* returned the fire, and the Chinese immediately circulated the rumor that British guns had killed thirty thousand townspeople and had destroyed three or four million dollars in property. A local boycott against British trade promptly developed and continued for nearly two years. It came to a halt then only because Donald prevailed upon his old friend, Marshal Wu Pei-fu, who had retired to rule Szechwan Province,[4] to call it to a halt. He convinced Wu that the claims concerning British destruction of life and property had been ridiculously exaggerated. When the boycott ended and agreements were made to resume trade, the British ordered a ship to sail for Wanhsien. After it arrived, the Chinese gave it an indignant look and put the boycott back into effect. The British had rubbed salt into an old wound. They had sent the *Cockshafer*!

The two conferences had brought no immediate results. Throughout the months of deliberation, the delegates looked upon China as a problem child. They recognized one thing alone—China's state of disrepair in the absence of a strong and authoritative government, the presence of banditry, civil wars and rule by war lords.

Yet, as Donald had warned so many times, the roadblocks against changes could not be maintained for long. Four years after the conference, in 1929, after a new and stabler Chinese government had been established, the United States, Great Britain and ten other nations recognized, in theory, China's complete tariff autonomy. (In theory, because China went on paying thirty per cent of her customs revenues —about sixty per cent of her total national income—toward retirement of her debt to foreign bankers.) Left untouched, however, was the raw spot of extraterritoriality.[5]

By the spring of 1926, Canton, the old springboard for revolt, was getting ready to catapult a new force back into an old fight. The Red-indoctrinated Kuomintang placed Chiang Kai-shek in command of the Nationalist army and left the job of unifying China to him. T. V. Soong, a brilliant financial student, had returned from Harvard and

[4] At the start of the Sino-Japanese War in 1937, Wu was in Peiping (Peking) and there he repeatedly frustrated Japanese efforts to make him a puppet. Later, he was afflicted by an ulcerated tooth and, under the care of Japanese and German physicians, he died.

[5] Abolished nearly two decades later by the Powers as a gesture of friendship in the midst of World War II.

had become minister of finance in the southern government. Dr. H. H. Kung was minister of industry. There, too, was twenty-seven-year-old Mei-ling Soong, youngest sister of "T.V." and of Madame Kung. The forty-year-old Chiang began to court her. At first she seemed distant, but he was determined to marry her.

Politically, Chiang was also having his troubles. The old associate of Sun's, Dr. Hu Han-min, the foreign minister, had been driven away when Chiang had begun to fear his influence. Wang Ching-wei, the slight, handsome poet around whom violence always seemed to center, had been elevated through Sun's wishes to political leader. But if Chiang had feared Hu who had been on the right, he eyed Wang, the leftist, and the shadow of Borodin, no less anxiously. There was the uncomfortable feeling that the price for Soviet friendship had not yet been paid.

The southerners took inventory of their political and military stock pile and, on the advice of the Russians, announced that their reshuffled government was representative of all China. All the while, the vaudeville of government had gone on in the North. But in Canton, fighting spirit was high, and in June, the northern expedition to unify the country began.

Chiang found the way had been paved in the initial stages of the campaign. Many a petty war lord was ready and waiting to welcome the southerners. Everywhere the cry of antiforeignism was heard, for the Borodin brand of propaganda found eager voices and attentive ears. As the movement, with Soviet strategists riding its fringes, progressed north, a representative of M. Karakhan, the Russian ambassador to China, called at Donald's office in the Bureau of Economic Information to inquire hazily about some elementary matters. The call was indicative of the esteem in which he was held even by those to whom he was an antagonist. It turned out that Mr. Karakhan wanted to see Donald, whom he knew of as a keen observer, although no friend of communism. Like so many Russians, however, his approach had been Oriental and indirect.

Donald was asked almost apologetically if he would be willing to visit the Soviet Embassy. He laughed, said he would, and the next day he had tea with the tall, suave, immaculately dressed Red diplomat.

Karakhan eyed him sharply, but seemed friendly. He tugged at his black goatee. He was the man through whom Borodin had received his funds and the encouragement to continue inflaming reckless mass demonstrations by students. Because of this, Donald had been instrumental in urging Peking newspapers to attack him and insist upon his withdrawal. He wondered whether Karakhan would allude to this. The diplomat asked, however, what the opinion was of Russian efforts in China.

Donald, concise neither in writing nor talking, and who bristled always under interruption, took three hours to answer the question from both the foreign and Chinese points of view. In his estimation, the Russians had failed.

"You've got every door shut against you," he explained. "If you've got every door shut, there is failure. You've antagonized the world. How can you expect to win in China or any place else?"

Karakhan's handsome face was inscrutable. He inserted a long cigarette into a paper holder and lit it.

Donald went on, "The failure will be emphasized as soon as your people get to a position where they must direct the Chinese armies if they want to succeed in sovietizing China. There is the rub. There is where you are blind. You will find this out at the precise moment you begin to dictate to the Chinese. They will not stand for foreign dictation."

The ambassador said: "It is not true."

"Well," Donald grinned, "the time will come when you will be kicked out of China."

"Ah," Karakhan put in, "the Imperialists will be kicked out before us. Anyway, we have no commercial stake in China. We have nothing to lose."

"Wait and see," said Donald. "Wait and see who gets kicked out first."

Later he was in Shanghai. Karakhan was there preparing to leave for Moscow, unaware that he was going home to be shot as a Trotskyite. His mission in China was over, although the extent of his failure was not yet apparent. On the day before he left, Donald was having tiffin with the wife of the British consul-general at Shanghai and remarked that he had visited Karakhan that morning.

The British woman, known for her insatiable curiosity, said at once that she would like to meet a Bolshevik, and asked Donald to fix it for her.

Donald listened in amusement. He answered, "For you to meet Karakhan would create consternation in Shanghai and international complications. It might cause your husband to lose his post. Don't you realize that under cover Russia is your enemy, that she's trying to drive you out of China?"

Nevertheless, the woman insisted, and when her husband, the consul-general, joined them, she told him what she had asked Donald. He paled and then protested with an air of futility. Donald left and walked over to the Soviet Consulate where Karakhan, eying him a bit skeptically, agreed to have ice cream that evening with an "interested lady." He did not ask who it was.

At the introduction, Karakhan revealed his astonishment only by a slight raising of his eyebrows. After she had chatted animatedly for a while, she arose to go. Donald escorted her to the British Consulate and then returned to Karakhan.

"My God!" the ambassador exclaimed. "Was that all she wanted to do—just look at a Bolshevik!"

"Exactly," Donald grinned.

Karakhan chuckled.

Donald knew that he did not have to ask the Russian to forget the incident, although he was aware that the diplomat realized he could have ruined them by simply supplying the Tass news service with a paragraph stating that the wife of the British consul had called at the Soviet Consulate. Karakhan kept the secret. People did things like that for Donald.

As the Chiang Kai-shek forces moved up toward the Yangtze Valley, Peking sought to fight its way out of its customary confusion. In the far North, Russia and Japan were up to their old trick of pressing against each other, the situation having a direct relation to developments in the Peking area. There, Chang Tso-lin, financed by Japan, had combined with Wu Pei-fu, double-crossed several years before by Feng Yu-hsiang, to drive Feng northward into Mongolia. Feng had had Russian support. The victors prepared to meet the advancing army of

Chiang Kai-shek, the man whom Donald had known only casually for the last fifteen years and whose program he was not yet ready to endorse.

Both war lords had men aplenty, but what was needed was money. Then, as if the government did not quite understand what Donald stood for, as if it suddenly confused his pro-Chinaism with willingness to be a tool, it turned to him.

The minister of finance had sought to borrow seven million dollars from customs receipts to finance the fight against Chiang Kai-shek. Sir Francis Aglen had said no, there would be no loans for purposes of civil war. The minister decided that the way to the funds was to push Aglen from his generalship of the customs.

One night the minister of the interior called on Donald and began a discussion of the possibility of removing Aglen. Donald protested, arguing that any effort to remove him or what he stood for might bring disaster. He said flatly that the customs stood as security for foreign loans and that their safeguarding was of paramount importance to China's world position. The minister then announced that it had been decided to confer upon him the most important office a foreigner might hold in China.

"The minister of finance," he said, "has instructed me to invite you to take over Aglen's post. It pays nine thousand dollars a month plus your house and servants, you know."

Donald laughed and answered that there wasn't enough money in China to make him accept.

Still thinking it a joke, he later hailed Sir Francis with:

"Who do you think is to be your successor?"

Aglen answered slowly, "I don't know."

"Well," Donald laughed, "they're going to appoint me."

He waited for Aglen to smile, but the inspector's eyes were hard.

"I hope you enjoy the job," he said icily.

Donald's jokes did not often backfire, but this one had. He retreated and called on Teddy Edwards, chief secretary of the cusoms. Since Donald refused to take the minister's suggestion seriously, they joked about the fantastic changes Donald would make when he took over.

He next called on the finance minister to emphasize his refusal.

"Oh," the minister said, "let's not bother about Aglen and the customs. I have a far better plan. China now wants to make you head of the salt administration."

"What!" Donald exclaimed. The situation was almost incredible. Within twenty-four hours he had been offered the two most lucrative, most coveted positions in China. He looked at the minister with the sort of eyes that see through people and things. He could read his mind, small, petty, twisted and corrupt.

He laughed, then said seriously, "There's a point you may have forgotten. The British Legation has the option on the appointment of the head of the salt administration. Sir Ernest Wilton, you know, is the present head."

"Let's not bother about him. He's visiting in London. You're a British subject and you're qualified to take the position. Once in, you might find it competent for us to secure a loan from the salt administration's surplus."

Donald reminded the minister that there had been no surplus for several years. He left after refusing to accept the appointment. Chinese officials insisted, however, that he take one or the other of the posts, and sent him a scroll several yards long decorated with seals and red ribbons. It commanded Donald to appear at the salt administration the following day to be inaugurated. When he showed it to Aglen, whose pride was now scorched, the Britisher eyed it solemnly.

"Good Lord!" he groaned. "You'll have a bit of trouble with our government. Britain will not like this."

Donald tossed the document aside and snapped, "What's Britain got to do with this? I don't care what the British minister says. I'm resisting because I will not be made a tool of by anyone."

Aglen looked horrified, and Donald remarked that if the British minister made any objection, he might take the job in spite of him.

The next morning, Donald, of course, did not appear at the salt administration. Flowers had been set on the desk he was to have occupied, and the minister's deputy hovered near—just in case. But Donald was somewhere off in the Western Hills, riding his favorite horse.

By late August, 1926, the trained, well-equipped army of Chiang Kai-shek had seized a portion of the Yangtze Valley, and the Nationalist government had been moved from Canton to Hankow. Borodin's influence was stronger than ever, and a Communist regime for all China seemed nearer a certainty. As the months went by, Donald watched events even more anxiously. What was happening would not bring about the sort of China he had hoped for. Writing again to the Rathvons in early December of 1926, he expressed his feelings.

I am glad to see that friend Silas Strawn is getting things off his chest over there, and I hope that it will do something in the direction of awakening American thought to the realities of the situation out here. There has been so much humbug talked over there about the gallant Nationalists that it is time the other side of the picture was shown. We are having a hectic time of it. Hankow is threatened with grave trouble [a few days later a Communist-inflamed mob overran the British Concession] and we are all watching the development there with curious interest. If the striking laborers can get away with murder there, then we are in for bad times. The truth is that the southerners have loosened forces which they cannot control, and the danger is that these forces will run amok and include wealthy and intellectual Chinese in their list of national enemies. A redistribution of wealth on the original Bolshevik lines would please the masses and there are numerous Chinese now wondering why they encouraged the onslaught on the "Foreign Devils" and fostered the campaign to get back the concessions. . . .

The Russians are pushing ahead the propaganda against the "Imperialists" and it is difficult to determine if they really know what they are doing. Their present policy is one of crippling British trade with the hope of getting Britain to recognize them and deal with them on an equal basis. They think Britain might be blackmailed into such a situation. . . . In one way, I am not pessimistic about the advent of the South. Once they are in power, they will have to have revenue and a large loan, and they can only get funds through commerce and through foreign markets. So the war on the capitalists will have to cease. . . .

At Hankow, Chiang had barely paused. He had swung sharply to the east and seized coastal areas. All the time he knew that the break with the Reds was inescapable, that Borodin and his fellow travelers would not quit easily, that they would have to be driven off if China was to be saved from communism.

After their defeat south of Shanghai, the northerners retreated to

Nanking. Chiang's forces followed and seized the old city on March 24, 1927. There, Chiang's troops began looting, rioting, attacking foreigners and their possessions. It was a combination of customary banditry and antiforeignism nurtured by communistic propaganda. American and British gunboats bombarded the city, then evacuated their nationals. It was an embarrassing spot for the young generalissimo who had hoped in his effort at unity to make a good showing to the world. Before he could make a statement, the Red government at Hankow announced that the northerners were to be blamed. This was obviously false and served only to add to Chiang's embarrassment. It topped a series of incidents which had embittered the more conservative supporters of Chiang. He wired T. V. Soong at Hankow to break with the Borodin crowd. But Soong was not able to effect the break. Chiang and his supporters then set up a regime at Nanking, giving China for a time three governments—the northern regime in Peking, the Red government at Hankow, and Chiang's at Nanking.

Immediately, Chiang began an anti-Red movement which culminated in massacres in Shanghai, Canton and Nanking. Secret societies under his direction sought out Communists and alleged Communist sympathizers, arrested thousands and beheaded hundreds. The act was foul and bloody, typical of the depredations through which China had wallowed for centuries. At Hankow, a disintegration set in, and many Chinese who had thrown in their lot with the Communists began to realize that the Russian intention from the beginning had not been philanthropic. The price for their help was the sovietizing of China. T. V. Soong and Mei-ling had already left when in July the Kuomintang divorced itself from the Reds, and the Borodin clique was driven to Russia. But China was not done with them, nor were they finished with China.

Donald eyed the floundering—perturbed, annoyed, conscious that much of it might be avoided if they had good counsel. But in this fracas, he had been an outsider. He would have it no other way. The element of radicalism in the movement had been too deeply ingrained for him. H. B. Elliston, who had been on the staff of his bureau but now was in England, heard about it in the following letter, written from Peking in mid-October 1927:

. . . Politically, things are as obscure as ever. . . . The Kuomintang are now trying to settle their differences but it will not last. Nothing can last in China. Even graft will come to its end when everyone is bled white. . . . You are lucky to be out of this mess here . . . and to be in a civilized part of the earth. . . .

By late autumn, the Hankow and Nanking regimes had joined, one of the compromises being, however, that Chiang resign as commander of the Nationalist army. He complied and departed for Japan where he pursued his courtship of Mei-ling. Mrs. Soong was there, and Chiang had to overcome her traditional Chinese antipathy to a soldier as a son-in-law. He was successful and, in Shanghai on December 1, 1927, Mei-ling became Madame Chiang Kai-shek.

The ceremonies were hardly over before the Nationalists at Nanking begged Chiang to return as commander in chief and finish the northern expedition. There was no one else to do the job. Troops from Peking were threatening, and in the South, at Swatow, the Communist menace had reappeared. In April, 1928, Chiang renewed his march northward. The old Christian general, Feng, back from Mongolia and Russia, was at his side as well as Yen Hsi-shan, the war lord of Shansi Province. After difficulties with Japanese troops in Shantung, Chiang reached Peking on July 3. The largest portion of China now was under control of Chiang forces. Another battle in the revolution that began in 1911 had ended.

The young Chinese who had rallied to Chiang wanted none of the mustiness of the old reactionary capital. Governmental machinery was moved to Nanking, and from that time on, Peking (northern capital) was known as Peiping (northern peace).

The new government looked bleakly at the rubble, then began to pick itself up. It found that it was standing on the brink of change, that social forces, set in motion long before it or the Communists came along, were calling for attention. In the government itself, some of the faces were new but much of the stuffing was the same. The war lords, the reactionaries who once had been scattered, were now congregating at Nanking.

They referred to themselves as Nationalists, but Donald, with his flair for the cruel truth, was soon to label them the *Nationalusts*.

chapter

20

MANCHURIA AND THE YOUNG MARSHAL

*Better a diamond with a flaw
than a pebble without.*

H. B. Elliston once wrote of Donald that he was the only adviser in China who never felt that he had to sing for his supper and, more, he was incorruptible, likewise a feat in China. Both of these virtues were in the foreground when, in late 1928, he could no longer stomach the snarls of the new Nationalist government which had tried to turn his Bureau of Economic Information into a propagandist organ.

At the time, the small amount of wealth that he had managed to accumulate in the previous twenty-five years had all but vanished. He had blocked an effort at "squeeze" by a former minister of finance, and funds for his bureau had been cut off. He had then paid for the bureau's operation out of his own bank account until he could pay no more. As a consequence, he was owed seventy thousand Chinese dollars, and the new government had given no sign that it intended to repay him. It is known that for awhile he considered abandoning any further work for China and had asked American friends to search for openings for him, but the mood appears not to have lasted long.

It was after this that Donald took on one of the biggest jobs in his career—the remaking of a man whose reclamation was to mean a better, more unified China. He told of prior events in a letter to Elliston from Shanghai, in December of 1928:

I am writing a few lines to let you know that I am still alive and that the bureau is pretty well dead. I have had a long haul since the time when you left. The minister of finance sought cash (squeeze), at first $5,000 a month, later reduced to $1,000. I refused all overtures, and eventually got away with it. They tried to get me to appoint a Chinese codirector. I refused. The fools forgot that they had the power to do that, and that I had nothing to do with such an appointment. However, I did not enlighten them. While the old government was after money, they never tried to break the bureau up. That has been left to the enlightened *Nationalusts* to do. . . . I contrived to be taken over by the minister of industry, commerce and labor. Dr. H. H. Kung, the minister, professed sturdy protection for the bureau. He swore that he would see to it that its work continued unimpaired. His swears were not worth a continental damn. He meant well, but God save us from the people who mean well! . . .

I resigned on October 10, thus celebrating the anniversary of the revolution in which I so heartily participated to bring in the government that is so rapidly proving itself impossible. But perhaps I am wrong to condemn the government. The ministry mean well but they are not free, as you might be able to understand when you remember what the radicals are, what the party (Kuomintang) is, and how the party rules. Kung came especially to Shanghai when he heard that I had resigned, and both he and Dr. C. T. Wang refused flatly to let me go. Nevertheless, between October 10 and now I have resigned three times in writing, and about six times orally. . . . So now I am going to do what the average Chinese official does when things get beyond endurance—flee. I am hoping that nothing will interfere to delay me. I am wholly fed up with this situation. If I get away, I shall go to Manchuria. They want me to work with them, and I must say that it interests me more than working here. This time I am going to try and get on the boat first and resign afterward. . . .

Donald sailed, and thus this interlude in working for the economic organization of China was wound up. As his tender slipped quickly down river to the waiting steamer, he watched the black of humanity flowing in relief at the base of Shanghai's gray stone buildings. By foot, by ricksha, by barrow, in tramcar and in bus they infested Garden Bridge. By the thousands they bobbed in the river in tiny sampans, in lighters, in junks. The nearby looked up, their expressions less inscrutable than blank.

The great sludges of fellow man. Donald saw with a wonderment that a quarter century in China had not dulled. He thought, as he had so often: Just that one moment, that split second of ecstasy in an embrace is the why of all these people.

In Manchuria, Chang Hsueh-liang, known widely as the Young Marshal, had assumed the rule over the three great northern provinces left vacant through the assassination of his father, Chang Tso-lin, shortly before the Chiang Kai-shek forces reached Peiping. Incensed because the man whom they had always regarded as their puppet refused to resist the Nationalist army and China's growing unification, Japanese agents had blown up the old warrior's train just before he reached Mukden in his retreat.

For centuries, Manchuria technically had been a part of China; in language, customs, it had been identical. It was China north of the Great Wall. Yet, China's jurisdiction over it had been hardly more than nominal. The last of its powerful masters had been Chang Tso-lin. From the time of the Manchus' collapse in 1912 until he was assassinated in 1928, he had held this Asian tinderbox, this spawner of khans, in his own tight grip.

Now big changes were in store for Manchuria. The first came less than ten days after Donald arrived at Mukden, the capital. China's national flag—the flag of the Kuomintang—was hoisted everywhere. As it went up, Donald won another victory over the Japanese who had predicated their success in Manchuria, as in the rest of China, on preventing any show of national unity. They had sent special emissaries to wean the Young Marshal from any thought of unification. But they had found him more outspoken, less pliable than his father. Supporting Donald's policy of a solid Chinese front, he had replied: "I am Chinese. Manchuria is Chinese. I do not take orders from Japan." The flag went up, although complete unity—Donald's goal—was yet to come.

Little wonder that Donald was drawn to the Young Marshal. They held the same ideals for China: Political unity and economic organization. As a youthful commander under the Old Marshal, he had been known to Donald as a youngster of great courage and socially as one possessing a trait unique in China: frankness and the capacity for self-criticism. While recognizing him as a good leader, Donald realized, however, that Chang was still young, often impulsive. Some changes would have to be made. It became Donald's intention to see to the changes.

His first meeting in years with Chang Hsueh-liang had been a shock. He had heard he had become a drug addict, but he had not expected to find the physical wreck that sat across the desk from him. His face and his hands were thin and pale, and as they talked, his body occasionally shook convulsively. At the end of fifteen minutes, the Young Marshal excused himself. He needed more drugs. Donald turned to Lo Wen-kan, a doctor of philosophy and a personal friend of the Young Marshal's, and said disgustedly:

"That man is all shot up. He isn't worth a farthing to himself or to China."

"I know," answered Dr. Lo. "You've got a job on your hands."

Young Chang had become addicted to opium smoking in the summer of 1926 while he was commanding his father's troops in the fight against Feng Yu-hsiang. He had contracted influenza and, devoted to his men, had refused to leave for medical attention. Advised by an older opium-smoking general that opium then would be the sole substitute for hospital care, the Young Marshal turned to it, only to find later that he was unable to discard it. General Yang Yu-ting, crafty and ambitious, the man whom the Old Marshal had feared someday might strive to control Manchuria, advised the use of pavemal as a cure. But pavemal proved to be even more insidious than opium. At the time Donald arrived, two doctors were on hand at all times to administer the drug and there was hardly a spot on the Young Marshal's back free of needle prick. Donald looked bleakly at his new job. Had he come to Manchuria to be nursemaid to a drug addict?

The same day that he arrived at Mukden, he heard whisperings of trouble. The principals were reported to be the sinister General Yang, in charge of the arsenals, and a slightly duller confederate, thick-set, black-mustached, General Chang Yin-wei, director of railways. Donald's thoughts went back to Shanghai to a day just before he had left for the North. He had been visited by a man who had handed him a check for two thousand pounds, said that he represented Generals Yang and Chang, and asked Donald to accompany him to London to negotiate a fifteen-million-pound loan. He added that the money was wanted for development in Manchuria. Donald had laughed, remarked that since Manchuria could give no security, they would be wasting their time.

After his first conference with the Young Marshal, Donald called on General Yang and found him vague over what developments were proposed under the hoped-for loan. He began to suspect a familiar Chinese pattern, and hurried by train to distant Tsitsihar, headquarters of General Chang. Chang seemed nervous and confused under his questioning. Certain that a revolt was brewing, Donald wanted no part of it. He had had enough of wars and rebellions, of ups and downs, of the greedy and the ambitious, of militaristic stupidity. He wanted China only strong and united. He had hoped that the Kuomintang flag flying over Manchuria would hasten the end of civil strife. Depressed by the apparent hopelessness, he toyed with the idea of resigning and leaving China forever. But the predilection of a newspaperman —the urge to face, not to retreat from excitement—was triumphant. He wanted to be on hand when the crisis came.

Donald returned to Mukden on the night of January 10 after spending several days at Harbin. Met at the station by his interpreter, he was told that General Chang Yin-wei had preceded him but everything was still peaceful. He went directly to his hotel and there wrote letters to Generals Yang and Chang, stating that he could not consider any association with them. Later, he observed a group of the Young Marshal's officers huddled in a far corner of the lobby talking excitedly. He felt strangely out of place for he sensed that something big had happened, and few events took place in China without Donald being in the dead center. At six o'clock the next morning, his interpreter arrived with a headful of rumors of the night before, and Dr. Lo Wen-kan followed, talking as if he were intoxicated.

"There's murder!" he shouted. "Both Yang and Chang were shot last night at the Young Marshal's house."

Puzzled, Donald stared from his window to the streets. Mukden was as quiet as a graveyard. If two of the most powerful men in Manchuria had been assassinated, why was there no reaction, no rising of the troops? Either the story was false or the Young Marshal was stronger than other war lords he had known.

Donald left for the Young Marshal's and when he arrived he found him stepping into his motorcar. He invited Donald to accompany him on an errand. As they passed the home of General Yang, the Young Marshal said quietly: "Poor Yang."

Donald said nothing.

On the way home, they passed the general's house again. Once more the Young Marshal said: "Poor Yang. He owned all that property."

"I notice you use the past tense in referring to General Yang," said Donald.

He thought the Young Marshal looked a bit melancholy when he answered, "The past tense. That is right." Donald waited for him to go on.

"Some time ago," the Young Marshal began, "several of my father's old officers came to me and reported that General Yang and General Chang were conspiring to head a mutiny in Mukden on January 12. I was to be killed. They urged me to arrest and execute both of them, but I was reluctant to believe them guilty of conspiracy. At last, however, I summoned General Chang to Mukden."

He then told how Chang and Yang had arrived at his house on the night of January 8. First off, he had asked Yang for his reports on the arsenals under his command. Yang sparred, said he had misplaced them but would bring them to the next meeting. The Young Marshal then asked Chang for his year-end report on the railways. Chang had also hedged, promising to bring it to the next meeting. When they left, the Young Marshal was no more certain of the charges against them than before. Their attitude revealed only average inefficiency. The next day, however, his father's officers again urged the execution of Yang and Chang. That night, the Young Marshal brooded over the problem. He was still short of thirty years, and the quasi kingship of a land nearly twice the size of Germany weighed heavily. It had fallen to him, and he had taken it mainly because of his hate of the Japanese. They had killed his father. But he had no liking for the sordidness of politics, for the disagreeable business that now faced him. He took a dollar from his pocket and tossed it into the air.

"Heads for arrest, tails for execution," he said to his wife. It came down tails. He tossed it up twice more and each time it came down tails. His wife remarked that perhaps the dollar was heavier on the tails side.

"All right," he agreed, "tails for arrest and heads this time for execution." It came down heads three times.

Donald asked, "Who pulled the trigger?"

"I'm coming to that," the Young Marshal continued, relating how Yang and Chang returned on January 10, the night just passed. He lost no time in asking Yang for his report on the arsenals.

"I am running the arsenals," Yang replied unsmiling.

The truth came suddenly, knocking at the flushed temples of the Young Marshal. He turned to Chang and asked for the railway accounts.

Chang sneered, "What does a youngster know about railways?"

The Young Marshal jumped to his feet, strode to the rear of the room and flung open a door. In marched several of his officers. They drew their pistols and shot Yang and Chang each through the head.

"And that," the Young Marshal said to Donald, "was the end of a sorry and sad business."[1]

And that was Donald's introduction to Manchuria.

The quiet that he had noted on the morning following the assassinations continued. There were no reprisals by the troops of either Yang or Chang. Quickly and adroitly the Young Marshal had made compromises with possible antagonists, thus strengthening his position. He settled down to rule sprawling Manchuria.

Donald's determination to resign faded after several more conversations with the Young Marshal. Every day he was finding new qualities to admire. Here was timber for leadership. He would not leave him although the opportunity was always present. Not long after he arrived in Mukden, the Nanking government began to feel the loss of his counsel. They reached out to pull him back. The reach was in the form of Sir Frederick Whyte, formerly of the Indian government, now adviser to the Ministry of Foreign Affairs. Sir Frederick said that he had come to Mukden to convince Donald that his place was with the

[1] The Young Marshal personally gave the widows of Yang and Chang $100,000 each.

Nanking government and, he added jokingly, "If I fail in that, I am instructed to bring you back bodily."

Although Donald knew little or nothing of the man who sat before him, he had always felt a scorn for self-styled advisers, for men who had little to give but much to take from China. In all his years in the Far East, he had never referred to himself as an "adviser." He said:

"Let's talk no more about it. You haven't been in China long enough to understand China. I am involved in China in a way that would be hard for you to comprehend. I know what's best for China. I'm staying here for the time being."

Nevertheless, Donald was at a loss how to begin his help as long as the Young Marshal clung to the drug habit. He saw the dangers. There were young, ambitious officers who might be bold enough to strike for power if the Young Marshal continued to weaken himself. Subcutaneously, the older, conservative generals resented his show of national patriotism. In their code, this was rank radicalism. One day, Donald told the Young Marshal bluntly that he would have to stop using pavemal. Instead of stubborn refusal, Donald got a look of warmth and gratitude. At that moment, a comradeship was born—a comradeship that was to hold together through rough going. Already beginning to adopt some of Donald's mannerisms. He said cheerily: "All right, all right, let's have a go at it."

With Donald's help and encouragement, the Young Marshal struggled valiantly. Donald watched his diet, saw that he was fed on nourishing foods only. In the early morning, they took long walks over country roads or they were on the golf links doing eighteen holes. They rode horses in the hills. They fished, swam and hunted—everything that would tire the Young Marshal. Sometimes Donald believed he was only a step away from success. The crave for the drug would fall off until it was at least ninety per cent gone. He would say to himself: Just two or three more days, and I'll have it whipped.

But the young man would break, beg for the drug and, seeing his torture, Donald would relent. Finally, he consulted doctors who advised that the patient be closeted away from everyone for at least a month. However, the Young Marshal vetoed the idea on the grounds that rumormongers would spread a story of his death, encouraging revolt. He countered by inviting an opium-cure expert, Dr. Miller, to open a sanitarium in Mukden, giving him land and the necessary funds.

"When it is finished," the Young Marshal said, "I'll enter it and take the cure." But that was not to be.

The Young Marshal's youth had been crowded with romantic adventures, but under Donald's calming influence he gradually settled into a serious, administrative groove. Even his reading matter changed from light, illustrated magazines to books on political science and world affairs. Brighter, stronger, although still plagued by the drug, he began to set more of his radical ideas in motion. They sprang out of long conversations with Donald on all phases of Manchuria's economic questions; they sprang from his dreams as a youth. Bit by bit, they fell into place.

Obsessed with the incentive to train personnel capable in political, technical and scientific matters, one of his early acts was to donate nearly ten million dollars for the construction and support of the Northeastern University, at Mukden. He jarred old-school war lords by establishing a land reclamation bureau, disbanding soldiers to carry out his reclamation schemes. Still bruising militarists' knuckles, he converted a big arsenal into an industrial concern. Realizing the potentialities of Hulutao, he had it developed into a good harbor. He made it possible for famine victims in North and Central China to reclaim waste lands in Manchuria. Always, Donald stressed one point: Think in terms of China.

Japan watched nervously. The new spirit of reform and a solidifying China were not to her liking. Despite the old American enunciated Open Door Policy, she had considered Manchuria her own special reserve for development and exploitation. Once she had held it for a brief spell in the Russo-Japanese War, but the Portsmouth Treaty of 1905 had removed it from her grasp. She had never ceased to covet it. Under Chang Tso-lin, she had been mildly successful in infiltrating. Under Chang Hsueh-liang and Donald's shadow, she was blunting her stubby nose.

In the days of the Old Marshal, Japan had tried to secure the right to construct and operate a railway connecting Kirin Province with Korea. To Japan's militaristic mind, this was a fundamental necessity in the fulfillment of her strategical plans and was economically desirable as parallel competition to the Chinese Eastern Railway. With such a line, she could quickly spill her troops throughout Asia. The day when she was to do it was coming up fast. Just two years before, in 1927, Baron Giichi Tanaka, then premier of Japan, had laid before the Throne a memorial for the conquest of Manchuria, Mongolia, China, then the Southwest Pacific, so that in ten years they could dominate the whole world. He had advised a policy of blood and iron. Manchuria was first on the list.

They had been able to construct a portion of the vital Kirin-Korea line, but the Old Marshal had forced its suspension before it reached the border. From that moment on, Japan was his enemy and incident after incident developed. The Young Marshal inherited Japan's ill will, but he might have escaped it.

An enticement was offered one day when a Japanese diplomat called on him. Donald was present, puffing quietly on a cigar. The caller came quickly to the point, reminding the Young Marshal that his father had made many promises of concessions for Japan.

"You must redeem these promises," he said, drawing in his breath.

"For instance?" the Young Marshal asked.

"Well, let us start with the Kirin-Korea Railway."

"I know nothing of such promises," Chang snapped. "If your accounts are not forged, you can go to Nanking for collection."

The face of the Japanese clouded, but his speech was still smooth. "But we do not wish to go there. Neither do we wish to see you entangling yourself with those people. The Kuomintang is an evil thing. We want you to realize that before it is too late."

The Young Marshal saw Donald looking at him, chin forward, lips pressed tight.

The Japanese went on, "Should you keep aloof from those people, be assured our humble country will stand ready to render you help. Otherwise, we shall do what we deem proper whenever our privileges are impaired."

"I am certain I am detaining you," said the Young Marshal. "I regret your leaving."

When the diplomat had gone, Donald said, "Good lad! But you've just invited the biggest dose of trouble any man could have asked for. The Japanese won't stop. They want that railroad. They're headed hell-for-leather."

"I know," said the Young Marshal.

"It would have been easy enough for you to comply. They would have rewarded you with support of your position, honors and wealth."

"And the hate of my countrymen," Chang put in grimly.

By early 1930, China's politics had been frothed up once more. In October, 1929, two separate revolts against Chiang Kai-shek's Nanking government had broken out. The more serious resulted in the establishment of a separatist government at Peiping by Yen Hsi-shan, Shansi's capable governor; Wang Ching-wei, who had retired several years before in favor of Chiang; and the old war horse, Feng. Chiang swept his armies out against them and looked hopefully to Marshal Chang in Manchuria. He had sent delegates to Mukden, as had the independent government at Peiping, to solicit support. The Young Marshal listened, then took counsel with Donald.

Together they had set up an anti-Civil War policy, and they were hopeful of maintaining it. But the delegates persisted, and the pressure grew. Before each meeting, Donald would caution, "Don't make any commitments. Hold tight. The time may come when you'll have to go into this war. But go in only on a basis on which you can help China."

Then, in an act unprecedented, the Wang-Feng-Yen government seized the foreign-manned Chinese maritime customs in the North and installed their own men. B. Lenox-Simpson, a brilliant Britisher who wrote *Indiscreet Letters from Peking* and a score of other volumes under the pseudonym of Putnam Weale, was made commissioner at Tientsin. In his Peking days, Donald had known Simpson, and a marked lack of cordiality existed between them. A columnist on a Peking newspaper, he had twitted Donald more seriously than jokingly for enriching himself through his numerous adviserships. To Donald, this was the summit of insult.

One day, Donald and the Young Marshal were on the golf links, and as Chang sunk a putt, he said, "A high Kuomintang man—General Wu Teh-chen—is calling on me tonight."

"Well," Donald said quickly, "this stupid war has gone too far. The time has come for you to declare yourself. Now you must become part and parcel of China's recognized government—the one run by Chiang Kai-shek." He holed his own shot, straightened up. "But," he cautioned, "you demand that they alter the organic law of the Kuomintang. You get them to do some housecleaning."

They were standing by a sand trap now. "You mean that if this were the Kuomintang," the Young Marshal answered, drawing a square in the sand, "the other parties (he drew smaller squares outside) should enjoy the same rights as the Kuomintang?"

"Exactly. You demand that, and you demand the end of civil war in China."

Early the next morning the Young Marshal told him that Nanking had agreed to his terms.

"All right," said Donald, "you send a circular telegram advising the separatists at Peiping to halt their war against Chiang. Make them realize that if they don't, and if they don't dissolve their government, you will send your armies against them."

"Will it work?" he asked.

"Of course," Donald said confidently.

The Young Marshal sent the telegram, and that day, September 18, 1930, the unification of China was complete. From then on, the Chiangs owed Donald gratitude. Had he advised the Young Marshal to back the separatists, the Chiang government might have gone down, never to rise. However, faced by a powerful threat to their rear, the rebel government collapsed and Chiang returned to Nanking.

At this time, young Chang told Donald of having received a letter from Lenox-Simpson. Donald looked up sharply. Chang was a practical joker, and once or twice before Donald had found himself tangled up in one of his jokes. Expressionless, Chang told how Simpson had offered him two million dollars cash and a million dollars monthly if he would sustain him in his post as customs commissioner. The Britisher was to arrive the following day to discuss details.

"That's bribery," Donald said acidly. "Simpson must have a poor opinion of you. I hope you take care how you answer him."

On the way home after golf the next day, the Young Marshal said, "I'm seeing Simpson this evening."

"Watch yourself," Donald said. "If he thinks that you can be bribed, and you let him think it, well, then, there is only one end to this. You may gain yourself another friend, but as certain as God made little green apples, you'll lose this one!"

The Young Marshal laughed. At the entrance to his house, they stopped. A boy came out with a calling card which bore the name of Lenox-Simpson. Donald walked off.

The next morning, the Young Marshal told him what had happened the night before. Simpson, the writer-turned-administrator-turned-adventurer, had exclaimed, "Marshal, I'm glad that you agree with me."

The Young Marshal had answered, "Agree with you? Where did you get that idea?"

"Why, you sent for me after I laid out my plan to you."

"Yes, I sent for you to tell you to hand over the customs."

Simpson had looked a bit gray. "What!" he had said. "You don't agree with me?"

"I don't touch your sort of filthy money," the Young Marshal had snapped.

Simpson had been nervous. "If you won't support me, what'll I do?"

"Ask Yen Hsi-shan."

"He's run away."

"Run after him."

"Will you give me two weeks to straighten out my affairs?"

"I give you two weeks to rob the customs? I give you now the order to hand over the customs to the proper authorities."

As the Young Marshal finished his recital, Donald looked at him with the air of a doctor whose patient had just passed a crisis. He had turned down millions of dollars—a deed which, as far as Donald knew, was without parallel in his China days. If he had had doubts about the character of this whimsical, thin-framed, hollow-cheeked man, they were now and forever dispelled. He could take advice. He had integrity. He had courage. He had wisdom.

"Han Chen," he said, using the Young Marshal's courtesy name for the first time, "why did you call Simpson up here?"

Han Chen grinned. "Don," he answered, "I wanted to see how badly an Englishman can lose face."

Simpson returned to Tientsin. There, a few days later, he was shot to death by a Chinese underling who had discovered that Simpson had set aside three hundred thousand dollars against his retirement. The underling decamped with it.

On October 10, shortly after his return to his capital, Generalissimo Chiang Kai-shek announced that Marshal Chang Hsueh-liang had been rewarded by his elevation to vice commander in chief of the National army, navy and air force. The next month, with Donald, the Young Marshal flew to Nanking in his trimotored Ford where he was received with unprecedented cordiality. He participated heartily in the Kuomintang conference then being held. He liked Nanking. Nanking liked him. Pleased as an old schoolmaster, Donald stood happily in the background. While they were there, however, rumors were circulated by Japanese news agencies that Chang Hsueh-liang had been arrested, that he had been imprisoned, that he had been slain, that he would never be allowed to return to Mukden because of a movement against him by his father's henchmen. The stories were baseless. He returned to his capital early in January, 1931, and remained until May. Then, with Donald still at his side, he flew again to Nanking to attend the National Assembly. It was a demonstration of the sincerity of his feeling about national unification. Once more, Nanking greeted him enthusiastically.

But as the assembly convened, the South, bubbly as a pot of boiling porridge, bubbled once more. A group of dissatisfied leaders in Canton sent a telegram denouncing the government, denouncing Chiang as a dictator. They scored him for his hastiness in expelling Borodin's colleagues so completely. Students once more went on the rampage. Before the month was out, the southerners, Wang Ching-wei among them, had set up a new government. Chiang maneuvered adroitly to avert civil war.

By this time, Marshal Chang Hsueh-liang had headed north for Mukden. There was trouble in his realm, too. Japan was baiting a trap and standing by to spring it. Everything was opportune: The trouble in the South was now coupled with a dissension the Japanese had developed among rival generals in the North. They had caused Koreans to attack Chinese farmers. They had raised an uproar over a missing explorer who existed only in fiction. Thus, on Japan's home front, the mood for war was being funneled into cities and villages, into bankers and peasants.

But the Young Marshal never reached Mukden. At Peiping, he was stricken with typhoid fever and entered a hospital. Donald continued on and saw the unmistakable signs of what Japan was up to. The old enemy was pawing the ground, getting ready. He sent a sharp warning to his friend, Dr. C. T. Wang, now foreign minister at Nanking, that the Japanese military were ready "as soon as an excuse could be manufactured" to invade Manchuria. They calculated, Donald stated, that they could effect occupancy within eleven hours.

It was mid-September when he hurried back to Peiping to determine whether the Young Marshal could return to Mukden. He found him improved and on the afternoon of September 18, 1931, the first anniversary of Manchuria's complete unification with the rest of China, the Young Marshal left the hospital. That night, both he and Donald had dinner at the British Legation. Afterwards Chang attended the theater where Mei Lan-fang, the greatest of Chinese actors, was playing. Donald went home.

At 1:00 A.M., his phone rang. It was the Young Marshal.

"The Japanese are in Mukden!" he shouted.

Donald reeled a bit. The fact that he had seen it coming was no cushion now for the impact. This was it. This was the beginning of the march, the first step along a path the Tanaka Memorial had charted. This was the culmination of pages of sorry history—the pages that Donald had watched flipped one by one. The hates born out of competitive commercialism, the intrigues with the Manchus, the conspiracies in the Twenty-One Demands, the plottings with unsavory factions, the pitting of war lord against war lord.

Before Donald could leave for the Young Marshal's, Jimmy Elder, the young Scotsman who was Chang Hsueh-liang's personal treasurer, burst in. Elder reported the spread of Japanese in and around Mukden, the seizure of the airdrome and arsenal, and added that the Young Marshal was in direct communication with the city through the Mukden telephone operator. Donald sprang to the phone and called Nelson T. Johnson, the American minister, and Sir Miles Lampson, the British envoy, informing them of the attack.

Manchuria was tottering. The eleven hours the Japanese had set had been accurately calculated, for it was still in the early hours of the morning when the Mukden operator said, "I can talk no more. The Japanese have entered my office." He cut off, and a silence settled over Manchuria.

In the days and months and years that followed, Japan explained the coup with bales and tons of propaganda. The Chinese, they said, had blown up a section of railway track. They had acted, of course, in self-defense.

Donald watched the sweep of the Japanese over Manchuria, certain that this rashness was the beginning of the end for them. In a remarkably prophetic letter to his sister in Australia a few days after Mukden fell, he wrote:

. . . . In my opinion, the Japanese militarists are biting off more than they can chew, and are likely to bring about the complete breakdown of Japan in the end. Japan cannot afford to have China hostile. The market is Japan's mainstay, and to garrison a hostile and stubborn land like Manchuria, and at the same time have a hostile and antagonistic country like China to deal with, will be more than Japan can manage. The Chinese will retire to the interior, live on their own resources, carry on guerrilla warfare, and devote the years to keeping Japan fully occupied. . . .

chapter

21

JAPAN ATTACKS

*If you continually grind a bar of iron,
you can make a needle of it.*

THE biggest of Asia's storms had begun. In a prelude to a universal
cataclysm, Japan's army had swept into Manchuria, stood looking
southward over the Great Wall.

Her military had moved at the most opportune of times. The United
States was entering the depths of depression, Britain was off the gold
standard, and the failure of the most important Austrian bank threatened all Europe with bankruptcy. Except for the position taken by the
American secretary of state, Stimson, the jingoes had carte blanche to
ravage Asia. Britain had remained virtually silent, and once again
Donald spoke bluntly against her policy, noting that her indifference
had encouraged Japan.

The situation within Japan, also, had made it opportune. The army
clique had been engaged in a fight with several political parties seeking to cut down on military appropriations. To triumph on the home
front, it was necessary to fight on a foreign front, and in China there
had been excuses aplenty, real and manufactured. Thus, the army
whose bible now was the Tanaka Memorial had struck.

The Manchurian attack had not been many hours old when Donald
took steps to bring help—if only moral—to China's side. With Nanking government representatives in Peiping and other influential men,
he and the Young Marshal went into hurried conference. Donald
proposed that League of Nations aid be immediately invoked. He
argued that China, like the bamboo, would have to bend with the wind.

The bulk of the Young Marshal's two hundred and fifty thousand troops, which had been garrisoning south of the Great Wall at the time of the invasion, was not equipped to fight Japan's modern war machine. Resistance by any or all of China's armies would be national suicide. Donald hoped that the League would approach this, its first major case, zealously. Nanking followed his advice, appealed to the League, then waited.

As the Japanese army, fighting virtually a nonexistent enemy force, glorified itself in communiques, the Japanese navy watched jealously, fearful that it might be on the short end of the forthcoming military budget. By January, 1932, outside Shanghai, it had begun to work itself into a war fever, and as it did, Donald once more made one of his timely arrivals. The drama began to piece itself together in the early hours of the twenty-fifth.

Donald was in Nanking. The night before, he had attended a Boxer Indemnity meeting, planning to leave the next morning for Peiping. He was asleep in his room when General Wu Teh-chen, mayor of Greater Shanghai, burst in with the report that there was serious trouble in Shanghai. He urged Donald to go down and help him.

Donald asked a few questions as he dressed, and in the gray of a weary dawn that came hesitantly from behind the hills, he hurried with General Wu to the train. As they rolled out of Nanking station, the mayor went over the growth of trouble brought on by the mushrooming of anti-Japanese boycott associations which had sprung up in retaliation against the Manchurian affair. Japan was being hurt in a severe way commercially. She was demanding satisfaction.

The two old friends reviewed the increasing ugliness and new unruliness of internal politics. Students, with their usual lack of acumen, were making a show of themselves again. They had commandeered a train at Shanghai, driven it to Nanking and there pummeled the minister of foreign affairs, Dr. C. T. Wang, for lack of a strong anti-Japanese policy. In Canton, the rebel southern government formed in 1931 again had rebuked Chiang for "truckling to Japan." However, Dr. Hu Han-min, Sun's old confederate, who had been arrested by Chiang, then released, had convinced the South they should abandon attempts to overthrow Chiang by force and instead negotiate for government reorganization. The two factions had met in October, and while the Japanese stood menacingly in the North, they wrangled. The outcome was that Chiang had gone out, supposedly stripped of all power, and the southerners had taken over. Into the premiership had come the son of Dr. Sun, Sun Fo, while the Foreign Office had been taken over by brilliant Eugene Chen, key figure in many a political explosion of the past. Disgusted by the chaos, the Young Marshal had submitted his resignation as a member of the military affairs commission. Wang Ching-wei had placed his well-trained Nineteenth Route army in command of the Shanghai and Woosung garrisons. Its real role was to protect the southerners in the government should any of them decide that Nanking's political climate was uncomfortable.

Immediately, Chen and Sun Fo had sought to develop a strong policy against Japan, but Chiang, theoretically without power, had said no. That was that. Within a short time, the two southerners, along with their partisans, resigned, and the shuffle had begun all over again. Wang Ching-wei now was premier. Dr. Lo Wen-kan, the man Donald had met on his first day in Manchuria, became foreign minister. Chiang had returned as chairman of the powerful National Military Council—the real core of the government—but the confusion continued depressing.

As the train rumbled through the snow-sprinkled Yangtze Valley, Donald listened while Wu told of Japanese being beaten up by the Nineteenth Route army men. Here was an ominous tone. Donald knew that China was not ready for war, but war might be knocking.

Wu paused. Donald watched the dreary countryside crawl by. He saw two farmers crouched on their skinny haunches by an irrigation ditch, excreting. He knew what they would do when they finished. They would fertilize their land with it, as their ancestors had done for centuries. The wretched farmers were not faring a whit better than when the revolutionary armies had surged over their lands twenty-one years before to free them of the Manchus and supposedly find for them a better life. Ah, yes, the government talked of elaborate agricultural improvements—and talked and talked and talked. The train ground in to Chinkiang, ground out again. The same unpretentious station was there where he and Anderson had signed a chit for a locomotive to dash up to Purple Mountain. He wondered about Mr. Pope.

Donald felt the Mayor's eyes on him, felt him waiting for an answer to the problem. "You'll have to give in to Japan's demands," he said. "Take my advice, close the boycott societies and eat some humble pie. Otherwise, Japan will shut them by force, and you'll be in the soup. That'll mean military defeat for you."

Wu looked dismayed. Donald's suggestion meant serious loss of face.

When they alighted at Shanghai, Donald noticed a small, stooped figure stepping down from a rear coach. Amused, he watched the man approach—a little more wrinkled, a little grayer than when he tried to trick Chow Tzu-chi one night at dinner seventeen years before. Donald looked down at Mr. Funatsu.

"Well," he asked mischievously, "up to some more of your monkey tricks, Mr. Funatsu?"

Mr. Funatsu froze and shot Donald a startled glance. Then he smiled and gave a jerky bow. "Ah, so, Mr. Donald," he said. "So sorry, but I am no longer a diplomat. I am merely president of Japanese Cotton Spinners Association in China." He bowed once more and walked on.

"Who's that?" Wu asked, puzzled.

"Oh," Donald laughed, "he's a b-b-bloody b-b-bastard!"

He watched Funatsu disappear into the crowd. Three days later, Japan's navy began to erase a part of Shanghai from the map.

In those three days, Donald worked perhaps harder than he ever had in his life. He called on American and British officials in the International Settlement, on French leaders in the French Concession, at their homes, in their offices, exhorting them to apply pressure against Japan and against what to him were obvious preparations for war. From some he got indifference, from some a shrug of despair, and from others cheerful but futile co-operation. With Mayor Wu, he worked to prepare the Chinese public, now in no mood for appeasement, for a humiliating about-face—acquiescence to Japan's demands. It was slow, tortuous work. On January 27, with the boycott associations still unclosed, the Japanese navy sent a twenty-four-hour ultimatum. Donald and Wu worked fast. By noon the next day, the doors of the societies were finally shuttered, and in the afternoon, Chinese and foreigners

were guests at the Japanese Consulate General for an exchange of
cordiality.

Japan professed satisfaction. Her diplomats promised no war. But
still under the tension of the past days—of sandbags, soldiers marching
into defense positions, and hurriedly evacuating Chinese civilians—
Shanghai breathed only slightly easier.

That evening, Donald had dinner at Mayor Wu's. Just before midnight, he returned to his room at the Astor House. The city was dark
and quiet except for the pad of feet and the creak of rickshas. Chinese
were still fleeing from Chapei where lived a million. Then, as if a
door had been opened on a house of pandemonium, machine guns
began to chatter a few blocks away, and he heard rifles popping like
corn. In the river, Japan's naval guns began to bellow. He phoned
Mayor Wu, opened his window and for a moment hung the mouth-
piece outside. Then he hauled it in and said:

"You've got another war on your hands. Now you have to fight with
what you've got—which is blessed little."

In Chapei, where the world first heard of checkerboard bombing
being applied, the Nineteenth Route army under tall, angular General
Tsai Ting-kai struggled for more than a month against the combined
Japanese marine and army forces. The world did not know it then,
but here was the obliteration pattern for Barcelona, for Warsaw, for
Coventry and for a hundred Chinese cities. Chapei was pulverized.
Even in this crisis, Chiang's anger at the South for having maneuvered
him from power surmounted the need for patriotism and unity. His
personally trained Eighty-eighth and Eighty-seventh divisions were
ordered to Shanghai, but hardly for purposes of war. For weeks, they
sat camped at a safe distance, a dagger at the back of the southern
troops. When they did take part, the Nineteenth Route army had been
torn badly, and an armistice was but days off.

Like Donald at Shanghai, the Young Marshal at Peiping watched
the ineptness of Nanking, the continued thrust for power and the sulk-
ings. At the height of the confusion, he sent the following wire to his
adviser:

WHY DON'T YOU LET THE HEROES SOLVE THEIR OWN PROBLEMS STOP YOU
CAN'T TELL THEM ANYTHING STOP COME BACK.

But Donald stayed to assist the Chinese delegation in the armistice proceedings. The two adversaries, with yards of gold braid and dancing epaulets, met with representatives of foreign powers. Japan's ambition was to secure a large demilitarized zone (demilitarized by the Chinese) which she could occupy and administer adjacent to Shanghai. However, the Powers—jealous of their own commercial stake—were not to countenance any such surrender by the Chinese. They were aware of Japan's objective: to establish a footing on China's mainland as a first step in developing herself as a continental power.

Day after day, the disquisitions dragged on, even though the outcome was a certainty. Conscious that she faced the prospect of winning nothing from her military victory, Japan sought to save her face with lengthy and ornate speeches. Before long, the foreign diplomats were bored and restless. Donald was not at the spacious conference table but seated directly behind Sir Miles Lampson. One day he tapped the British minister on the shoulder.

"How do they get the hole in macaroni?" he whispered.

Sir Miles stared blankly, then grinned. "I don't know," he answered, "How do they?"

"Haven't the foggiest idea," Donald said.

The table awoke in a quiet way to the intriguing question. No one, however, bothered to include the Japanese. Nelson Johnson, the American minister, said softly, "Let's ask Ciano. An Italian should know." Sir Miles quickly scribbled a note to Count Galeazzo Ciano, Mussolini's son-in-law, and shoved it across the table. Ciano read it, chuckled, wrote, "I no savvy" and passed it back.

The note then went from one diplomat to another. Tokyo's delegation stirred restlessly. Its speakers stopped, eyed the flurry, then went on. Was some plot being formulated against them? Not once did anyone pass them the note. Finally, Ciano let it be known *sotto voce* that he was dispatching a secretary to his consulate to ask if anyone there knew how the hole was put in macaroni.

While he was gone, macaroni—favorite dishes and favorite restaurants—was discussed in pairs and trios. Japanese irritation grew. Again their spokesman paused. Lampson tiptoed from the room and returned with a mysterious book. It was the Encyclopedia Britannica. He quickly read up on the subject, then spoke his findings to Johnson. The whisper was repeated in the ears of everyone but the Japanese. The encyclopedia had told all about macaroni except how the hole was created!

Finally, the secretary, flushed and perspiring, returned, reporting quietly to Ciano. The Italian cleared his throat and in the mock dignity of a professor announced in a voice easily audible to the Japanese:

"Gentlemen—it is put in by machinery!"

Everyone but the Japanese laughed. They sat looking bewildered. For them, the commotion was never explained.

Meanwhile, the unending melodrama of Asia went on, the shuffles, the changes, the torpidness and the hotheadedness. Even as Nanking flipped its political pages, a political change took place in the North. Japan had spirited the one-time boy emperor, Henry Pu Yi, from Tientsin to Manchuria and there had made him Emperor Kang Teh (Exalted Virtue) of the puppet state they had carved out of Manchuria.[1] Renamed Manchukuo, it presented a brazen, tawdry backdrop for the forthcoming study of the whys and wherefores of this forerunner to world collision.

Answering China's appeal, the League of Nations had dispatched an international commission headed by Lord Lytton to probe the Manchurian affair and to set the blame. It had arrived in Shanghai shortly after the Japanese had blundered into war and had proceeded to Peiping for initial studies. There, upon the conclusion of the peace conference, Donald joined it as counselor to the Chinese group that was to accompany the mission to Manchuria.

This journey was to see him solely in the role of an adviser. He no longer was a newspaper correspondent. At the outbreak of the Manchurian trouble, he had resigned from the London *Times* and from a more recent post with the Manchester *Guardian* on the grounds that since he was an employee of Manchuria, there would be those who might suspect that he could no longer write without prejudice. Yet, long before he had removed himself as dean of Far Eastern correspondents, his reputation had been established internationally. Diplomats and businessmen, military officers and tourists were advised to "see Donald" whenever they visited China. Magazines sought articles

[1] Pu Yi's throne tumbled for the third time at the conclusion of World War II.

and book publishers sent letters that implored him for his memoirs. They sought to tempt him with lavish advance royalties. Donald politely spurned them all. Acquaintances who knew that he had not only absorbed the lore of the Orient but was a solid part of its history insisted that he write of his experiences. Many failed to comprehend his reluctance, his strong sense of right and wrong that forbade him from writing anything but the whole truth as he saw it. And sympathetic, understanding of their follies and foibles, he could not tell the truth about some of his Chinese friends.

But there were even broader considerations. The night the train left Peiping for Mukden carrying the Lytton Commission, a number of the members, including Donald, settled in the lounge car. Lytton, whose one-time viceroyship of India had made him sensitive to all Far Eastern problems, asked Dr. Wellington Koo a political question which Koo was unable to answer. Donald spoke up with his customary bluntness, "I will answer that question." And he did, tracing it back in great detail.

Lytton listened attentively, then asked, "Why don't you write a book?"

"Oh," Donald answered, "everybody asks why I don't write a book. If you want to know, I'll tell you why. Then you can give me your advice as to whether I should."

He described the events leading up to—and the outbreak of—the 1911 revolution, told how he went to Everard Fraser, Britain's consul at Shanghai, how he maneuvered him onto his side, how he sent the warning to Japan, how under his initial influence the British pulled Japan off China.

"Now," Donald asked with a twinkle, "do you want me to tell the world that the British meddled in China, that they won the revolution for the Chinese, or that I got the British consul into my pocket and jockeyed him into my plot?"

Even if the international situation had been considerably less delicate, no doubt the Englishman and Dr. Koo still would have been as emphatic in their chorused "No!" The subject of Donald as an author came up again several years later at dinner with Sir Miles Lampson and Dr. T. V. Soong. Not betraying his mirth, Donald admitted that he might do an autobiography, noting that his central theme would be how the British really won China's revolution.

"Good Lord!" Sir Miles exclaimed good naturedly. "Let's say no more about it." Laughing, too, Dr. Soong agreed.

That was why "Donald of China" continued as something of a legendary figure, as a man whose exploits were hearsay, as a man whose strong influence in Chinese affairs remained known to only a select few.

From the moment the commission set foot in Manchuria, the way was not easy. Japan, its agents like clumsy stagehands dropping their props, bobbed up behind the scenes. Spies followed every member, Donald in particular, since he was the most feared of the Chinese delegation. Once a Chinese friend asked for him at his hotel and was immediately clapped into prison by the Japanese and released only after Donald and the commission had left. Another annoying incident happened when Donald returned to a store where he had purchased cigars the day before. The proprietor begged him to leave and never return because the Japanese police had visited him after Donald's first call. They believed the Australian had brought a fortune with him to finance a revolt by Manchuria's Chinese and they were looking for a "go-between." After that, he never entered a Mukden shop without being conscious that he was shadowed continually by Japanese agents.

One night in Harbin, he spun around, seized two such men by the arms, marched them back to his hotel and turned them over to a man he knew to be their chief.

"Better find some others," Donald cautioned. "I know these fellows."

White Russians then were detailed to follow him, but in time he picked them out and hustled them back to the hotel. The chief was embarrassed.

"I'd commit hara-kiri if I were you," Donald snorted.

His experiences matched those of the rest of the commission. Lord Lytton, for instance, once caught the head of the Japanese delegation, a Mr. Yamato, searching his desk when he entered his hotel room. The commission's was a rotten business, anyway. On the spot, facing a *fait accompli*, they felt the impotency of the League. They were irked by the Japanese. They were tired and they wanted to go home. Even before they left for Peiping to write their report, the Japanese press employed its usual tactics against opponents, vilified the commission, accused it of consorting with prostitutes, then refusing to pay their bills. Of Donald, the papers said that he had a different Russian girl with him at each meal and still another for his "dream world." For Donald, the most careful and meticulous of men, the charge was coarse.

While the commission had gone through the sham of studying man's ills, Donald had had twinges of conscience. It had been he who had advised that China lay her problem before the Western world and ask for the justice that had been guaranteed not only at the Washington Conference but also under the League Covenant. Yet, he was able to console himself with the knowledge that China had had no other course. She could not then, now, or for years to come defend herself. Japan was on top, riding the tiger. No one wanted to be a tamer. One day, just before he left, his old friend, E. W. Frazer, still a businessman in Japan, called him at his Harbin hotel. Donald invited him to tiffin, and Frazer accepted but a moment later said, "Oh, no, Don. If I do, the Japanese will see me."

There was only a split-second study of his friend's reply. He understood the problem the American faced—a man doing business in Japan and lunching with him, emissary of the opposition. Yet he knew that men like Frazer and thousands of other foreigners in the Far East would have to have courage to face what was to come. He could not help but administer a mild spanking:

"Business is more important than friendship. Remember that, if you people are to hang on by your teeth in the days ahead." He paused while Frazer mumbled an agreement, then went on, "And now I'm going to say something to you, and then I will say no more. You are going to a Rotary convention in America and you take my advice and say to the Rotarians that the end has come for the brotherhood of man. They must urge their governments to arm themselves to take part in the biggest war the world has ever seen. If they don't, they will be fools and they will lose."

At Peiping, the commission's report was written, it being made public in October, 1932. The capable Lord Lytton wrote it himself, and while it branded Japan definitely as the aggressor, it admitted in effect the League's inability to do anything about the aggressor. Even the careful language of the report, however, was too much for the French delegate, General Claudel, since France then was playing the coquette with Japan. Lytton sat by, enraged, as what little bluntness there had been about Japan was rounded off, and Claudel then affixed his signature. While Donald watched, the Italian delegate, Count Aldrovandi-Marescotti, signed, followed by the American, General Frank McCoy, and Dr. Schnee from Germany. After protest, Lytton angrily wrote his signature, then threw down his pen.

"Now," he said, "I'm free to tell the truth. And damn it, I will!" Lytton's voice was heard again when the League censured Japan early in 1933. Japan's answer was to walk out, and the covey of men at Geneva was as powerless to stop her as they were to halt with words her march southward on the map.

Throughout the summer of 1932, Donald had kept in contact with China's ragged politics and with the Young Marshal. Chang, still addicted to drugs and the butt of attacks in the "mosquito"[2] press which accused him of everything from chicanery to promiscuous love affairs, once more had been dovetailed into the government. Yet his enemies—mainly because of his liberal views—were increasing. This annoyed Donald as did the revival of communism in China. In his opinion, communism never could be the solution. While its protests were nearly always justified, its reforms were often false. It never seemed interested in the indigent masses, which it might be forced to serve, but always in the wage-earning proletariat which could serve it. For China, preponderantly indigent, the advantages appeared obscure. He believed that China's salvation lay in establishing a republic in fact, not name alone, with a sound constitution, a bicameral parliament, suffrage for the people, and a civil service, patterned after the United States system, to provide a higher standard of worker. There would have to be freedom for capital and for foreign investment, and social-istic ideas would have to go hang.

There was no guarantee of any of this in the communism that, after its initial suppression in 1927, had bobbed up again, at first

---

[2] Dealing in sensation and unconfirmed stories.

spottily, then with a strength that began to menace the reactionary Kuomintang—still referred to by Donald as the *Nationalists*. While Chiang's campaign against the Reds had been proceeding desultorily for some time, he now decided to divert the public mind from Japan and turn it against the Red menace by a full-scale attack. But Chiang's communiqués which told of "stamping" them out and "routing the remnants" were false. The Communists merely moved from the central and southern sections to the northwest where they established fairly substantial strongholds.

Added to the bad blood on all fronts was the bitterness developing between Premier Wang Ching-wei and the Young Marshal over the latter's decision not to send his troops against Japan. Chang, following the policy that he and Donald had set together, could not be budged. Chiang sided with the Young Marshal, and Wang, the chronic in-and-outer, resigned and went to Europe. Meantime, rumors of new plots afoot and new governments in the making rippled the land. Feng Yu-hsiang, mentioned as a conspirator, denied them, affirmed his loyalty to Chiang, and again for a few months tranquillity came, hovered, then departed.

In January, 1933, Japan's restless military again began to crowd downward on the continent. They bombed Shanhaikwan, eastern gate of the Great Wall, and late in February, they stormed into the province of Jehol, once refuge for besieged Chinese monarchs. As they moved across the border, T. V. Soong, the Young Marshal, Donald and several German military advisers hurried from Peiping by car to Jehol. They hoped to encourage the governor, General Tang Yu-lin, to stand against Japan's continued voracious appetite for China.

Still impossible was a national resistance, but the Young Marshal and Donald were now convinced that at least isolated opposition would have to be made. They drove day and night through blinding blizzards, then finally reached Chengteh, the capital. There, they saw their first Chinese soldiers, their first guns. Both were guarding General Tang's opium factory in the city's center—and that was all. The governor was an old Manchurian reactionary, corrupt. He listened indolently to their pleas and did nothing. The Japanese swept in, following the route laid down by the Tanaka Memorial, and on March 3, Chengteh was taken. Manchukuo now had bulged deeper into China, and the Japanese grip was tighter than ever.

Under the new defeat, China stirred angrily, and the South once more ballooned its hatred for Chiang, accusing him of dealing secretly with Japan. The situation in the North was tense. How quickly would Japan strike again? The clamor for some action grew. On March 6, three days after Chengteh was occupied, Chiang Kai-shek hurried north. Someone had to be a whipping boy. The Young Marshal was it. Chiang asked for his resignation. After long conferences with Donald which dealt with national unity, the Young Marshal, on March 10, at Paotingfu, near Peiping, handed over his army, planes and materiel to Chiang. It was the first time since the founding of the republic that a commander in chief with a feudalistic background had with good grace retired in obedience to a government order. It was another important notch in the career of this strange young man. But from the national government there were no thank-you's. A civilian, Chang Hsueh-liang faced his troops and spoke with a patriotism that was rare at Paotingfu, this old military academy which had always housed a succession of personally ambitious war lords. He made it brief:

"We came into China proper to effect national unification, but the result is that we are now homeless. Although our sacrifice is great, it is worth while. After my departure, you must obey Generalissimo Chiang's orders and support the government unanimously. You must all be aware of the fact that in permitting me to resign the generalissimo wishes me good."

The Young Marshal went on to exhort his troops to remember their duty to their country whenever they thought of him. "Thus," he concluded, "we can attain our objective of recovering the lost land and returning home armed to the teeth."

Donald was happy that the Young Marshal was free of all military and political duties. At last there was a chance really to help the hollow-cheeked young man. Still convinced of the timber for leadership in his protégé, Donald decided a trip to Europe would broaden him, mold him into a better leader. Before Europe, however, Donald had a job—a big job. The time to begin work had come.

The day following their return from Paotingfu, Donald told him: "Tomorrow we're going to Shanghai. You're coming along. No arguments."

Chang at first appeared puzzled, then shrugged. In their four years together, he had learned the practicality, the wisdom of Donald's ways. Time and again, when he needed it, he had drawn upon his vigor, his intenseness. Looking at Donald, he saw, as he had in times of crises, the determined, the unyielding jaw.

The next day they left for Shanghai—Chang, his two wives, several children, a retinue of bodyguards and secretaries, and Donald. On the morning they arrived, Donald called on Dr. Miller, who before the Manchurian affair had begun, but never finished, his Mukden sanitarium.

"I have a patient for you—a man you know well, doctor," Donald said. "I want to take him to Italy within a fortnight. Can you lessen the influence of the drug on him?"

The doctor smiled confidently. "Not only that," he said. "I now know how to cure him."

This was more than Donald had expected. Buoyant, he returned to their Avenue Haig house and informed the secretarial staff that a cure for the Young Marshal had been obtained. He sensed a strange indifference. Of the large group, only one spoke. He said, "You can't do anything without his permission."

Donald snapped, "He's going through with it! All of you, now, run along and tell him what's up." A few minutes later, he followed to find them attempting to dissuade the Young Marshal from seeking a cure. As Donald entered, he looked up pleadingly.

"Let's wait," he said. "Let's wait."

"No waiting," Donald said. "This is your big chance. You'll take it." He walked out. In the hall, he met the chief of the Young Marshal's bodyguard, General Tan.

"General," he said, "we've got to get rid of the secretaries, the two doctors who have been feeding the young fellow his dope, and all the servants. I believe that for years they've been in cahoots to keep him on drugs. They've made money on it."

General Tan patted his holster. "I'll shoot them all if you tell me to," he said seriously. Donald never asked any questions thereafter, but the entire household staff disappeared before the day was out.

That night, Dr. Miller arrived, went quickly about his work, and shortly the Young Marshal and his two pavemal-addicted wives were put to sleep. The doctor then made large blisters on their stomachs, and from the blisters he removed a liquid, injecting it into their arms.

"They'll sleep for about three days," Miller said. "After that, we might have some trouble."

The vigil began. A cot for the doctor was placed inside the bedroom, while Donald slept immediately outside the door. This was his big project. He wanted no slips that it might be within his power to prevent.

On the morning of the third day, Miller received an urgent outside call, and after he had left, Donald heard a disturbance in the bedroom. Running in, he found his patient struggling with a male nurse. Donald barked at him, the Young Marshal stopped and glared belligerently.

"Get into bed!" Donald commanded, and Chang, after hesitating a moment, obeyed. Once in bed, he began to fight Donald, flailing at him with arms and legs. His adviser held him in a bear grip.

"You'll stop," he said, "or I'll lay you out."

The Young Marshal looked startled, then relaxed. It was plain that he had not entirely emerged from his stupor. His eyes were sick and glassy.

"Don," he mumbled, "are you a Christian?"

Donald straightened up, laughing. "If I weren't, I'd have chucked you in the lake a long time ago."

Chang smiled weakly, went back to sleep. In a few days, both he and his wives were completely out of the stupor. They were cured. There was no craving for the drug. They never went back to it. Even before they sailed for Italy, the three had added weight, were looking better.

They arrived in May, the Young Marshal's step springier, his cheeks fuller. The ocean voyage had breathed new life into him, and he had been a gay, lionized figure all the way. He showed himself adept at cards, at amusing tricks, and to have a knack for jollying children. But what perhaps caught his eye more than anything was the figure, the asplike charm of the heavy-lidded green-eyed Countess Galeazzo Ciano—Edda—the daughter of Mussolini. The count, his tour of duty over in China where he and Edda had been at the top of the swirl of Shanghai society, was returning to become Italy's foreign minister. Edda, then an enchantress, commanded much of the Young Marshal's time. But to shipboard gossipers, Donald only cluck-clucked.

Chang began his European adventure at Rome. Coached by Donald, he met the right people, said the right things. Overnight, he was a great success socially. More than ever, he was full of humor, full of play. There was none of the brittle brightness or the vacant-eyed sagginess of the drug addict. Donald watched, pleased. He was with him every step, his good nature always at hand. One night, they had dinner at the restaurant of Alfredo, known as the noodle king. Alfredo served his customers personally, with flourish, using a gold fork and spoon given him by Douglas Fairbanks and Mary Pickford. When he came to Donald and the Young Marshal, he handed them his guest book and asked to be honored with their signatures. At first, they begged off, but Alfredo implored, and Donald said, "Well, if you will tell me why a noodle is called a noodle, I will write in your book."

Although Alfredo confessed he could not answer, Donald, who throughout the years had never lost his enthusiasm for concocting limericks, wrote:

> Though Alfredo is known as the great Noodle King,
> Of the whyfores of noodles he knows not a thing.
> Ask him if you will why a noodle is a noodle,
> He'll reply, "I don't know but it brings in the boodle."

After leaving Rome, they spent six months touring Europe, motoring in and out of the major countries. They played golf, they swam, they rode horses. Within a short time, the Young Marshal was in perfect condition. Donald had succeeded. His charge was taking a keener view on matters of import. He was less impulsive, more deliberate. In each country, Donald worked with him, studying political, economic, educational matters. For awhile, Chang was caught by the glitter of the reforms in Italy and Germany, particularly by Mussolini's "rejuvenation" schemes. He believed that he was witnessing a resurgence of a great people and a parallel for China. When his enthusiasm would reach too high, Donald would caution:

"Go easy. All is not gold that glistens."

Before some of his exhilaration had tapered off, the Young Marshal wrote a letter to an acquaintance in China. Translated, it read:

The rejuvenation of Italy and Germany is due chiefly to their peoples wholehearted support of their leaders who, therefore, have sufficient strength to overcome the obstacles on the way to national rejuvenation. It is not the case with China. When a leader has just shown his ability to lead the people, there spring up jealous people to engineer his downfall. This has been responsible for the civil wars and foreign aggression. If our people wish to work for national salvation, they must have implicit faith in their leader and support him. . . .

In this, Chang was advocating support for the man who had given him no thanks for his unprecedented gift of an army. But that is why the Young Marshal was strange—strange for China.

By November, they had reached Copenhagen. There, a wire came one day from the Young Marshal's office in China. It read:

REVOLT HAS BROKEN OUT IN FUKIEN STOP THERE IS A MOVEMENT UNDER WAY TO GET US TO JOIN FACTIONS AGAINST CHIANG KAI-SHEK STOP COME BACK AT ONCE.

Chang wanted to leave immediately, but Donald advised him to wait while he went in advance to determine how delicate or how dangerous the situation. He would wire him when and if he might return. Donald sailed from Venice. At Singapore, a newspaper headline greeted him: T. V. SOONG RESIGNS AS MINISTER OF FINANCE. He knew that when such a man as Soong, the most capable of China's financiers, left the government, there was real trouble in the wind.

He resumed his journey to Shanghai, plagued by the curtain of gloom that never seemed to lift.

chapter

22

DONALD AND THE CHIANGS

To dig up a tree, you must begin with the root.

❖

THE situation was cankerous when Donald stepped into Shanghai early in December. There was animosity and the feel of pending upheaval on all sides. Throughout the summer and autumn, the passion against Chiang Kai-shek had mounted. The North wanted his downfall. So did the South. The big question was which way the troops of the Young Marshal would go—the troops which had only sullenly accepted a nominal control by Chiang. But a projected drive against the Nanking leader had not materialized. Chiang had moved strategically in Hunan Province, and the South, lacking adequate support, temporarily shelved its plans. Thereupon, the North quieted down.

By November, a new plot had arisen—this time in Fukien Province, fomented by the Nineteenth Route Army's General Tsai Ting-kai, who had reason aplenty to hate Chiang. Tsai and rapier-tongued Eugene Chen set up the "Federal Revolutionary Government of China" and then looked hopefully to the North, South and West for support.

They were still looking when Donald arrived in China to stir, as always, a flood of rumors in his path. No casual tourist, Donald's appearances had significance attached to them by both Chinese and foreigners. On his first day, one paper reported that his mission "held high political importance," while another stated, "It is even whispered as a telltale straw in this troublous wind that W. H. Donald has held conferences with Vickers, well-known munitions makers." Chinese political eyes were on him, and just as intent were the Japanese, whose

286

fingers were always wetted for China winds, especially if they might be directed toward their newly acquired Manchukuo.

Donald's first move was to call on T. V. Soong. He found that the minister had quarreled with his brother-in-law, Chiang, and had resigned because Chiang, who was completely barren of economic understanding, wanted to use a disproportionate percentage of revenue for military expenditures. Soong stood for financial orthodoxy, a balanced budget and expenditures for the military within the nation's income. Donald listened intently, noncommitally.

He made other calls, and when he returned to his hotel, Mr. Yakichiro Suma,[1] roving listening post for the Japanese Legation, was outside his door. He followed Donald in and Donald, facing him, kept him standing.

He spoke abruptly to the burly Japanese: "I suppose you want to know if the Young Marshal is coming back. I want to tell you that he will come back. He will not ask the permission of the Japanese."

Suma stood uncomfortably. He attempted a polite smile. He wanted to know, all right, as did his government. Tokyo was agitated by its inability to learn whether the Young Marshal had plans for the recapture of Manchuria and whether he might have secured financing in Europe.

Donald gave him no chance to speak and, looking at him as one might contemplate emptiness, he continued: "I'm going to tell you something and then you may toddle on. What Japan has always needed in China is a good adviser. With one, you could have had China in the cup of your hands."

Suma jerked his head in annoyed agreement. "Like you, I suppose," he said.

Donald ignored him and went on: "Japan is wrong in her thoughts, in her aims concerning China. She has an enemy where she could have a friend. But, then, that is her manner. She's always kicking people in the pants. Anyway, we know what you are up to. You do not fool us."

Donald opened his door for Suma. "That's all I have to say," he said, "and that's all the information you need."

[1] Later in the Tokyo Foreign Office, and subsequently ambassador to Spain.

In the next several days, Donald held conversations with representatives of all factions, pro- as well as anti-Chiang. From these talks, it appeared that the Young Marshal was the balance of power. Whichever way he and his armies went, so would go the nation. His high-ranking officers needed only his word to scuttle their allegiance to Chiang. Nanking was swimming in its usual political crosscurrents. Its reactionaries still sputtered a hate for the radical Young Marshal. Nevertheless, by the end of the fourth day, Donald had drawn his conclusions. He had decided what was best for China. He held a press conference and announced:

"The return of the Young Marshal to China is desired by his officers. But, in view of conditions now prevailing in this country, it is difficult to say when he will return. I have a strong feeling that he may go to Soviet Russia."

That was enough, he knew, to do the trick. Two little words, Soviet Russia. The hint was broad. That night, he wired the Young Marshal: "You can come home now." The next day, Nanking representatives were camped on his doorstep, cordial. He had frightened them.

The Young Marshal returned on January 8, 1934. Donald had met him at Manila, and when they stepped off at Shanghai, two hundred bodyguards closed about them. Donald was taking no chances with malcontents. His decision to co-operate with Nanking was now widely known. On the way north, the two had discussed the wisdom of linking up again with the Nationalist government. Donald saw it as the only solution for national stability, and the Young Marshal had agreed.

"But," Donald said, "joining up means we're taking on a big job. We've got a lot of cleaning to do. Nanking is stagnant."

From Shanghai, they went to Nanking and to a meeting with Chiang Kai-shek. The generalissimo had just completed suppression of the revolt in Fukien. When it had become apparent that the Young Marshal's troops were not to join with his antagonists, he had moved with speed and surprising air and ground power, wiping out the Nineteenth Route army, heroes of Shanghai, and scattering the Separationist government.

The meeting between the granite-faced, solemn Chiang and the ambitious, effervescent young man got off to a fiery start. Chiang said that he supposed the Young Marshal was wondering what job he was to be given.

"I'm wondering more how China is to make herself behave," the Young Marshal answered briskly. "Europe doesn't think much of either you or China."

Chiang's expression never changed. He said that he and Madame Chiang were leaving the following day for Hangchow, a resort to the south. Would the Young Marshal and Donald join them there?

They accepted and, when they were again alone, Donald said to the Young Marshal, "Good. Now we'll tell the old war lord a thing or two."

The four sat in a private room in a restaurant that faced the lovely shallow blue pool of Hangchow's West Lake, girt by green hills, watched by graceful pagodas and crossed by willow-draped causeways and moon bridges. The generalissimo, imperturbable, pate glistening; Madame Chiang on his left to translate; the two strange partners in front of them. It was seven o'clock when Donald pinned Chiang with a polite, pleasant stare and began to talk. Four hours later, he was still at it.

"I'm going to tell you what's wrong with China," he said. Mei-ling stirred and looked quickly from Donald to her husband.

The Young Marshal coughed.

"Don't interrupt," Donald said to him. "You'll have your innings." He began what no man had had the courage to do before.

"First off," he said, "no high official can reform China because there is a lack of understanding of what to reform. You people sit in your yamens, and your horizon is your window sill. You are ignorant because no one dares to correct you. You might lose face and, what's more, someone might lose his head. You've retreated into your intellectual ratholes, leaving exposed only a posterior of vanity. Goddam it, sir, you've all become insufferably stupid!"

Donald paused. Madame Chiang translated. The eyes in the stone face of the generalissimo blinked once.

"This country is ridden with graft," Donald went on. "It's full of swindlers who will steal anything from American Red Cross funds to a squeezing, a rake-off on every government or private transaction. It's gotten to the point where a man is apologetic if he cannot steal for himself a fortune overnight."

"I will tell the generalissimo your opinion," said Madame Chiang. Chiang's bright eyes burned into Donald.

"You damn well know, as I do, that opium is flooding the country," Donald continued. "It flows up and down the Yangtze right past your front door. Thousands die of it every month. Thousands, yes millions, die because there is no flood control, because there are no guards against pestilence, because China, a nation of farmers, is really a poor farmer. There is no protection against disease, and epidemics sweep like the wind across the land. Millions more die, and thousands and thousands of others die because you cannot stop killing yourselves in civil wars."

Mei-ling interpreted, and Donald jabbed once more. "Where are your schools?" he asked. "Where are your fine highways and where is the network of railways you should have? Where are the industries, the steel, the hydroelectric power? Where are your trained, technical men for engineering projects, and where are your skilled administrators? Above all, where is there decency and nobility for the common man?"

He halted and eyed Madame Chiang. "China should be ashamed," he said. "There is the staleness, the obeseness of wealth on one hand— the hog wallow of poverty on the other. The ricksha man and the wharf coolie are worse off than the horse and camel in many another land."

The Young Marshal took it up at that point. He berated the Generalissimo for an indifference that seemed to sanction corruption, inefficiency and the presence of unprogressive elements. He spoke harshly and vigorously.

It was near midnight when the two rebels ended their separate monologues. The generalissimo stayed to confer with his staff while Donald and Chang escorted Madame Chiang to her hotel. As they walked, she hooked Donald's arm. "You were wonderful," she said. "We needed that."

They stopped in the lobby. "Why don't you come to work for us?" she asked. "We need a brain like yours."

"I don't work for women," Donald smiled. "Why should I try to advise one of heaven's whimsies? They can't take it."

"I can take it," she answered. "If I couldn't, I wouldn't have dared translate everything you said."

"That's right," the Young Marshal agreed. "She even put in your goddams."

Donald laughed. "I'm going to write you some letters," he said. "If you can get the generalissimo to act on them, then some day I might be working with you."

For the next hour, Donald walked along the shores of the enchanting little lake, thinking of the generalissimo and his wife, of what the generalissimo might think of him, of what was to be the fate of the Young Marshal as the result of their outburst. The moon was bright and the scene before him beautiful. It had been an inspiration for China's poets from the Sung dynasty on.

For awhile, Donald lingered by the shore, watching fishermen drag in their catch. Then he returned to his hotel and, since he had a mind as agile and flexible at midnight as at noon, he dashed off a bit of spicy rhyme. He addressed it to the gay, convivial mayor of Hangchow whom he had met that day and had liked. This is what he wrote:

A Warning to Elephant[2]

When night had come upon the lake,
When only prowlers were awake,
And little fishes free from fear
Were feeding where street lights were near,
A savage came with net in hand
And hauled the little fish to land.
They lost their lives because at night
They lingered looking at the light.

Let this a warning be to you:
All brilliant lights and lures eschew.
There's danger in the lamp's bright glare,
In maiden's eyes, and lips, and hair.

[2] The characters in the mayor's given name were also the characters for elephant.

Where lights are red be doubly sure
That if you fall you know the cure,
For many a sweet and charming miss
Is loaded down with syphilis.

Lest unsophisticated you
Should find yourself right in the stew,
Beware the nets spread all around
To drag you down upon the ground.
If you'd escape the fishes' fate,
To bed go early—ne'er stay late,
And maybe you will live quite long
Just like the foreign devil "Don."

The next day, the Young Marshal was notified formally that he had been appointed vice commander in chief of the Bandit Suppression troops in Honan, Hupeh and Anhwei. Headquarters were to be at Hankow. The two rebels had won the first round in the fight for better government.

What began to happen now almost certainly left the Chiangs gasping. Donald plunged into a whirlwind campaign to clean up China even before he left for Hankow and soon, the fur, as he put it, began to fly in the Yangtze Valley. Matters under the command of Dr. H. H. Kung, now minister of finance, were the first to come under Donald's big guns. He called Kung's attention sharply to the fact that smuggled goods were finding their way up all avenues of trade under Japanese protection, and he urged an immediate widening of the customs police service. Donald promised to investigate the matter thoroughly as soon as he reached his new headquarters. Quickly, he turned to China's broader problems.

While his river steamer was between Nanking and Hankow, he wrote comprehensively, emphasizing many of the points he had made at Hangchow and bringing up new ones:

February 24, 1934

Dear Madame Chiang:

I am going to Hankow with the Young Marshal and there will begin investigations of Yangtze commerce and industry so that you may in course of time have some adequate idea of the obstructions which confront merchants and industrialists.

Whatever can be done to promote the flow of commerce and the establishment of industries for the manufacture of those things which China now imports, the sooner China will be restored to her rightful position in the comity of nations.

Today on the river I saw three batches of barges being towed up river toward here loaded with Fushun coal. Does it not strike you as peculiar that Japanese coal, mined in so-called Manchukuo, can be brought by rail from Mukden to Dairen, thence to Shanghai by steamer, thence by barges up the Yangtze and be able to compete with Chinese coal? Really, it is a disgrace, but it is due to the fact that the mines cannot operate properly because of official neglect of their interests.

Every energy of the rulers of China should be bent to the one object of manufacturing all those things that Japan exports to this country. Surely, China has brains enough for that; has the competent labor; has the energy. Of course she has, but she also has the officials who care not one iota for the country or its well-being; who regard it as a bonanza for their exploitation; who bleed it white.

League of Nations' advisers are not needed to tell what is wrong with China. Perhaps they would not tell. But you must know the truth if China is to be saved, and the truth is rotten officialdom—squeeze, corruption, militarism, overtaxation. . . . I am sure that it can be removed. I am sure that you can help remove it. But you will have to be ruthless, and hard, and uncompromising. A big stick can cure a lot of ills in China. The Chinese people are oppressed beyond belief. They are waiting for someone to give just a lead in saving them. Can't you find a big stick lying about somewhere and use it without scruple?

Unless you or someone initiates a move to install honesty quickly, China will die. It is dying now. . . .

Donald and the Young Marshal took hold of their new tasks with vigor. With the Australian advising, Chang began to put teeth into his tri-province post, with scourging of the Communists and economic rehabilitation foremost. Before many weeks, the Central China Economic Investigation Bureau was set up, with Donald as director. Patterned after his bureau of similar name in Peiping years before, the new office began to probe ways and means of rejuvenating trade in the interior and developing natural resources.

Donald's fame for getting at the core of bad situations had preceded his arrival at Hankow. First to call on him was Bishop Logan H. Roots, an American missionary whose reputation was wide for loving all humans quite indiscriminately. The bishop, who headed an anti-opium league, unfolded shocking tales of how the drug was being ferried down river from Szechwan, aided and abetted by the military and police, how large quantities were actually sold by them. To Donald, the story was old, the details new.

Since its introduction into China, opium had become a steadily increasing problem. In many areas poppy cultivation was virtually the only means of livelihood. Because it was profitable, farmers turned to it when and if the opportunity was afforded. Donald remembered once having visited, in the company of a group of newspapermen, a district where a dam built with American funds had been opened to irrigate wastelands and to provide the people with agricultural opportunities. What they saw accented the depth to which the fruitlessness of effort to assist can go. In the new fertile lands they saw not rows of cabbages, beets or leeks but fields of nodding red poppies—opium poppies.

Newsmen had exposed the "agricultural development." Embarrassed, the government had ordered troops to mow down the poppy fields watered by the dam. Left without an opium crop, many of the farmers and their families had starved that winter.

After the bishop left, Donald wrote Madame Chiang, itemizing the corruption that existed among officialdom in the opium traffic. He pointed out that the statue of Dr. Sun Yat-sen overlooked the biggest opium shop in Hankow. On the shop's window was a large sign that read: CHEAP SALE OF OPIUM—THOSE WHO MAKE EXTRA LARGE PURCHASES WILL BE GIVEN FREE TICKETS IN THE NATIONAL GOVERNMENT LOTTERY. Madame Chiang was told that newspapers were heavily bribed not to publish material unfavorable to opium, that banks were used solely for opium collections by the merchants. He offered a solution.

Within twelve hours from the time she received the letter, the generalissimo issued his first anti-opium manifesto. Chiang stated that he considered it one of the vilest of evils and ordered all opium-smoking shops closed. But the opium traffic went on. It continued to come down river in undiminished quantities. Once again, Donald blasted out with a stinging denunciation of it, excoriating officials. Chiang met the challenge by ordering decapitation of all persons caught dealing in narcotics.

The day after the order took effect, Donald saw a postal van loading opium in parcel-post packages in the center of the city. He knew now that Chinese alone were not to blame. He knew that foreigners were involved as well. The next day, the Hankow *Herald*, a Kuomintang paper, carried an unsigned article by him in which he noted bitterly: "Yesterday, I expected to see on the Bund the decapitated heads of a number of persons, including the British commissioner of customs and the French chief of the post office. But there were no heads there at all."

All the while, Donald was whipping out on all sides. Even as he fought opium, he seized upon one of China's most shameful situations: agriculture. Essentially an agricultural country, China could not feed herself, and every year her imports of rice and flour mounted by millions of dollars. The Chinese farmer, burdened by medieval methods and the indifference of the government, was sliding deeper into a morass. Donald insisted upon attention for him. Then he turned to the salt revenue of nearly two hundred million dollars a year and the flagrant dishonesty in its collection:

HANKOW, April 13, 1934

Dear Madame Chiang:

. . . If salt taxes are administered with a big stick, you can increase the revenues tremendously. I know the difficulties—but Roosevelt had them and he is flogging them out of sight as well as democracy. Most people who exist are ready to be governed and they will accept a *fait accompli* the world around. If a few *faits accomplis* are established here, they would be accepted in a surprisingly short time. . . .

Make graft, corruption, squeeze, or whatever one might call it, a capital offense, and shoot a lot of people and soon there would be a change. But start high up and not among the unhappy low salaried unfortunates. . . .

From earthy matters, he switched to the psychological. At Hangchow and in repeated letters, he had urged the Chiangs to give thought to the stamping out of face. Always its opponent, Donald now became its greatest enemy. He had been at Hankow less than two months when he suggested a New Mentality movement, a new national psychology to complement the New Life movement.[3] And forthwith he began an anonymous campaign in the newspapers, supplying them with material which, he pointed out to the editors, contained the idea that could save China. In such articles and letters to Madame Chiang, he noted that the proposed movement would remove the barricade to greatness and to decent respectability as a nation.

Remaining always in the background, mysterious in his ways as ever, he urged through articles in English, as well as those translated into Chinese, that China's millions give thought to how face had contributed to the demoralization of social and political relations. He wrote that "to face and its craziness you can trace all manner of ills and particularly the failure of patriotism in China." Put on a false basis, he argued, were the relations between man and man, between group and group, no one daring to tell the truth if face was involved. In one article he declared that "The whole civil service (if it can be called that) of China is crammed with dead wood, eating up small salaries amounting to millions, because face would not allow the sacking of the worthless." Again, he wrote that he himself had no face in China because he carried his own parcels and belongings, and because he did many of his own chores.

Before the campaign was many weeks old, the generalissimo issued a solemn statement to the nation on the evils of face.

Bound by no isms, Donald was able to hunt and peck the good from the bad at random. As the New Mentality idea developed step by step, he turned to the matter of China's national spirit which, although improved by two decades of revolution, was to him sadly weak. To illustrate his point, he drew upon his recent trip to Italy and Germany. While he had cautioned the Young Marshal against the obvious iniquities of their political theories, he felt that the national spirit they engendered might well be encouraged in a land that had none. He

[3] Based on four words familiar to the sages: Propriety, Justice, Integrity and Conscientiousness. It was designed to correct the morals and the manners of the entire population. Generalissimo Chiang was officially credited as the movement's founder, but Madame Chiang was the dynamo behind it and Donald was the dynamo behind her. Many believe that Donald himself was its creator.

felt that China could build a spirit, and to the Chiangs he said that their household was where it should begin. He was out to combat defeatism. He wrote insistently time and again that the generalissimo should plead for a self-inventory among the people. He wanted groups started that would talk honestly without thought of face and would extend searching criticism through all avenues of social, business and political life. "Let us stop talking in polite but empty phrases," he declared. "Let us be honest with ourselves and we will be honest with our country."

He hammered home the idea at the Chiang doorstep: "I am certain that you can do in China in time what has been done in Germany, Italy and Turkey. It is merely the development of another kind of 'Boy Shouts', though bigger boys. Pride of country and personal pride must be developed to save China, and if the Kuomintang was worth its salt at all, it could be the instrument or the machine to work up this plain, straightforward national movement."

How close to treading on thin ice Donald may have realized he was is not known. Certain it is that he wanted no brand of earth-shaking politics or the development of a super-race. There was, of course, no question of his awareness of China's political immaturity and of her unpredictable emotions. But Japan was bearing down, Tanaka Memorial in hand. Perhaps he felt the urge to lean to the extreme in order to combat a national apathy that continued to squat as a fog on the land. Perhaps he was motivated as he had been many times in the past: When great issues are at stake, great risks are called for.

Donald next swung to the subject of exploitation—not by foreigners, as was the cry of the Communists, but from China's union leaders:

HANKOW, April 18, 1934

Dear Madame Chiang:

I hear nothing but tales of woe regarding labor conditions. All strikes and "Go Slow" movements are run by grafters and troublemakers. It is what is called in Chicago a "racket."

Only yesterday when talking about the coolie work on the Bund, I was told that of every dollar paid for carrying, only forty cents went to the poor coolie. Who gets the rest? The fat, grafting compradores who exploit them.

In factories, labor conditions are appalling since the laborers are under the thumbs of union bosses who graft on them and use them for extortion and political purposes. . . .

Another paragraph in today's paper says that the Japanese are blocking the arrest of the strike leader at Tongshan coal mines. Of course the Japanese are interested in disturbing everything in China in general and North China in particular. They MUST be able to tell the world that they alone can restore order in this distracted country.

CURE FOR LABOR STRIKES: Set up an arbitration court to make awards in all labor difficulties. Penalize all strike leaders. Indeed, make it a capital offense. Wipe out the union bosses and let labor get what it earns and much of the trouble in China would be wiped out. Get foreign advisers at work to support the judges—who MUST be honest. Or would that be loss of face?

Ten days later, the following story, typical of those in other newspapers, appeared in the *Central China Post*:

NANKING, April 28. Generalissimo Chiang Kai-shek issued yesterday identical orders to the chairmen of Hupeh, Honan, Kiangsi, Anhwei and Fukien provincial governments with instructions that the authorities shall prevent all labor unions from collecting membership fees in order to lessen the already heavy burden on workers. At the same time the generalissimo ordered that, while working hours be increased to ten, maltreatment of workers is strictly forbidden.

Donald kept up an almost day to day bombardment of the Chiangs with detailed studies of China's aches and economic and political ills. To him, ideas for reform were not new. He had first preached them to the Manchus in the South, then to Dr. Sun. The little doctor, in turn, had expounded them dreamily in after-dinner speeches, but no one had listened. Thereafter, Donald had urged them upon a succession of Chinese governments, but met always the patient smile, the deaf ear. Was it possible that now, after more than thirty years in China, he was to see the first glimmer of success?

The "idea factory" at Hankow ground on. He called for the creation of a Sino-Foreign Railway Reconstruction Board to reorganize all railways and substitute efficiency for neglect in order to be able to repay foreign loans. He attempted to shame the government by pointing out that Japan, as soon as it seized Manchuria, had paid off railway loans made by Britain. He prodded it on the need to revamp mining laws and thus encourage foreign capital into mining enterprises. Almost to the point of harping, he dwelled on the need to employ foreign technical help, to establish technological schools. He proposed foreigners for tax collection boards and offered a scientific method for tax collection. For the farmer, for whom he always had the deepest pity, he had new ideas to make his work more profitable. In addition, he asked that China abandon one of her most unwholesome practices: the use of child labor.

But he never lost sight of Japan. Wherever her ambitions bobbed up, he pointed. He saw in some of the labor unrest the machinations of Tokyo, whose industrial profits went up whenever China's factories closed down. He watched her military and her diplomats, suggested counter-propaganda as Japan preened herself before the world as arbiter of affairs in China. When Japan's army, rolling westward in North Asia, began to reach for Inner Mongolia, Donald took steps to spy on its movements. With Madame Chiang's permission, he reached deep into Mongolia (so deep that it took eleven days by horse and cart to deliver the telegram after it arrived at the nearest telegraph station) to bring out a man to do the job. He was the famous F. A. Larsen, a Swedish missionary, known as Larsen, Duke of Mongolia. Larsen, who had been given royal standing by Mongolia's rulers, was flown to Hankow where Donald expounded his idea for formation of a border patrol, patterned after the Canadian Northwest Mounted Police, the Texas Rangers, and the former Swedish Gendarmery in Persia. Once before—twenty years before—he and Larsen had met in the North and had talked of such a project. He wanted it officered by Swedes, with a Chinese codirector. Besides riding herd on Japan's ambitions, he saw the gendarmery as a club to quash Chinese banditry.

But Donald's criticism of China and Chinese went beyond his efforts at reform. He left the Sinophile to his romantic dreams while he, the realist, spoke sharply of a major emptiness in Chinese character—the inability to handle emergencies.

"The test of a superior man," he once told Ed Hunter, editor of the Peking *Leader*, "is not how intelligently he talks, how cultured he is or what he does in normal circumstances. The test is how he meets crises."

Donald went on, "There is where the real inequality exists between

East and West. The Chinese meets them badly. Suddenly, he seems paralyzed. He differs from the Westerner who leaps into gaps and immediately has the confidence to command. Take the American, for instance. He meets famine and flood, hurricane, war or fire, at home or abroad. He meets them alertly, quickly and efficiently."

Thus Donald showed himself a more severe critic of China than many would have thought. Yet, as he told Hunter, he had to be. "These people," he said, "always want to hear the best about themselves. But I never tell them how right they are, but how wrong. That's the only way I can be a good adviser."

China was in his thoughts all his waking hours, as he was jogged along in his ricksha over the mile of unshaded road between his house and office; at his work; during meals and at the odd times he found for golf. As at Hong Kong, Shanghai, Peiping and Mukden, he took no interest in clubs and around barrooms he steered a wide path. He dropped no calling cards on his compatriots and their wives. By now, he had abandoned what he had regarded as his major dissipation—ten to twelve cigars a day. He had decided with customary abruptness that he had had enough.

He had arrived at Hankow in February, 1934. It was now June. In that time, he had become an anonymous *enfant terrible* in Central China. His correspondence with the Chiangs, of course, was confidential, and only a few could detect his touch in newspaper articles. A Chinese government was hearing more constructive suggestions for reform than any Chinese government had ever heard in the past. Some of his proposals had taken hold, for how long he did not know. Others were like holes in beach sand, quickly filled by the backwash. He was now fifty-nine, still vigorous, although understandably weary from his great effort. Momentarily, the outside world beckoned. Perhaps it was the quiet of the back country of his native Australia, or perhaps the solitude of the carefree South Seas. He looked longingly, then told of his thoughts in a letter to Elliston on June 23:

. . . The Young Marshal is at the moment at the Anhwei front where troops under him are fighting the Communists. If he goes on as he is going (and if he survives), he'll be quite a factor in China one of these days. I have done my best for him, anyway, and am tired of it all, so I'm thinking somehow of breaking away with a ream or two of paper with the object of getting out of my memory the events of the past thirty years or so. It is all a jumble and a miserable business. . . .

Politically, things in China seem to have advanced a bit since the days when there were so many elements about capable of flinging the country into the throes of civil war. Most of the chiefs of the armed coolies, who call themselves marshals or generals, have disappeared. The Young Marshal has set a fashion and that is to talk straight out from the shoulder. He is all for a dictatorship on the basis that the people do not understand anything necessary for a popular government. He wants the Kuomintang wiped out if it will not readjust its views and cut out the capers. He went against a lot who tried to get him to join in the overthrow of Chiang Kai-shek on the basis that any attempt to force Chiang out would be defeated in course of time, but while the war was going on, China would be lost.

The gang at the head of affairs in China have now agreed among themselves to face the facts, to realize that it is not the unequal treaties or imperialism or foreign devils who have ruined China, but the Chinese themselves. And so they listen to the truth, talk frankly, and try to cure the ills. But the inertia of the mass is terrific. How poor old China is ever going to get ahead of it, it is impossible to say. The Young Marshal thinks only the methods of the Bolsheviks will do anything—chop the heads off a million or so. He says that the only thing to do is to hand the country over to some foreign power and let them run it for twenty-five years or so. . . .

The stage is getting set for either an upheaval or a very quiet transition from the rottenness of today to a dictatorship with more rottenness. . . . We shall see what we shall see.

But Donald's thoughts of breaking away from China were soon swallowed up in the continuing welter of work. In October, 1934, Generalissimo and Madame Chiang arrived at Hankow on their way to open a new branch of the Central Military Academy at Loyang. Madame Chiang invited the Young Marshal and Donald to join them for a three-day trip. At first, Donald tried to beg off on grounds that he was too busy, but under her insistence, he relented. The morning after they left, he was sitting in what was formerly the private car of the old dowager empress when Madame Chiang came in, her tiny frame almost smothered in an armful of letters and documents. She set them down on a desk and looked wearily at Donald.

"It's too much for me," she said and plopped into a chair.

Donald smiled warmly. To some, she was glamorous, frightening, a beautifully cold statue, efficient and precise, but to Donald she was frail and delicate, intelligent and pretty, an elf with a dynamo. He had known her since she had worn pigtails.

"Relax," he said, "and I'll tell you some stories." He did—tales of the Manchus before their overthrow, of how he had helped her father plot that overthrow, of days with Anderson and their cannon before Nanking's gates. In the afternoon, Mei-ling came back with another load. She looked at him with warm, almost moist eyes. She said, "I cannot do these. Why don't you help me?"

"That might be difficult," he answered. "I'm in another's camp."

"There's nothing in China that's closed to you," she replied quietly.

"Nothing?" he asked.

She smiled and pushed a pile of letters toward him. He went to work, making memos for the generalissimo, answering queries from a variety of sources, typing them all swiftly. His decisions were quick, his judgments sound. She watched in quiet admiration. Donald did not know it then, but this was the beginning of a task from which in the years to come he was to find little relief. He was to be closer than ever before to the point where he could apply the starch Petrie Watson once had said they needed, to the role of Dutch uncle to tell them "which way is up wind and which way is down."

On the third day, the Chiangs, the Young Marshal and Donald were having tea on the train before starting back to Hankow. Donald turned to the generalissimo.

"If you will order the engine hooked onto the other end of the train," he said, "we'll be in the city of Sian by tiffin time tomorrow."

Madame Chiang looked eagerly at Donald, then translated his remark. The generalissimo stared questioningly.

"You have never been in Shensi Province, the cradle of the Chinese race," Donald said. "It is about time you went there. It would be a shame to miss it now that we are so close."

Chiang nodded. At Hangchow, Donald had said that no ruler could guide China properly because no official knew where reforms were needed. What happened in the provinces rarely reached the ears of central authority, and no ruler had ever taken the time for personal investigation.

But there was more to Donald's plot than Sian. He was accomplishing with a China leader what no one else had, and he was going to make the most of it. He was going to teach a Chinese something about China, even if he had to do it by the most diplomatic of kidnapings.

At Sian, they were greeted enthusiastically. Instead of a few hours, they spent three days, and for the first time the generalissimo heard firsthand statements about the maladministration of the country. He heard them from all nationalities in the missionary body at a meeting Donald had Madame Chiang call. Both speaking eloquently, the generalissimo in Chinese, Madame Chiang in English, they outlined China's aims. They spoke earnestly of co-operation with the missionaries and asked that it be made mutual. They stressed the efficacy of the New Life movement and wondered if Christian teachings might be dovetailed with it. Donald stood by beaming. Here was a new day in China, perhaps a new era. He could see the astonishment spread from face to face. At the end of Madame Chiang's talk, she invited them to speak frankly on what they thought of the administration in the districts in which they lived. The missionaries, who long before had resigned themselves to nothing better than official toleration, looked even more astonished. No one spoke. Donald rose and said:

"What Madame Chiang is asking is that you tell them to their faces what you have said behind their backs many a time."

Finally, one rose, then another, each telling the story of bad government. When the meeting ended, missionaries and representatives of the New Life Movement formed a joint committee with the stamping out of opium as their foremost objective.

As a member of the religious Soong family, Madame Chiang was at home in Christian gatherings. This, however, was the first time the generalissimo, who had been converted by his wife to Christianity only a few years before, had ever met with a missionary body. But in Donald's plans there were more such meetings to come. These plans got under way immediately. Before Chiang could offer formidable resistance, Donald and Madame Chiang had an itinerary set out. This time they flew, heading for Lanchow, on the edge of the thickly settled parts of the Northwest, in Kansu Province.

There, the foursome, Donald, the Chiangs and the Young Marshal, walked through the city every day, talked to the people, learned their views on politics and economics and engaged in a variety of small talk. Donald watched the generalissimo closely. He could sense a change day by day. Small as it was, it was there—a growth, three dimensional. His face was more relaxed and, if only infinitesimally, more animated. Hitherto, this far western territory had been something of a menace to him—the breeder of rebellions and mutinies. Now he found that he could walk about without fear, almost an idolized figure.

Before they left Lanchow, the missionaries had been called together, and as at Sian and in places they were yet to visit, an anti-opium league was formed. As they prepared to take off, Chiang made a futile effort to return to Nanking, but Donald and Madame Chiang prevailed. The plane flew them this time into remote Ninghsia, the Mohammedan quarter between the Gobi and Ordos deserts. Never had anyone so highly placed in a Chinese government visited so deep into the heart of Asia. From there, they returned to Sian and struck by train into provinces to the west and south, where the Young Marshal left them, then to the north and east, finally to Peiping. There had been no rests in Donald's tornado-like Cook's Tour, and feeling the need of a physical checkup, the trio entered the hospital of the Peking Union Medical College, where Dr. Sun had spent his last days. There, they came under the attention of M. D. Willcutts, an American naval officer attached to the hospital. In their short time together, Donald and Willcutts formed a friendship. Donald had no idea then how much this friendship would mean at the end of the next turbulent decade.

All the while, there was the unending blizzard of paper work in the center of which Donald would find Madame Chiang. She would look up, chewing the frayed end of a pencil, and he would laugh, scoop up an armful and go to work.

From Peiping, they flew to Kalgan where they met the Mongolian prince, Teh, lineal descendant of Genghis Khan. Throngs greeted Chiang warmly, as they did later when the party visited Suiyuan Province and Taiyuanfu, in Shansi, where Donald and Sun had once visited during the doctor's triumphal railway tour. In all these places, Chiang spoke forcefully, criticizing malpractices.

At Taiyuanfu, the generalissimo left them, flying back to Central China where urgent military matters concerning the Communists awaited him. Dr. H. H. Kung, who had been visiting his spacious ancestral home near by, joined his sister-in-law and Donald, and by easy stages they returned to Nanking. Donald did not go back to Hankow.

It was December now. They had been gone two months, had covered thousands of miles and nearly the length and breadth of China. The propaganda effect of the tour, as Donald had foreseen, was tremendous. Yet, it had been more than just a political success, more than just a stumping of the country, more than the American equivalent of hand-shaking and baby kissing. Chiang in two short months had grown in stature. From that time on, he began to understand economics, he began to understand that there was a China beyond the tip of his bayonet. For the first time, one man now stood out as a leader. The unification that began to jell throughout the land was not the result of long years of revolution and counterrevolution. It was born in that trip, with Donald the unassuming progenitor.

Inevitable, but hardly perceptible, was the transition Donald was now making. Inevitable because in Madame Chiang he was confident that an avenue had been found through which China might be strengthened, the avenue through which corruption, inefficiency and defeatism might be wiped out.

When they arrived at Nanking, he went to live in the generalissimo's bungalow, just outside the East Gate. Stacks of correspondence had preceded him. He went to work immediately. Several days later, the Young Marshal arrived from Hankow and telephoned Donald.

"You damn old man," he said, "I never see you any more!"

Donald invited him to tea that afternoon. "You'll learn why you never see me," he answered.

When the Young Marshal walked into the bungalow, Donald was at a typewriter at one end of the desk and Madame Chiang was using one at the other. Tea was served, and over it Madame Chiang and the Young Marshal discussed Donald in Chinese. Donald read letters, scribbled shorthand notes. After awhile, the Young Marshal walked over and slapped him on the back, and smiled.

"It looks," he said, "as if I've lost you."

"Yes," Donald answered. "I damn well think you have."

"I'll miss you," the Young Marshal said, still smiling.

Donald gripped his hand. "Tommyrot."

From the day at Hangchow when he and Chang had spoken their minds to the generalissimo, Donald had been drawn slowly toward the Chiang Kai-sheks. A strong friendship was developing, and because he had a quirk for brevity in some things, he had soon reduced "generalissimo" to "G'issimo," and Madame Chiang became "M'issimo." In speaking of them to others, Donald always mispronounced their name, as he did all Chinese names and places. It was almost as if he wanted to exaggerate his inability to speak the language. He referred to them as "Chee-ang" instead of, correctly, as "Jong." In turn, Chiang called him "The Adviser," while to Madame Chiang he was, as he had been for many years, plain "Don."

Of the two, he was interested more in Madame Chiang's approach to the heavy problems facing the country. It was during their tour of the provinces that he paid her his greatest compliment. "M'issimo," he told her, "you think like a man." The generalissimo, taciturn, monosyllabic, was difficult to fathom, although gradually Donald found that his point of view was somewhat different from what he had supposed it to be, different from what his enemies alleged it to be. Still, he wondered how well he would ever know him.

As Donald settled into his new job, the Young Marshal pushed the campaign against the Communists with, Donald suspected, a growing lack of enthusiasm. Japan watched, hoping China would bleed herself into exhaustion. Then, with the stage set, she struck in the North, in Chahar Province, bit off a piece, then shifted her attentions directly south, hoping to repeat the performance in a more important area. Turning first to Hopei Province, where she had clashed several times with the hostile Northeastern army under command of the Young Marshal's officers, she presented Chiang Kai-shek in May, 1935, with a list of commands that nearly equaled the Twenty-one Demands in their ferocity. Japan wanted the Young Marshal's army and the governor, an appointee of his, removed. In addition, she demanded that military training of students be halted and, among sundry other items, the dissolution of the antagonistic provincial and city Kuomintang headquarters. Chiang weighed the problem, consulted Donald, made his decision. China still was not ready to fight. He ordered the governor dismissed, banished the Northeastern army to Kansu to pursue retreating Communist forces. The Young Marshal's command was expanded, and he was shifted to Sian to establish new headquarters. Although his dissatisfaction was mounting, he obeyed. But the itch to turn his forces against Japan grew more insistent.

The Donald-Chiang combination moved along smoothly. The adviser continued to toss up ideas, put words in the generalissimo's mouth, make them sound like his. One project was the People's Economic Reconstruction movement, which embodied all the economic ideas he had been fighting for. For weeks, Donald, through Madame Chiang, had worked with the G'issimo on it, shaping his thoughts, reasoning, drawing diagrams, showing him how it might be done. Then, as they stood one day with newspapermen on a Communist front in Kweichow, Donald felt that the time was appropriate for Chiang to spring the latest thought on how he was to rejuvenate the Chinese race. Chiang enunciated Donald's reconstruction plan which, like his New Mentality Movement, would complement the New Life Movement. The announcement was greeted enthusiastically. If this could be accomplished, the papers editorialized, China would catapult into the position of a first-class power.

A few days later Donald headed northward by plane, accompanied by Chinese and foreign friends, among them T. V. Soong and Willys Peck, American chargé d'affaires at Nanking. Flying over Communist territory, they narrowly escaped being shot down. Donald relieved the tension by suggesting that they idle away the time in storytelling and limerick writing, at both of which he excelled. Life, no matter how grim, was never entirely grim for Donald. He could emerge from the most harrowing of experiences with an infectious laugh, a laugh that always drew a circle of adoring friends about him. They vied with each other to ride in the same car with him, in the same plane. He polished off this particular session with:

T. V. Soong and Tommy Lee,
Willys Peck and Wang and me,
Mounted Pegasus and sang
"Now we're off to Kiukiang."
Bright the sun and blue the sky
As o'er the Yangtze we flew high.
Verdant fields below were spread
Like mosaics that giants tread.
Serene we soared in pinions wide
Above the Yangtze's yellow tide,
Until a restless brain began
Some limping limericks to scan.
Peace quickly bowed to Tumult's reign
As brain began to vie with brain.
Words flew in ghastly disarray
But not kind tributes to convey.
The champion was the poet who
Most quickly his opponents slew
With defamation crude and cruel—
Or drove him off to use the stool.

Donald's new position had made him the cynosure of many eyes. He was in the inner circle of a ruling Chinese dynasty. He slept in the same house with them, and he ate with them, although never their Chinese food. He was the first white man ever to attain such a standing in China. Thus, it is easy to understand how he came to be hated by some, envied by others. Chinese reactionaries were angered by his influence with Madame Chiang and the reforms he was able to have instituted. Foreigners who suspected that he was attaining wealth through his position were covetous, and there were the inevitable attempts to unseat him. Few knew that Donald accepted as salary hardly more than his living expenses were costing him, and that what was left over, he spent freely and generously.

He rarely paid attention to such maneuvering, although there were times in which his conceit was nettled. One such instance was when he visited Hankow with the Chiangs where he ran up against something that made him make plans to leave China once and for all.

As a routine courtesy, he had called on Merrick Hewlitt, the British consul, whom he had known for a number of years. He had always regarded him as an old-school and a school-tie sort of a fellow.

Hewlett said to Donald, "You know, my boy, I will be joining you soon."

"What's this?" Donald asked, startled.

"Well, the generalissimo has asked me two or three times to join him. The generalissimo has said he will give me a house to live in at Nanking. I'm to retire soon, you know. I want to stay in China. I feel that I can help the Chinese."

Donald winced. Had he done all of his fighting just to have this happen? Was the generalissimo's headquarters going in for more fumbling, *status quo* thinking? Wasn't there enough already? He clapped on his hat. He said, "Well, good-by."

He walked down the street. The decision came suddenly: Now I will build my yacht. Now I will clear out of China. If Hewlett is to be made an adviser, then there is no further use for me.

At a British machinery importing firm, he asked them to order a motor from London. Then he wired a Mr. Edward Cock, manager of the Hong Kong and Whampoa Dock Company, at Hong Kong. He instructed that a boat be built for him, giving specifications that had been in his mind for a long time for a small cruiser. Then he headed back for the residence where he and the Chiangs were staying. He thought: Now I'll write those damn memoirs. I'll get away from this blasted country.

That night, he said nothing to either of the Chiangs about the day's developments, but in the weeks that followed he went ahead with his plans for the yacht. Yet, there was not much to do until it was built, and that would take at least six months.

Summer found him once more at the Communist front with Generalissimo and Madame Chiang, and there the Hewlett problem tagged after him in the form of a letter from the consul himself. Hewlett was anxious. Apparently, he had not yet received a formal invitation from the generalissimo. Donald replied tartly that he noted that the Britisher was eager to become a member of the Chiang family as he was and to live with them as he did. "But," he wrote, "I want to tell you that the kind of life I lead is one you would never be able to lead. There are no clubs where I go. There are no pubs. There are no bright lights." He added that he worked all the time, sometimes from dawn to dark, that it was "all work and no play, traveling by all means at all hours, in all directions without any relief."

After several weeks, two letters arrived. One was from Hewlett, with strong implication that Donald was crowding him out of a coveted post with the generalissimo. The other was a letter Hewlett had written Dr. Kung which the finance minister had forwarded on to Madame Chiang. In it, Hewlett stated flatly that he had been invited to join up, that he wished to do so without pay and to receive only generous allowances for the many missions he hoped to perform. Donald said nothing, but Madame Chiang jumped up excitedly and ran into the generalissimo's office. Returning, she announced that the generalissimo never at any time wanted to do more than to offer Hewlett a house and for reasons of friendship alone.

"I will write a letter for you and tell Mr. Hewlett that he has made a grave mistake," said Donald.

Later, the cagey adviser received a letter from a friend who was head of the salt administration at Chengtu. Hewlett had been in the city and at a dinner had remarked that Donald was jealous of him and had caused him to lose his post with the generalissimo. Donald replied by asking his friend to read Hewlett an accompanying letter in the presence of "whoever will listen to it." He stated bluntly that Hewlett was responsible for his losing about twenty thousand Chinese dollars, since he had ordered an expensive boat built when Hewlett had said that he was to become an adviser to the generalissimo. "Therefore," Donald wrote, "since Hewlett cannot carry out what he said his plans were, he owes me that much money, and I propose to sue him for it." That was the end of the affair. Donald never heard of Hewlett again.

Through the tortuous heat of a West China summer, Donald had followed the drive against the Communists with Chiang, his influence as persistent as the sun. Madame Chiang would fly in to join them from time to time. After Kweichow, where Chiang had denounced a rascally administration and had supplanted it with Nanking men, the campaign moved into Szechwan. There was little fighting. The ragged bands of Communists or bandits without ideology fell back quickly, more interested in a haven than in anything else. Everywhere Chiang went, he made an effort at reforms. The reforms, however, were only temporary. They collapsed when he withdrew his army.

Yet in Chiang many saw a glimmer of hope for the future. A foreign resident noted the change that had taken place:

At one time he seemed not far different from any other militarist, seeking his own ascendancy by fair means or foul, enriching his relatives and friends, merging himself with the corrupt surroundings in which he found himself. But owing to the critical times and partly no doubt to his own innate greatness of character, Chiang Kai-shek has come out of his long ordeal a different man. He has been made modest and humble by the task ahead of him.[4]

It was on a day early in September, after he had returned to the Szechwan capital from a reconnaissance trip with Chiang, that the first real trouble came to Donald. That evening, he was struck by chills and every muscle began to ache. The next morning, he was worse. Madame Chiang came in, worried. She found him feverish and weak. Tests were quickly taken, but no diagnosis could be made.

"I must have been bitten by a Communist bug," Donald said.

A plane flew him to Shanghai where he entered the well-equipped Country Hospital. The chills persisted, the doctors being as much in the dark as those in Chengtu. Despite this, Donald kept up his furious campaign for reform. It seemed an obsession. There was almost a daily letter either to the generalissimo or his wife. He told of approaching the government in India, of persuading the new British ambassador to China, Sir Alexander Cadogan,[5] to loan China experts in opium control. He advocated that the government abandon its reluctance to permit Pan-American Airways to use China as a terminal, pointing to the prestige that would accrue from partnership in trans-Pacific flight. He had comprehensive plans drawn up for gold mining in Szechwan, and for ways and means to co-ordinate work on the always tangled problem of flood control. He presented the Chiangs with an armload of unsolved questions—on banking reforms, on protection of credit—and then, apologizing for having snowed them under, he sailed for Hong Kong late in October to claim his yacht.

[4] Berkov, in *Strong Man of China.*
[5] UN delegate.

His decision to leave China forever had been amended. He planned only to cruise, rest, perhaps write a bit, then return. En route to Hong Kong, he wrote Madame Chiang:

I appeal to the generalissimo, through you, very carefully to look at this whole problem from a new point of view. You, I know, recognize more than anyone the vital necessities, so what I am saying is not so much for you personally as it is food for thought for the generalissimo. China has been drifting for a long while, but now she should awaken and make up her mind to take control of her direction and her destinies. . . . So I wish you well in this stimulating job that has been thrust upon you, and I hope soon to see that China has emerged from the dark shadows. I look forward to reading it in some paper or other very shortly and for you all I meanwhile pray.

At Hong Kong, he was disappointed to find that his boat was not ready, and so with American friends whom he had joined at Shanghai, he set out by regular steamer for the Dutch East Indies. There, for more than a month, he basked in the sun, his health seeming to improve. But in China, the improvement that he had hoped for was not taking place. At Batavia one day a wire came from Madame Chiang urgently requesting his return. He left immediately, but the day before he touched at Hong Kong, the fever and chills returned, and he placed himself in the War Memorial Hospital there.

His condition grew worse. Doctors thought he would die. They asked if he had friends in Hong Kong, persons who might be notified—just in case. Donald's thoughts went back over the years, those cramped, stuffy years in Hong Kong.

"I refuse to have friends in such a place," he said and let it go at that. In relating the story later, he told how one "genius" decided to try to reduce his fever by treating him for malaria. The fever fell off, and the doctors looked at him in astonishment. Gradually, his condition improved and once again his thoughts were on China and the *Mei Hwa*, the name he had given to his yacht. He had selected the characters carefully. They could be translated as either "plum blossom" or "a thousand times beautiful." Also, "mei" was the first character in "Meiling," Madame Chiang's given name.

After repeated requests to hurry "home," Donald left Hong Kong, in March, 1936, but not before the *Mei Hwa* was launched, and he had taken her out on trial runs. She was a good ship. She handled well and had all the comforts of home miniaturized. There was even a desk at which he could write his memoirs.

Donald returned to Shanghai, but feeling shaky still, he re-entered a hospital there. After three months, he bolted, when his condition failed to improve. He flew to Nanking, and when he stepped from his plane, he knew he had found his remedy. Madame Chiang was waiting and beyond was the bungalow where he was sure work was piled almost ceiling high. After a few days of sun bathing, his improvement verged on the miraculous. In a week, he played a round of golf, and within several days he felt better than he had in years.

By midsummer, the South was astir again. Leaders in the provinces of Kwangtung and Kwansi had called on Chiang to mobilize against Japan. He had refused. Then, under the ruse that they themselves would march against the enemy, the southerners made a move to drive northward. Actually, it was a plot against Nanking, with the objective of unseating the generalissimo. The plot, however, died aborning. Gone was the day when support could be mustered for every common garden variety of revolt. Telegrams poured in from Chinese all over the world urging the nation not to split but to stand firm and united.

More confident, more sure of himself than ever before, Chiang flew to the South and quickly dissolved the autonomous movement in Kwangtung. Kwansi, however, for reasons of face, remained obdurate for a long time, refusing to align itself with national policy. Donald and Madame Chiang went with the G'issimo, and Donald played a major part in pacifying the rebels, preaching the need of a solid front for the chaotic days that lay ahead—the time when China would have to fight Japan.

Together, Mei-ling and Donald returned by air. As the plane winged northward, they sat and talked of the day when China would walk shoulders square, chin up, the time when a new psychology would replace face and give the country strength. She must have liked the way he talked, brisk, sparkling, good-humoredly, to the point. Her eyes were dark, searching, always eager for knowledge. He thought of her intelligence and her courage. He pulled a scrap of paper from his pocket, marked off some squares and said, "Let's play ticktacktoe."

Mei-ling won two out of three. He turned the paper over. "M'issimo," he said, "I'll write you a poem. Not for you—but for those who should be like you." As the plane hummed over the valleys and hills green with rice paddies, over yellow rivers that tore and rent the land, he wrote:

The "Patriot's" Soliloquy

or

That Great God Face

As soon as winter winds arrive,
And blow from tempest-ridden skies,
I fly as fast as motor goes,
And buy some foreign-devil clothes
To be ill-dressed is a disgrace,
And I must never lose my face.

They say that China's in distress,
That creditors upon us press,
That we must now reorganize
And follow foreign enterprise.
Pooh! Pooh! I say, that's a disgrace,
So I fight that, thus save my face.

I have my job, my friends have power,
Rich gifts on them I always shower,
Reform to them means irksome work
And work is what I always shirk,
Reforms aren't needed by our race,
So I'll grow nails[6] and save my face.

They say the Japs will soon be here.
Oh, lucky man I've nought to fear,
For I have Nippon friends galore
And they will use me, that is sure,

[6] Donald appended his own footnote: "Long fingernails were grown to distinguish the 'gent' and the literati from the toiler."

Ha! Ha! I'll then set up the pace,
And I'll have lots and lots of face.

And a Lament—

God in His wisdom suffers fools
To cut strange capers, act as tools,
For wicked people, plunged in crime
And some whose lives are lived in slime.
What puzzles me is His sweet grace
To silly fools who live for face.

chapter

23

THE KIDNAPING OF CHIANG

*Rivers and mountains may easily change
but human nature is changed with difficulty.*

IN THE nearly two years that Donald had been associated with the generalissimo, he had come to understand better, and even to appreciate, some of his characteristics. The savage pace of the early months had slackened, and he had time to look back, to reflect upon those whose destinies he had begun to shape. His principals were a man and a woman as complex as China herself—each balanced in varying degrees with the old and new in curious confusion.

The generalissimo had emerged from middle-class stock. His early education had been conventional. It had been based on a studious devotion to the classics and a strict adherence to the cultural lines of old China. This had left him with a circumlocutory system of thought —a cautious approach to new ideas and to matters beyond his ken.

Donald soon saw the scars that, for better or for worse, had been deeply cut. Chiang had developed a defensive manner which was manifest in a dogged determination to grip tightly to what he believed right. Step by step, he fashioned for himself a Gibraltar of stubbornness. To Donald, this stubbornness, as he once wrote, "cemented the plinth on which he stood." It prevented a breakdown in his character. It drove him to intense and intenser silence. The toughening which he was administering to his own hide was to enable him to withstand pressure, even though such obstinacy promised danger to himself.

Donald was sure that here was a quality upon which China some day would draw.

Chiang's handicap always was that he had to deal with foreign problems through interpreters. This handicap often caused adverse foreign reaction and led to misunderstanding. In such instances, Donald felt a deep sympathy for him. Sometimes he would find him grappling stoically in solitude with weighty problems, bewildered and confused. His best interpreter was Madame Chiang, for she, better than anyone else, could reach into the deep entrenchments of his military mind with a clear picture.

The three—the Chiangs and Donald—had become almost inseparable partners. They went everywhere together, with no doors, few conversations shut to the Australian. They became something of a "closed corporation," and few reached the Chiangs without first having been screened by Donald.

When the three were not together, then it was Donald and Madame Chiang by themselves, talking and planning, with Donald pointing to how her theories on reform—with which she had been surface-polished brightly—might be translated into action. Using her husband's influence, he was master-minding her integration more and more into the government. The American-educated woman had become another in his magnum-size schemes. For an age that lacked heroines, he had one. He had the material—beauty, courage, intelligence. Only a sculptor's touch was needed to produce a First Lady of the World. He began to mold patiently, carefully. Whatever she said "on the record" was prepared by Donald or under Donald's direction. She made few decisions, took few administrative steps without first consulting him. When she tackled a job without him near by, there would be the echo of his oft-repeated admonition: "Think in a straight line, think clearly, and never talk nonsense."

As Chiang pressed his secret preparations for eventual resistance against Japanese aggression, Donald turned his attentions to the highly corrupt Aeronautics Commission which some day might have to pit its air force against Japan's. At Hangchow, the Central Aviation School had been established to train Chinese pilots, theoretically under American experts. The customary muddles had developed through squeeze and dissension, and so in October, 1936, Donald went there. He struck immediately at the core of the trouble, and with the shadow of Chiang's authority in the background, he chopped out the Chinese deadwood and placed the Americans in complete authority. Before he had finished, he had created a near riot, but he had won out. Returning to Nanking, he immediately provoked a reorganization, a cleanup in the Aeronautics Commission. He had Madame Chiang made its chairwoman, and together they went to work to wipe out squeeze within its ranks, to strengthen it for the inevitable war with Japan.

Donald always had been as much an enemy of squeeze as he was of face. He had fought it constantly, no matter what form it took, against the lowly ricksha man or against the highest of officials. But always, his friends knew, he butted a stone wall. Nevertheless, his tireless battle infused Chiang with a like spirit, and many a time Donald saw him, white faced, confront his officials, roaring out a denunciation for the corruption among them. But when Donald and Madame Chiang unearthed a scandalous squeeze plot in the aviation group, the generalissimo refused to weed out the dishonest, claiming it would leave him without an air force.

Donald was angry. He turned to Madame Chiang and spoke impatiently: "You get out of this damn business. You resign. If you don't, you'll be blamed for the entire mess someday."

Madame Chiang resigned.

Before this, however, an event took place that held the world breathless and sprang Donald into a role that won him world-wide attention. Out of it came the seemingly impossible: The reconciliation, if only temporarily, of two old enemies—Chiang and the Communists.

On a day late in the fall of 1936, the Young Marshal flew down from Sian and called on Donald. Slumping into a chair, he said:

"China is no place for an honest man."

"Well, when did you find that out?"

Chang made a despairing gesture. "I'd resign," he said, "if my homeland wasn't lost and if the Japs weren't tramping on my father's grave."

He told of his futile efforts to persuade Chiang to accept a Communist offer to join forces and fight the Japanese. "Chiang's got a head like a rock," he said. "All he'll say is 'I am the commander in chief. I have given orders. You and everyone else must obey!'"

The Young Marshal arose, his face troubled. He stared out of the window. "So," he said, "I don't know what to do. My men won't fight the Communists. It isn't Communist bullets they're afraid of. They listen to what the Communists say to them, and the Communists say 'We are Chinese and you are Chinese. Why do you fight with us? Your officers get rich. They don't pay you your wages. They have their motorcars, their concubines, their silk gowns and you get nothing.'"

He eased into his chair once more. "Everything they say, of course, is quite true. But what can I do? Old man Chiang says we've got to fight the Communists."

Donald advised him to write out his complaint and hand it to the generalissimo. He did, then returned to Sian. Shortly afterwards, the generalissimo, with a staff of high-ranking officers, flew there, to investigate the rumors of disaffection among his troops, took up residence at near-by Lintung, a famous hot springs.

Early in December, Madame Chiang, then still chairwoman of the Aeronautics Commission, was in Shanghai on commission business. Donald also was there, and on the afternoon of December 12, he returned to his room in the Park Hotel to find his table littered with telephone messages urgently requesting that he call Madame Chiang. He located her at the home of Dr. Kung who told him in a hushed voice to hurry over. When he entered the house where a few of the Soong clan had gathered, she said breathlessly:

"There's been a mutiny at Sian! The generalissimo has been kidnaped and killed!"

"I don't believe it," Donald answered quickly. "I don't believe first that the Young Marshal would mutiny. Second, I don't believe the generalissimo is dead."

Donald's unshakable confidence never failed to impress them, and for a moment they looked hopeful, as if by some magic he had suddenly learned the truth. Then they walked nervously to the window and looked out as though the real answer might be found somewhere on the street.

That night, the Kungs, Madame Chiang and Donald left for Nanking. The plan was that Donald would hurry on to Sian to find out the truth. It was significant that he had been trusted with such a mission—significant because it was evident that a Chinese would not trust a Chinese in negotiations of a scope no one could measure. If Chiang was dead, the empire of the Soongs might come clattering down and plunge China backward into warlordism. Before the party left Shanghai, Donald wired the Young Marshal not to bombard his plane on the following day, for the story then was that Sian was on fire, Red flags were flying, soldiers were digging trenches abreast of Sian's walls and, in general, terror existed.

The four were having breakfast at Nanking the next morning when the rest of the government walked in, headed by soldiery, arrogant General Ho Ying-ching,[1] minister of war, a long-time military intimate of Chiang's. He was the leader of the reactionary group, which included a strong pro-Japanese element, that clustered about the generalissimo. He was one of Donald's most bitter opponents. More composed than she had been the day before, Madame Chiang told him that Donald was to fly into Sian.

"No one," Ho replied, glaring at Donald, "is going to Sian. We are attacking Sian. The generalissimo is dead."

Donald returned the glare. "You say the generalissimo is dead, and I say he isn't. You cannot attack until the truth is learned."

"He is dead," Ho snapped, "and we are ordering the attack."

But Donald knew his protégé too well to believe him guilty. Yet as the morning wore on bringing no reply from the Young Marshal, his anxiety grew. Madame Chiang also had wired that Donald was to leave, but out of Sian came only silence.

Donald waited until noon, then, after telling Madame Chiang that no further time must be lost, he left secretly when it became evident that Ho might try to stop the flight. Loyang was four and a half hours from Nanking, and he set down there, listened to a flood of rumors, then made arrangements to hop off for Sian at dawn the next morning, December 14. Just before he left for the field, the phone rang. It was Madame Chiang. A telegram from the Young Marshal finally had been delivered. He was asking that Donald come at once.

[1] Delegate, United Nations, 1946.

"Hurry," Madame Chiang pleaded. "You must save the generalissimo."

Sian was an hour and a half distant. They flew direct over the Huashan Mountains, and at Lintung they came in low to see if any activity could be detected where the generalissimo had been living. Everything seemed quiet and between there and Sian there were no soldiers on the road. The city gates were open. There were no Red flags, no trenches. The streets appeared normal, people moving about unexcitedly.

At the field, there was only a solitary figure when Donald's plane roared in, and as he stepped out, the figure shouted, "You're the only man in the world who could have got through!"

The voice belonged to Jimmy Elder who had continued on as the Young Marshal's personal treasurer. Elder was fluent in Chinese dialects, and he and the Young Marshal had gone to school together in North China.

They shook hands and Donald asked:

"What's the trouble up here?"

"They have the generalissimo."

"Is he alive?"

"Of course he's alive. He's over at General Yang Hu-cheng's. Yang's the big boss here now. He staged a mutiny and took over a few days ago."

As they drove toward the Young Marshal's, Donald told how Nanking throbbed with rumors of Chiang's death, and Elder, in turn, gave a sketchy picture of the developments. When Donald walked in, the Young Marshal had just emerged from a conference. He looked worried and tired.

"Did you get my telegram?" he asked. "I sent it as soon as the damn business happened."

Donald replied that he had not heard of it until shortly before he left Loyang.

"Then someone held it up," the Young Marshal answered angrily. "There's something rotten in Nanking."

"That I know," said Donald. "But more important—what's rotten here?"

Even as the Young Marshal began to talk, the outside world, inspired by the utterances of the Nanking reactionists, was heaping condemnation on him. The words "traitor to China" were heard over the air and read in the press. But Donald, making an actual shorthand transcription of his statement, was hearing the real story—a story that was not to go beyond the walls of the room in Sian, for later Nanking was to close the Young Marshal's mouth, and Donald, the keeper of confidences, was bound to secrecy. The generalissimo, however, was to tell his story in his published diary, *A Fortnight in Sian*, and Madame Chiang was to present her case in *Sian: A Coup d'Etat*," both somewhat expurgated. The Young Marshal's story began this way:

"For a long time I had been distressed because we wasted our strength fighting Chinese instead of fighting Japanese. When the generalissimo came here, I asked him why not begin to resist Japan. I said the Reds were Chinese."

Chiang, as customary whenever challenged, had flared up and accused him of being a Bolshevik. Chiang had emphasized that the time to fight Japan had not arrived.

"I do not say that you are wrong," the Young Marshal said he had retorted, "but at the time of the Manchurian trouble, you declared that we must prepare and in two years we could drive the Japs from China. Five years have elapsed. We cannot go on saying to the people that we are still preparing, for the enemy is digging deeper into the country. Now, the government is like a bank. If it defaults, confidence is lost. We only talk, and, therefore, we default. Sir, there are only three choices—we fight the Japanese, we retreat, or we submit." The generalissimo had turned livid at this and had screamed that he would never surrender.

Then, interrupting his story temporarily, the Young Marshal remarked that he was certain Donald knew that he had strong ideas on the steps necessary for the country's salvation.

"As you suggested," he continued, "I wrote a long letter to the generalissimo. I said that he had better change my position. I asked to be allowed to go north to fight the Japanese. I said that if he wanted to fight bandits or Communists, then let other troops do it, as my men were unwilling to fight anyone but Japanese."

Chiang, nevertheless, had reiterated his command to push the war against the Communists, and the Young Marshal had warned that this would only provoke desertions. He said that he had also called the generalissimo's attention to recent wholesale arrests in Shanghai.

"You put many patriots in jail—just like Yuan Shih-kai," the Young Marshal had told Chiang. "You have killed or exiled men just because others charged they were Bolsheviks. But these people are just Chinese, like you and me." At that, the generalissimo had become incensed again. He had shouted that it was plain the Young Marshal thought him wrong and that there wasn't anyone anywhere who could think that of him.

The first disturbance after the generalissimo's arrival began when the students at Sian decided to parade as a protest against the government's failure to resist Japan. The Young Marshal pointed out to General Yang that the parade should be stopped as the generalissimo disliked the idea. But it was held one day just as snow began to fall.

"At first," the Young Marshall explained, "I refused to see the students because I did not want to give the impression I was fostering such a demonstration. Later, the police, presumably following the sentiment of the generalissimo, fired on the marchers, and there were several casualties. Angry, the students fought to get out to Lintung and confront the generalissimo. It was late now. I was anxious about them. I did not want to see them sleep by the road all night in the snow. I went out and, unlike the generalissimo, I was able to reason with them. I said that I would talk to the generalissimo and finally they agreed to that. They returned home."

That night, the Young Marshal had attempted to speak to Chiang on their behalf, but had found him in a wild rage. He accused him of supporting the student demonstration. On the following day, December 11, the Young Marshal, in company with General Yang, again tried to open conversation with Chiang. The generalissimo stormed, pounded the table and cursed him in what the Young Marshal said was vile language.

Back at his Sian headquarters, he had told a meeting of officers, "I am afraid this may mean the end of my association with the generalissimo. I cannot stand for such disgraceful treatment."

General Yang had put in: "There may be a way out. I'll bring him into the city and then he'll have to listen to what we say."

The Young Marshal had expressed alarm. "Your troops are ex-bandits," he had pointed out. "They might either kill or hurt the generalissimo. That must never happen. Let me send my bodyguard out to bring him in and if, after we talk to him, we cannot settle the matter, I will take the blame. But if the generalissimo agrees that things can be settled, then you can have the credit."

Accordingly, the Young Marshal's bodyguard was sent that night. Shooting accidentally broke out, and several of Chiang's officers were killed. Thereupon, the generalissimo was told that a mutiny was under way, and, in his underwear, he jumped from a rear window. He scaled a ten-foot wall, then stumbled into a deep moat, wrenched his back, clambered out and ran until he was tripped by brambles. He fell into a hole and there, shivering in the December cold, an officer of the Young Marshal's staff found him.

Chiang asked that he be shot on the spot. The officer replied, "We do not want to shoot you. You are the generalissimo."

The Young Marshal looked at Donald's growing pile of shorthand notes, then went on: "The generalissimo finally accompanied my men into Sian. They brought him to Yang's headquarters. I found him extremely angry. He managed to blurt out a demand that if I were not responsible for the affair, I must prove it by sending him back to Nan-king at once. He said that if I didn't, then we were enemies, and I could shoot him then and there."

The Young Marshal had told the generalissimo: "Your bad temper always is the cause of trouble."

Chiang had crackled, "I don't want to talk to you."

"Never mind. I want to talk to you."

The generalissimo was begged to change his ideas, the Young Marshal stressing his belief that China faced oblivion if action was not taken.

"I never change my ideas," Chiang had answered. "My ideas are all right. Anyway, you talk too much. You always talk too much. All I will say to you is: Either kill me or send me back to Nanking. I don't care which."

"I know you don't care. I admire your courage. But this whole thing is not one of individual ideas. It is a national question. We are willing to obey you because we are patriotic, but we are not idolizing you."

The generalissimo, who had been facing the wall, turned and screamed:

"Go away! You're my enemy and I won't talk. If you want to shoot me, do so at once."

After two hours, the Young Marshal left.

He next told Donald how immediately upon the detention of Chiang, he had underscored the fact that everything had to be done openly. As a result, they had sent a circular telegram notifying Nanking. The telegram had demanded a reorganization of the Nanking government in order to permit a greater participation by the people as a whole in political affairs, principally in the matter of national salvation. It did not call for immediate war against Japan, but it did ask that fighting against the Communists be halted. Then he went on to describe to Donald how he had spent the rest of that day and the next pleading with the Generalissimo to readjust his views, but had met only stony silence.

The Young Marshal looked wearily at Donald. "My intelligence officers have informed me," he said, "that Nanking has ordered Sian attacked. This means they want the generalissimo killed. Either they will try to do it with bombs, or they hope that someone here will be inflamed enough to do it. They're using this, of course, as a means to seize power. They have cut telephone communications and have ignored my requests to have them restored."

He then said that he had rented a modern house next door with steam heat and other facilities Chiang now lacked and had asked the generalissimo to move in, but the proposal had been curtly rejected.

Donald stood up. "Let's go see the generalissimo," he said.

Before they left, they went into the next room to talk with General Yang and the other officers. Addressing the group, with Jimmy Elder interpreting, Donald admonished them for seizing the generalissimo since the act would have a bad effect on public opinion in China and throughout the world. Speaking pungently, he urged that Chiang be released as a demonstration of China's new unity, adding that a refusal would play into the hands of Japan.

Spokesman for the group, Yang replied, with customary indirectness, that they were all in this cabal together and no single officer would be permitted to take separate action. Donald knew for sure then that the Young Marshal could not personally release Chiang.

They drove to Yang's headquarters where Donald found the generalissimo in a small room on a wooden bed, blanket over his head, face to the wall. The room had dirty hangings and no sanitary facilities. In one corner was a bucket, in another some brooms.

Donald said, "Hello, G'issimo."

Chiang turned over, sat up. Tears came to his eyes. "I knew you would come," he said. The Young Marshal translated.

"I have come," Donald answered, "and Madame Chiang also is coming."

The color leaped to the Generalissimo's face. "You cannot bring her here," he shouted at Donald. "You cannot bring her into this den of thieves." Once more, he turned to the wall and pulled the blanket over him.

Donald looked at the Young Marshal, then out of the window. For several minutes, both stood in silence. Then the Young Marshal said to Donald, "Say something to him, say something."

"I have nothing more to say," Donald answered icily. "I do not like anyone to jump down my throat."

"He's been jumping down my throat for days."

"Well, all right," Donald answered and, turning to the generalissimo, he remarked, "I think you should leave this room. It's no place for you."

The generalissimo rolled over once more, pulled the blanket from his head and glowered. The room was uncomfortably quiet. After awhile he said, emphasizing his last word, "I will go with you."

They waited outside while Chiang dressed, and when he emerged in full uniform, sentries clicked to attention, saluted as the trio walked to a motorcar. As they rode through the city, the generalissimo was tense and gripped Donald's hand fiercely. Once in his comfortable new quarters, he asked the Young Marshal to sit down, but the latter refused. He stood at attention, and the generalissimo began to address him harshly. Donald noticed that the Young Marshal was so tired he was hardly able to stand. He had had no sleep since his chief's detention.

Eventually, Donald tugged at his coat, suggested that he go home to dinner. As the door closed, the generalissimo turned to Donald with a look of despair and, waving his arms excitedly, exclaimed: "Finished. It is finished."

Donald was both surprised and puzzled—surprised by Chiang's sudden outburst in English, puzzled by the words. But Chiang said no more, and Donald left the room to arrange with servants for the generalissimo's care. Then he joined the Young Marshal at his house.

After dinner, Donald said, "I've brought along something you must read. It's Chiang Kai-shek's diary." He handed it to the Young Marshal, who began to thumb through it as Donald continued: "I believe you'll find him a greater patriot than you have supposed." He waited for a long time while he watched his friend read. When the Young Marshal looked up, he went on: "Now, there are other things you must do. You must tell your people that their future depends upon saving the G'issimo, that the Nanking crowd want him removed so that they can take his place. They will run the government and you will be rebels or outlaws. To avert that, to put the responsibility where it belongs, to sheet home the blame, you must save the G'issimo at all costs."

The Young Marshal laid down the diary. "I see," he said slowly, "that Chiang all along has been secretly preparing for war against Japan. I'm beginning to see him in a new light."

"Good lad," said Donald.

The Young Marshal promised to follow Donald's advice.

It was still the night of December 14. Donald knew that the world press, without accurate information, would be flooded with rumors and conjectures. He was right. Headlines were announcing that the generalissimo had been murdered, that his head was sticking on a pole on the main street of Sian, that Nanking had started bombing, that the Young Marshal had reverted to the drug habit and had gone berserk, that Sian was bathed in blood and the soldiers had run riot and killed a number of foreigners.

For the first time, the pace had eased off sufficiently for Donald to send the truth of the situation to the outside. He dispatched a telegram to Madame Chiang, along with one from the Young Marshal, informing her of the generalissimo's safety, then sent news telegrams to Hallett Abend, of the New York *Times*, to Reuters and other agencies. The telegram from the Young Marshal invited Dr. Kung, along with Madame Chiang, to Sian to negotiate a settlement. But at Nanking, the sincerity of the messages was discounted and a cry was sent up that the Young Marshal only sought additional hostages. Although Mei-ling anchored a deep belief in the validity of Donald's telegrams, she was bewildered by the misinterpretations and the flood of sensational reports they produced. Consequently, she wired Donald to send no further stories for publication. However, as she related in her diary, correspondents and newspapermen were so accustomed to hearing from him, no matter how far away he might be, that they could not understand his silence and, again, many rumors sprang up. One maintained that Donald was being held a captive, another that he was actually directing the campaign against Nanking.

Donald stayed that first night in the generalissimo's new headquarters, as he was to do for nearly a fortnight. The next morning, the Young Marshal arrived with a copy of eight demands contained in the original circular telegram. He told Donald that he was reluctant to present them, but Yang, more powerful than he, had insisted. Yang had argued: "I'll lose my head among my own men if I let him out without some understanding."

Together, they went into Chiang's room and, standing stiffly, the Young Marshal read the plea for a housecleaning and the end of civil war. As each point was read, Chiang rebuked the Young Marshal. He would consider no demands in his present circumstances. The Young Marshal stood reddened, humiliated. Donald could see the anger that must have existed at the beginning of the incident. He marveled at his control.

Donald then took over, asking the Young Marshal to translate. He began by speaking of the clique, with which the generalissimo surrounded himself, whose policy it was to suffocate liberal views and many of whose members were secretly pro-Japanese. He spoke of the wisdom of listening to the people of Sian in order to appreciate what right they might have on their side. He spoke of the need for the generalissimo to abandon his stubbornness, so that the way might be paved for him to quit Sian.

Donald referred next to the generalissimo's attitude, his ill-humor, irascibility and actions that bordered on megalomania.

"Wait!" the Young Marshal cut in. "I can't translate that."

"Why not?" Donald said sharply.

"He'll think I put you up to it."

"I'm not allowed to have any views," Donald asked, again sharply, "because they coincide with yours?"

"I won't translate. You can say what you like through Jimmy Elder."

Elder came in, translated the rebuke, and then Donald began a discussion of the eight demands. He pointed out that he saw nothing wrong with them. The generalissimo seized on number seven which asked that Dr. Sun Yat-sen's will be carried out.

He said: "If I agree to that one, then I'd agree to all of them. I have no intention now of agreeing to any of them."

Donald answered: "You carry out Dr. Sun's will, and the rest will take care of themselves."

He walked out, followed by the Young Marshal, and announced that he intended to fly to Loyang to telephone Madame Chiang and tell her that everything was all right.

When he took off, snow was falling. The ceiling was low. The plane crept over the mountains, picking and poking its way through the gorges of the Yellow River to Loyang. It was like flying down the center of a big city street. Their wings almost touched the cliffs. At Loyang, he telephoned Madame Chiang, reported on the generalissimo's condition and urged her to work hard to prevent a bombing of Sian, since it might mean the sacrifice of the generalissimo's life.

Madame's voice sounded far away and plaintive. "Please," she said, "you come to Nanking. If Sian is bombed, you may be killed."

"I can't," he answered. "I've promised the generalissimo and the Young Marshal that I'd return." He added that she was not to give up hope, that there would be a way out.

"Be careful," she called. "I'm having a difficult time holding back our power-hungry clique."

Bad weather delayed his return, and he took off the next morning—

December 16—after Madame Chiang had called him twice. Snow was still falling. As Donald boarded his plane, he saw twenty bombers sitting near by, each loaded with bombs and being readied for take-off. Once he was in the air, they climbed after him, one by one, settling on each side of his plane, under and over. Then, for no apparently sane reason, they began to unload their bombs. Some fell on empty fields; some fell on railway stations. Donald expected that at any moment one would crash against the roof of his plane. His discomfort grew. This was the work of the Nanking clique. He had a hunch that if he detoured along the crest of the mountain range, flying off the course to Sian, they would not follow. They would not risk a waste of gas. Hours late, he arrived with only a few gallons to spare. The bombers never reached Sian.

Snow was deep as Donald motored to the generalissimo's. There, he reported on his conversations with Madame Chiang, particularly on the two they had had just before he took off in which she had asked if T. V. Soong would be acceptable in place of Dr. Kung, since Kung was now acting head of government. It was discovered that Soong would be satisfactory to the Sian officers, and Donald radioed their acceptance. The Young Marshal came in while he was telling the generalissimo how Nanking bombers had trailed him, of their bombing of the railway, and how they had failed to lift over the mountains to attack Sian. Chiang's eyes lighted and he looked out of the window.

"Do you think they will make another try?" he asked eagerly.

Donald looked at him blankly. He thought: My god! Will I ever know this man?

The next day, he and the Young Marshal found the generalissimo standing impatiently before the same window. He was mumbling something, and the Young Marshal told Donald: "He's saying, 'Why don't they bomb us, why don't they bomb us?' "

The two exchanged glances, and Donald walked to the window. "Look, G'issimo," he said, "there's snow on the ground, and it's still falling. That's why they don't come. For some inscrutable reason, God is protecting you. If the planes could get in, they'd finish you off in a hurry."

The G'issimo shrugged. He replied, in effect, that to give up his life for his country was a price worth paying for the destruction of Sian, the enemy. He said that he was seriously considering sending, by some means or other, his ideas on how Sian might successfully be attacked and destroyed.

The Young Marshal and Donald left. "He wants to be a martyr," the Chinese said. "Nonetheless, my opinion of him is improving. I've read some more of his diary."

After several efforts by the Nanking authorities to prevent his take-off, Soong arrived at Sian on December 20. He went into session with the generalissimo, emerged to announce that their leader was still un-wavering in his determination not to agree to anything while he was detained. A few hours later, Donald hopped off in the Ford trimotor plane for Nanking.

The ceiling was still low, the clouds loafing around the mountain peaks. As they wound along the valley of the Yellow River, the port engine sputtered, then stopped. The pilot began to look for a landing place while Donald, seated on a couch, his feet on the back of a chair, gazed calmly out of the window. Finally they swooped down onto a flat river bank covered in a snow blanket and bumped to a stop. The pilot came back to find Donald in the same position.

"So help me," he exclaimed, "you're an extraordinary fellow! You knew one motor was gone, and yet you looked as if you were on a picnic."

They found that the trouble could not be fixed, and at Donald's suggestion, they took off on two motors. Neither liked the prospect of freezing there in the desolate wasteland.

Such episodes left little or no impression with Donald. He never glamorized them, he never elaborated on them. Behind him was a personal history at times as thrilling as a blood-and-thunder novel. Yet to friends he would often remark, "Nothing exciting ever happens to me."

The next morning—December 21—he was at Madame Chiang's house in Nanking. After some discussion, it was decided that they would go to Sian the next day. The pattern for release was now taking better shape. As Madame Chiang later related, Donald had laid the foundations, Brother "T.V." had built the walls, she would put on the roof.

As they headed north, the Nanking military was below them, pushing up the rail line toward Sian, hindered, however, by tracks smashed by their own bombers and by mountainous snow drifts. Madame Chiang was nervous, and as they neared their destination, her nervousness increased. Just before they taxied to a stop, she slipped a revolver into Donald's hands.

"Please promise to shoot me," she pleaded. "Please shoot if any soldiers touch me."

He looked at her patiently. "M'issimo," he said, "no soldiers will touch you."

"Please," she replied.

Before the plane stopped, he reminded her what her attitude was to be with the Young Marshal. They had decided that she would talk to him as if nothing had happened. "We want no bad feelings," he cautioned.

The Young Marshal, looking tired and perhaps a little contrite, was the first to greet them. General Yang was immediately behind him. Then, as if it were just an ordinary Tuesday in the affairs of government, they drove to the Young Marshal's. "I must have some tea," the M'issimo said, "before I see the generalissimo." It was all casual—on the surface. Then everyone went next door.

When she walked in, the generalissimo cried, "I knew you would come. I was reading in the Old Testament this morning that Jehovah will do a new thing. He will make a woman protect a man."

The doors closed behind them. When she reappeared, she reported he was still resolute, still unshaken. She, "T.V.," and Donald walked out into the garden, and as they paced the snow in the fading light, they weighed their growing problem. While it was plain that the Young Marshal was against continued detention, his voice was only one in a group whose stubbornness equaled the generalissimo's.

The next day, December 23, "T.V.," after a long session with the Sian officers, reported that he believed he was on the verge of maneuvering a quick release for the generalissimo. The gloom that had hung over them vanished, but on Christmas Eve it was back again. Sian had changed its mind.

As night fell, the Young Marshal, now wholly in the Chiang camp, came in with a plan. He wanted to disguise the generalissimo and drive him to where his troops were stationed. Donald and Madame Chiang would fly to Loyang where the generalissimo would later meet them. "If we don't," he said, "I'm afraid we might have to fight our way out. That would be disastrous."

Madame Chiang opposed this plan. She wanted the generalissimo to leave with dignity, not as a criminal.

The Young Marshal looked defeated. He left but came back after awhile to say that there was a man in Sian who, if Madame Chiang would talk to him, might use his influence to secure the generalissimo's release. "He's a Communist," the Young Marshal said quietly, "His name is Chou En-lai."[2]

A Communist? Neither she nor the G'issimo had spoken to a Communist in ten years. She looked to Donald.

"Shall I see him?" she asked.

"Don't talk nonsense," Donald said. "See him, of course." He did not add that the new development had been his idea.

Chou arrived later that night, a shrewd, confident man in his late thirties, the son of a one-time mandarin. The army of the people he represented still was camped at a distance from Sian. It had had no part in Chiang's detention. He and Madame Chiang talked for several hours, Chou describing the problems of the Northwest and relating the age-old story of bad government. Madame Chiang pressed the point that China must unify to strengthen herself.

"We Chinese must stop fighting each other," she said.

"I know," Chou replied. "We Communists have been telling you that for years."

He left after emphasizing his belief that apart from the generalissimo, China had no one capable of leading the country at that time. He promised to see what he could do with General Yang.

The next morning, Christmas Day, the household, depressed when it had gone to bed, rose on a note of cheer. The thoughtful touch of Donald did it. At the fireplace, two of his golf stockings hung and attached to each was a string. At the end of one string was a portable

[2] In 1947, "minister for foreign affairs" in the Chinese Communist government. In their diaries, both Madame Chiang and the generalissimo ignore his part in their release.

typewriter for Madame Chiang. The other held a steamer rug for the G'issimo. Chiang laughed for the first time since he had been detained.

But more cheer was ahead. They felt certain now that they would be released that day. Word had filtered back that Chou En-lai, the Communist, the man whom Chiang had fought so energetically, had been successful. They packed their bags. The Young Marshal came in and dropped a satchel beside Donald's.

"Pretend this is your bag," he whispered. "I'm going on the plane to Nanking with you."

By 2:00 P.M., it was definite. Chou had convinced Yang.

Before they left the house, the Young Marshal and General Yang appeared before the generalissimo at his express command. They stood rigidly at attention as he admonished them, this time quietly and gently. When he was through, he singled out the Young Marshal.

"Han Chen," he said, using his courtesy name, "you stay in Sian with your troops."

"No," the Young Marshal answered, "I have been accused of mutiny and of murder. I'm innocent of both charges. But I'm going on the plane with you to stand court-martial for what has been done here. I suppose if you order me to stay here and I go, I'll actually be guilty of mutiny. But I am doing what I am doing for the sake of the country."

In a little while, they took off. Royal Leonard, the pilot who flew the historic plane back to Nanking, observed his passengers' moods.[3] The Young Marshal's features were drawn and strained. The generalissimo, face haggard, was asleep on the plane's single lounge. Madame Chiang looked out of the window, a faint smile of happiness on her lips. Donald chuckled to himself. T. V. Soong occasionally looked at some papers.

They set down at Loyang, met an enthusiastic welcome, spent the night there, then took off the next day for Nanking. As they glided in on the capital's airfield, Donald could see thirty to forty thousand persons along the bordering streets and on the field. The city was rejoicing. The welcome was tumultuous. Firecrackers had started popping the night before, and they were still exploding. The party was

[3] In his book, *I Flew for China*.

weary and needed rest, but they got little. Correspondents swarmed around, assailing them for interviews. The well-wishes seemed genuine, even those of War Minister Ho Ying-ching.

Four nights later, Captain Walther Stennes, one of the Generalissimo's German military advisers, walked into Donald's bungalow, machine gun in arm. Donald looked at him queerly.

"Going hunting?" he asked.

"No," the German replied. "I just thought I should stay with you."

"What for?"

"Oh, just in case. There's a rough crowd in this government, you know."

Donald belittled the idea that his life was in danger, but when a note came informing him that Madame Chiang had left for Shanghai, he caught a night train for the same city. When he arrived, he was handed a translation of an editorial from the *Central Daily News*, a Kuomintang paper. Donald was accused of being a traitor to China, a confederate of the "rascally" Young Marshal. The paper demanded that he be sent out of China under military guard. "He must never return," the editorial declared. Donald sent the clipping over to Madame Chiang. Angered, she flew to the generalissimo who was in Fenghua, Chekiang, his birthplace. She told him what Donald had told her: He wouldn't mind if they succeeded in running him out.

The generalissimo took quick action. He made the *Central Daily News* apologize, as well as others who had editorialized similarly, then sent some editorial heads rolling.

Humbled, the Nanking generals, who had been encouraged to attempt to oust the Australian adviser by Japanese agents (Donald heard that Yakichiro Suma, who once had shadowed him at Shanghai, was among them), never forgave Donald for his part in the Sian coup or for the retaliation they had suffered for their effort to discredit him. Sharing the reactionaries' disappointment that Chiang had escaped with his life were the Japanese, who stood to profit more than anyone else by the removal of China's strong man, and by the chaos that would have resulted.

In the days that followed, there was a general face saving. The reactionaries, of course, had their's scrubbed. Chiang, viewing himself as a failure, repeatedly resigned. There was no time lost in granting the Young Marshal's plea to stand before a military court. Donald, the clique's enemy and regarded as the Young Marshal's closest friend, could offer nothing in his defense. It was a sad day for him when the young man walked into the courtroom. This, perhaps, was the end of a career that once held promise, the end for a man he had worked hard to shape.

"Take it easy, lad," he said to him.

The Young Marshal knew that if he held his peace, he could, like the others, have his face saved. But, no stoic, he quickly lost his patience.

"The only one of you all who is worth a damn is the generalissimo!" he shouted. "None of the rest would be any loss to China. If I get out of this, I'll start a revolution!"

He didn't get out. He was promptly put under Kuomintang "protection" for ten years, sent first to Chiang's birthplace to live under surveillance, and, finally, moved to just outside Kweiyang, in Kweichow Province. The original sentence had been imprisonment and the denial of all civil rights, but an order from Chiang softened it.

After it was all over,[4] in January, 1937, Donald wrote a letter to his old friend, Harold Hochschild:

. . . . The kidnapping was on the twelfth, I left Nanking by plane the next day, got to Sian on the morning of the fourteenth; heard the Young Marshal's story; cursed him; went and saw the generalissimo and cursed all and sundry for giving me so much trouble. . . . The Young Marshal was not the prime mover in the matter, though he takes full responsibility for it, and it came about that he was put in that position in order to save the generalissimo and prevent harm coming to him personally. . . . He looks well and does not regret anything, and is highly amused to see that all he demanded has now been agreed to. The chief thing was cessation of fighting with the Reds. The fighting stopped automatically and negotiations are now coming to a head to wind up the whole business. . . . So, in principle, the Young Marshal won out. . . .

[4] For Donald's part in the Sian Incident, Chiang Kai-shek awarded him the Order of the Brilliant Jade, Grand Cordon of Blue.

chapter

24

WAR AND FAREWELL

When the wind is great,
bow before it. . . .

🎴

THE Sian drama was the beginning of the rapprochement between Nanking and the Communists which materialized in February of 1937. Shortly after Chiang's release, Nanking broke its icy aloofness toward China's Reds and Chiang himself invited Chou En-lai to the capital. While various branches of the government condemned the Reds for purposes of a smoke screen, negotiators went quietly ahead patching old wounds, paving the way for the united front that was to face Japan. Common ground for agreement was Japan. Other matters, it was tacitly decided, could wait until the case against the older enemy had been prosecuted and filed away.

The unpublicized about-face that Nanking now began to make verged on the sensational. Bit by bit, the Kuomintang adopted a policy that coincided in almost all respects with the Young Marshal's program and Communist proposals. Political prisoners were set free, newspaper censorship was abolished and a conference was called to consider steps in a fight against "foreign aggression." The Communists tossed in their chips, promising not to call themselves Communists. In addition, they changed the names of their government and army in order to give the illusion that they were a solid part of Nanking.

Chiang Kai-shek's plans for eventual resistance against Japan had gone deeper than either the Japanese or the Reds suspected. The air force was growing and, more important, the once-ragged armies were better equipped and were being whipped into fighting trim by 140

German officers, many of whom were regarded as Germany's finest military men.[1]

Late in May, Donald happened across the chief of the German military mission, General Baron von Falkenhausen.[2] That day, unhappy rumblings had come out of the North concerning Japan's new intentions toward China, and China had sensed, as a farmer does rain, that a blow was about to fall.

Falkenhausen expressed supreme confidence in China's ability to meet Japan. He admitted that organization at headquarters was somewhat deficient but insisted that, with a pulling in of the slack there, China would be as ready as she ever would be. "In fact, my friend," he said, tapping Donald with his swagger stick, "if Japan attacks, she will be defeated."

Donald made no reply, but he watched the events as they marched down the calendar toward a day in July. Incidents were crowding in upon one another rapidly. Some were obviously staged, just as the Manchurian episode had been. Others were just what the Japanese charged: outbreaks of anti-Japanese feeling by Chinese.

Across the Yellow Sea Tokyo was looking fearfully at a picture that had reddened since Sian. The idea that China might be drawing closer to Russia was horrifying. To add to its alarm, two major reforms that Donald had fought for had come to pass: (1) The currency had been stabilized, a central bank was operating, and Europe was granting China sizable loans; (2) China was strengthening herself economically, her industry rising to compete with Japanese. Further, Japan was aware that China's military power was on the increase. For Tokyo, it was now or never.

On July 7, 1937, the third and the greatest of Sino-Japanese wars broke out. It was not to end until eight years later, not until American aerial and naval might and two atomic bombs had brought a demoralized Japan to her knees.

This was it—the big show was on, the big bayonet charge to pin

[1] In 1938, after the start of the Sino-Japanese War, Japan complained to Berlin that it was being hurt through German generalship of Chinese troops. Hitler ordered the German military mission to return home.
[2] Military Governor of Belgium during World War II.

Japanese culture and co-prosperity spheres on a world that needed such enlightenment! The Tanaka Memorial had said so, and the Tanaka Memorial not only was a bible to Japan's militarists but it was the Son of Heaven's gospel to the industrialists and the bankers, the farmers and the fishermen.

The fighting began when Japanese army units opened fire on Chinese at the Marco Polo bridge, ten miles outside of Peiping. For the next three weeks, desultory wrangling went on as the Nipponese moved in troops and supplies. Nanking speeded defensive preparations. Then Japan struck with power. Peiping fell on July 29 without the firing of a shot, Tientsin followed, and then, as in 1932, fighting broke out spontaneously at Shanghai. This time, Chiang did not stand aside as he had done five years before. He poured in a tough fighting force which fought doggedly until November. It was the biggest battle the world had seen since Verdun. A total of four hundred and fifty thousand Chinese were killed, and then the retreat began.

The Japanese swarmed on toward Nanking.

Donald had switched all his energies from reform to world propaganda to arouse sympathy and pity for China and antagonism to Japan. He gathered several capable men and women around him. Their job was to build about the tiny frame of Madame Chiang the sparkle, the words, the voice to command the compassion, the dollars and the moral support of democratic people everywhere. He was a dynamo that began work at 8:00 A.M., shirt sleeves rolled. The dynamo did not cease until midnight or later. Leagues and societies, clubs and religious bodies, government offices and propaganda outlets the world around received, over Madame Chiang's signature, words full of confidence or kid-gloved rebukes for the continued sale of war materials to Japan.

She and Donald were busy not only on the international front but on the domestic front as well, particularly in morale work with China's troops. Shortly before the Shanghai front collapsed, Madame Chiang, Donald and an aide-de-camp left Nanking for the big city. They were to visit wounded soldiers along the way. It was dangerous, for the roads were pockmarked with shell craters. Japanese planes kept a sharp lookout for cars and attacked everyone in the hope of finishing off persons of importance. Dressed as she usually was on such occasions—in blue slacks and a shirt—the M'issimo was chatting animatedly with Donald when their open-top car hit an obstruction, and the rear tire blew out. The car went out of control, struck another bump, careened off the road and overturned. Donald was spilled out, but not before he saw Madame Chiang hurled over his head. Neither he nor the aide-de-camp was hurt, but she was in a ditch nearly twenty feet from the car, unconscious, her face smeared with mud.

He stooped over her, shook her. "M'issimo!" he shouted. "Wake up!"

There was no sound from her. He thought: Oh, Lord! She's a goner.

Scooping her up, he carried her toward a farmhouse. Then she stirred. He could feel her breathing. In his relief, he began to parody the old Chinese custom of shouting loudly to frighten away devils that come to claim lives. He sang in a deep, booming voice: "Oh, she flies through the air with the greatest of ease, this daring young girl who fights Japanese. . . ."

She opened her eyes and Donald laughed and said: "You can never say that I didn't pick you out of the gutter!" Then he told her to change her clothes in the farmhouse, wash her face and put on some make-up.

Farm women helped, but Donald kept knocking at her door, hurrying her on. She mentioned that her side hurt. He did not want her to give in to pain in the open country far away from medical help. She came out pale and weak, and she held on to his arm tightly as they sat once again in the car, which had been righted. "Do you want to go on and visit the soldiers?" he asked.

She considered for a moment. "We'll go on," she answered.

He supported her as they made the rounds of a few camps, and several hours later they were in Shanghai. A doctor found that she had a broken rib and confined her to her Shanghai home for a week. Then they returned to Nanking where strenuous work for both began again.

Japan was doing her utmost to concentrate efforts against government centers. Town by town, village by village, she was beating her way along the old familiar warpath in the Yangtze Valley, past Soochow, past

Chinkiang, until Nanking, the capital, could hear the sound of heavy guns. Donald, often with Madame Chiang, watched the Japanese planes push the pulverizing of the countryside closer and closer. Day by day, they saw the diminutive air force which they had fought to strengthen shrink into virtual nothingness. They saw the Russian unit in the international section quit to a man after losing one pilot in their first combat.

Donald sat in on the meetings of government bureaus, of war councils. He saw expectancy on the face of every official. In their eyes, he read: "Do we surrender now?" But no one put the question into words. They sat waiting to hear something from the silent man in the office whose walls were covered with maps. They heard nothing. He sat grim, stubborn.

By late November, most of China's national government had been scattered, some of the offices to Hankow and Changsha, others deep into the West at Chungking. Events had marched so fast and so inexorably that the corporation of Chiang, Donald and Chiang had not given a thought to where they would go. It was now the first week in December. Japanese forces were approaching the city and its fall was imminent. Late one night, Donald suggested to the generalissimo that he had better order his plane to stand by. Chiang nodded. He answered: "We leave at dawn." Just as a grayish haze crept over the field, Madame, Donald and the generalissimo climbed aboard their Sikorsky and took off.

"Where shall we go?" Donald asked the still-silent man. Several hundred miles southwest of Nanking, he answered: "Here." They were over Poyang Lake.

The big flying boat settled on the water, and an anchorage was found. The three stepped out lightheartedly, Donald and the M'issimo bantering each other. No one would have dreamed that they had just lost a capital. The party threaded its way in sedan chairs along a pathway leading up to a hustling mountain torrent. There, where the generalissimo had a house, they stayed for more than a week relaxing, their only contact with the war the generalissimo's telephone communications with his generals at Hankow. They climbed the mountains, strolled the shaded paths, as Donald wrote friends, "never thinking of adversity or defeat, never discussing the startling events of the war, never bothering about it."

Then, several days before Christmas, they hopped off in their Sikorsky once more, and in a few hours, dropped down on a lake near Hankow just at dark. During the flight, Donald had heard the generalissimo quietly humming his Chinese poetry. It was a thing he often did, and now, as his taciturnity became more noticeable, so did his humming. Donald thought: Humming is the balm of Gilead to him.

The fall of Nanking had brought high hopes to the Japanese camp. A poor judge always of human reactions, myopic to what lay ahead, Japan had begun the war with two strategical errors: (1) She had charted a campaign to last not more than three months. (2) She had branded Chiang Kai-shek a bandit at the head of a riffraff army and vowed never to deal with him. For that, the man who was equipped almost solely with stubbornness, never forgave them. As the campaign dragged from three to six months, Japan, despite her vow, took her first step to negotiate with Chiang.

The generalissimo had set up temporary headquarters at Hankow, and there the German ambassador, Dr. Oscar P. Trautmann, telephoned one day to ask if he might call as he had an important communication from Berlin. The generalissimo murmured to Madame Chiang, "He wants to talk of peace. I won't see him. You, Kung and Donald meet him."

Ambassador Trautmann came in, suave, heel clicking. He held a long document—Japan's terms of peace. He read them aloud. They were the terms of the victor. Concluding, he said, "I am instructed by my government to hand this in without comment."

Dr. Kung said nothing. Donald watched Madame Chiang. She smiled and replied, "I should think so. How are your son and daughter?"

Dr. Trautmann bowed like an automaton, smiled under her icy shower and retreated.

As the years went on, the Japanese tried repeatedly, through one medium after another, to open peace conversations. They never succeeded. Not only did the generalissimo refuse to speak, he often refused to listen. Both J. Leighton Stuart,[3] president of Yenching University, and British ambassador Sir Archibald Clark-Kerr[4] at later dates and separately sought to act as intermediaries. Chiang faced each, polite but silent. When Sir Archibald called, the Japanese had just installed Wang Ching-wei, alternately Chiang's friend and antagonist, as puppet president of China, with Nanking as his capital. Wang was attempting to sue for peace on behalf of the Japanese. Sir Archibald carried the message. Chiang had Donald tell the ambassador: "There will be no peace while a Japanese soldier is on China soil or while Wang Ching-wei also remains on it."[5]

Near him every day, Donald observed the generalissimo's sphinxian stolidity, his sometimes almost maddening imperturbability. He saw the actions of others, their timidity, their indecision. A conviction became deep rooted: Had anyone else been leading China, the war would have ended in favor of Japan after six months. It was his hardheaded, unyielding and uncompromising stubbornness that kept resistance going. It had made for the impasse at Sian with the Young Marshal. It held together now the remnants of a country that seemed to be supported only by bamboo thatch, glued and patched at the seams.

Days with him were like the silence of a lonely Arctic night. When he did speak, there were only single-syllable questions. Often there were not even those as the trio took daily walks along country roads, Chiang alternately quiet and humming softly. Their walks were long, and sometimes for an hour Donald and Madame Chiang would discuss in detail all phases of the war, physical and psychological. But from Chiang would come no comment. Donald sometimes would think: I'd like to ax this fellow's head open and find out what's inside.

Occasionally, Donald would clap his hands in order to jar him from his peculiar nirvana. Chiang would incline his head slightly to Madame Chiang and ask slowly, "What's he saying, what's he saying?"

At times when matters appeared pressing and there would come no

[3] Born in China, he has spent fifty years of his life as either missionary or educator. He is known widely for his liberal views. At the conclusion of the Sino-Japanese War, he was named U. S. ambassador to China.
[4] Now Lord Inverchapel, British ambassador to Washington.
[5] When the war ended, Wang was not on it, he was under it. Death had claimed him before a wrathful Chiang did.

word from the high ivory tower, Donald would ask Madame Chiang: "M'issimo, do you know what your husband is thinking?" Donald would see a look of helplessness and would think: Good God! Doesn't he even talk in his sleep.

The war raced on through skeletons of Chinese cities and towns, China fighting a war of attrition, Japan biting off bigger and bigger chunks. Tokyo had struck in South China, and early in October, 1938, she began to move on Canton. Shortly before this, Donald had been stricken with a fever and had gone to a hospital in French Indo-China near where he had discovered the Russian fleet thirty-three years before. When he left the hospital, he flew to Kunming where a message awaited him. Chiang was asking that he speed his return to Hankow.

On the way, however, he received a radio message to delay his arrival because the Hankow field was being bombed. He was told that two Japanese pursuits were hovering near by, presumably waiting for him. He set down then at Ichang just before dark and was greeted with the startling report that Canton had fallen. It turned out later that Japan had used "silver bullets," the polite Chinese term for bribes.

China's plight was mounting. The encirclement was widening. Only the West was now left and thither millions of Chinese had been fleeing for months. Donald thought: Poor Generalissimo—now he's really in the soup.

He took off at dawn the next morning. It was still early when his plane came in for a landing at Hankow where an empty field was covered with a strange blue fog. As they set down, feeling conspicuously lonely in the morning calm, one of the field staff was seen coming toward them as fast as he could pedal a bicycle, signaling frantically all the time. Before he arrived, however, Donald had stepped out to smell the "fog." It was the smoke from freshly exploded bombs! He could see the craters now. The rider came up and yelled that a raid was still on. Donald quickly yanked his satchel from the plane which cleared the field in a hurry. Just then, more bombs began to fall.

He learned that seven enemy bombers had gone up river after the first raid. He could not understand how they had missed him unless the mists hanging over the Yangtze had acted as a shield. Had the Japanese encountered him, it would have been the end. There would have been no escape. The whole country between Hankow and Ichang was swamped in the usual floods.

When he arrived at the Chiang residence in Hankow, he found the generalissimo and his wife pacing the garden. They were astonished to see him alive. Madame Chiang's eyes were moist. In awhile, the generalissimo said, "Canton's fall has opened up our flank. Now we must leave here." Donald thought: He speaks of losing a city as one might a pawn in chess.

The generalissimo added, "Now we shall go someplace else. Now we shall change our strategy."

Briefly, he told Donald that he had decided to adopt mobile warfare to replace positional warfare. China hereafter would select her own battlegrounds, thus robbing the Japanese of their advantage in artillery, tanks, heavy arms and planes.

They were facing south. They could see smoke rising from burned-out villages five or six miles away. "When shall we go?" Donald asked tonelessly.

"Tonight at nine," Chiang replied.

The Chiangs resumed their walk. Donald stood for a moment, marveling at the caliber of a man who could go on peering from behind his pile of bombed wreckage, who could absorb the jolt of defeat without a visible wince. Canton was gone. Hankow's fall was only hours away. Here was the loss of two great cities and thousands of square miles of territory. Could China even hope to survive? Her armies were being pushed back into the mountains, completely cut off from the coast, deprived of all shipping connections.

He walked off by himself and, shortly, met several of the German military advisers. He found them desolated. They saw nothing but surrender. Nothing in their super-race catechism offered a key to the understanding of the generalissimo. Donald retraced his steps, remembering what he had heard the generalissimo once say: "I am not disturbed by the loss of cities. If we lose too many, we shall build some more."

A letter for Donald had arrived in his absence. It was from the Young Marshal—the man who ached to fight the Japanese—ebullient, patriotic as ever, his written English not yet perfect. He read:

Kweiyang, Kweichow
October 20, 1938

Dear Old Friend Don:

Thanks for your letter and also thanks to your boss. I know that both of you have good heart and kindness for me. But what kind of man I am I think you know very well. I would not return evil for good. I hope you people do your best help poor China. I never droop. Please do not worry too much for me.

Han Chen

Donald smiled, then murmured to himself: "Goddam everything."

At nine that night, the trio walked onto the field. The generalissimo's request was translated to Donald: "Ask the pilot if he knows where Heungshan airfield is." There was a rush for maps. It was found, but there was some question concerning its exact location. "We'll go look for it," said the generalissimo.

They set off up the Yangtze in the pitch black of night, heading for Hunan Province. Before they were halfway there, however, the plane's radio failed, and they were forced to turn around and fly toward their enemy. By midnight, they were back at Hankow. The Japanese now were closer to the city. Their artillery shells were splashing on its outskirts. Unruffled, the generalissimo walked the field, humming, while a new plane was readied.

In two hours, they were off again, and at daylight they arrived at Heungshan which, until December 8, 1938, was their headquarters. They toured all the fronts, the generalissimo delivering his usual cliché-studded, Spartan addresses; his wife dispensing charm. Then they left for Chungking, China's capital for the next seven dreary years, a desolate, damp, cheerless spot.

The rush of refugees westward now multiplied. From the east to the west of China, the biggest human migration that ever occurred took place; more than fifty million people were on the move. They filled the highways and trails for months, tramping, tramping ever westward On their shoulders or in wheeled vehicles of all types, they carried their possessions, their tools and many of their industrial plants. They set them up in the West, to endure under calamitous odds.

Once again, the furious pace, the daily grind began for Donald and

Madame Chiang. From an idea tossed up by two American writers, Edgar Snow and his wife, Nym Wales, the Chinese industrial co-operatives had been born. They were small, movable industries, using salvage tools and employing the vast armies of the homeless who had surged into the West. Madame Chiang had a hand in their promotion, working with other members of the government. Donald guided and assisted. Soon they were thriving, providing muscle for China's deplorably weak economy.

A big task before the government was the continued effort to win the sympathy of democratic nations, the United States, Great Britain and France in particular. China wanted munitions and financing, and she wanted the world, especially America, to halt its war material sales to Japan, to cease making a profit from the spilled blood and the shattered homes in China. No one was naïve enough to believe that the United States or Britain would enter the war against Japan. Hope was held only that some moral, some economic action would rise out of stricken consciences. China expected the League of Nations to implement its resolutions; she wanted democracies to withdraw their ambassadors from Tokyo as an expression of their unwillingness to rub elbows with militarists who dealt in inhumanity.

This was Donald's self-appointed job: to fight a battle of words, to confront the world with the tragedy of China. He pointed to the failure of the Powers to uphold treaties and showed them how their passiveness was permitting Japan to tear their investments into shreds, and to uproot the economic stakes they had striven so hard to drive in the last century. It was a fierce fight he put up and, also, an adroit one. He did not win, of course. The world went on much as it had, taking quick profits, flying blind. But it cannot be said that he lost entirely. Slowly, perhaps almost imperceptibly, as he waged his fight from a little office in the backwoods of Szechwan Province, some people in the world began girding for the inevitable fight against totalitarianism. How big or how small a part Donald had in the molding of opinion may be difficult to weigh, but slowly and surely pity was coaxed Chinaward in the dying days of the thirties.

As he and Madame Chiang plotted, there was some comfort in the thought that even though governments had turned their backs, the small man in the world was behind them. Day by day, Donald worked to foster the illusion of a tiny living statue in the midst of carnage, giving to her a cry of appeal for all the world to hear. Madame Chiang on the air, in photos, in released statements, became the symbol of distressed China—valiant, frail yet sturdy—calculated to tear at the heartstrings of a gentlemanly world.

But the failure of the democracies to step in finally gave the reactionaries in the government the lever they wanted. The pressure grew for orientation toward Germany and Italy. It was hard to counter their arguments while the West remained mute to China's appeals. At last, the time came when Madame Chiang was forbidden to write or broadcast that China was lined up with the democracies. For Donald, the zenith of insult was reached when the pro-Axis faction accused him of being a British agent and the accusation was not rejected by Chiang.

But his struggles were not against political reactionaries alone. There was at China's core, as always, the lassitude of the wealthy, the greed, the lack of patriotism. At times he faced the shocking indifference red faced, damning. One time, he stood mute.

He had seen an ambulance provided by American funds stop before a bank in which one of the government officials had a heavy interest. It was when the Japanese were pressing down upon Hankow. Through the crowd of spectators that had gathered to watch the ambulance cart away a part of the official's huge fortune, a murmur ran that here was proof that Hankow was to be abandoned to Japan. It was the pattern, centuries old, that the man-in-the-street recognized: the moneyed barons fleeing, possessions their first thought, the plight of people no concern of theirs.

That afternoon an American, the president of a Chinese university, called Donald.

"Someone has to tell the Soongs and the Chiangs to put a stop to this nonsense," he had said. "Some of their official family are making money hand over fist in the exchange market. Lord, haven't they any sense of decency!"

Donald had walked briskly to the Chiangs'. He had taken Madame's arm gently, led her into the garden and in quiet but sharp tones he had told her that she would have to order a halt to such ostentatious and vulgar display of wealth while the nation tumbled all about them, while the cries of the hungry and the suffering mounted. He cited in particular the wife of one official. But Donald had hit too close to home. Madame, who had listened coolly up to then, had turned on him in a blaze of anger, saying: "Donald, you may criticize the government or anything in China, but there are some persons even you cannot criticize!"

Donald had stood silent for a moment, then had walked quickly off as he felt the blood leap to his cheeks.

Now he took inventory of his further usefulness to China. He began to think of the *Mei Hwa* bobbing at anchorage in Hong Kong waters. It was 1940. Germany, after attacking Poland, was digging deeper into Europe. The speeches that he was writing for the generalissimo became more and more pungently anti-Hitler. One day, Chiang sent one of them back with a notation: "I'm not at war with Germany."

Hotly he retorted: "I am."

He walked briskly over to where Madame Chiang was living. He said good-by to her alone. That night, he caught a plane for Hong Kong, and when he stepped from it, it was almost exactly thirty-seven years from the day that, full of hope and zeal, he had walked up a Hong Kong street for the first time.

Now he stood looking at the *Mei Hwa* and to the ocean beyond.

chapter

25

THE ROAD BACK

Sooner or later the weariest dragon
will mount to Heaven. . . .

Dᴏɴᴀʟᴅ walked out on a jetty and, climbing aboard the *Mei Hwa*, ran an expert, appreciative eye over her sturdy lines—the poise of her forty feet from bow to stern, the chestiness of her eleven-foot beam. He glanced up at his Bermudian rig, walked over and spun his helm with the studied air of a connoisseur sampling wine. In front of it was the brightly burnished compass that Madame Chiang had given him. Everywhere there were the warm expressions of friendship that had accumulated since the yacht was built: A wireless set, a fine log chip with speed indicator, silverware, and an assortment of knickknacks.

He sat down before his desk and ran a sheet of paper in his typewriter. He began a letter:

Dᴇᴀʀ Mᴀᴅᴀᴍᴇ Cʜɪᴀɴɢ:

Once I told you there were all sorts of roads out of China and that you need only say the word and I would kick up a dust so fast it would be as a locust cloud in retreat. Well, at last I am on a road, a big highway. . . .

He pulled the paper out and tore it up, climbed back onto the jetty and walked swiftly to the office of his friend, Teddy Cock, who had built the *Mei Hwa*.

"Hong Kong's not far enough away, Teddy," he said. "I'm going to the Solomon Islands."

For awhile the two discussed the trip, then finally decided how it should be made. Since the *Mei Hwa* was not equipped for long sails between ports, she was to be shipped aboard SS *Yunnan*, a steamer bound for the Solomons. Donald spent the next several weeks gathering supplies and acquiring a secretary to help with the memoirs he hoped to write. She was the pretty eighteen-year-old daughter of a Chinese merchant in Hong Kong who was an old friend of Donald's. A tour of the romantic South Pacific? The bright eyes of Ansie Lee sparkled at the thought. Accomplished in English and in shorthand, she would be ideal.

They sailed late in the summer of 1940, and in November, the *Mei Hwa* was lowered into the waters off Tulagi. By day, they poked into strange, jungled coves; cut between islands that twenty-one months later were to be battlegrounds for American and Japanese forces; skirted reefs and wound in and about in the manner of a pencil sketching. They listened to the stories of British overseers of copra plantations, and, because there was little else to do, they went on the trail of some of the tall tales. They heard that at Savo Island there was a man who would whistle and sharks would race in from the sea like a pack of friendly dogs. But at Savo, they never found the man nor did they see a shark. There, however, they were told that in the waters off nearby Malaita was a forty-foot shark that sprinted in when a resident shouted. Laughing, they took off, found the man who gladly accommodated with a shout. But no shark showed up.

"It's probably his day off," the man grinned. "He's like everyone else —on a forty-hour week."

They had planned to sail south to the New Hebrides, but old blackbirding laws prevented them from taking from the Solomons the native crew that Donald had trained. Late in December, the *Mei Hwa* was reloaded on a steamer bound for Hong Kong, and Donald and Ansie took a coastal ship to Port Vila, in the Hebrides. From there, a Dutch liner carried them to New Zealand where they caught another vessel to Fiji. They had no intention of returning to China. Life was too serene, too pleasant in the lazy tropics. They had completed some work on the personal history. They would do some more. He had dictated notes on the monarchy of Yuan Shih-kai, some reminiscences of the Twenty-One Demands and a few reflections on Dr. Sun Yat-sen.

From Fiji, Tahiti beckoned, and they sailed for the Society Islands aboard a sugar boat, arriving there in February, 1941.

Donald found Tahiti a paradise made dreary by the fall in copra prices, its old glamour almost a myth. Still, it was quiet and restful, and they had days on end of swimming in the surf and bicycling along country roads. Even before he was settled, however, he began to hear the call of an old Lorelei, a call from an old land that had wedded itself to him as much as he to it. He told about it, and made some predictions in the following letter to Elliston, written from Papeete on June 3, 1941:

. . . . I came here because I fondly thought that it is the farthest spot from China where one might live in peace for a time, but alas and alack! before I arrived here Madame Chiang Kai-shek wrote me a letter asking me to fly back. I wired that I must have from four to six months' notice to catch a steamer. Then I jumped on a schooner and went for a month's cruise of the Marquesas. Upon my return, I found a wire to "go to some more accessible place or go back to Hong Kong." The telegram added, "We do not wish to interfere with your rest!"

. . . . That it has taken almost four years for America and Britain to recognize what the Chinese resistance to Japan has meant is regrettable, but it is good to see them now supporting China. In a little over a month, the end of the fourth year of fighting will arrive. The Japanese are making a desperate effort to claim some kind of a victory over China before the arrival of that date. They will not be able to do so unless some collapse takes place inside of China. The Communist armies are making some kind of a fight to get definite districts to govern, but that will not be agreed to. In the meantime, they do not fight. As a matter of fact, they never did fight. Rather, they have bluffed at it, have had good publicity when they have captured a Japanese transport section or when they made a raid or two, but they have been conserving their strength so that when the war is over they will be in the position to take advantage of the mess that will surely result to try to extend their communism over the country. Russia is doing a similar thing in world politics. In my opinion, Russia will never fight unless some of her territory is actually threatened. She wants to have all her strength when the war is over and the participating nations are bled white and are fed up. Then she might try a hand at communizing the world. . . .

In the letter, Donald also told how once again he had discarded the idea of writing his memoirs because "I would have to do too much debunking and hurt too many people."

But China was not alone in reaching into his retreat to claim his services. In Australia, a clamor was being set up in the press to name him as Australia's first minister to China. He heard of it and was amused. He a diplomat—bowing, using the formal, velveted language, intriguing for one nation alone and not a cause?

More letters and more wires arrived from Madame Chiang. They told of a change in policy. The new policy would be more to his liking. The reactionaries appeared to be exerting less influence. Chiang was less inclined to listen to the Axis. Donald would read, file away the letters and go for a swim.

By midsummer, however, he noticed that he was listening more and more to daily short-wave news broadcasts which detailed the march of ominous events. Suddenly, Tahiti no longer interested him. He was convinced that the Pacific was about to burst into flame. Another letter had come from Madame Chiang. She had plans for a good-will tour of the United States. She wanted him at hand for the guidance that she knew she needed. He replied: "I am returning."

Honolulu, crossroads of the Pacific for air travel, was his and Ansie's immediate destination. There, they could begin island hopping, touching at Wake, Guam, Manila, and then into China and to Chungking. But a quick check of Tahiti's limited steamship agencies showed no listings for the Hawaiian city, and for several weeks they waited vainly. Donald's anxiety deepened day by day. The difficulties had commenced. For him, they never ended. Incident upon incident was to build a unique story. A thousand were to keep a secret.

The road signs pointing to war now were more readable. Japan was openly eying French Indo-China and the Dutch East Indies. Troop movements had begun in occupied South China. One day, Donald in desperation hustled his secretary aboard an interisland cargo ship and headed for an island to the south and west. From there, they caught a ship to New Zealand, and from Auckland they sailed for Honolulu.

At Honolulu, Pan-American Airways advised that priority for air travel in the Pacific had started and that they would have to make application to Washington. By then, it was the first week in November. They applied, and once again they waited. Each day, Donald read headlines in the Honolulu *Advertiser*:

JAPAN SEIZES MERCHANTMEN ALONG CHINA'S COAST
KURUSU AND NOMURA TALK PEACE AT WASHINGTON

He was sure that the jig was about up. On November 17, he wrote a hurried letter to Hochschild:

. . . . The heat of war in the Pacific is steaming up. Whether or not Japan will risk an encounter with America and Britain will be known in a week or so. There are some Japanese army folk who would not mind. They have great arrogance, and they have great belief in their own might. A conflict with America or Britain will teach them a lesson, for the end is certain.

I am sure that the navy of Japan is no better than the army and their air force is worse. The Japanese have been overrated by the world and they have overrated themselves. China pricked the bubble of their invincibility as far as their army is concerned and if the American fleet gets after that of Japan, they will find themselves with naval victories such as they have never had the chance to get before. . . .

Two weeks after they arrived in Honolulu, they sailed aboard a freighter, SS *Robert Dollar*, loaded with arms and equipment for Canadian troops at Hong Kong. The next day, with Hawaii three hundred miles in their wake, the radio operator handed him a message:

PRIORITIES FOR TWO GRANTED YOU VIA TRANS-PACIFIC CLIPPER.

It had come twenty-four hours too late, and what a difference a day was to make in the lives of a vigorous man and a pretty girl. For many a person in the world, the twenty-four hours had meant only the daily routine at the office, home to dinner, to bed and to the office again. For Donald and Miss Lee, however, it was the end of one life, the beginning of another.

Donald tore up the message and watched the wind scatter the pieces.

It was December 8, Orient time, when the captain came to him. They were just south of Amboina, in the Dutch East Indies.

"Pearl Harbor has been bombed," he said, as if not quite believing his words. "There's war. The Japs have bombed Pearl Harbor."

Donald stood nodding his head as if he had known it all the time. "Better run for Singapore," he advised.

"No, I'll put in at Manila under the American flag."

"You'll lose your ship," Donald said and turned away.

At sixty-six, the pattern of his character was unchanged. He advised, but never argued. His intuitive sense of what was inopportune and what was not was still strong.

The captain turned his ship north, and they picked and poked their way up the long Philippine Archipelago, finally docking at Manila.

Ashore, a fusillade of chaos spat about the Australian and Ansie Lee. Japanese troops had been hurled onto Lingayen Gulf beaches, and now they were funneling rapidly down the broad Luzon Plain toward Manila. The sound of guns was audible. General MacArthur was beating a fast retreat into Bataan. Trucks piled high with supplies and American and Filipino troops roared through the city. Merchants were frantically boarding up fronts of stores.

Japan, the old enemy against whom Donald had steered China repeatedly, was on the rampage—and here he was in what inevitably would be her camp.

As Donald and Ansie paused in the midst of Manila's hubbub, debating which street to take, a Japanese fighter buzzed the rooftops, strafing. Two days before, Manila had been declared an open city, but the declaration had been ignored. With the United States Air Force knocked out, Nipponese planes were droning leisurely above. Ansie watched one unload its bombs far to the northwest.

"If we had taken the plane—" she began.

"That's spilled milk," Donald answered quietly. "No crying."

He sought out Chinese friends, and before nightfall, a house had been found for the two at San Francisco del Monte.

Thus, the secret a thousand were to keep began.

The house was near the Sulphur Springs resort, which already had been converted by British residents from China into a voluntary internment camp. Across the street was Manila's most famous movie studio, its gay scenery standing bizarre and incongruous amidst the growing panic and suffering.

And then the Japs came, their tanks clanking down the roads, soldiers running from house to house, squatting, peering, running on again. Ansie and Donald stood behind a curtained window watching. They saw them set up a garrison in the movie studio.

"If they find you," Ansie said, "you know what that means."

"I know," said Donald. He knew, all right. It was easy to guess to what extent the old dossier on him had grown for it had become almost legend that the Japanese wouldn't mind having him, dead or alive. To them, he was "The Evil Spirit of China," and they had christened him that.

He took her arm, and they went out the back door, down an alley and reached the Sulphur Springs camp without being challenged. The Japanese had not yet taken it over.

Mr. Dahlan, the owner of the converted resort, an American-natural-ized German who had fought for Kaiser Wilhelm in World War I, looked up as Donald and Ansie entered the camp office. He smiled pleasantly, and then the smile froze. He picked up a dog-eared copy of the *Saturday Evening Post*—a March, 1938 issue—and he looked at a picture accompanying the story he had read earlier that day. The story was "China's No. 1 White Boy," by H. B. Elliston, and the photo-graph—

He stared at the man before him. He said, "You're Donald of China."

It was characteristic that even in an emergency Donald did not evade the truth. He answered, "Yes. My name is Donald."

"I gather from this article," Dahlan said, "that the Japanese have a price on your head."

"I suppose so."

Dahlan opened his camp registry. "I'll register you," he said. "The Japanese should be around shortly." He directed that Ansie Lee be taken to the women's quarters, and motioned to Donald to follow him. Outside the door were three Britishers, former residents of Shanghai. One of them exclaimed:

"Why, you're Donald of China! I'd know you anywhere."

Donald halted, smiled. "Yes," he said, "but please don't broadcast it."

"Righto," the speaker replied, and Dahlan led Donald to a cabin on the far side of the spacious estate. He gave him details on the food problem and saw that he was comfortable. Before he left, he said, "I'll store your luggage separately from the others."

The Japanese took over, and slowly the rations dwindled to a bowl of rice and stewed fish heads. But Donald, a rugged man who looked twenty years younger than his age and felt even younger, kept going. More important, his secret had not leaked out. Everyone of the nearly four hundred men and women in the camp was aware that the famed Donald of China was among them. A man's life was at stake, and each knew it.

Dahlan had remained on as something of a custodian under the supervision of a Japanese commandant. One day, one of Donald's British friends insinuated that Dahlan's World War I record might be cause to watch him. But Donald took no stock in gossip.

"I think he's pukka sahib," he declared.

His faith in Dahlan was justified a few nights later when Dahlan came to him a bit troubled.

"You've just had a close call," he said. He related how Japanese "gestapo" had suddenly appeared and demanded an inspection of the camp. Dahlan had led them from one building to another, unlocking those that had to be unlocked.

"Then we came to the house where I had stored your luggage," the former German soldier said.

"Yes, then what?" Donald asked.

"Well," Dahlan grinned, "I fumbled with my keys for awhile and said that I must have forgotten the one for this particular house." He explained that the Japanese then grunted that they would kick in the door but he had suggested that it would save wear and tear on them if they would wait until the end of the tour when he would find the key and they could go back. However, Dahlan had conveniently forgotten about the key and the Japanese had not remembered to ask.

Donald smiled. "The papers in my bags would have been enough to hang me."

The protection for Donald grew, and the secret was still watertight. He had been in the camp for months, and he had not seen a Japanese nor had a Japanese seen him. When Nipponese guards or inspectors would start in the direction of his cabin, internees would sidle up and whisper, "The Japs are coming over the hill." Donald would wander in an opposite direction.

Then a pulse-quickening rumor filtered through the camp one afternoon and by evening it had become the truth: A group of the Sulphur Springs internees was to be moved that night to Santo Tomas University, the center of internment activity, staffed by high-ranking Japanese officers mainly from the China Theater. Donald was among those to go. As the truck stopped for inspection at the university gate, the Australian was maneuvered into the center of the group, his face shielded from view. Guards momentarily swept the internees with flashlights, then a curt order moved the truck along.

He began a new life among faces new to him. Assigned to work in the university bookbinding shop, he was in daily contact there and on the campus and in the quarters where he lived with two hundred to three hundred persons. The word "Donald is here" spread. It had seemed to him fantastic that every internee at Sulphur Springs had kept his secret. It was almost too much to ask of human nature that the secret again be kept from Japanese ears. Although there was a feeling of warmth in the continued protection that sprang unbidden about him, there was each day a chill in the thought that a Japanese hand might drop onto his shoulder and a voice might hiss, "You're Donald of China. Come along." But if the feeling of not knowing when the end might come was disquieting, Donald did not show it.

Yet the end almost came for him one night as he slept. This time, it was not his friends but the gross stupidity of the Japanese that saved him. The army's "gestapo" had swept into the camp and had demanded that the Japanese commandant produce "W. H. Donald, of Chungking." From somewhere overseas a tip had come that Donald, the old foe of Japan, was in the Philippines. The commandant thumbed through the camp registry until he came to the entry made by Dahlan. It read: "William Donald, Edinburgh."

"We have no W. H. Donald," said the commandant.

The "gestapo" chief snapped, "We want no mistakes. We want this man. Think hard. Here, I have a description of him. He is a youngish man of, say, less than fifty. He is strong and muscular."

"You are on the wrong track. My records show that the William Donald we have is sixty-eight years old."

They stormed out in search of a new lead.

Donald heard of the incident the next day from an American, Mr. B. B. George, a truck driver for the camp. Mr. George had a Japanese interpreter who had overheard the conversation between the "gestapo" and the commandant. He had described the scene to Mr. George.

The secret was still good. Counting those at Sulphur Springs and the circle in which he worked and lived in Santo Tomas, at least seven hundred knew his identity. But the seven hundred had sealed their own lips because they wanted a man they liked, a man they knew was held in high respect in Chinese and international political circles, to go on living.

In the outside world, every precaution was taken in order that his whereabouts should remain hidden. In Australia, his brothers and sisters made no effort to communicate with him, and everywhere—in China, the United States, Britain and India—friends were cautioned against trying to write to him. When infrequent batches of mail arrived through the Red Cross, there was none for the Australian, and he was glad of it. Then one day a letter was handed to him. With a start, Donald noted the address. It was not to "William Donald." It read, "Mr. W. H. Donald"! And it had passed through Japanese hands before reaching him. Close friends in the camp knew of the letter, and for days they expected to hear the heavy tramp of army boots followed by the sudden departure of their friend, but the police did not come.

Easily adaptable to any surroundings, Donald had quickly fitted himself unostentatiously into life at Santo Tomas. Yet his quiet magnetism could not help but make him the hub of what little opportunity there was for intellectual pursuits. With others, he organized a small group which met twice a week to discuss world economic and political questions. At each meeting, a different member would read a paper on some particular subject. On these occasions, his simple but profound common sense, combined with his wide experience, time and again clarified matters in which a snarl would develop.

For him, there was never anything less than warm cordiality from the inmates, and from some, adoration. So trusted was he that those who possessed secret radio sets hardly thought of listening unless he was present. There was no trust higher than that in a Japanese internment camp. Children knew him as "Uncle Don." To one American lad, six years old at the time, Donald is today still his most vivid memory of four years under Japanese guards. Donald entertained him daily with his fairy stories of "Winkie Doodle," interspersed with bits of his own true life story on China—all told simply and amusingly. On his sixth birthday, Donald invited him to his shanty for a birthday dinner. It was no mean invitation when every mouthful was weighed carefully. Also the privations of the camp had now begun to cut deeply into him. He had lost considerable weight and a tired feeling was creeping over him.

Elsewhere, the story was developing much as he had predicted. The American flag was being carried across the Pacific with amazing rapidity. The United States Navy was winning the victories he had foreseen, Japan's air force had proved itself greatly inferior and the Japanese army's defenses of islands were frequently shoddy. American army, marine and naval units had fought through the Solomons, the Gilberts and the Marshalls, had seized Saipan, retrieved Guam and were knocking heavily on Japan's wobbly frontier gates. Japanese communiqués to the contrary, Donald and his friends, listening in on secret radios, knew the truth.

Despite the cheer from the outside, Donald felt that his life might be more secure in some place other than Santo Tomas. There was always the chance that he might come face to face with a Japanese officer from the China Theater, which might easily be his undoing. Japan had credited him with being a major factor in stirring Chinese resistance, and she knew that he had not only helped to chart military strategy against her but had supplied much of the brains behind China's economic warfare. Donald set wheels in motion to arrange his transfer to the Los Banos camp, located in an agricultural college high in the hills. There was an element of danger, the risk of identification through the necessity to reregister, but he took it one day in 1944. He had heard that Ansie had finally been brought to Santo Tomas, and just before he left, they met briefly.

At Los Banos, he settled down to something of a better life. The air was clearer and cleaner, but the food was just as scanty and lacking in nourishment. He was still losing weight and the feeling of tiredness persisted. Then one day, as he walked, a sharp pain seared through his chest, and he stopped and sat down, short of breath. After awhile, the pain passed and he went on with his walk.

Rounding a turn in the road, he came upon a group of Japanese army officers walking briskly toward him. Donald stopped and eyed them calmly. This would be his first face-to-face encounter with any Japanese since internment. Was it to be the end of his secret that now was being kept by a thousand persons? They passed, however, paying him no attention, with the exception of the ranking officer. He shot Donald a fleeting glance, paused and looked again. Donald recognized him as Major General Tanaka. He had been Captain Tanaka when Donald had seen him forty years before during the Russo-Japanese War. Tanaka had been public relations officer for the army, and, as such, it had been his job to buoy up the flagging spirits of foreign correspondents. He and Donald had been particularly friendly.

Had Tanaka recognized him? Donald did not know. Forty years is a long time to remember a face. The general had looked at him as one might look at a fence post, a tree, a rock, and walked on. But no "gestapo" followed the Tanaka inspection.

The months dragged, then late in October the word seeped through that Leyte had been invaded, and Los Banos waited jubilantly for the blow that would free Luzon and Manila. It came several months later, on January 9, 1945, and the internees knew, as did their Japanese guards, that liberation was near.

On the morning of February 23, Donald rose at six o'clock as usual, and at six forty-five he was seated by the side of the road awaiting roll call. The morning sun had just swum up from behind a hill when he heard the faint roar of motors; then quickly a dozen large planes came screaming toward the camp.

"God stone the crows!" Donald exclaimed, suddenly remembering half-forgotten Australian slang in his excitement. "What's this!" He saw that the man next to him had his mouth open and was staring blankly at the planes as they roared in low. Then, as if a riot of white flowers had blossomed against a blue wall, parachutes, white and dancing, came drifting down in the sun's path.

Donald jumped up and ran toward the camp buildings, shouting that rescue had come. By this time, Filipino guerrillas and American paratroopers already were snipping barb wire and clambering through, guns blazing. Internees ran out, then quickly threw themselves to the earth, noses pressed hard against it, Donald among them. For more than half an hour, bullets sang and ricocheted. Then quiet came as swiftly as it had been broken. A paratrooper, chewing gum, sauntered up and stood near Donald.

"Okay, folks," he said. "You're all out of here now."

Thus, the secret ended, but for Donald the battle was not over.

A United States Army field hospital had been set up in the Holy Ghost College at Manila, and there he went for observation of the ailment that had begun at Los Banos. Dahlan came to see him one day with one of Donald's handbags which held the most valuable of his papers. He pumped the Australian's hand and tossed the bag on the bed.

"Here it is," he said. "I'm tired. I've been carrying the damn thing around for nearly three years."

He shoved fifty pesos into Donald's hand and left. Donald never saw him again.

Before he sailed for the United States in May, Donald met General Douglas MacArthur, and for an hour and a half the general listened with interest as the Australian summed up the Pacific, its fears and its problems, over which he said would hover, as he had predicted before the war, communism's ubiquitous threat. Just prior to his departure, he saw Ansie. She had weathered the more than three years of detention well, and there was to be a happy ending. She had met an American internee, a banker, and they had made plans for a wedding.

By the time Donald reached San Francisco, he had gained weight, but his breathing seemed to become more difficult every day. He had hoped to find adequate medical treatment, but his trip turned out rather to be a visit to scores of "Old China Hands" from San Francisco to New York. In midsummer, he visited Harold Hochschild at his home high in the Adirondacks, where he spent a number of relaxing weeks, and he saw another old steadfast friend, K. C. Li, at his Long Island home.

While he was at Hochschild's, Madame Chiang arrived in New York, and at her request he visited her. What they talked about is not known, but friends concurred in their guesses. Observers already had noted that there seemed to .be a relation between the fall of China's as well as Madame Chiang's popularity in world democratic quarters and Donald's departure from the China scene. She had made a whirlwind tour of the United States in 1943 in what was a prime opportunity to win the good will that China then so badly needed, but her approach had been wrong, her technique bad. There was, of course, charm and beauty aplenty, but something was lacking. Perhaps it was the Donald touch. She had addressed a joint session of Congress and had criticized the war strategy agreed on by the United States, Britain and Russia. Thereupon, the White House had blown a chill in her direction. Later she had appeared before a rally of twenty thousand in New York's Madison Square Garden and had read an academic treatise setting forth her conclusion that the Roman Empire was a democratic republic! Americans had left with the feeling that she was pretty and that was about all.

Friends concluded that Donald had said when he saw her: "You must not talk nonsense."

By now, peace had come in both Europe and the Pacific. However, the scars inflicted unwittingly on "Donald of China" by the old enemy, Japan, had not gone. But Japan was not around to gloat. She had not conquered China. The Tanaka Memorial was nothing but a tawdry scrap of paper. The dossier she had kept on one "W. H. Donald" was out of her hands, and she was staring ruefully at the scattered bones of the imperialism he had so long opposed.

Although Donald's first conclusion regarding his health had been that he was suffering from malnutrition, this theory seemed unsubstantiated when, after months of normal diet, he was still tired. There was still the strange feeling in his chest. Believing that a warmer climate might help, he sailed in October for Tahiti.

There, one day in January, 1946, he pedaled his bicycle to Papeete's

French Hospital. A doctor tapped his chest, looked at him queerly and put him under a fluoroscope.

Then he told Donald that he had only one lung. He called a nurse, they inserted a syringe needle into the good lung. After that, he eyed Donald painfully. A quart of water, he explained, had just been drained from his only lung. He advised Donald to hurry to America, and the Australian wired Madame Chiang. The Chiangs acted, and one day a flying boat, at the orders of Pearl Harbor, winged out of Samoa and landed in the waters off Papeete. Donald was put aboard, and soon he was installed at the Aiea Naval Hospital at Pearl Harbor.

It was by chance that the United States Navy had come to his rescue so quickly. At Pearl Harbor, Commodore Willcutts, head of the Pacific's medical force, the same Willcutts that had attended Donald and the Chiangs on a day in 1934 at the Peking Union Medical College, had read a carbon copy of the message that flashed from the Chiangs to Washington. His eyes had clung to the name "Donald" and he had remembered back twelve years. He snipped red tape and had Donald hustled up to the finest hospital west of San Francisco.

As attendants lifted him from the plane in a stretcher, Donald smiled his thanks at the commodore.

"It's reciprocity," Willcutts said. "You've been doing things for Americans in China for years. Now it's our turn."

That night, Bill Hutchinson, night editor of the Honolulu *Advertiser*, phoned me. I was the paper's editorial writer and columnist.

"Selle," he said, "W. H. Donald is at Aiea. Since you're the only one of us who has ever lived in China, I had the idea you'd like to call on him. He should make a good story."

On the way to the hospital the next day, I stopped at the office of Commodore Willcutts where I heard the news. Donald had just been given a thorough examination.

"I doubt if he'll live long," Willcutts said. "He has an inoperable cancer involving his lungs."

"Does he know it?" I asked.

"Yes, he's the sort of fellow that wants the truth. I have given him my diagnosis. I told him he need not be too hopeful."

I walked down the silent corridors, through the customary numbing, strange smells, past wheel chairs where sat quiet men who had been blasted at Saipan or Guam, at Iwo or at Okinawa. I rapped on a door.

A cheery voice, a little bit nasal, called, "Come in."

I went in. He was sitting there, grinning, a big palm extended. He was cheerful, confident as ever, with the same certainty, the same clearheadedness concerning the future. "Hello," I said, "what are you doing here?"

"Oh," he answered in the poetic way he often spoke, "I'm sitting here looking at the green hills. I've been watching the sun and then the rain against my windows. And I am waiting to die."

I made what I thought a courteous, protesting remark.

He smiled. "I never argue with people," he replied.

We talked for hours, he gusty, breezy as ever. He would swoop down upon a subject, pick it clean as a hurricane might dust off a prairie, talking always of China, seeing her more clearly than any man, seeing her better than China could see herself. He felt strongly the need of American support for the Chiang Kai-shek government rather than for the Communists, since he doubted the sincerity of their leaders. However, he felt that the success of that movement was, in part, an expression of justified popular dissatisfaction with the generalissimo's administration. He pointed, as he always had, to the muck of corruption and reaction. Once he had made his roar heard in the Yangtze Valley for a housecleaning of the Kuomintang. Now he sat there, a crusader, dying. The echo of that old roar, although now faint, was still firm:

"China, the old leopard," he said, "is still spotted. And he'll not change overnight. If people think that China is to wake up and reform in a day, a month or a year, their calculations are a long way off. The old standpatters have their hooks in so deep it's going to be a damn hard job to get them out."

He watched the long leaves of a banana plant brush his window. "But," he continued, "if China has the wisdom of the serpent—and I think she has—she will houseclean. She will do this and many other things. She should profit more from the war than any other nation because she has been further behind. She should jump a span of a hundred years in perhaps ten." He went on to explain how China could pick up all the scientific developments and other Western improvements, thus leaping decades without the detours of trial and error. "She can buy experience," he said. "She will not have to wallow through it."

"In such a picture, where will the Young Marshal fit?" I asked.

"I think he is the strongest personality in China today," he answered. "You will hear more of him."

I went back the following day. He was reading a letter from Helen Rathvon. General Marshall had arrived in China several weeks before to attempt an unraveling of the tangle of China's civil war, and Mrs. Rathvon was asking what were the hopes for success.

He studied the letter, then began to talk as if he were dictating a reply: "I think Marshall will find for himself only heartbreak. Night and day cannot be made the same. The positive and the negative cannot be made one. The opposites are the Kuomintang and China's Communists. They will never join peacefully."

He went on to remark that the Communists never would consider coalition government, that their aim was only to honeycomb and honeycomb into government until it, a shell, collapsed. And he thought it strange that so many writers, particularly American, had fallen for the sham—after a "Cook's Tour" of Communist areas—of what he referred to as the so-called "advances" of the Chinese Reds. None of them, he knew, saw the danger to Asia and to the world of what a solid Communist front from Moscow east and south to India would mean.

Before I left, I said, "I'd like to write your memoirs." Immediately, I sensed the strength of his feeling as one hears the hum of a dynamo. I felt that at that moment (although at other times I was to witness qualms) he wanted it more than anything else in the world. But there was a cloud in his voice:

"How? Many people have said that before. But how can it be done now?" He looked meaningfully in the direction of Willcutts' office and the ominous prognosis there in his files.

I stole a line from Donald himself. "That's easy," I said.

The next day, January 28, I returned with a dictaphone. "It's a propitious day to begin," I remarked. "If I remember rightly, the Shanghai war began fourteen years ago. Where were you that night?"

"Let's see," he answered. "I was leaning out of my window at the Astor House. I was holding my phone so that Mayor Wu could hear the firing. Where were you?"

"It's a good thing you didn't drop the phone," I laughed. "I was walking past the Astor House just as the firing began."

His condition would not permit strenuous work. At times when he was strong enough to sit up, we talked for an hour a day every other day. Then the day would come when the pressure in his one remaining lung was so great that he had no breath for speech. The doctors would come in with their long needles, tap a quart, sometimes more, from the lung, and for several days I would not see him. After that, I would come in with my wife, and we'd find him chipper and breezy again. This lasted for a month. Steadily, he weakened. One day, I found him morose, and in a way so subtle that I was not aware of it until I returned home, he let me know that he had been waiting in vain for weeks to hear from Madame Chiang. In all his talks with me, his abiding admiration and affection for the M'issimo were evident. It seemed plain he felt that she, who had used so much of his strength, now might supply some for him. I wired her, not omitting a sting.

A week later, Hollington K. Tong, biographer of Chiang Kai-shek and one-time director of a Shanghai newspaper of which I was city editor, bounded into Honolulu from Tokyo or Washington, London or New York. Tong, a buoyant, charming bundle of nerves, was front man for the Chiangs wherever the Chiangs needed a front. He had important news. Permission had been received from navy doctors to fly Donald back to China. That was what Donald wanted. Before Tong arrived, we had talked on and off about it. We would talk about the trip by air across the Pacific—the quickness, thirty hours, with which he could be landed in Shanghai.

"I guess I have enough of those people in me," he would say, "to want to go home to die." He never thought of Australia as home. He had not been back in the forty-three years he had been away. He did not want to go now.

The take-off in a special navy plane, equipped with berths and nurses, was set for the night of March 15. Several hours before the ambulance was to carry him to the field, my wife and I came in with flower *leis* of carnations and tube roses. She draped them around his neck and in the custom of Hawaii kissed him.

He hid his emotions. "Do I have to wear these?" he asked in the quaint, rising inflection that was uniquely his.

We told him that he must not break the tradition of the Islands, that he must, as he passed over Diamond Head, somehow toss them from his plane. That, according to belief, would cause him to return some day.

"Ah," he said with quiet fervor, "I shall do it."

But Donald was not to return. Eight months later, in November, 1946, he was to die in the Country Hospital in Shanghai.

The plane's four motors were warming up when he came on the field. A small crowd had gathered, including the Chinese consul-general, Mr. Mui King-chow. My wife and I were the only ones who were not Chinese. He was lifted aboard amid a shower of presents. He smiled a Rooseveltian smile, waved a broad Panama hat. We were the only ones to follow him in. She stooped and kissed him. He gripped my hand tightly. He held on, and the seconds ticked.

"Good-by, old man," he said. The last two words were faint.

We walked out, numb and heavy. The Chinese were chattering gaily, a brittle, strained gayness.

The door clanged shut behind us.

The port motors burst into a roar. Then the starboard ones screamed even fiercer.

The plane taxied down the field and into the night.

BIBLIOGRAPHY

Berkov, Robert *Strong Man of China*. Boston: Houghton Mifflin Co., 1938.

Blythe, Samuel G. "The Flying Wedge." Philadelphia: *The Saturday Evening Post*, April, 1917.

Chiang Kai-shek, General *A Fortnight in Sian*. Shanghai: The China Publishing Co., 1937.

Chiang Kai-shek, Madame *Sian: A coup D'Etat*. Shanghai: The China Publishing Co., 1937.

Crow, Carl *China Takes Her Place*. New York: Harper & Brothers, 1944.

Elliston, H. B. "China's No. 1 White Boy." Philadelphia: *The Saturday Evening Post*, March, 1938.

Gunther, John *Inside Asia*. New York: Harper & Brothers, 1939.

Hahn, Emily *The Soong Sisters*. New York: Doubleday, Doran and Co., Inc., 1941.

Hart, Henry H. *Seven Hundred Chinese Proverbs*. Palo Alto. Stanford University Press, 1937.

Reinsch, Paul S. *American Diplomat in China*. New York: Doubleday, Page and Co., 1922.

Russell, Bertrand *The Problem of China*. London: 1922.

Seeger, Elizabeth, *The Pageant of Chinese History*. New York: Longmans, Green and Co., 1944.

Semenoff, Vladimir *Rasplata*. St. Petersburg, 1906.

Sues, Ilona Ralf *Shark's Fins and Millet*. Boston: Little, Brown and Co., Inc., 1944.

The pamphlet, *American Relations with China*, report of the conference held at Johns Hopkins University, Baltimore, Johns Hopkins Press, 1925; the periodicals, *Time* and *Oriental Affairs*.

Index